Contents

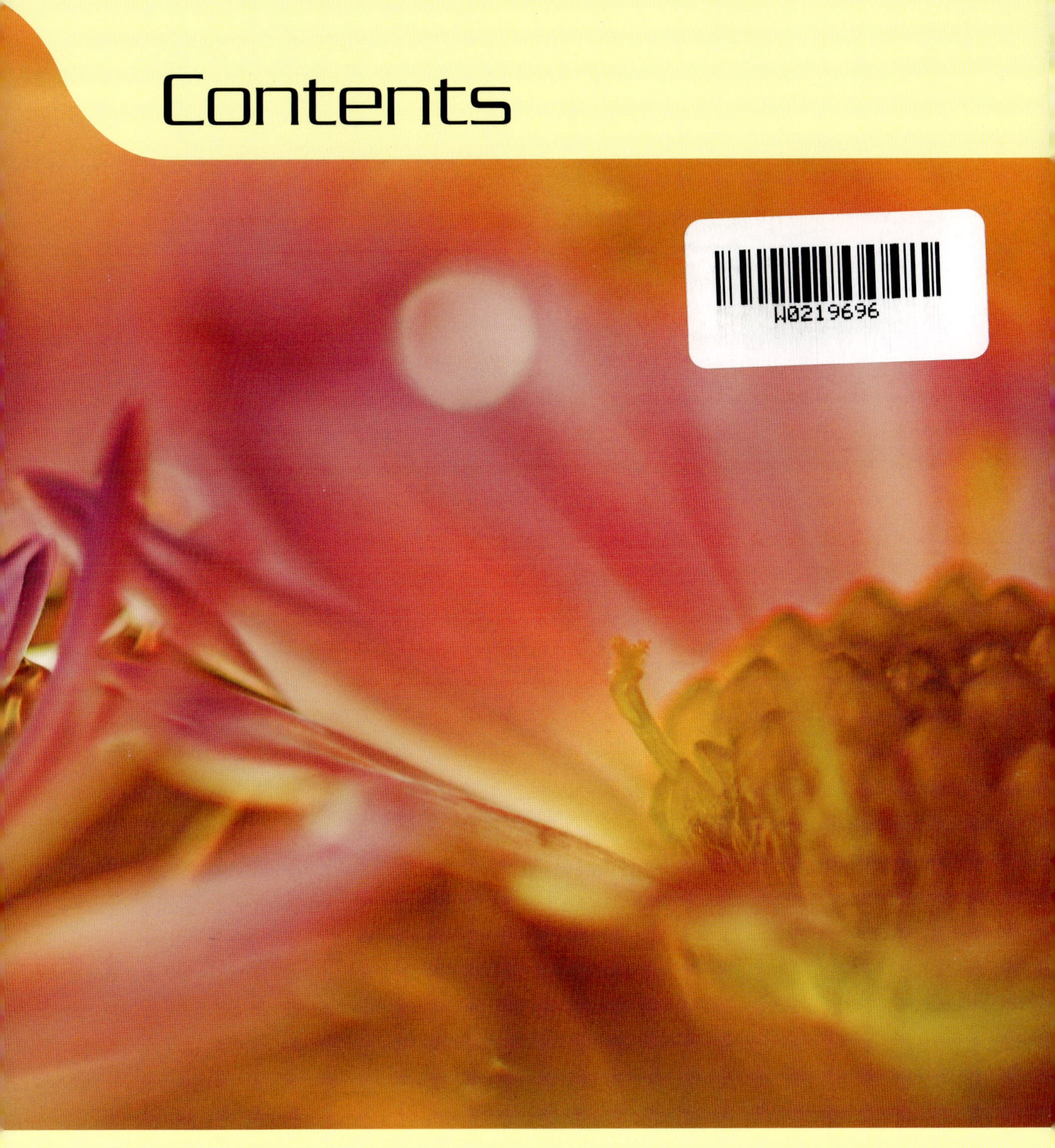

W0219696

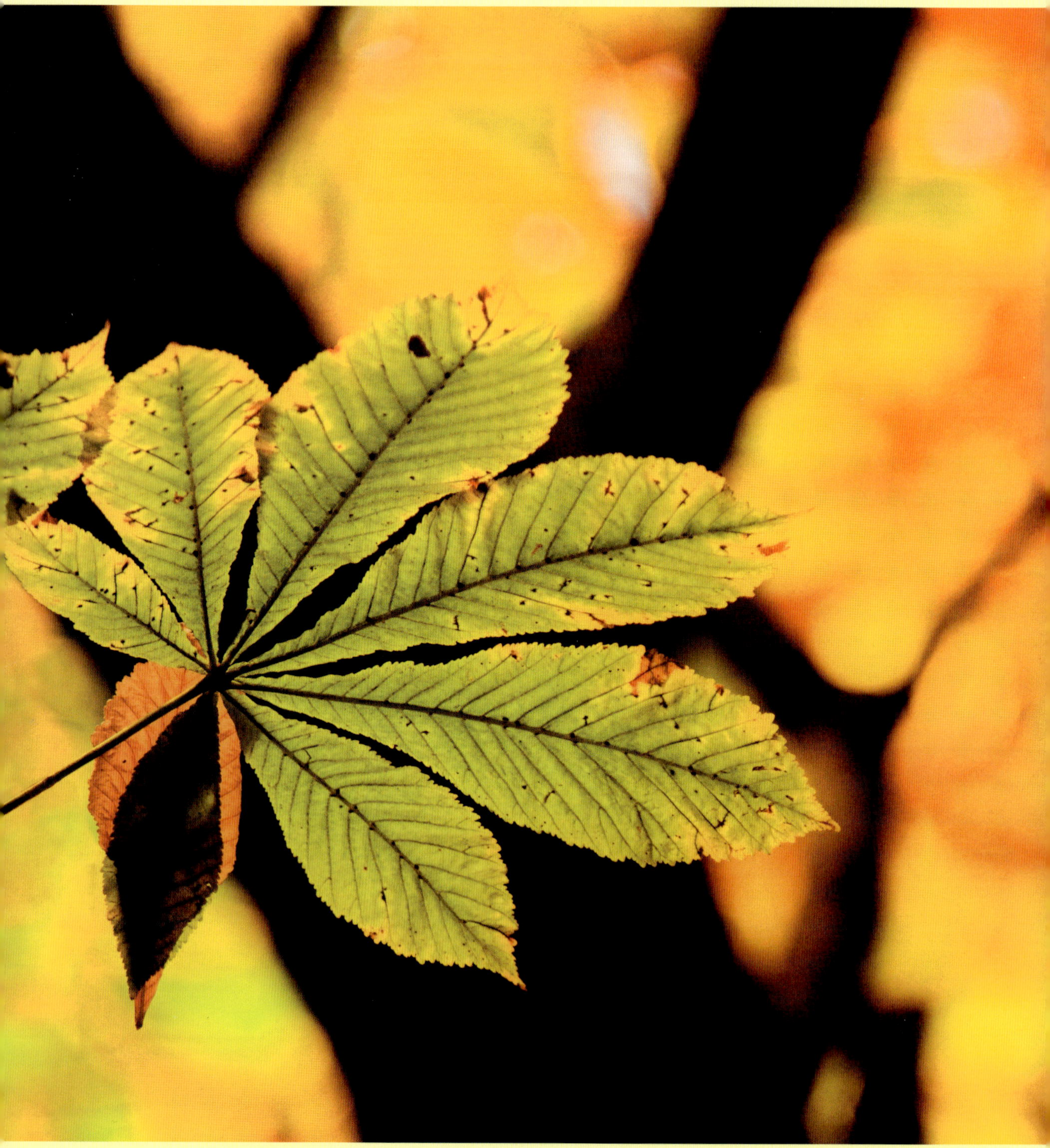

Introduction

he Essential Color Manual for hotographers is a comprehensive uide to the technical, practical, nd inspirational aspects of color hotography. Whether you are just eginning your journey into the world f photography, want to know how to et the most from your digital camera, r are an experienced photographer vishing to hone your skills, you will nd plenty to inspire and instruct you hroughout. Whether you are capturing nages on film or digitally, we discuss he many techniques and tricks you an use to add impact or subtlety to our photographs.

From the warm glow of a sunset o the glorious impact of summer lowers, color is often the first thing hat attracts us to a scene or subject. olor plays a huge part in how we eact to or feel about an image. ompared to black and white, color hotography is often seen as easy— fter all, we see in color, not in black nd white. However, translating the olors that we see into photographs s not simply a matter of pointing the amera and clicking the shutter.

The art of color photography relies on three main factors. First, there are the colors themselves, what they are, and how they fit into our perception. This topic is part-science and part-psychology, involving the actual color of the subject, the reactions and emotions that each color imparts, and the way in which different combinations of color work together. Second, there is the color of the light falling on the subject. Every light source has an effect on the color that the camera or we will see. Third, there is the camera itself. Whether it is film or digital, the camera will record color in its own way.

Starting with the theory behind colors and light, you will discover how you can use color in your images to best effect and why some colors work together and others don't. You will also cover how your camera records color, why it doesn't always match what you see, and how you can get the best results from your photography.

The rise in popularity of digital imaging has brought a whole new range of possibilities and challenges to color photography. The introduction of the "digital darkroom" has provided an unrivalled range of control and creativity for your photography. However, digital cameras capture images very differently from their film counterparts, and this is explained in detail throughout the book. These new technologies are covered in easy-to-follow guides on how to make the most of the features in your imaging software, and how to produce the best colors from your ink-jet printer.

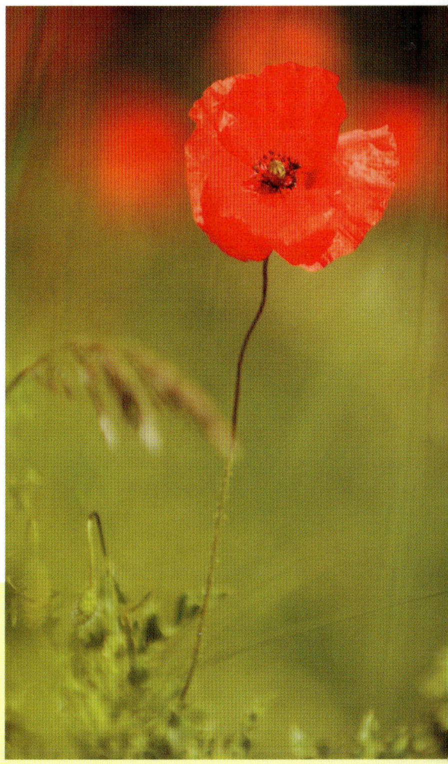

Capturing and using color in your photographs is the key to producing eye-catching images. Whether you are dealing with a single color combination, such as the red and black of a field of poppies, or a riot of color in the fall, the challenge lies in translating what you see into your photographs.

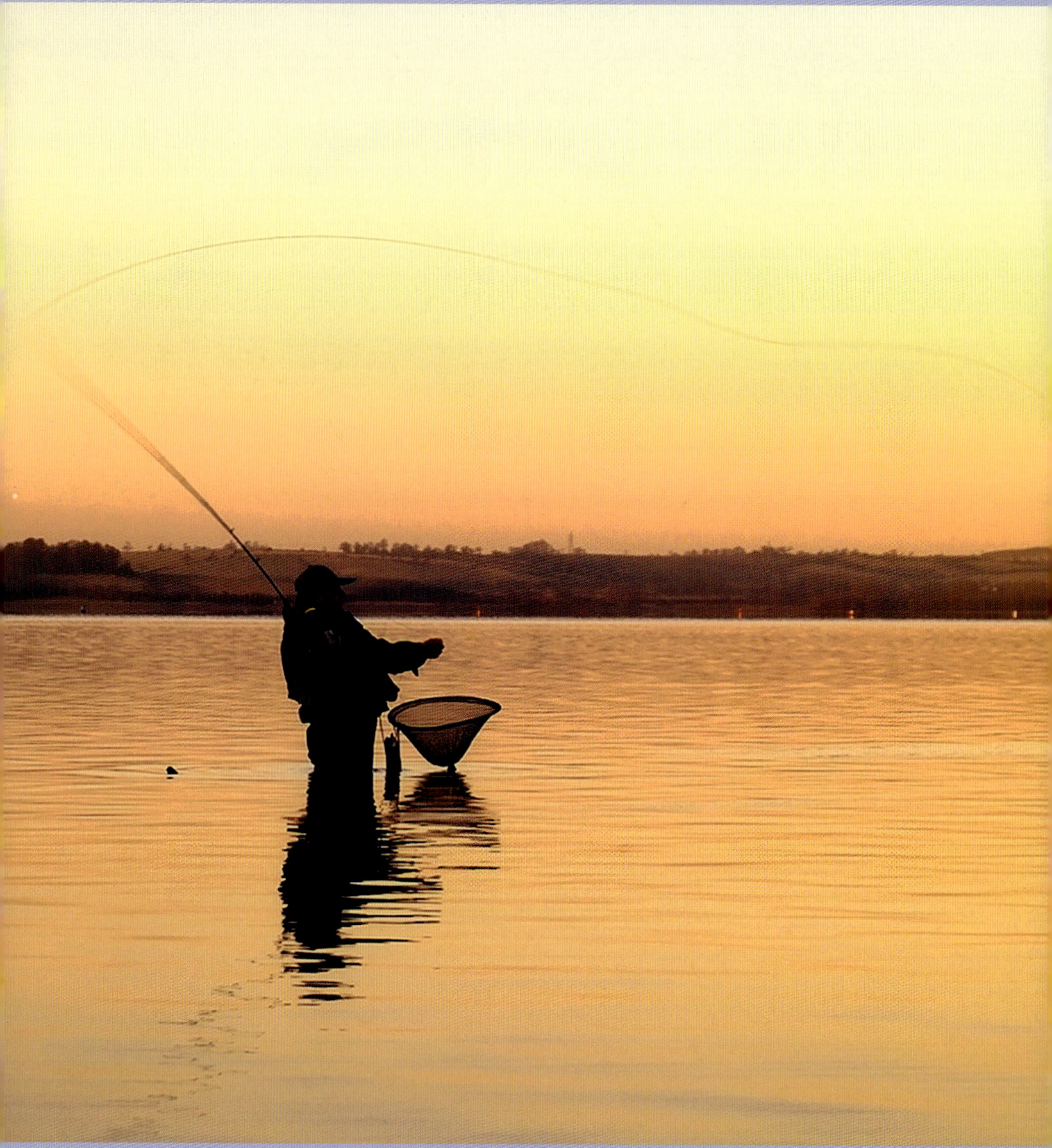

The Color Image 01

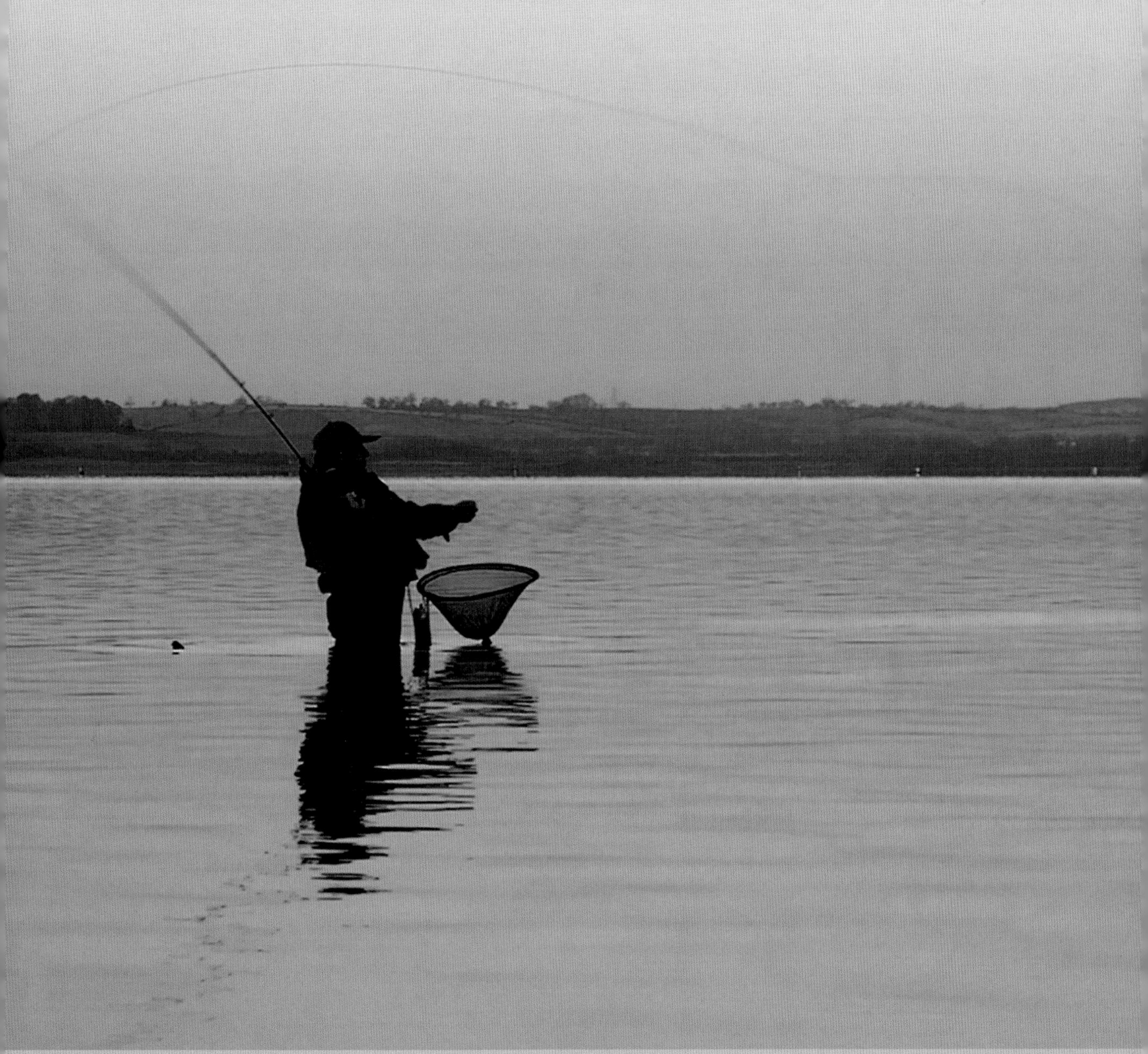

Introduction

It is easy to take color for granted; after all, it is how we see the world every day. But color plays such an integral part in our emotions and in our perception of a scene that knowledge of the nature of color and how to capture it in your images will give impact and expression to your photography.

Painters and designers learn how color can be used to their advantage at a very early stage, but for most photographers learning about this issue is often a question of trial and error. Traditionally, this has been because photography did not offer the same artistic license as other visual media. Simply capturing the world around them meant that there seemed little point in photographers learning how to mix colors and use color contrasts. However, digital photography has opened up a whole new world of creative possibilities, by offering everyone the opportunity to create their own vision of the world around them, including the ability to adjust or even to change colors.

Traditionalists may not hold with this level of manipulation, but does anyone object to black-and-white photography? That is surely the greatest manipulation of all, and it has been at the heart of photography since its very beginning. Even capturing images on color film is not a pure recording medium. Film does not "see light in the same way as we do; as soon as you press the shutter you are manipulating reality, so make the mos of it and use color to your advantage.

Knowing how to use color effectivel will expand your creativity and your awareness of why some images work while others fall flat. It is also valuable to know about the more technical aspects of the subject: color accuracy and knowledge of light sources will make it easier for you to capture the image accurately in camera. This mixture of artistic

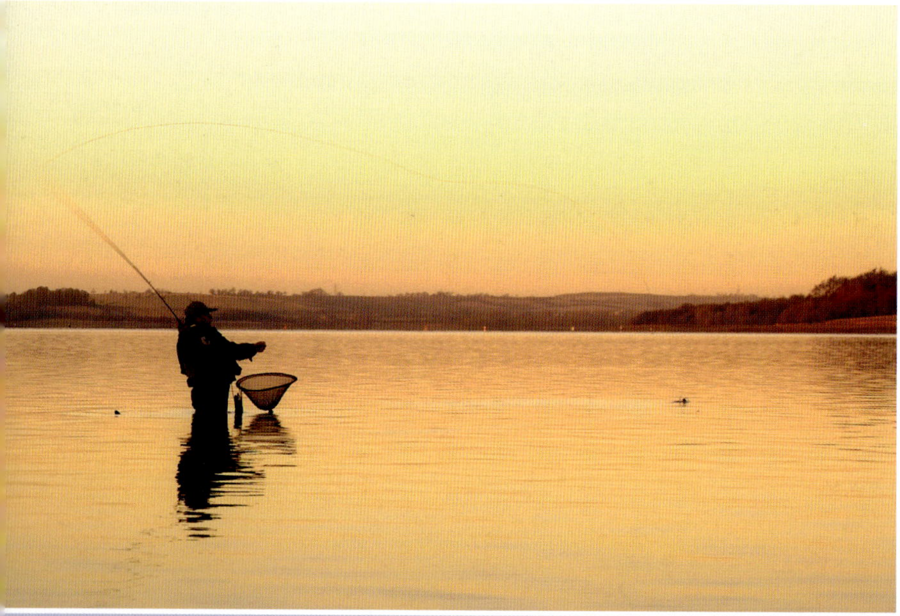

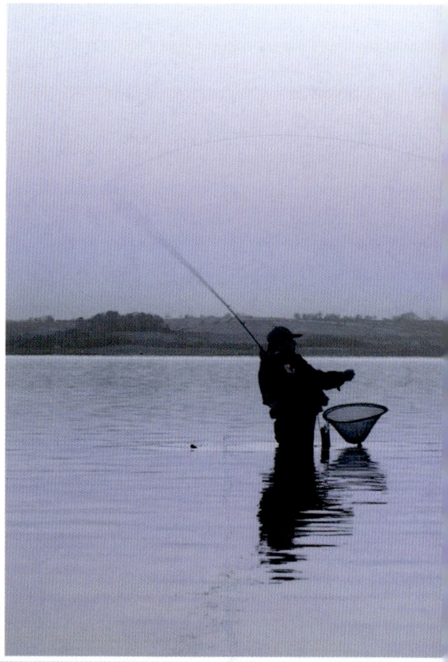

nd technical aspects lies at the eart of photography. Concentrating olely on the technical factors of your nages—the exposure, sharpness, and o on—can result in dull and contrived nages. But without some technical nowledge, you will struggle to get the nost from your photography. This is specially true of color and how you se it effectively in your images. If you oncentrate solely on getting the color echnically correct, you will miss out n a whole world of images.

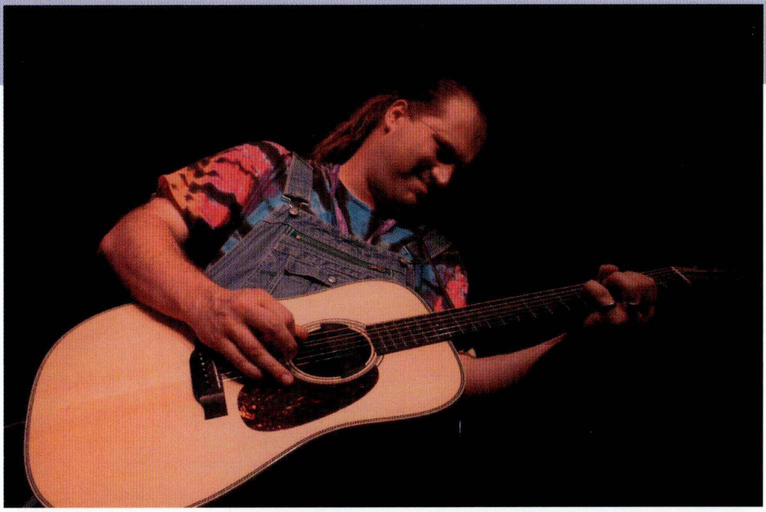

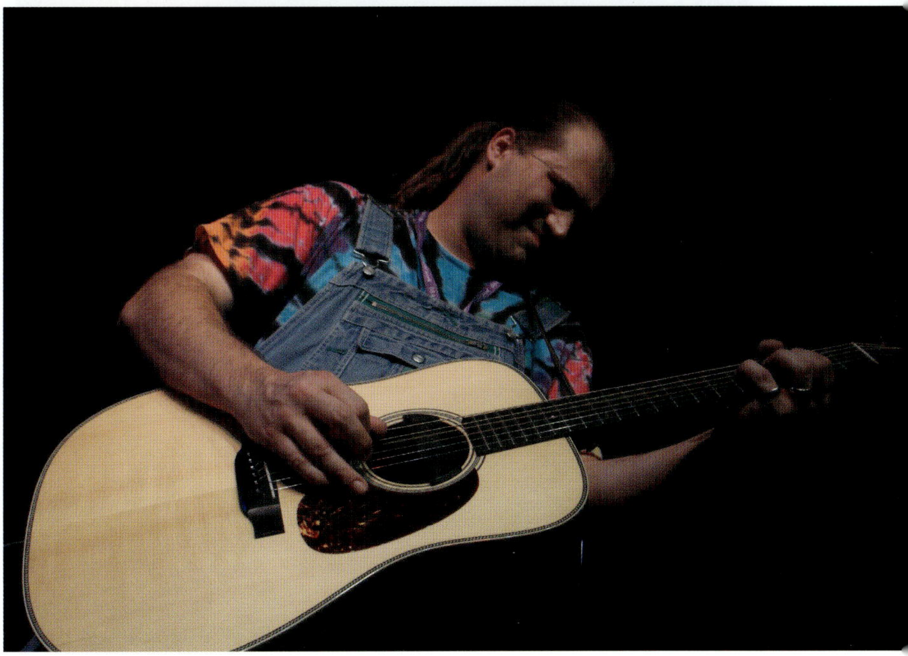

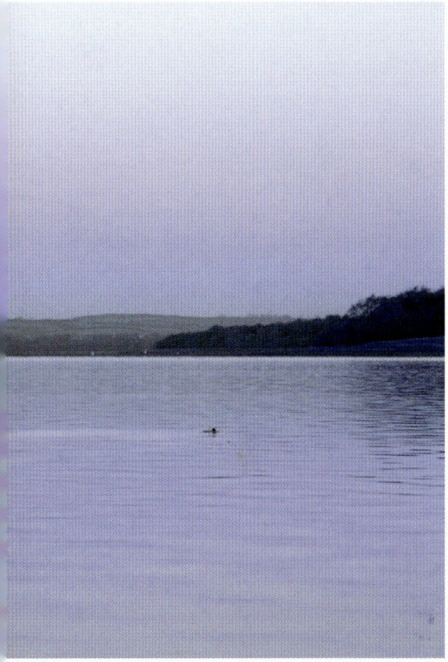

It is easy for us to identify the colors of this image as wrong, but what has caused the color cast and how do you eliminate it? Without some knowledge of how colors appear and basic color theory, it would take far more trial and error to find a solution than is necessary. This is why it is important for photographers to learn something about how colors work before embarking on the more creative aspects of color photography.

The difference between these two images is simple: one is mainly orange and one mainly blue. However, the difference in the overall feel of the two is marked. The orange image is welcoming and warm. In the blue image, the whole scene looks cold and uninviting. Why these colors cause such differing emotions is largely psychological. The ability to measure the color differences and manipulate them allows us to capture more than a simple representation of a scene; it allows us to create a more personal view of the world.

You need to be able to spot the potential of the colors in a scene and then use them in your images. This process starts long before you even pick up the camera; it involves how you see colors and how they influence our perception of the world. Honing these skills, along with the ability to capture them to recreate the impact they had on you at the time, is the key to producing great color photographs.

Even when you don't have your camera with you, keep your eye in by looking at the scenes around you. You will soon see how many of the things we take for granted use the same color principles that you can use in your photography. This includes how nature uses color to attract or deter other creatures, and how designers and architects use color to create an emotional reaction when we use their products or buildings.

Be aware that, for all our knowledge and technology, there are still aspects of color and light that we do not fully understand. Even the way that we actually see colors is a mystery; although the basic physical aspects are known, how our brains interpret the information gathered by our eyes is still open to much speculation. For me, that is what makes color photography such an interesting medium. Color has the power to create moods, evoke emotions, or show the world in ways that would otherwise be invisible or lost to our everyday lives. By carefully selecting, adjusting, or manipulating the colors present in an image, it can be given a meaning that can be as blatant or as subtle as you like.

Before we get started on the photographic aspects of color, we need to find out what color is and why we react to colors differently. The following pages will investigate the basics of color theory, along with the science behind our vision, and how we have tried to quantify and categorize colors. It is, of course, possible to explore the creative use of color without this groundwork. But with more and more photographers taking control of the whole imagemaking process, from capture through to printing, the need for an understanding of how and why colors appear as they do is becoming more important. So let's see why colors look the way they do.

Nature uses color to send signals, deter potential threats, and to communicate. We may not know exactly what these colors mean to the animals concerned, but our reaction to the different colors is largely influenced by the world around us.

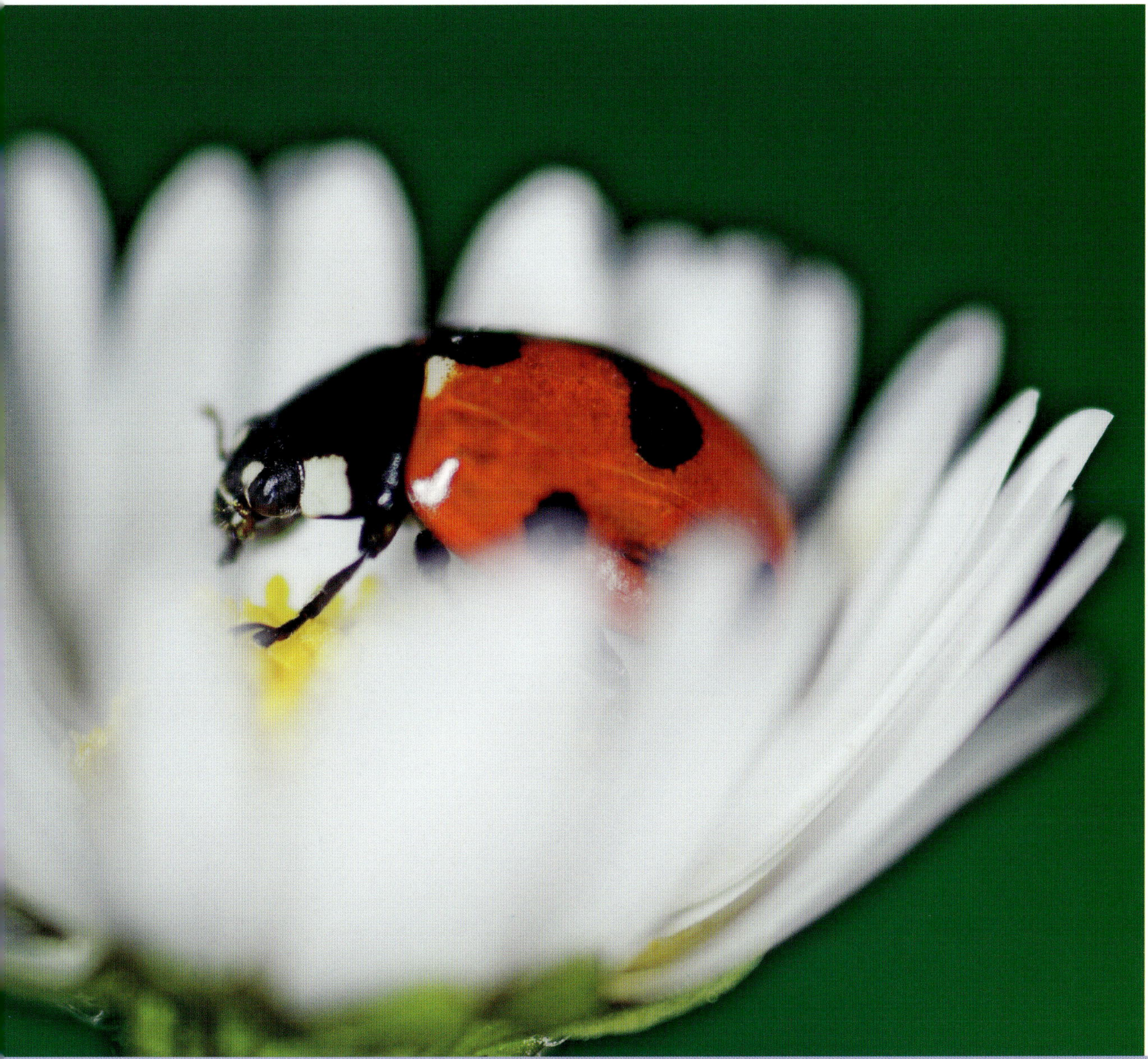

What is Color?

As long ago as the 6th-century in China, people have tried to understand how and why we react to different colors and how the various colors work together. This ongoing study has produced many theories about the nature of color, all with a similar theme at their heart.

Color theory is based around the existence of three colors that, when mixed together, can produce all other colors. These colors, known as the primary colors, vary according to their application. As photographers, we are mainly concerned with the properties of light, so that is what we will concentrate on here.

Additive Color

The three primary colors of light are red, green, and blue (RGB). Combinations of these building blocks can be used to produce all of the colors in the visible spectrum, and equal amounts of all three produce white light. Because these colors are added together to make white, they are known as additive primaries. Mixing equal amounts of two primary colors together produces what are known as the secondary colors. These are: yellow (red + green); cyan (green + blue); and magenta (blue + red). The easiest way to visualize these relationships is using a diagram known as a color wheel.

By placing the different colors around a circle you can see how the colors work, and how they influence each other. The primary colors are equally placed around the wheel, with the secondary colors placed between the two colors that, when combined, make that color.

The colors that are next to each other on the color wheel are known as harmonious or analogous colors. This is because when you see them together they give a sense of calm and peace, or harmony.

Colors opposite each other on the color wheel create the maximum contrast and are known as complementary colors. When viewed together, these colors can clash, creating a striking image.

These two relationships between colors lie at the heart of color theory. Color theory has been used by both scientists and artists for centuries, allowing them to categorize colors, or exploit them for visual effect.

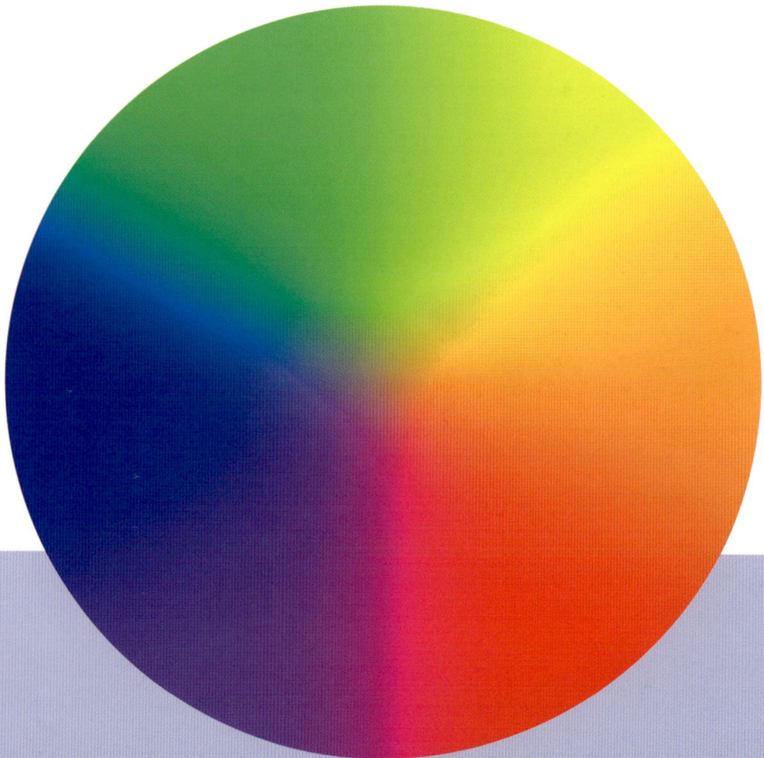

ıubtractive Color

ınfortunately, the red, green, and
ue additive primaries do not apply
every situation. To explain how
rinting inks produce different colors,
ɔu have to consider a different set
f primary colors: cyan, magenta, and
ellow (CMY). When combined in equal
mounts, these three colors produce
ack, and are known as subtractive
rimaries (in printing, these colors
e known as CMYK; the "K" stands
r black to avoid confusion with
ue, although originally "K" stood for
"key plate"). If you look at the color wheel diagram, you will see that this is simply a reversal of the primary and secondary colors.

Because cyan and magenta are not often encountered in their pure form in nature, subtractive color is best considered as a technical aspect of printing, rather than as a color theory for explaining color combinations. We will investigate it further when we discuss the process of color printing (see pp.68–71).

Another set of subtractive primary colors is yellow, red, and blue (YRB). This system is based on pigments and is therefore of most importance to painters. These three colors are those that aren't created by mixing any other colors, so are the primary colors. This produces a color wheel that varies slightly to the RGB model. But the colors are essentially in the same order around the wheel. So, despite the differences, you can apply both in a similar way.

Summary of the Uses of Primary Colors

With three different combinations of primary colors, it can be confusing as to which should be used. Here are the technical uses for each.

- Additive
  – Red, green, and blue (RGB): light, digital cameras, and displays
- Subtractive
  – Cyan, magenta, and yellow (CMY): commercial printing and some home printers
  – Yellow, red, and blue (YRB): painting and art theory

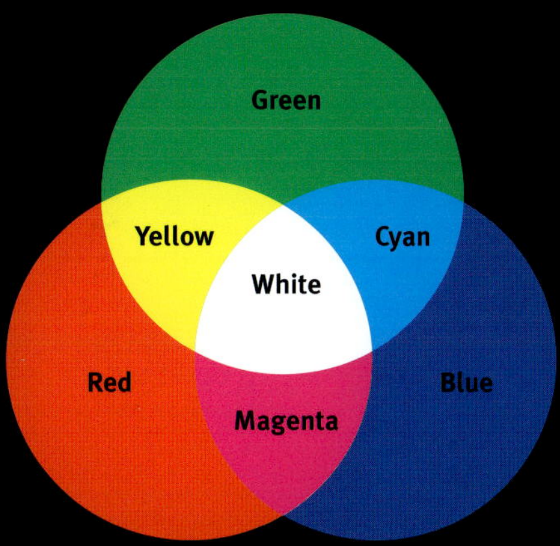

Additive Colors

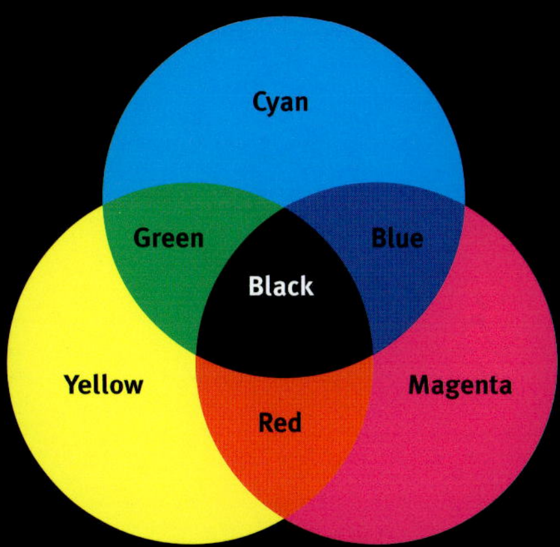

Subtractive Colors

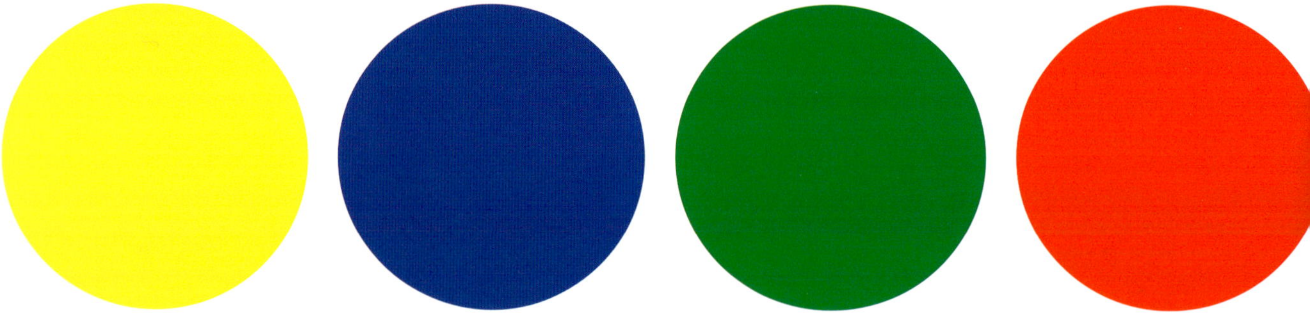

Despite being the same color saturation and intensity, the yellow swatch appears much brighter than the blue next to it. This discrepancy in our color vision plays a large part in how we react to certain colors in an image.

Which Color Theory is Best to Use?

As photography is concerned with the action of light, it is easiest to concentrate on using RGB as the primary colors. While there are differences between the relationships of the color in this and the YRB primaries, they both use colors in the same basic order on their respective color wheels. So neither is necessarily best to use, just more convenient.

Color Intensity

While the basic theory of primary and secondary colors is useful as a starting point, it does not fully explain how the colors work together. In this model, all the colors are presumed to be perceived equally. Unfortunately, our vision is not a precise instrument and we see colors differently, even though they have equal intensity.

For example, we generally perceive blue and green tones as being much darker than reds or yellows of the same intensity. This perception is partly physical, but is also due to the world around us. In nature, most blue and green objects, such as a clear sky or foliage, are non-threatening, so we don't need to pay so much attention to them. Red and yellow are more often encountered with objects that we need to pay attention to—blood or dangerous animals, for example—so we are accustomed to perceiving these colors as brighter and more eye-catching. These reactions mean that if we see an image with equal amounts of two primary colors—for example, red and blue—the red appears much stronger and more prominent.

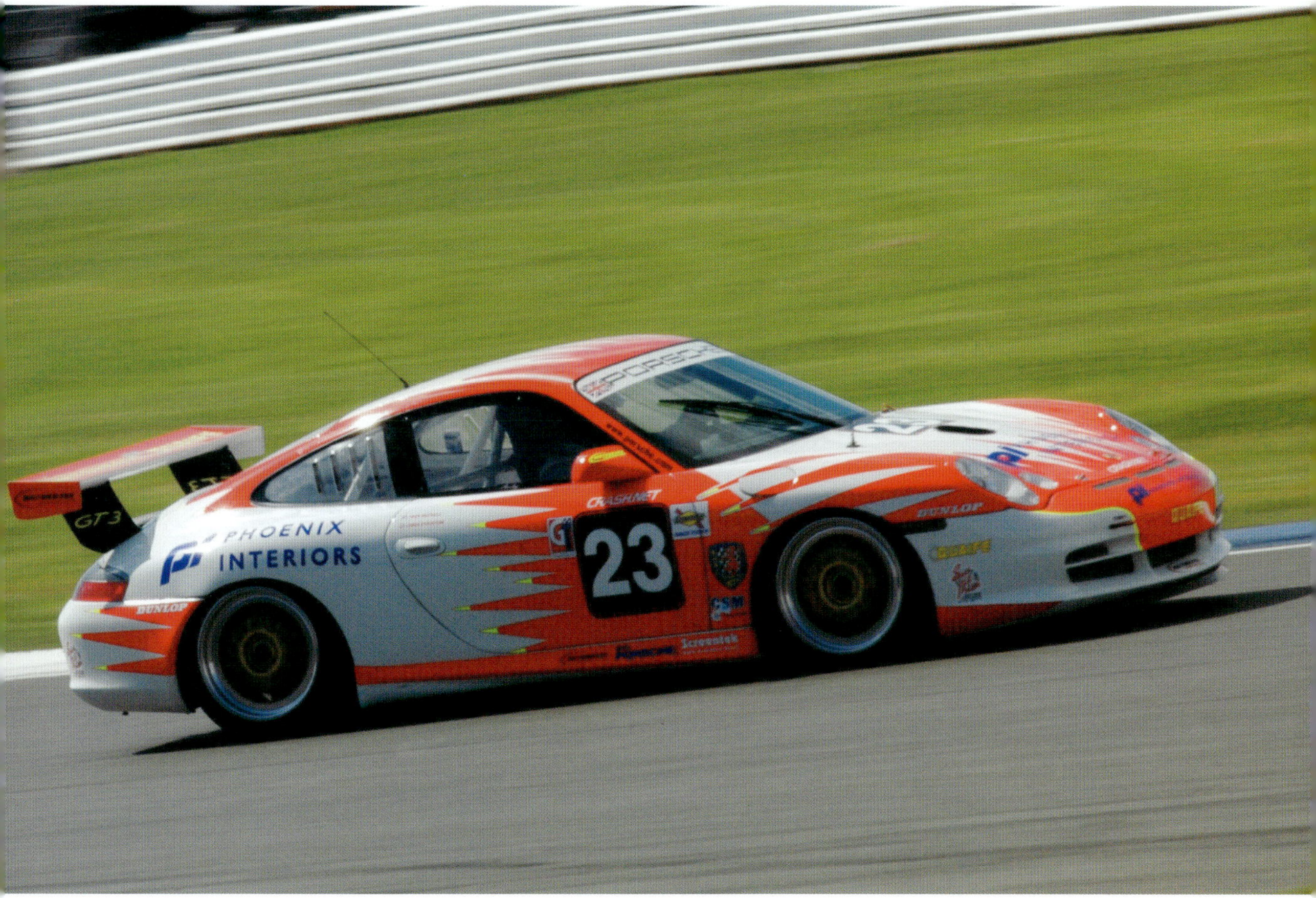

Red is a popular color for making objects stand out from green or blue backgrounds.

Light

We can only see (and photograph) color because of light. What we normally see as white light is actually a combination of many different colors. The rainbow we were all taught about at school is merely white light split into its constituent colors.

Much of our knowledge about light derives from experiments that the scientist Sir Isaac Newton (1643–1727) carried out in the 17th century. He demonstrated that daylight can be split into a series of colors. This sequence of colors—red, orange, yellow, green, blue, indigo, and violet—is known as the chromatic color sequence. Colors that are not part of this sequence, such as beige or burgundy, are known as nonchromatic colors.

The nature of light itself is still the subject of much speculation. Current theories explain light by giving it the properties of both waves and particles. We will deal primarily with the wave theory; this explains the aspects of light, such as wavelength and frequency, that concern us in color photography.

Light Waves

The easiest way to understand light waves is to imagine holding a string that is fixed in position at the other end. By vibrating this string, you create waves traveling along it. The faster you vibrate it, the narrower the distance between the crest of each wave. The slower you vibrate it, the longer this distance. This spacing between the points is known as the wavelength. It is this difference that creates the different colors within the spectrum.

The brightness of the light is due to the amount of energy produced by the light source. While this has an influence on photography, it does not directly affect the colors produced.

Light waves are the visible part of a much larger group of waves known as the electromagnetic spectrum, which includes X-rays and radio waves. The range that is present in daylight is shown below. This ranges from the short-wavelength ultraviolet to the longer-wavelength infrared, with the visible portion in between.

While our eyes cannot see ultraviol or infrared radiation, these can have an effect on the image produced by both digital sensors and film. In most circumstances, it is undesirable for the image to register radiation outsid of the visible spectrum. However, it is useful for both scientific and artistic applications for producing images of world beyond our visible experience.

The visible spectrum used in photography is only part of a much greater range of electromagnetic radiation.

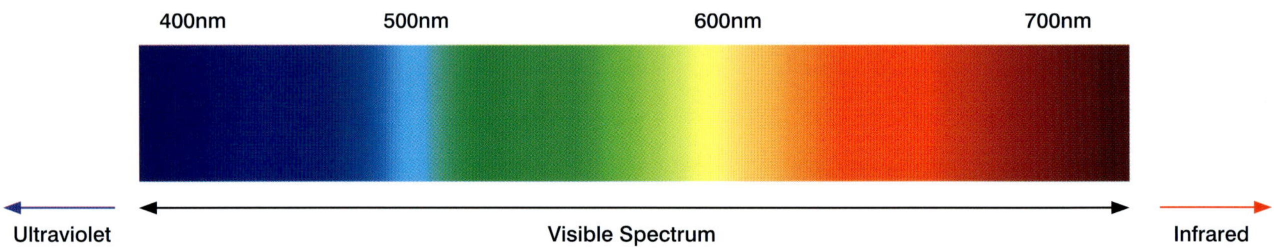

Vhy Objects Appear Colored

Vhen we see an object lit by white ght, its color is due to the object bsorbing some colors and reflecting or transmitting) others. For example, reen foliage appears to be green ecause it contains pigments that bsorb blue and red light and reflect nly green light.

It is a similar story when the light viewed through an object, such s a photographic filter. You only ee the part of the spectrum that allowed through. For example, a lue filter blocks red and green light, nd allows only the blue part of the pectrum through.

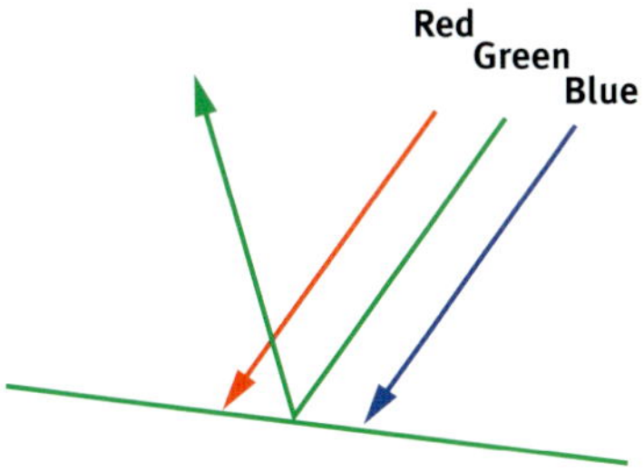

Reflected Color

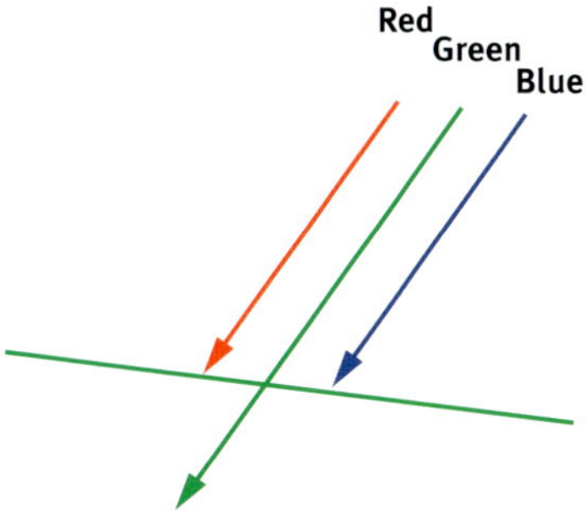

Transmitted Color

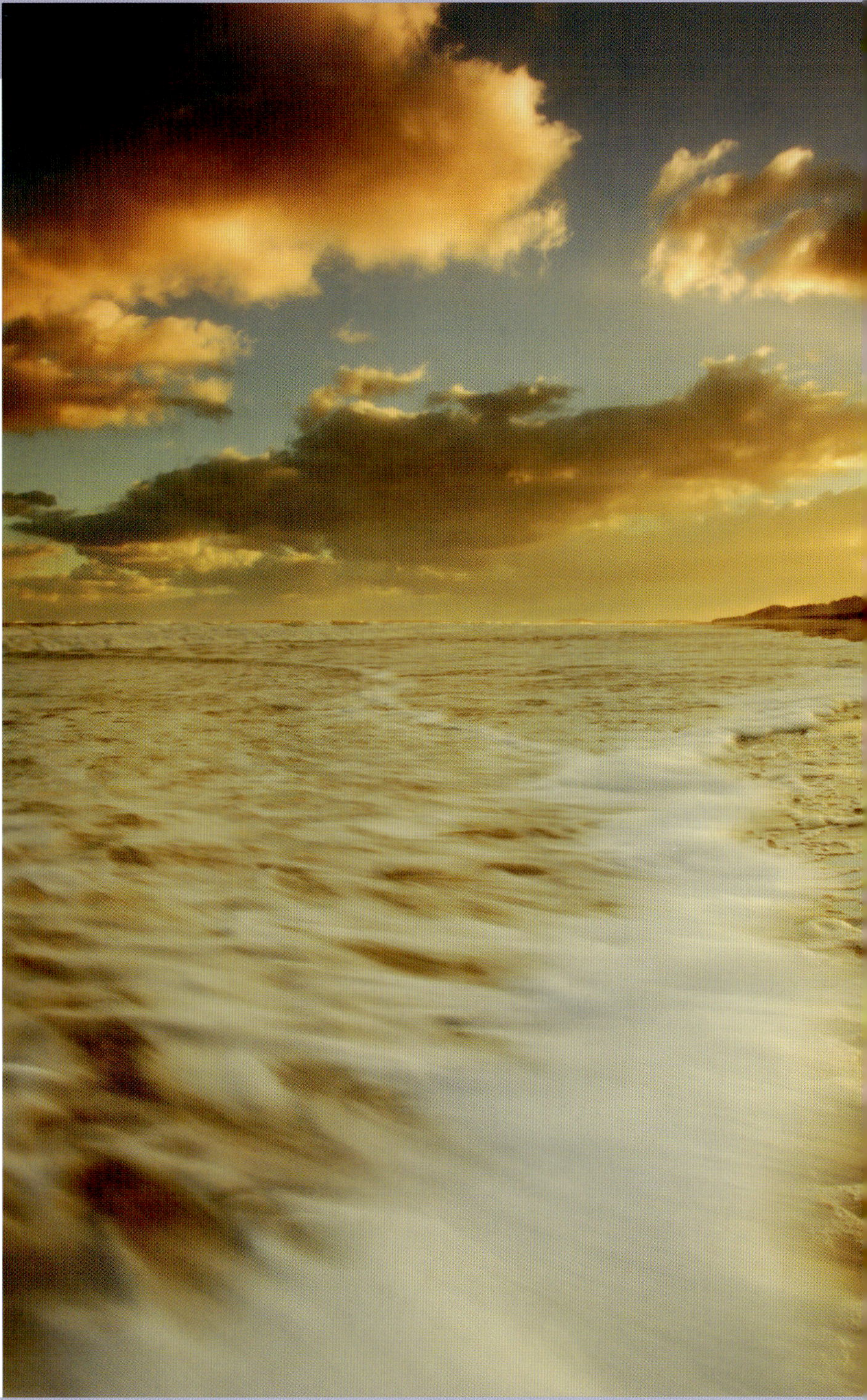

We only see the color and shape of the world around us because of the light either reflected or transmitted by each object we look at.

Measuring Colors

Human vision is very good at recognizing the differences between two colors seen side by side. However, it is a different story when it comes to accurately describing individual colors to someone else. Accurate color classification is an important aspect in color-management systems, which we discuss in detail later (see pp.72–75).

As an example, look at the colors of the flowers and background in the image below and try to accurately describe the two colors. Without being able to relate each to another color, you will struggle. You can say that the flowers are purple, or magenta, but it is almost impossible to relate that to someone who hasn't seen the color, even if they have a selection of colors to choose from.

There is also the matter of personal interpretation of different hues; as we will see in the section on how we see color (see pp.24–27), each individual has their own idea of what colors should look like. So, even if you have "perfect" vision, you cannot quantify the colors that you see without comparing one to another, and even this is open to massive differences in our interpretation of the color.

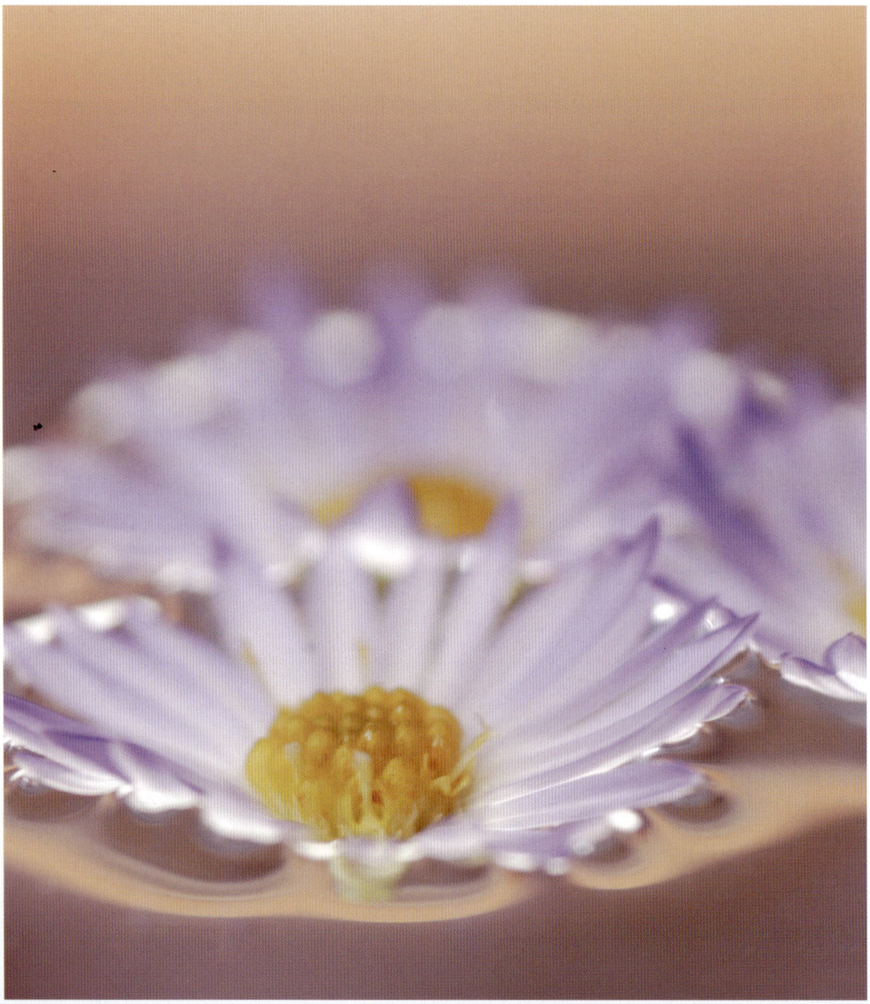

Describing Colors

To accurately describe colors for color matching, especially when we delve into the world of digital imaging and color management, we need a more reliable method. In order to describe a specific color, we need to break it down into three elements:

• Hue: the name given to the color itself. This is defined by the name given to the main wavelength contained within the color, such as blue, green, magenta, and so on.

• Saturation (or chroma): the purity of the color. In many instances, especiall in print or pigments, mixing black, gray, or white to a color will result in lower saturation.

« Even though we can see colors accurately, it is very difficult to describe them without a reference point to relate them to. That is what color measuremen is designed to do.

Luminance: the brightness of the olor. In pigments or print, this escribes how much incident light he color reflects; in the case of a ght source, it describes how much ght is emitted.

y using these three measurements, ny color can be described so that can then be recreated accurately hroughout an imaging system. An nderstanding of these measurements vill help you to understand the elationships between the colors in ne scene that you are photographing nd how these will be reproduced in ne final image.

There are two main systems used o define colors and give them a pecific numerical value: the Munsell ystem, and the CIE (Commission nternationale d'Eclairage) system.

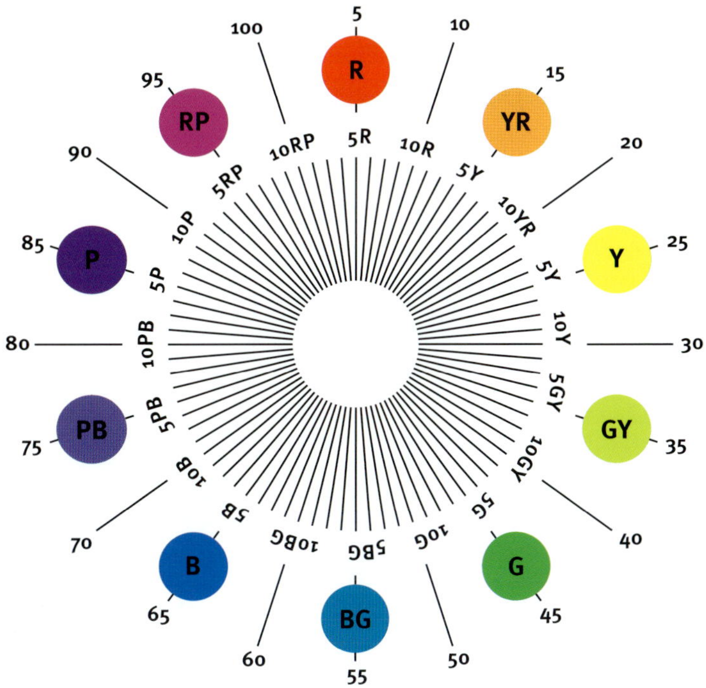

The Munsell System

Originally developed by American artist A. H. Munsell (1858–1918), this system was designed to classify standards for printing inks, color pigments, and artists' paints. It uses a collection of color charts made up of printed color swatches for each hue. Each color is assigned a number to define the hue (the chart that it appears on). Further values for luminance and saturation give vertical and horizontal coordinates to indicate where it appears on this chart. Therefore, as long as you have these three values, you can find the color on the Munsell chart and use it to ensure that it remains constant throughout an imaging system.

Because it is based on the pigments and inks available for printing, the Munsell system has only a limited use for photography. It cannot define many of the colors that you will come across in many situations—for example, the colors produced by a light source, or substances that have no direct pigment equivalent, such as fluorescent, or the phosphers used to produce the image on a computer screen.

However, the Munsell system is still in common use in the printing industry and some areas of graphic design; if you are producing images for magazines, you may come across this system for defining the colors that they are able to produce.

The CIE System

The CIE system is much more suited to classifying color in photography. It is usually shown in the form of a chromaticity diagram (see diagram below). It classifies colors by equating them to the quantity of red, green, and blue light that need to be mixed together to produce a color. This is shown graphically so that every color that it is possible to define can be placed by defining its X and Y values. Because it is based on the mixture of red, green, and blue light that forms the basis for most digital imaging, this system has become the standard for digital photography. This makes it the most suitable system for defining the colors in color-management systems.

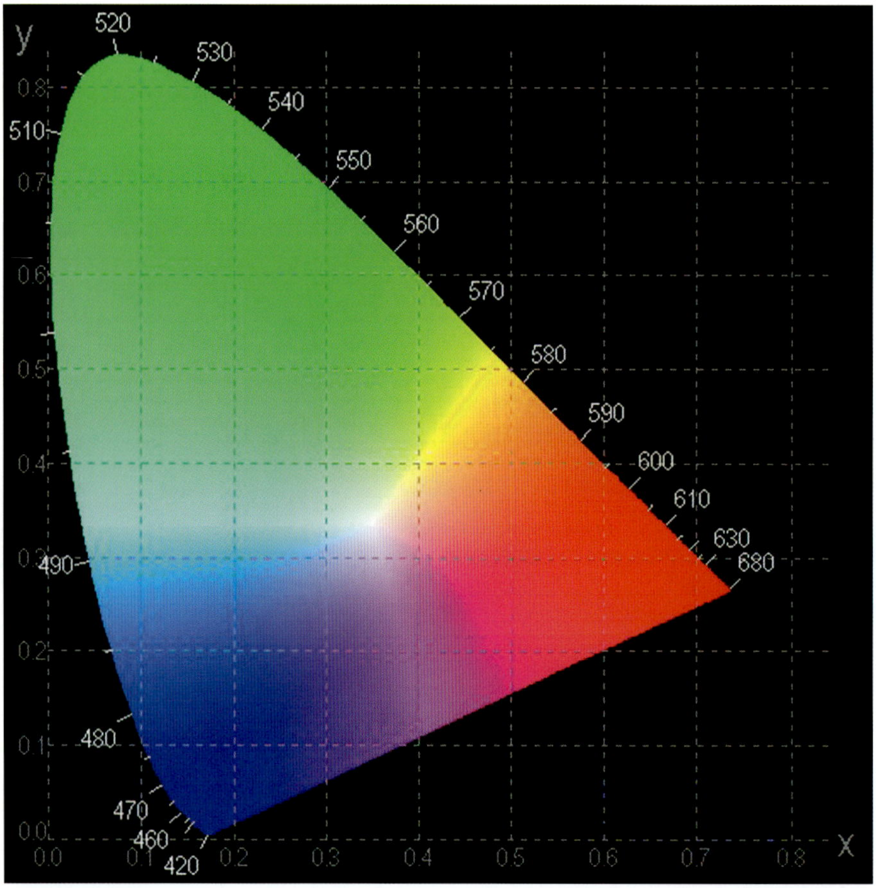

Why Do We Need Color-classification Systems?

When we photograph a scene, we will come across a huge range of colors and tones. Color-classification systems mean that it is possible to predict how these colors will be reproduced by each device that you use to produce the final image.

As a photographer, knowing how your camera, computer monitor, and printer will cope with the colors it encounters will help you produce the image that you visualized at the time. Knowing, for example, that your printer will struggle to reproduce the greens in the original scene means that you can try to adjust how you shoot the scene in the first place so you won't be disappointed in the final image.

/iewing

·ecause the color that we see is ffected by the color of the light alling on it, any color classification ased on color swatches relies on standard light source for viewing. o accurately assess any color in a rint, you need to view it under the ght lighting. The most common type f light is known as standard daylight, nd specialized viewing booths used commercial printing use lights esigned to produce a very accurate olor. These booths are beyond the neans of most photographers, but ou can buy daylight bulbs relatively heaply that are accurate enough for ll but the most critical uses. Try to set side an area of your workspace that oesn't contain any strong colors for ou to accurately assess the colors of our prints.

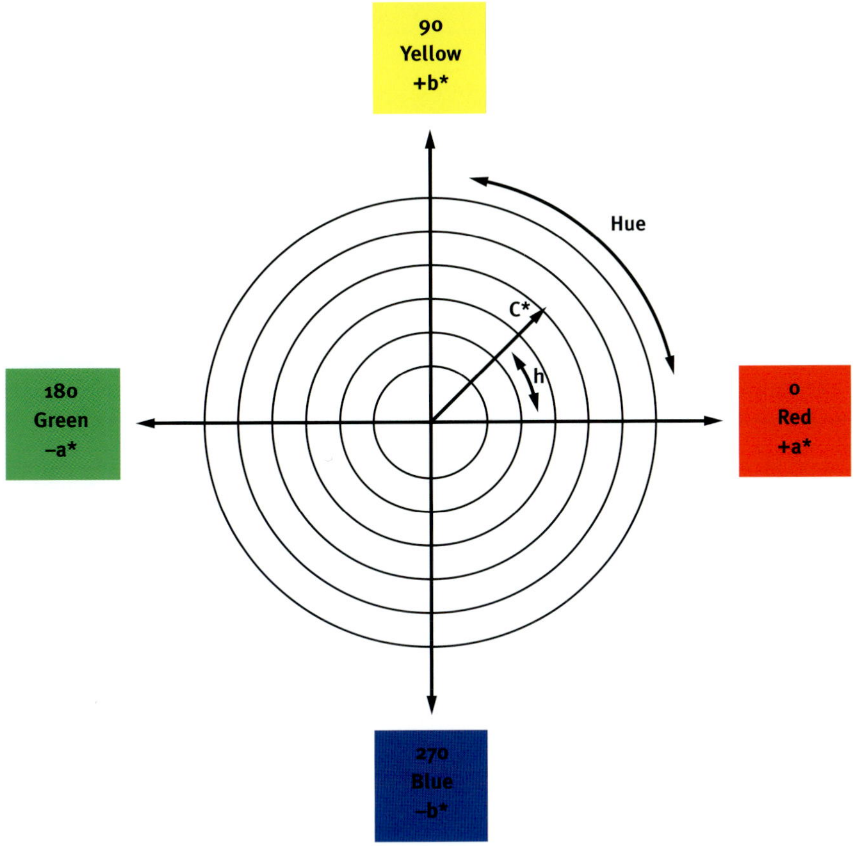

Color spaces can also be shown graphically around a circle. The hue is expressed in degrees around the circle and the saturation by the distance from the center of the circle.

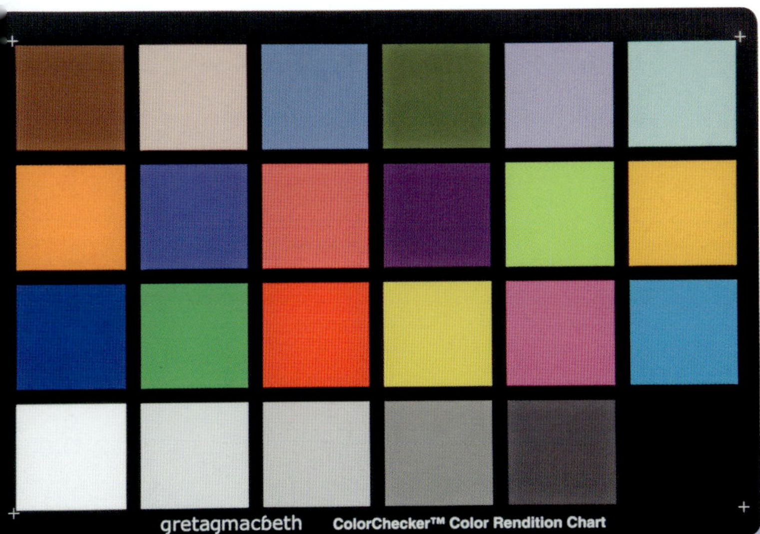

The Gretag Macbeth ColorChecker is the most commonly used standard for producing accurate results.

How We See Color

Trying to understand how color is recorded photographically without knowing how we see color is like trying to cook a meal without ever tasting food. While photographic materials record colors in a predictable and measurable way, it is how we see and react to both the original scene and the final results that makes or breaks the process.

While you may think that you see colors with your eyes, it is actually the brain's interpretation of the information that determines what we see. This can be influenced by personal and cultural factors (certain colors have specific meanings in different countries, for example). Despite these variable factors, there are also many deep-rooted reactions that seem to be almost universal, and these can be exploited in your photography.

Physical Aspects of Vision

Let's discuss some basic physical aspects of vision before describing how we use this information. As we have seen, light is made up from three primary colors—red, green, and blue—and this is basically how our eyes see color. The light-sensitive cells within the eye are split into two main types: rod-shaped and cone-shaped. The rods are the most sensitive to light, but cannot discriminate between different colors. The cones are less sensitive to light, but contain chemicals that allow them to see one of the three primary colors. The blue- and green-sensitive rods equate very well to the colors that we think of as pure primary colors, but the rods that we use to see red light are only sensitive to light that we would consider to be orange. The information given by these three types of rod is sent to our brain, which interprets the information to give us a mental picture of the scene. So, while our eyes play a major part in the physical aspects of vision, it is our brain that determines what we see.

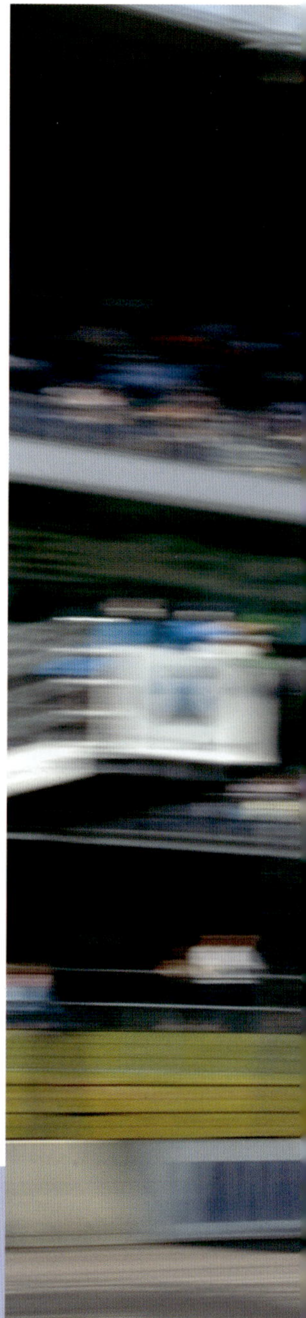

» **Your attention is immediately drawn to the red car in this image, despite the fact that it occupies only a small area of the frame. This is due to many factors, one of which is the fact that red is associated with danger. Consequently, we pay more attention to red than to the colors around it.**

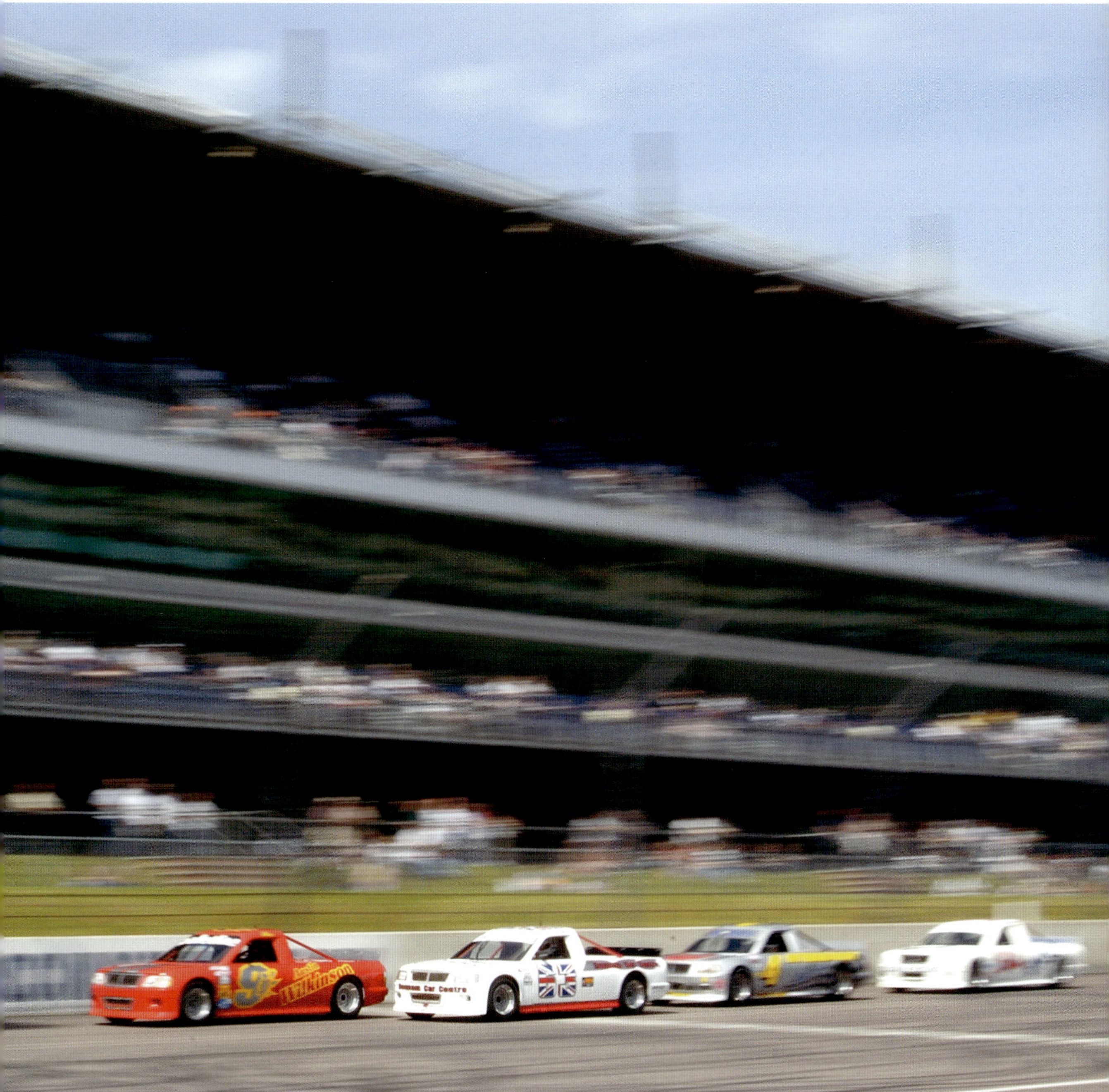
Wilkinson
Car Centre

Color blindness test chart.

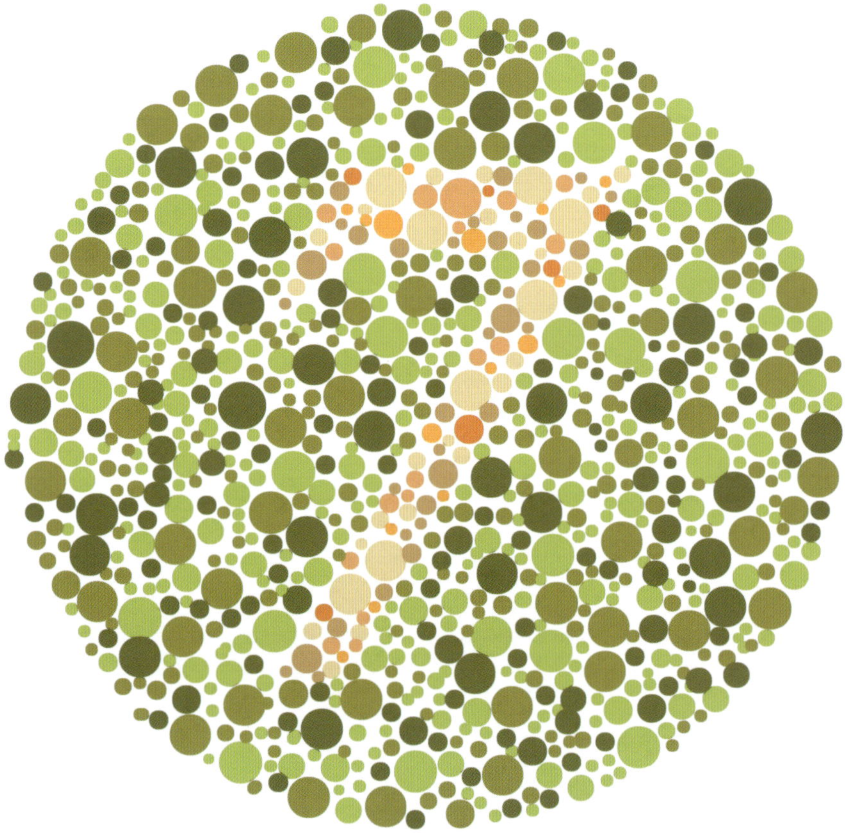

Limitations of Color Vision

There are many factors that mean that the colors seen by one person may not match those seen by another. Here are the most common problems to bear in mind when trying to assess color correctly.

Color blindness

As opposed to the psychological influences that mean we all interpret colors differently, color blindness is a physical aspect of the reaction within the eye. This can take the form of a slightly uneven response to the three primary colors, or can result in an inability to distinguish between red and green. Color blindness affects around one tenth of the male population, but is much less common in females. At its most severe, color blindness can cause problems with achieving accurate color balance, so it is worth checking out whether you suffer from this condition by using some of the charts readily available, or asking your optician.

Color memory

The human mind can be lazy at times; rather than making the effort of analyzing what we see, it often makes up information because it is easier to do so. If we see an object that we "know" should be a particular color, then the brain tells us that's what we are in fact seeing. For example, when you see a picture of a blue sky, your brain doesn't necessarily see the actual color, because you already know what color a blue sky should be. On the other hand, we take far more notice of the precise color of other objects, such as food or skin, because these are areas that, historically, we need to see precisely.

rightness and adaptation

ike the aperture of a lens, our yes have an iris to govern the mount of light allowed through. dark conditions, once the iris is illy opened, the eye increases its ensitivity to allow us to still see. his extra sensitivity is controlled by ie rod-shaped cells within the eye, so e get less and less information from ie color-sensitive cone-shaped cells. s the light levels drop, our sensitivity color shifts more toward the blue-reen end of the spectrum, until there no color information at all.

This adaptation is also partly esponsible for our ability to "correct" ifferent light sources. When you iove quickly from an area lit by aylight to an indoor situation lit by candescent light, the scene will ppear much more yellow. After a iort while in this lighting, your vision ill adapt, making the scene appear iore neutral. As we'll see in coming chapters, neither digital nor film cameras and materials react to light this way, so have to be adjusted to give a result closer to our vision.

Color fatigue

Our perception of an individual color can be affected by the color(s) surrounding it. This is partly a psychological reaction, but it is also due to the receptors in the eye becoming fatigued and influencing what you see. For example, if you place two identically colored objects against two differently colored backgrounds, the color of the object will often appear to be different.

Despite all these limitations, our vision is still remarkably good at assessing the world around us and how it can be captured photographically. The more you learn to see the world around you, the more likely you are to be able to interpret color correctly—and translate that into your photographs.

Although the blue area in both of these images is identical, because of the apparent intensity of the red around the bottom square, this appears darker than the one surrounded by the green. This color fatigue can greatly influence how your eye sees colors when working in an environment with one strong color, or when trying to assess colors on a computer monitor or print.

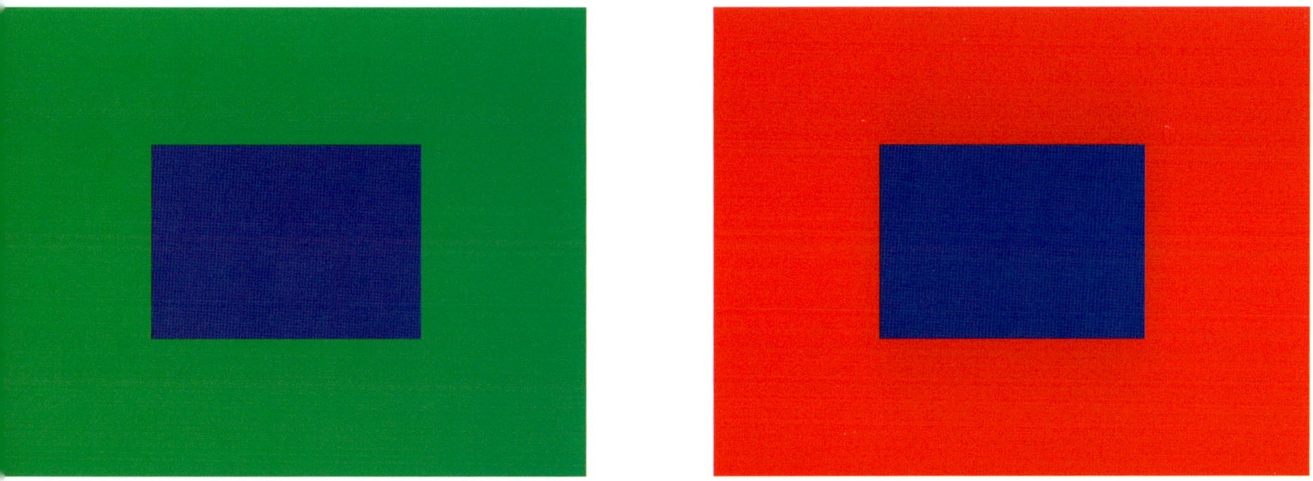

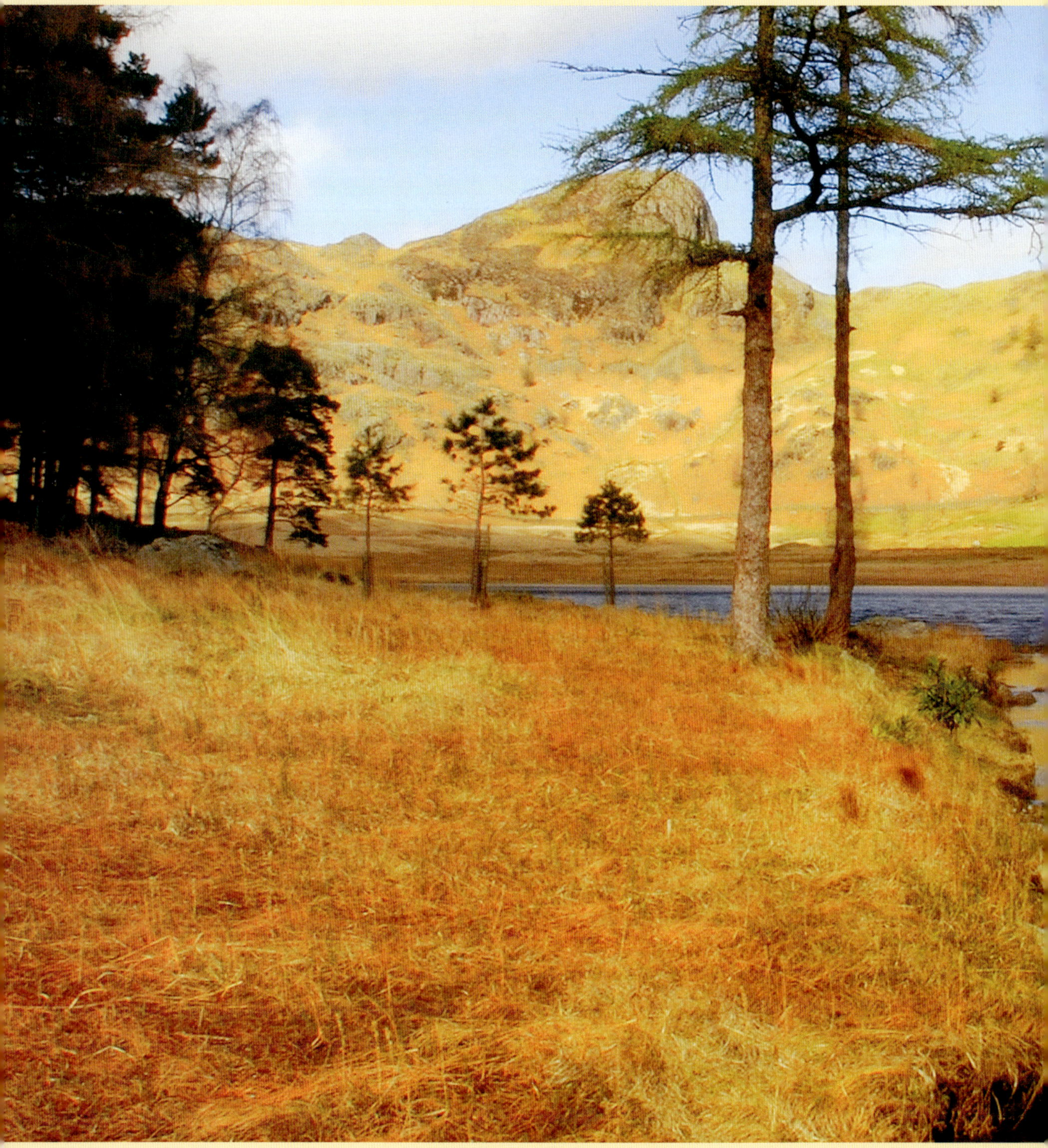

Capturing Color 02

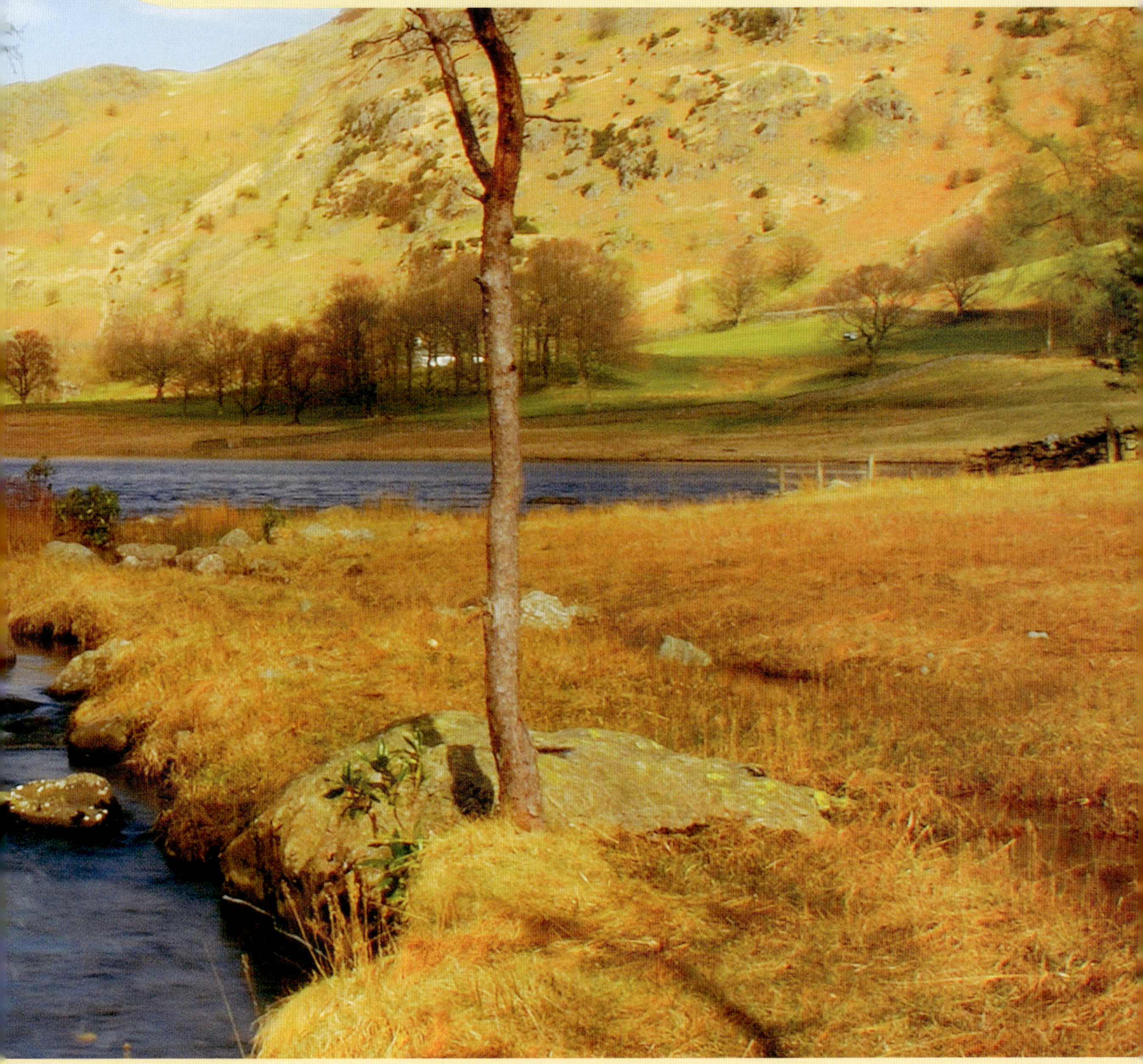

Digital Sensors

At the heart of every digital camera is the sensor. This array of millions of light-sensitive cells is what converts the light from the image into a signal that can be read and processed by a computer to create the digital image. So how does the sensor "see" color?

Imagine the sensor as a grid of millions of tiny squares. Each of these squares is an individual light-sensitive cell, or photodiode (PD). When the shutter is fired, the light falling onto each photodiode is turned into an electrical signal that is digitized—given a numeric value—that corresponds to the amount of light falling on it. At its simplest, this means that a cell that receives no light is given a zero value that corresponds to black, whereas one receiving a lot of light is given the maximum value and registers as white. The intermediate amounts of light are given values that correspond to different shades of gray. As long as the individual cells are small enough, viewed as a whole this would give an accurate monochrome rendition of the original scene.

To register the different colors falling on the sensor, the most common solution consists of a series of red, green, and blue filters covering each cell, so that it gives a signal for only one of the three primary colors. These filters are arranged in groups of four—one red, one blue, and two green. This design is known as the Bayer pattern mosaic filter. The extra green filter is used to mimic the extra green sensitivity of the human eye (see p.24). Each site only registers information about a single color; the signal from each photodiode is then processed by the CPU of the camera to form the fina image. To give the final color value for each pixel of the image, the data is combined with that from adjacent photodiodes. This process, called interpolation, relies on sophisticated software to assess the information gathered from nearby sites to assign the final color of the pixel. Because this process "guesses" some information for each pixel, it can lead to inaccuracies such as color artifacts and color casts if done poorly. This image processing is why two cameras with identical-looking specifications can produce very different results fror the same scene.

Bayer Mosaic Capture

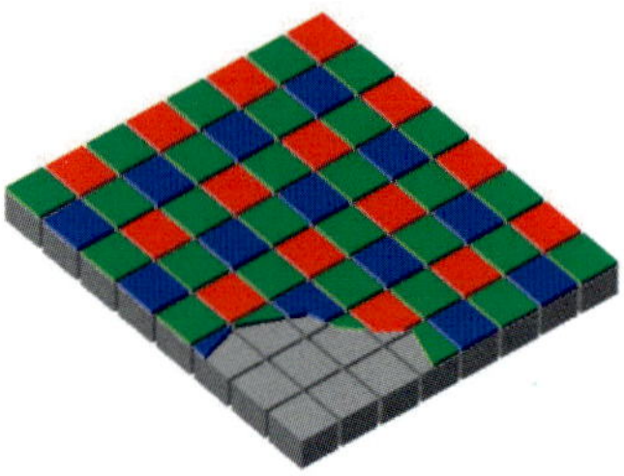

In conventional systems, color filters are applied to a single layer of photodetectors in a tiled mosaic pattern.

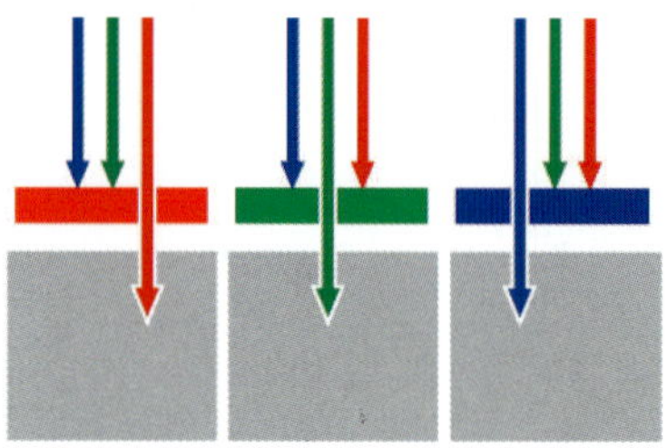

The filters let only one wavelength of light—red, green, or blue—pass through to any given pixel, allowing it to record only one color.

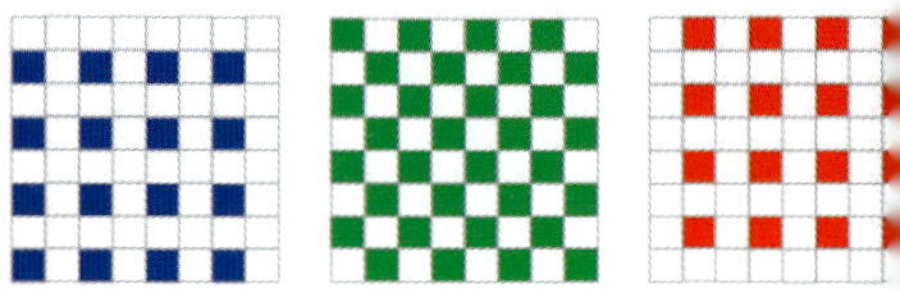

As a result, mosaic sensors capture only 25% o the red and blue light, and just 50% of the gree

The Bayer mosaic filter is used in most digital cameras.

·oveon Sensor

lthough the Bayer pattern mosaic lter is by far the most common type f filter used in digital sensors, there ; an alternative technology in use. he Foveon image sensor works in very different way from a mosaic lter. Instead of a single layer of hotodetectors covered by colored lters, the Foveon sensor uses three ıyers of photodetectors embedded n top of each other in the chip. This ystem exploits the fact that red, reen, and blue light penetrates silicon) different depths; the top layer is sed to detect red light, the middle ne green, and the deepest one blue.

The advantage of this system ver the mosaic filter is that every ıdividual pixel can detect all three olors. This does away with the need ɔr the image processor in the camera) interpolate (or guess) the amount of ıe other two colors. Because of this, ıe Foveon sensor can, theoretically, give more accurate color information and even sharpness from the same number of pixels. In practice, while there are some advantages to this, the more common mosaic filter gives adequate results.

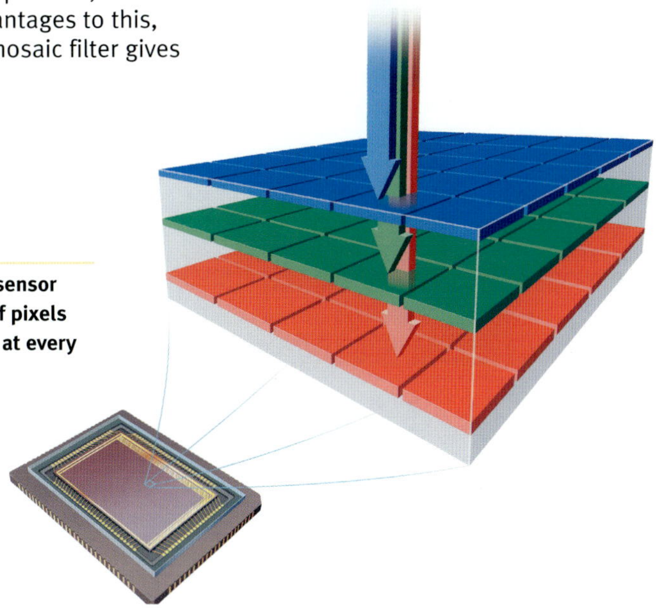

The Foveon image sensor uses three layers of pixels to record all colors at every sensor site.

ɔveon® X3™ Capture

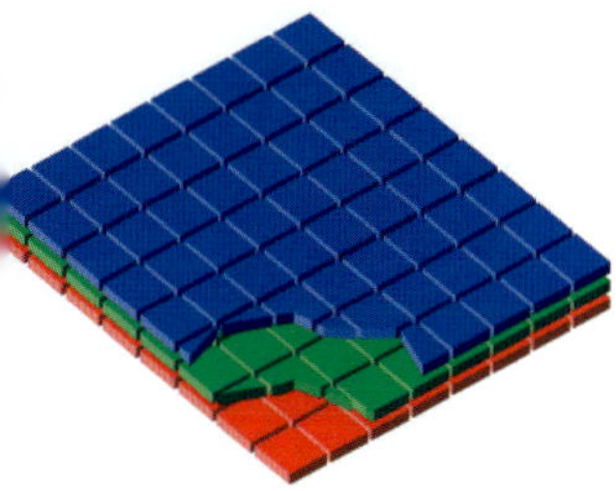

Foveon® X3™ image sensor ·atures three separate layers of ·hotodetectors embedded in silicon.

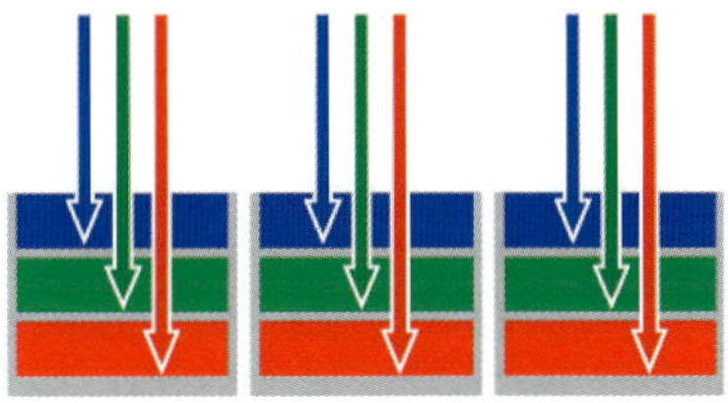

Since silicon adsorbs different colors of light at different depths, each layer captures a different color. Stacked together, they create full-color pixels.

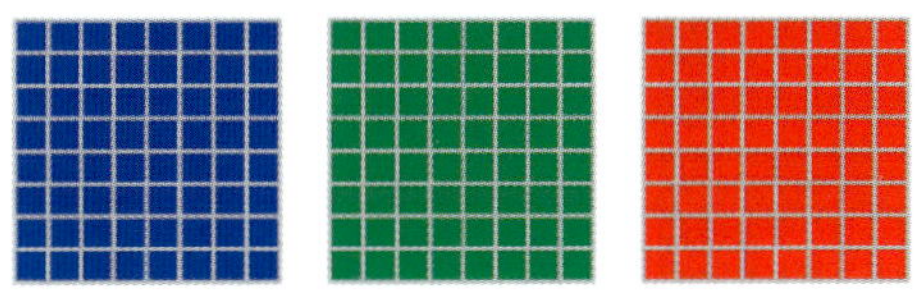

As a result, Foveon X3 image sensors capture red, green, and blue light at every pixel location.

In-camera Settings

Although the type of sensor in your digital camera is fixed, there are many ways in which you can influence the color of the results. To translate the light falling onto the sensor into a signal that can be read by your computer, the camera has to process the information. This in-camera processing can be varied according to your needs by accessing the setup menu of the camera.

Many of these functions will involve terminology that may be unfamiliar to photographers used to film cameras, and even the functions behind the more familiar terms can have a different effect on your images than their film equivalents. We will cover some of these in more detail in the following chapters, but here we discuss the main settings that you need to look out for.

File Format

This is one of the first, and most important, choices to make when you are using a digital camera. There are two main types of file format in common use with digital cameras: JPEG and RAW.

The advantages of using the JPEG format include:

- The smaller file sizes mean that more images can be stored per card.
- The format does not need conversion to be used in almost any software application.
- JPEGs produce the best results for printing directly from the camera.
- The image quality is good enough for all but the most demanding users.

Advantages of the RAW format include:

- This format offers the ability to change shooting parameters, such as white balance, post-capture.
- Conversion parameters applied by computer software can be more sophisticated than in-camera, so there is potential for higher quality.
- You can produce a JPEG file from a RAW file, but not vice versa.

The greatest difference between JPEG and RAW is the way that the processing is applied to the images. When the camera is recording RAW images, the data is taken straight from the sensor and simply translated into a format that can be read by the software. Any image corrections or processing (such as white balance, saturation, or sharpening) that is set on the camera is stored alongside the image in what is known as a header file. RAW formats can be saved as either compressed or uncompressed files, with any compression being "lossless."

When saving JPEG files, all of the image adjustments and processing is applied to the image before it is saved as a compressed file. The file is then saved in a "lossy" compressed format.

How the JPEG format affects color

- Lossy compression can cause subtle tonal information to be lost.
- All image processing is applied to the image before saving. This means that the camera settings such as white balance, contrast, and saturation are embedded in the image, so you need to set these for each individual image according to the conditions at the time of shooting.
- There is less scope for fine-tuning the color after capture without further loss of color or tonal information.
- This format offers 8-bit capture only (see pp.58–59).

How the RAW format affects color

- Files are uncompressed or use a "lossless" compression, ensuring that full color and tonal information is retained.
- Image processing and settings can be changed, even after capture, using the appropriate conversion software
- Adjustments in RAW conversion software can be carried out with only minimal loss of color or tonal information.
- Files can retain greater information thanks to 12- or 14-bit format.

How Compression Affects Color

A "lossy" compression format such as JPEG uses processing algorithms to throw away information in order to make the file smaller. When the file is reopened, similar algorithms are used to reconstruct the image. Because this process is not perfect, some of the color information that is discarded in the original image is lost forever. The higher the rate of compression (the smaller the file), the more information is lost.

The most noticeable effect is seen in areas of subtle tonal transitions such as blue skies, with a large amount of compression causing visible "steps" between areas of similar tones.

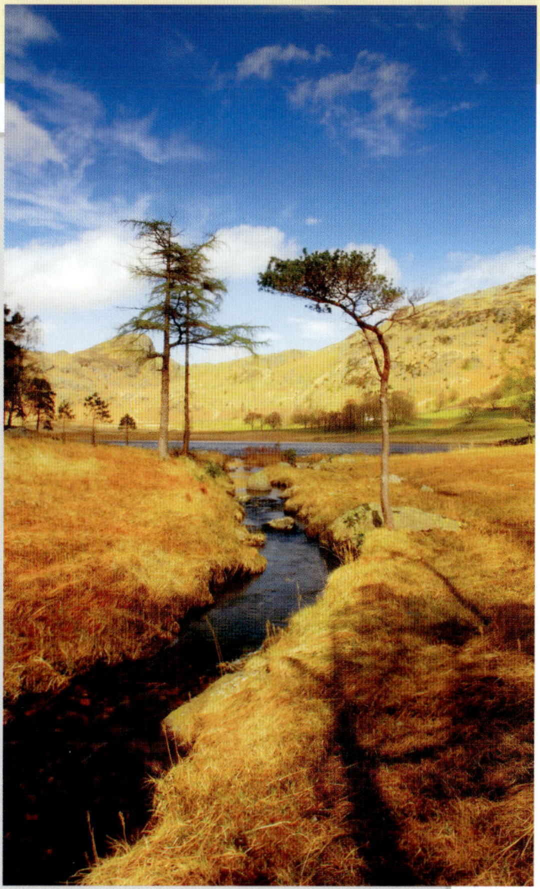

The file type you use affects the tones in your final image. Using an uncompressed RAW or TIFF file type produces the best results, as can be seen in the sky detail on this image. As a worthwhile compromise, the high-quality JPEG file is a good choice for many users, as the quality is almost as good as an uncompressed file. Avoid using the low-quality JPEG settings on your camera; they can produce results with visible artifacts where the color information has been lost forever.

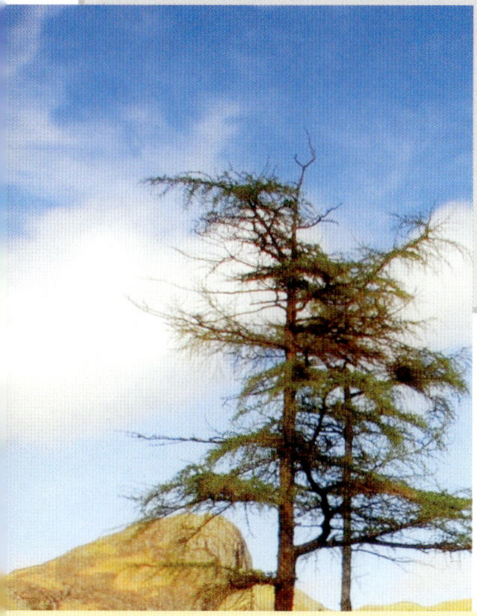

compressed TIFF

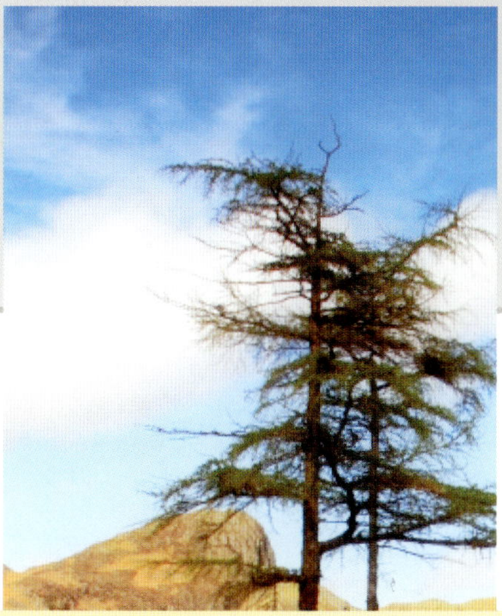

High quality JPEG

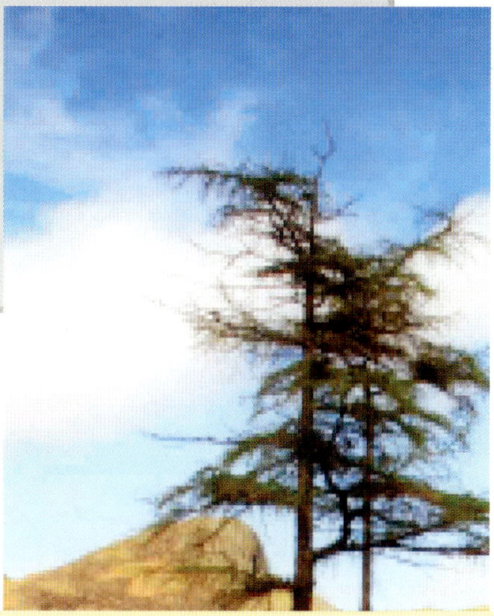

Low quality JPEG

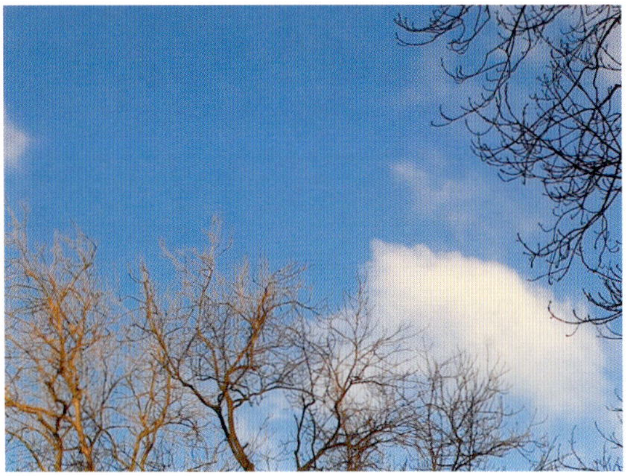

ISO 100

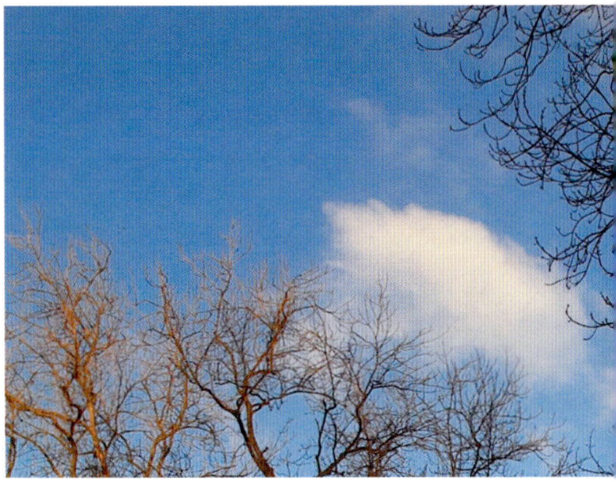

ISO 400

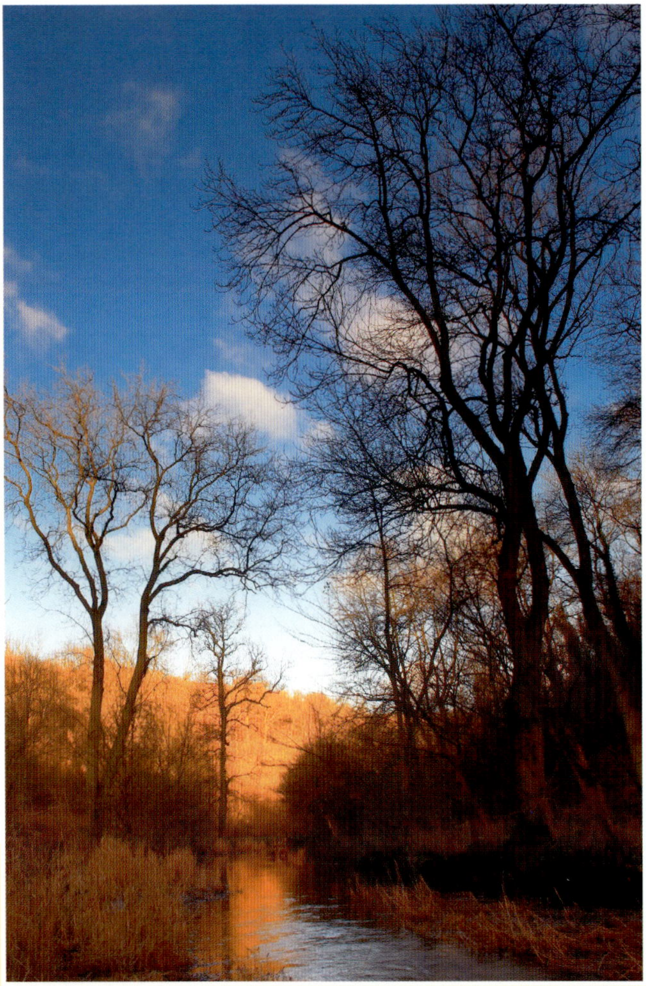

ISO Speed Equivalent

Used to allow you to shoot in varying amounts of light, this setting is often wrongly referred to as the sensitivity of the sensor. This sensitivity is fixed, and by increasing the ISO setting what you are actually doing is amplifying the signal. As with all amplification, this increases noise levels as well as the signal itself, giving lower quality as the setting is stepped up.

While noise is one problem with increasing the ISO setting, it also affects the color of the image. At high ISO settings, the color saturation and the ability of the image to retain detailed color information are reduced.

How significant these quality losses become is down to both the quality of the sensor and the image processing that is applied to it. Most modern cameras give acceptable results up to ISO 400, with the image quality dropping off above this setting.

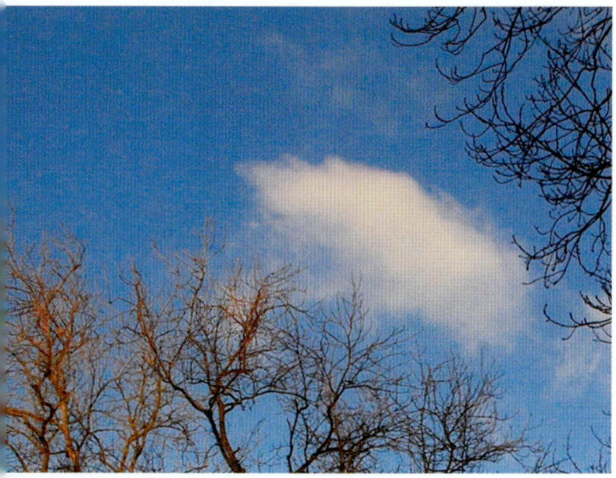

;O 800

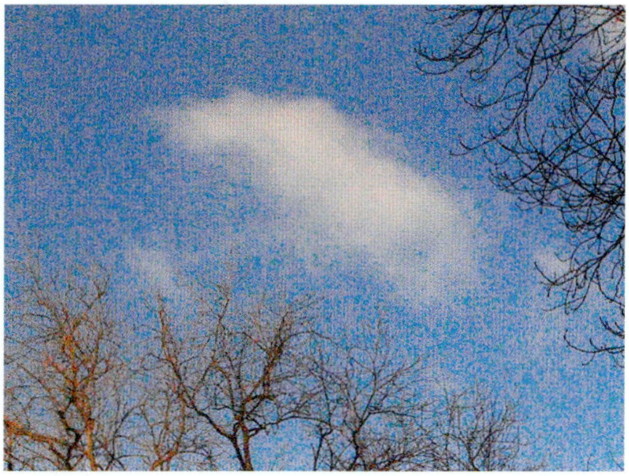

ISO 3200

The ISO setting that you use plays an important part in how the colors are reproduced in your image. The lower ISO settings produce the best and ost accurate results, with low noise and nooth tones. At ISO 400, the results are st starting to suffer from increased levels noise (the multicolored specks visible smooth areas), and the colors are less aturated than at the lower setting. At high O settings, the colors of the image are uch less saturated and the level of noise is eatly increased, so avoid using these for ost images.

Other Camera Settings

There are many shooting parameters available in the menu of most digital cameras. These allow you to fine-tune the image processing for individual images. While they can be handy for producing prints directly from the camera, it can be difficult to determine the best settings, especially in changing lighting conditions. When it comes to the settings concerned with color, unless you desperately need to use these settings, they are best left at the default values and any adjustments made in your imaging software. This gives much greater control to your final result. This advice applies to the following settings, which affect the color or tone of the image:

- Saturation: this allows you to increase or decrease the intensity of the color (see p.86 for using imaging software to adjust saturation).

- Tone compensation: this changes the apparent contrast of the image by adjusting the tonal distribution. In high-contrast lighting, use a lower tone setting, and vice versa.

- Hue: this is a means of fine-tuning the color of an image either by adding yellow for positive hue values or adding blue for negative values (see p.86 for how to use imaging software to adjust the hue).

- Color space: this is used to define the range of colors used and for color management (see p.56 for a detailed explanation of color spaces).

Tip

For the highest quality and best color rendition and saturation, use the lowest ISO setting available. Only use the higher settings when the light levels demand it.

Film

Low ISO slide films are excellent for landscape photography; they produce superb colors and fine grain.

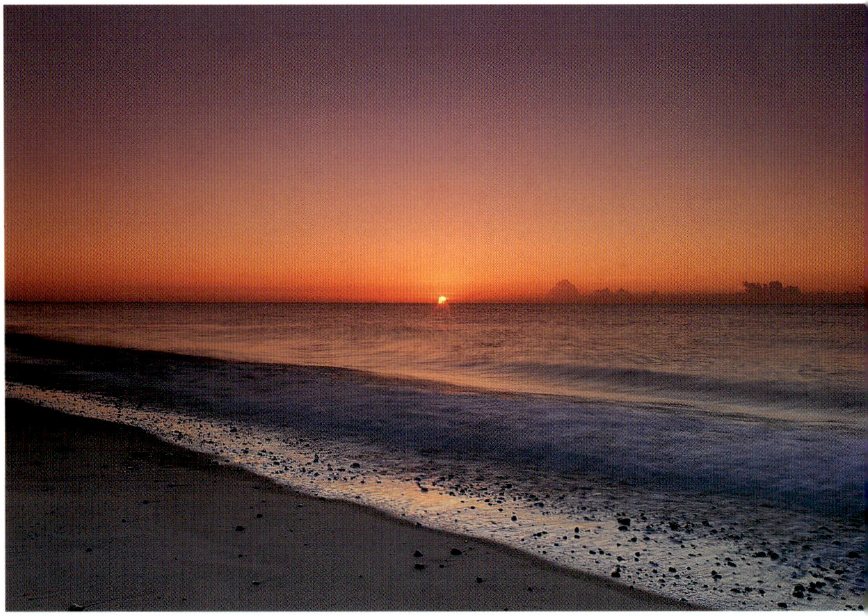

In an increasingly digital world, film still has a place in many people's photography. The choice of film plays a large part in the color of your results. The first decision is whether to choose print or slide film. Color print film is the most convenient option for most people, and there are some excellent films on the market, but they have a distinct disadvantage when you want control over the color of your images.

The automatic systems used by most commercial processing and printing laboratories adjust the colors of your images, often removing the effects of the quality of the light or any color filters you have used. You can have your images hand-printed to get the result exactly how you want, but this is expensive and not really convenient for most photographers.

This leaves us with color slide films. Because there is no printing process involved in getting your final image, the results are more predictable, especially once you are familiar with a particular film.

Whether you use print or slide film, there are some similar characteristics of the various options. One of the first choices many people make is the film speed. While for many uses this choice is made on the basis of the lighting conditions—a slow film for bright lighting and a fast one for low light—this choice also has an impact on the color of the result. Despite advances in film manufacture and design, a faster film generally gives lower color saturation than a slower film. Faster films also produce more "grainy" results that can also give the appearance of lower contrast and saturation. If you want to produce punchy, colorful images, choose the lowest film speed possible. In general, this will mean ISO 100 or 200 films, although in low light conditions you will need to steady the camera or use a tripod to ensure you don't get camera shake. The higher-speed films can also give acceptable results and allow you to handhold the camera in a wide range of lighting conditions.

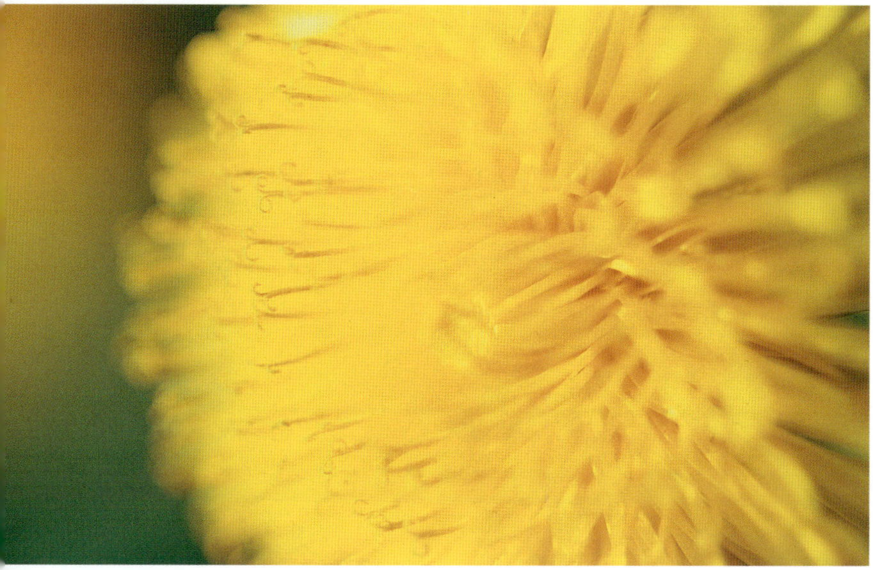

For the most saturated colors for flower and nature photography, use a slow film such as ISO 100.

:olor Balance

ll common color print and slide films re designed to give the correct colors 1 lighting with a color temperature quivalent to direct sunlight (5,500K). hooting in lighting that has any ther color temperature will produce olor casts on your images. Filters eed to be used to adjust the color emperature of the light to suit the lm (see p.50). These color casts are 1uch more significant on slide films because they simply record the light falling on the emulsion, whereas some adjustments can be made during the printing process for color print films. Unless you do your own color printing, or pay for individual hand-prints to be made, this can be a hit-and-miss process, as the automatic adjustments made by most laboratories can be fooled by strong colors in the subject.

Special Films

There are also certain specialist films available that you might want to experiment with.

Tungsten-balanced film

Becoming much less common, these films are designed to give correct color under tungsten lights with a color temperature of 3,200K. These are usually color slide films and are mainly used by studio photographers working with tungsten studio lighting.

Infrared

This is a very specialized film that is sensitive to infrared light, which humans cannot see. It has some scientific uses as it can "see" heat radiation, but for most photographers it is best left for special effects and for artistic uses. The color infrared films are much less common than the black and white versions, and impart completely unreal colors to even the most familiar scenes.

Faster films may be necessary for low light conditions, but the colors are often less saturated and the more visible grain detracts from the results.

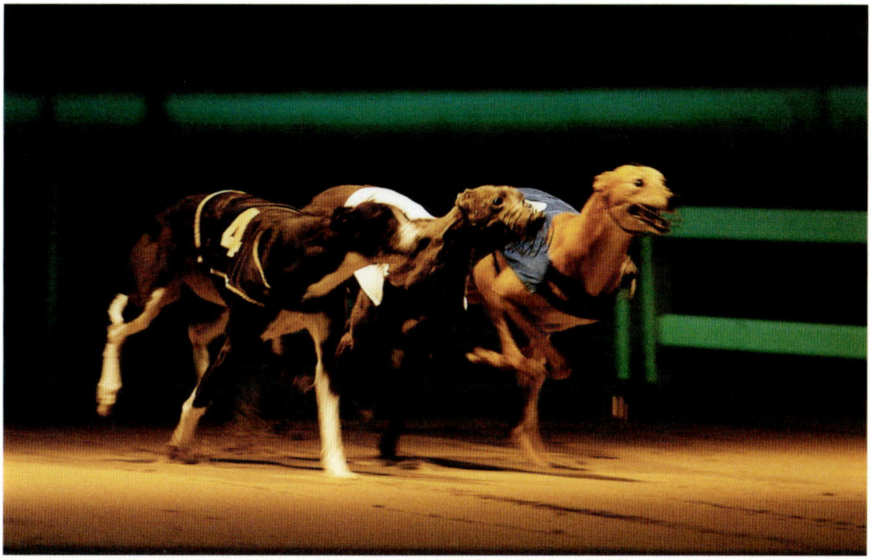

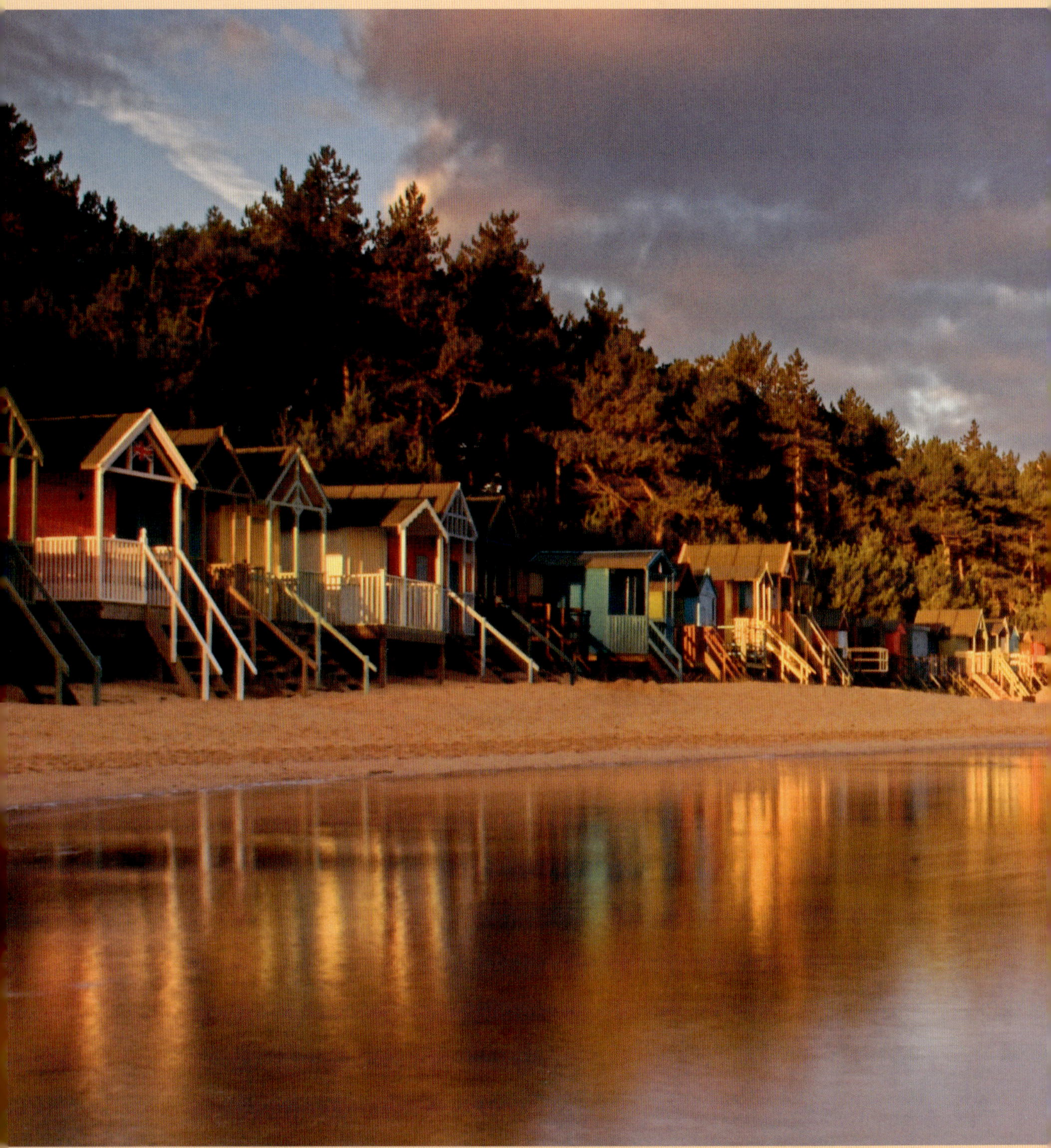

The Quality of Light 03

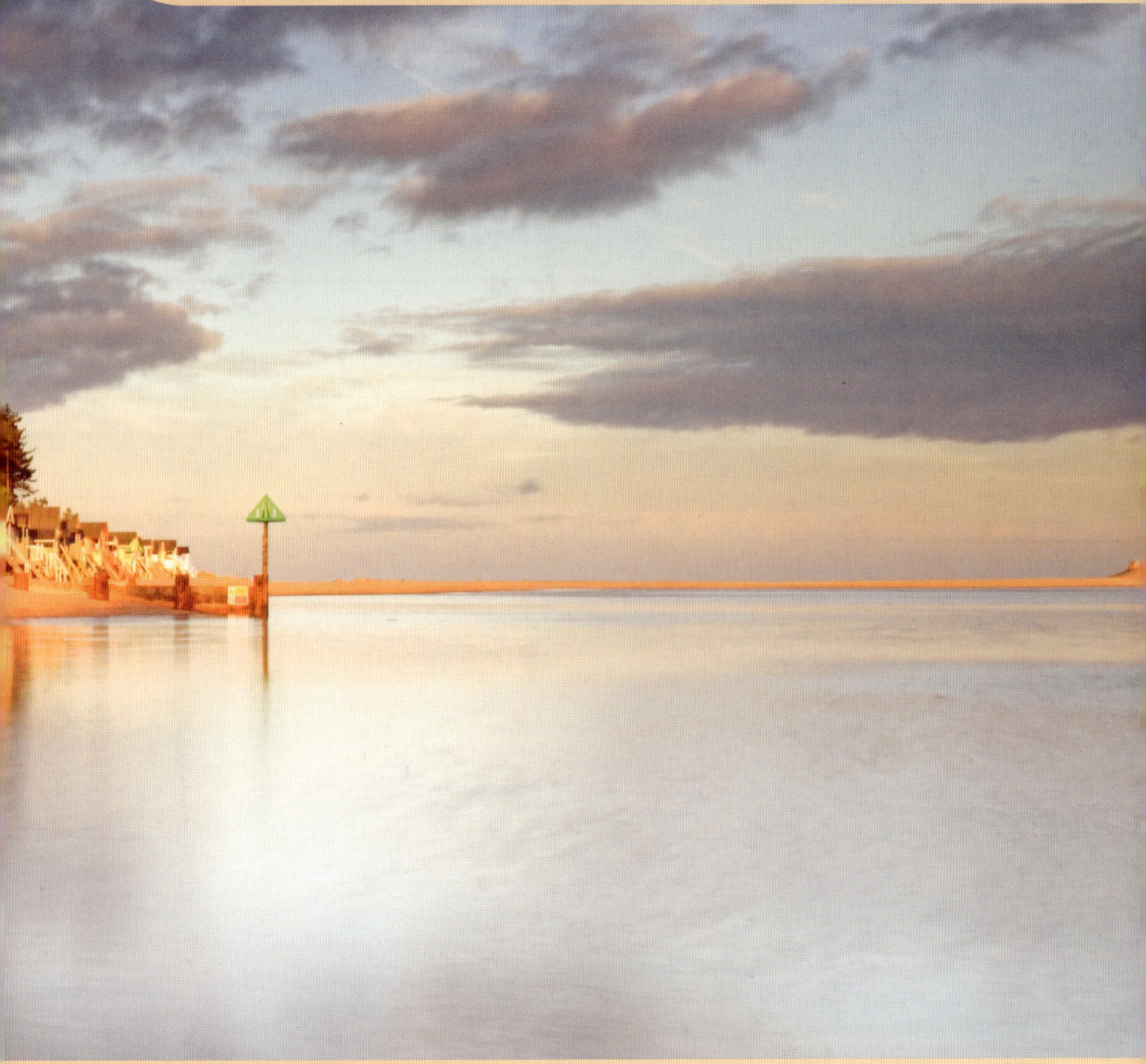

Color Temperature

The color from different light sources has an enormous effect on the way your photographs look. Even though our eyes can adjust to varying color, we can still tell that the light at sunrise or sunset looks much warmer than at midday, and the effect is much more noticeable on both digital and film images.

To make sense of this variation, the color of a light source is given a value known as the color temperature, which is expressed in units of degrees Kelvin (abbreviated to K). In the real world, this scale ranges from around 1,000K for candlelight to 10,000K for shaded conditions, lit only by a clear blue sky.

See the table below for the typical values of the most common light sources. In simple terms, the lower the color temperature, the more red light is present and the warmer the light will appear. Conversely, the higher the value, the more blue light is present, and the cooler the light appears.

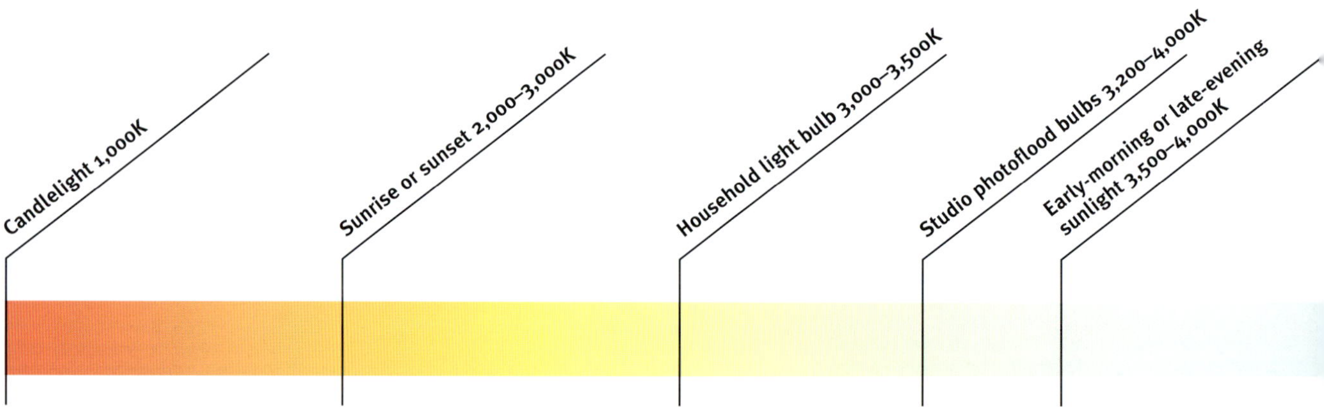

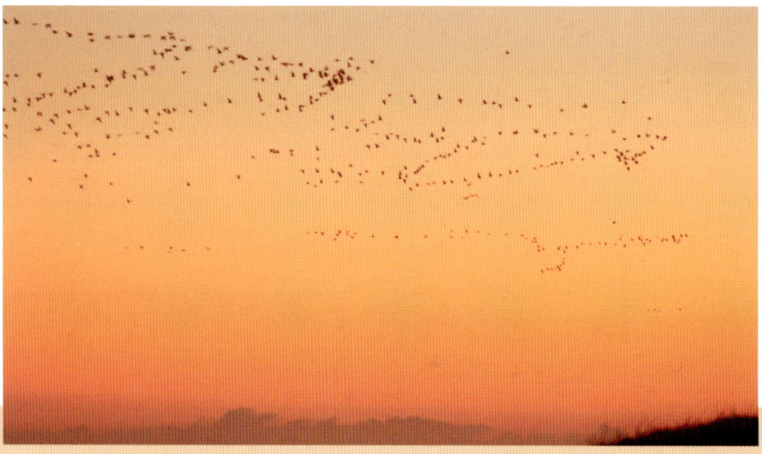

Sunrise: 2,000K. At sunrise and sunset, the color temperature of the light is very low, giving it the familiar warm glow that we all associate with this time of day.

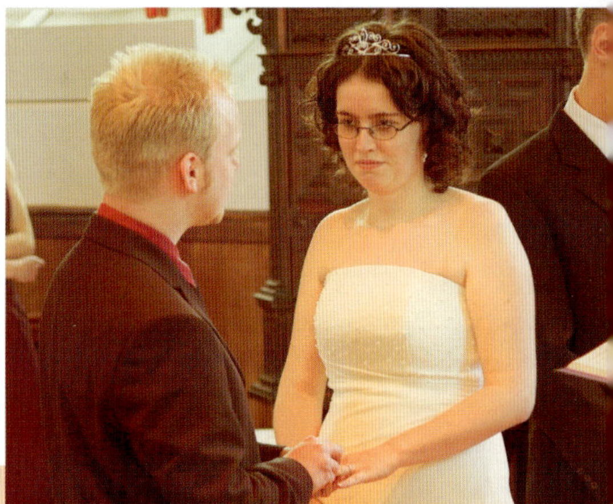

Indoor shots: 3,000K. The low color temperature of light bulbs causes a yellow or orange color cast on daylight film.

'he Kelvin Scale

his scale is named after the scientist ɔrd Kelvin (1824–1907), who came p with a temperature scale using bsolute zero as a starting point. his scale has been adopted to xpress the color temperature of light. ne science behind this scale uses the ıeory of heating an object known as a "full radiator" or "black-body." This is a substance that does not reflect any light, and radiates light perfectly when heated. The color temperature is the temperature in degrees Kelvin of this "black-body" radiator to emit light of the same color as the light source.

To make sense of this theory, think of an iron rod being heated in a fire. It starts off glowing a dull red at lower temperatures. As it is heated, it becomes more orange, until it finally glows "white hot."

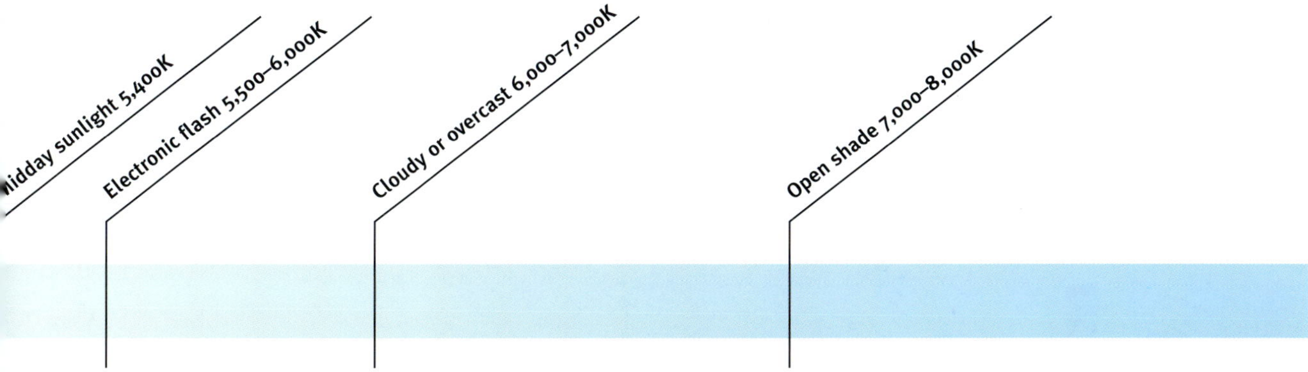

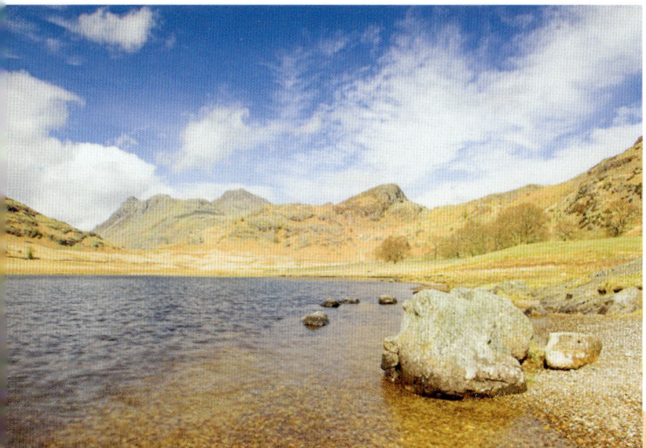

Midday sunlight: 5,400K. Light during the middle of the day gives accurate colors, as most color films are designed for use at this color temperature.

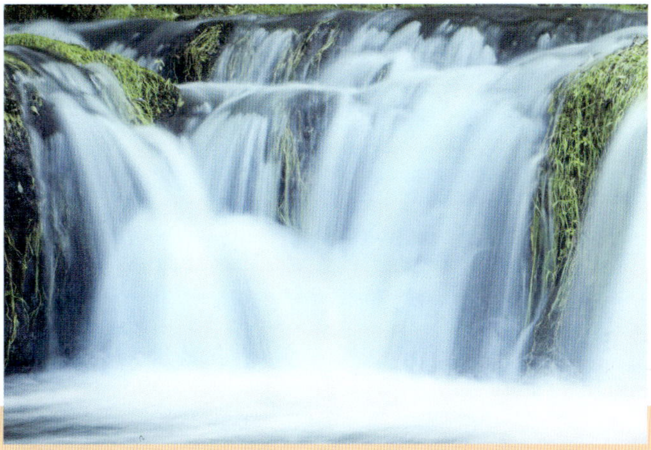

Cloudy: 6,500K. Cloudy conditions produce light with a higher color temperature than direct sunlight, imparting a cold-looking blue cast to your images. This is most visible on the water in this shot taken in heavily overcast conditions.

Measuring Color Temperature

There are commercially available color temperature meters for calculating the color temperature of any light source. These look like and work in a similar way to handheld exposure meters, reading the light falling onto the subject and calculating the color temperature. This temperature readout can simply give you the value in degrees Kelvin; alternatively, some models can be programmed with the film type to give a value for the filter needed to give the correct colors.

The mired scale

Although the Kelvin scale is the most common way of expressing colo temperature, there is another that yo may come across. This is called the mired scale, which is an acronym for "micro reciprocal degrees." Its main advantage over the Kelvin scale is that equal number values give equal variations in color. In the Kelvin scale, a 1,000-degree shift in color temperature from 2,000 to 3,000 degrees K cannot be compared to the same shift from 5,000 to 6,000 degrees K. In the mired scale, a 100-degree variation gives the same color change throughout the scale.

This makes the values on the mired scale a much better way of expressing the effect that colored filters have on the color temperature, as they can be given a single value that applies acros the whole color temperature range. This is known as the mired shift value of the filter. A yellow filter would have a positive mired shift value, whereas blue filters have a negative value.

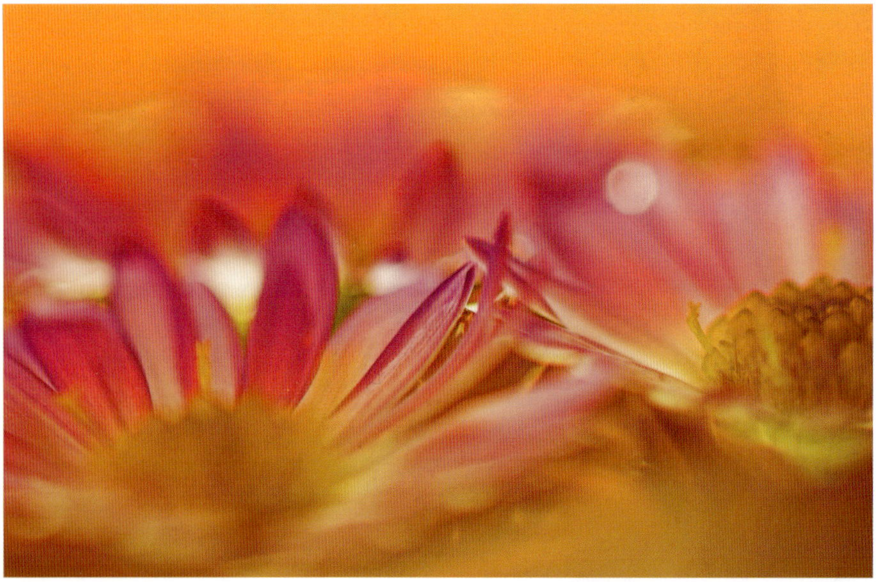

The mired scale is most often used when using filters as, unlike the Kelvin scale, the value is constant across the whole range of colors. Here, an 81B filter has been used to add warmth to this early morning scene giving a +27 mired shift. Experiment with other filters to accentuate the temperature of warm, late-summer light (above); dusk (opposite, middle) and the vibrancy of closeup work (far right).

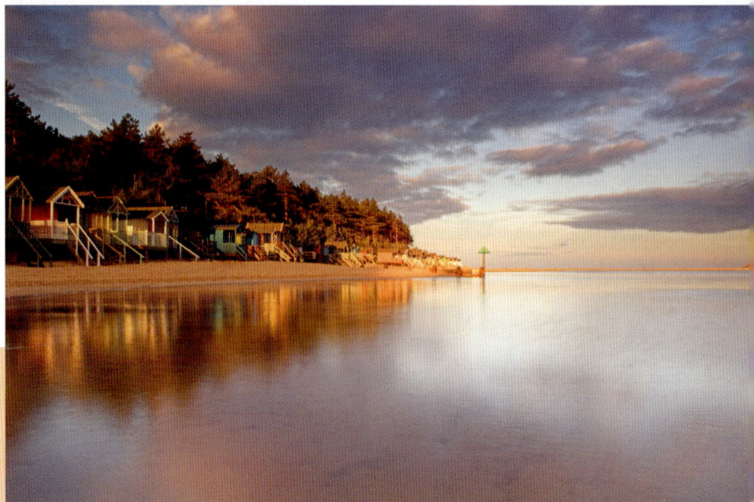

Even fluorescent lights designed to replicate daylight to our eyes have a strong green cast when photographed on daylight film. The light from these tubes does not conform to standard color temperatures, so requires careful filtration or digital correction.

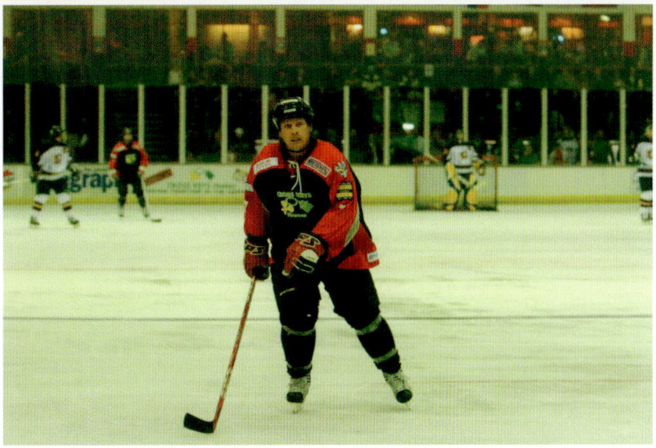

ıe mired value for color temperature ın be calculated from the Kelvin scale ׀ using the formula:

ired value = 1.000,000/Kelvin ›lor temperature

ired value	Kelvin value
›0	2,000
›0	2,500
›0	3,333
›0	5,000
›0	10,000

Limitations of the Color Temperature Scale

Although the color temperature scale works for most light sources you are likely to come across, there are some common ones that cannot be given a strict figure. These include fluorescent and sodium lamps. This is because, unlike most other light sources, they do not emit a continuous spectrum of light. The energy given out by these lamps is limited to very narrow bands that can be almost anywhere within the spectrum.

Luckily, many commercially available fluorescent tubes include a continuous spectrum as well as the bands of light produced by the fluorescent coating to give a more pleasant light. This means that they can be given an equivalent color temperature, although they can still produce a green color cast without either a filter or adjustment to the white balance setting on digital cameras.

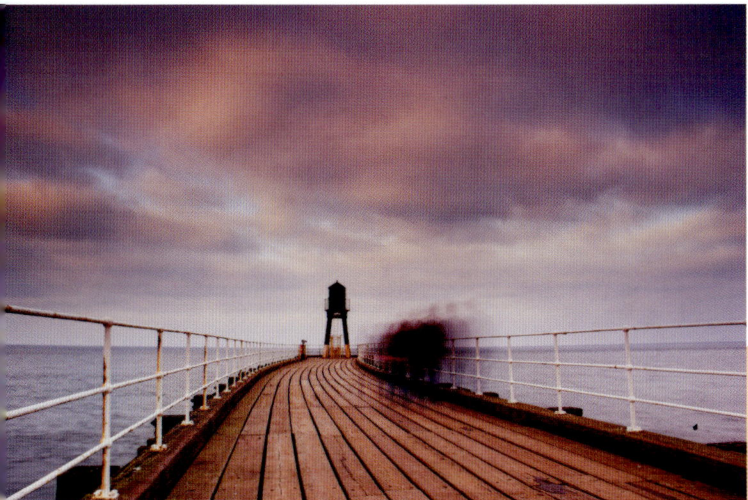

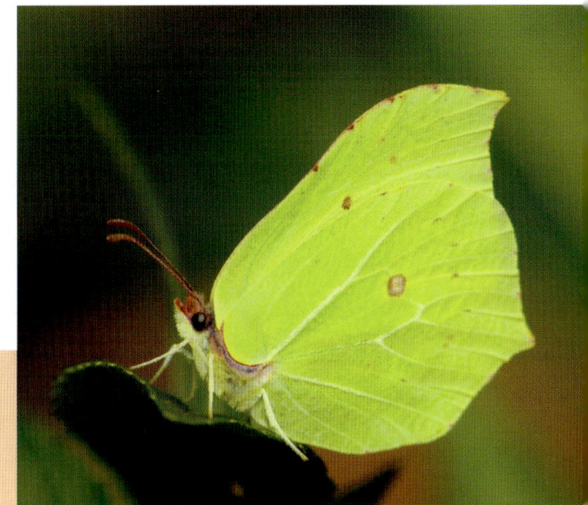

White Balance

As we have seen in the previous section on color temperature, the color of light can vary enormously. Without some way of compensating for this, even small variations in color are "seen" by the sensor, giving a color cast to the image. This is because the sensor inside the camera simply reacts to the light falling on it to produce an image.

While the initial image produced by the sensor may have a color cast, this is not the end of the story. One of the great advantages of digital imaging over film is the ability to adjust for these different lighting conditions in-camera. This setting, known as white balance, alters the ratio of red, green, and blue as the data is processed to give the final image.

There is a range of settings available within the white balance of most digital cameras, which we discuss over the next few pages.

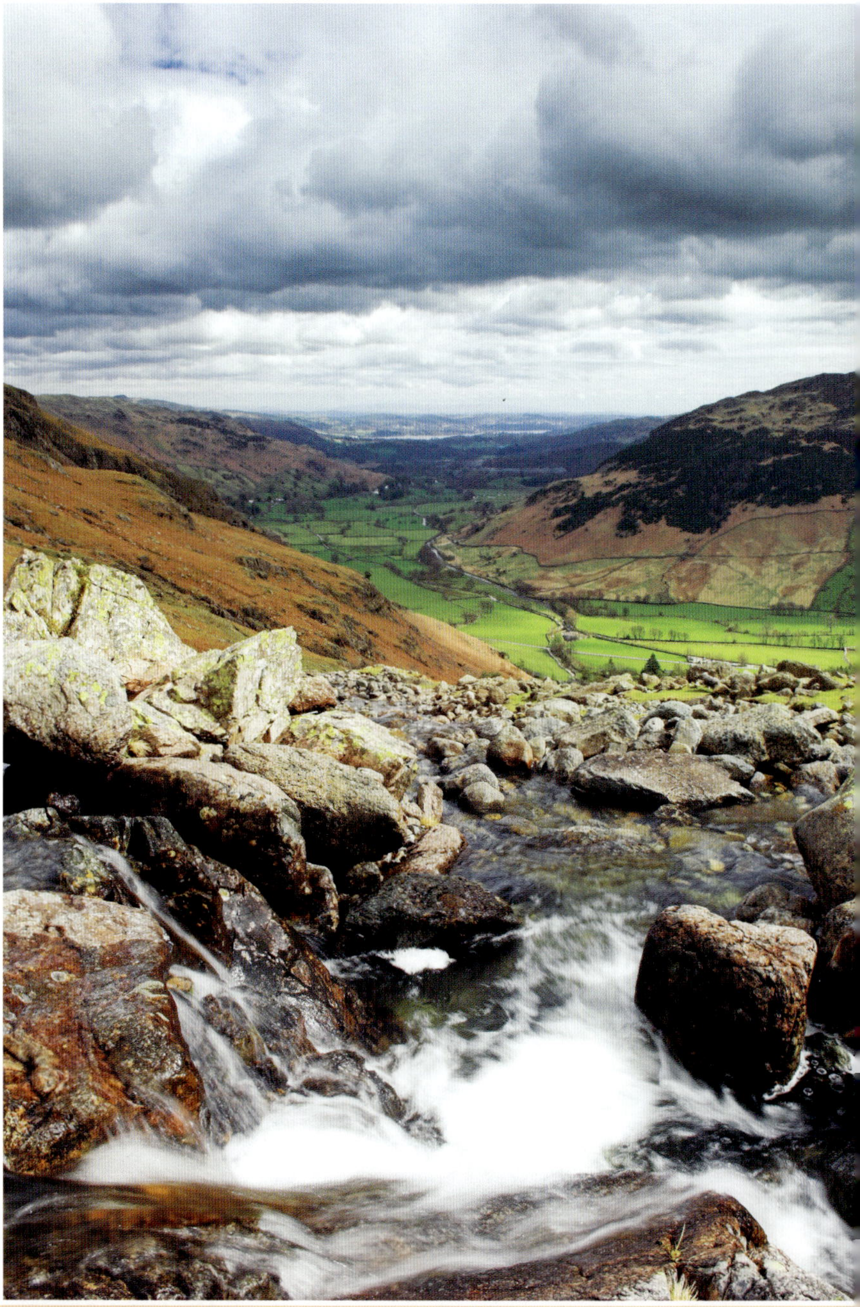

For average scenes in normal lighting, the automatic white balance produces accurate results.

ıutomatic Vhite Balance

ıe default option on most digital odels is an automatic setting where e camera analyzes the color of the ıage and sets the appropriate color mperature. This setting is good in ›neral lighting conditions, but, like l automatic systems, some lighting ›nditions or subjects can fool it. Many systems can struggle to fferentiate between the color of e light falling on the subject and e color of the subject itself. This especially difficult if the subject ıs a strong single color, as this can ol the camera into adjusting the hite balance to compensate for this ›parent color cast.

A few high-end cameras have a sensor on the top of the camera that measures the light falling on the camera rather than reflected from the subject. This system is more consistent than the through-the-lens (TTL) system used by most cameras, as it is not fooled by the color of the subject. Even this system is not infallible, however, if the light falling on your subject is not the same as the light on the camera. For example, you may be standing in the shade while your subject is in full sunlight.

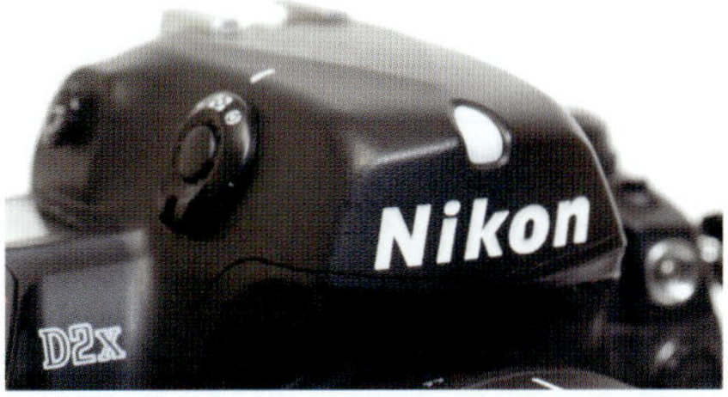

The small white spot on the top of the pentaprism is the external white balance sensor on the Nikon D2x. This sensor measures the color temperature of light falling onto the camera, so it is not fooled by strongly colored subjects.

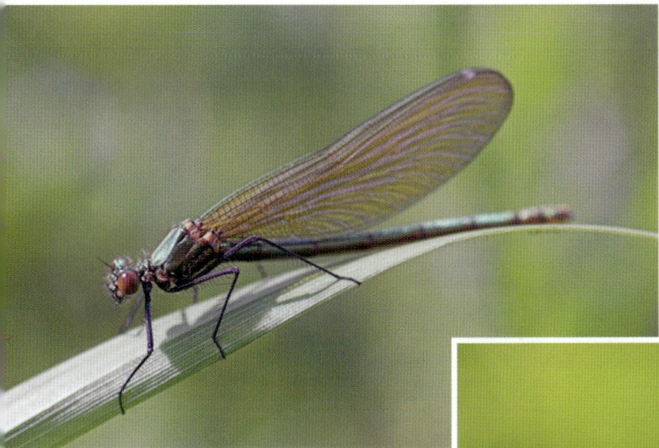

When the subject consists largely of a single color, the automatic white balance tries to adjust the color to give a neutral result. This produces unacceptable colors in the final image, as in the green foliage in this shot.

In these situations, you have to set the white balance manually to suit the light falling on the subject. In this shot, we used a Daylight setting to maintain the colors in the subject.

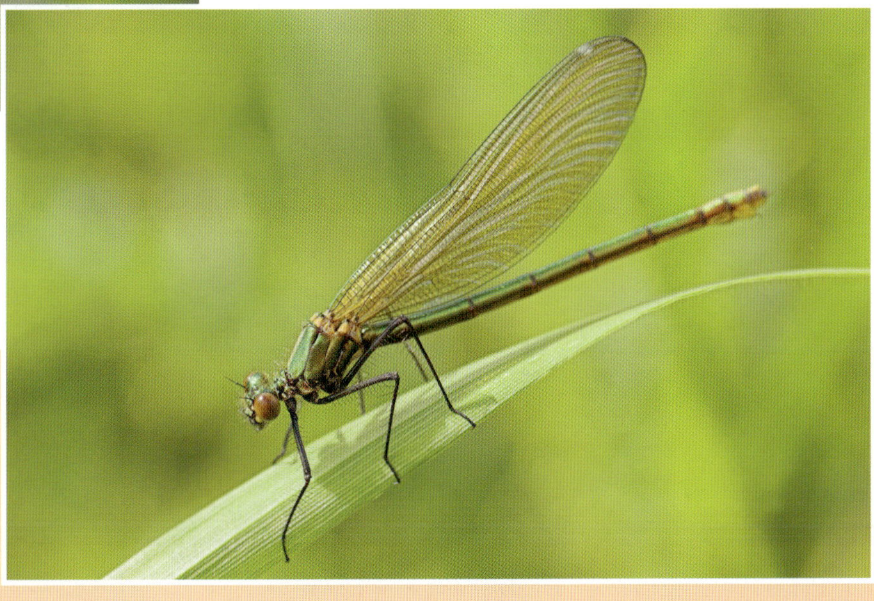

Tip

When using studio flash, use either Flash or Daylight white balance, as the short duration of the flash is likely to give inconsistent results with the automatic setting.

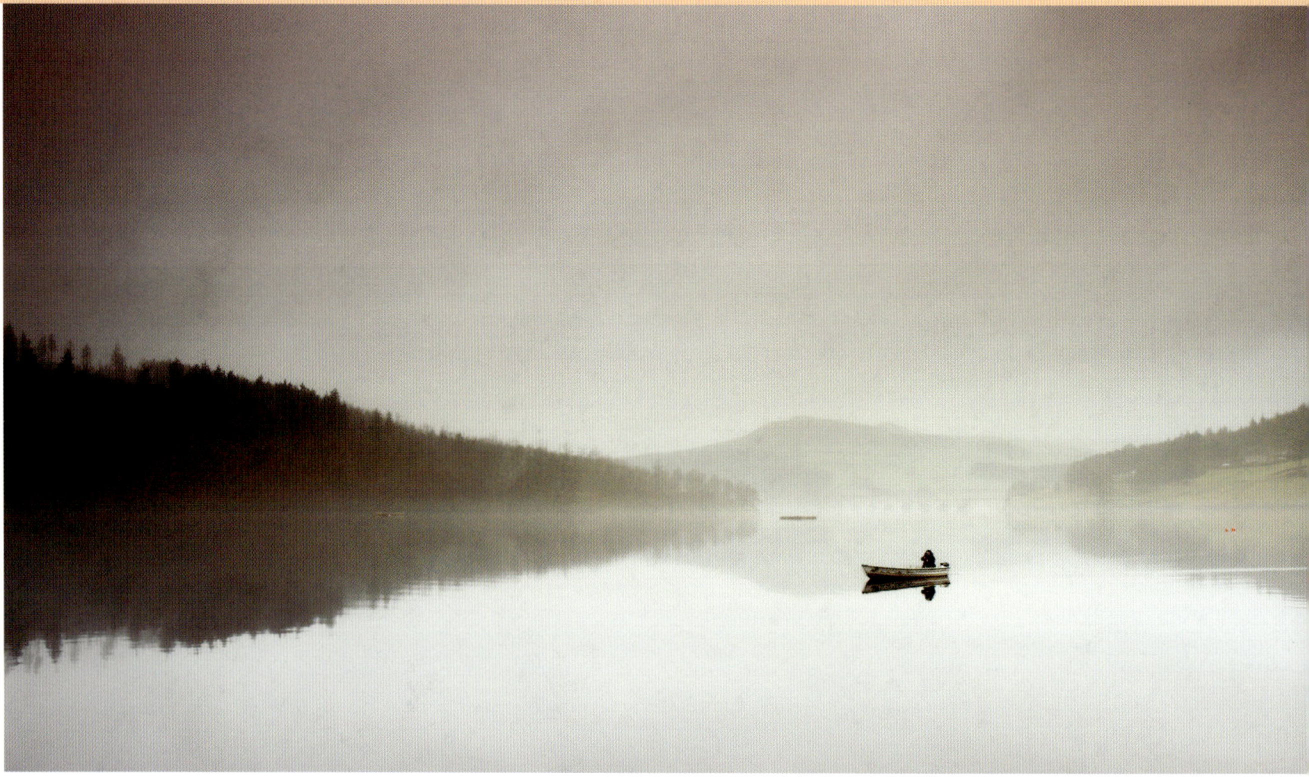

Manual Settings

In addition to the automatic setting, digital cameras give manual white balance options to put you in full control.

White balance programs
To simplify the task of matching the white balance setting to the lighting conditions, most cameras have a range of set options for the most common light sources. Although these are not the most accurate way of setting the white balance, they are sufficient for most conditions and will give a more predictable result than using the automatic option.

The exact settings vary between different cameras and manufacturers, but we set out some typical options below.

Incandescent
This setting is for shooting indoor scenes lit by household light bulbs with a color temperature of around 3,000K.

Fluorescent
Although fluorescent lights do not have a precise color temperature, this setting uses a color temperature of around 4,000K to correct for the most common types of strip light.

Direct sunlight
The digital equivalent to daylight film, this setting uses a color temperature of around 5,500K.

Flash
Although electronic flash has almost the same color temperature as daylight, some cameras have a separate setting with a color temperature of around 6,000K to compensate for the slightly cooler light given out by many flash units.

Overcast conditions: Although to our eyes the light on a cloudy day differs little from normal daylight, contains much more blue than rect sunlight. To record the cool ght of this overcast scene as utral, I set the white balance Cloudy.

Daylight: On bright, sunny days, set the white balance to Daylight rather than automatic. As long as the lighting remains constant, this ensures that the lors are recorded accurately.

Cloudy
his is for shooting under cloudy kies setting a color temperature around 6,000K.

Shade
his compensates for the blue cast eated when shooting in light hade; the camera sets a color mperature of around 7,000K.

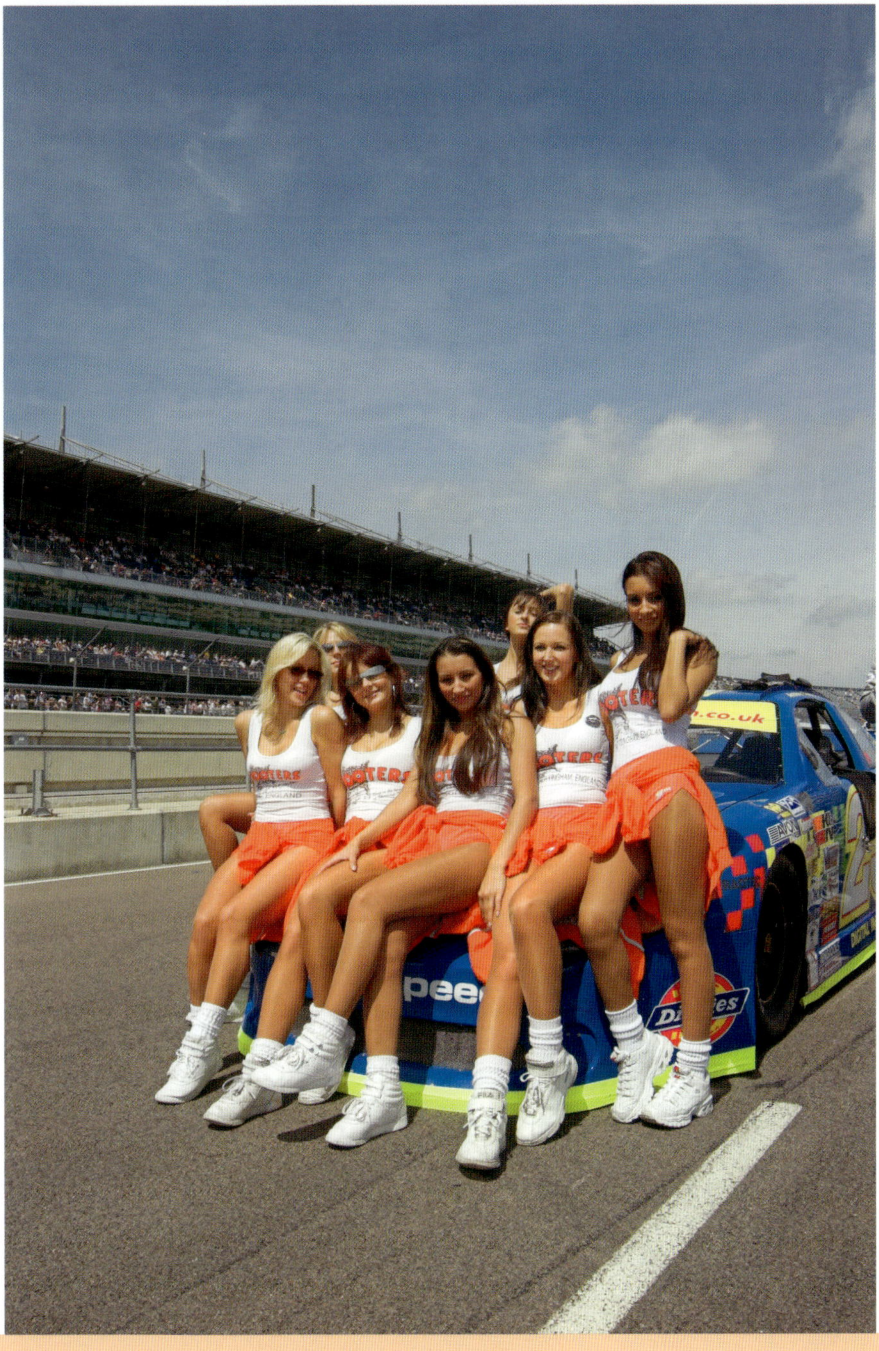

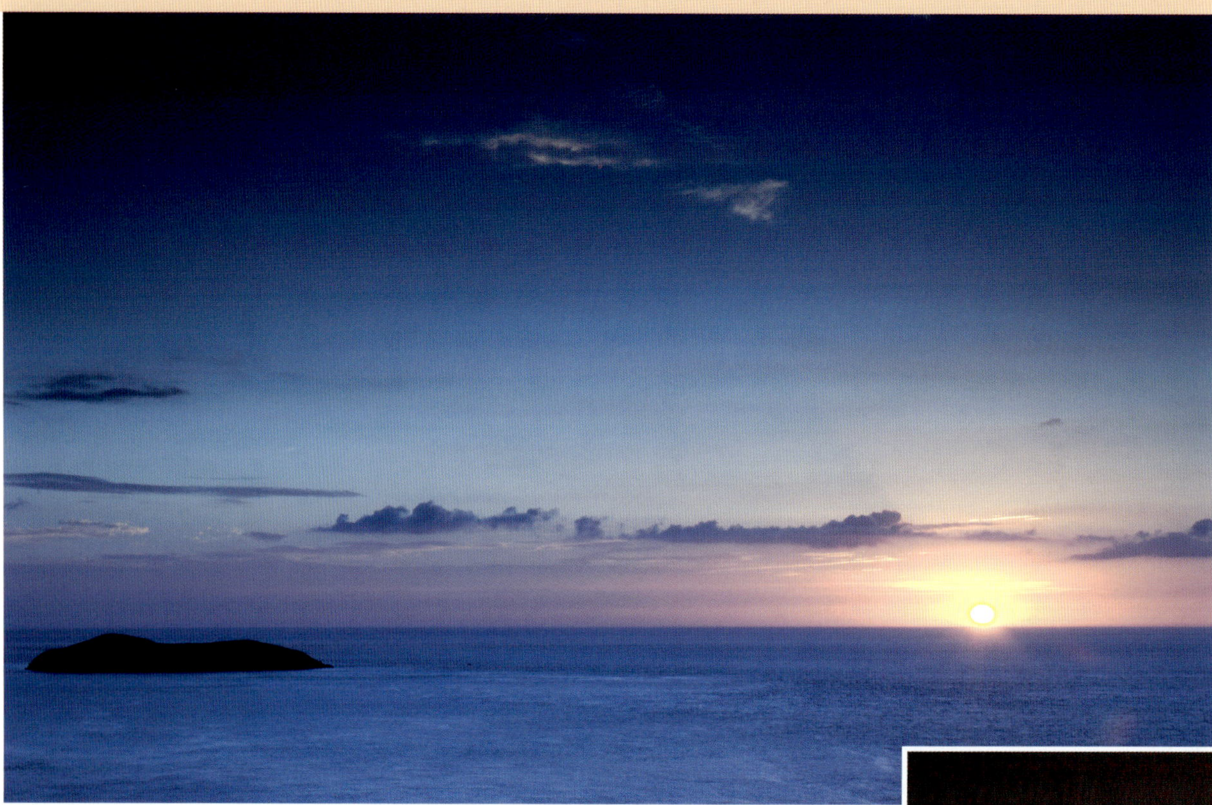

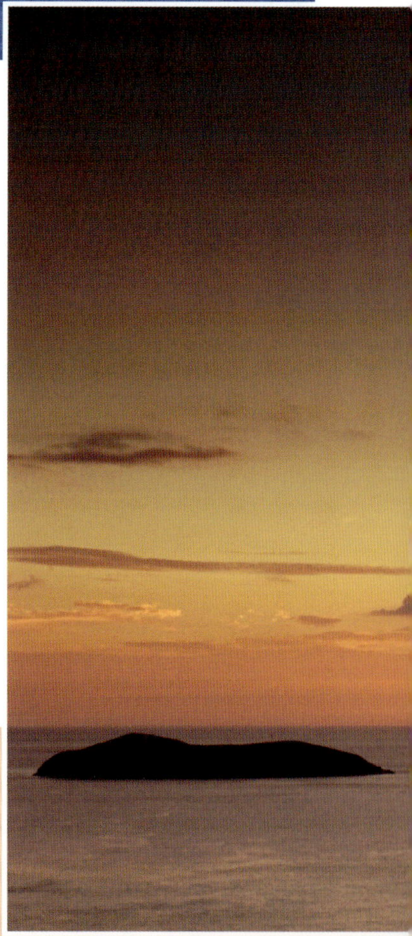

Advanced Settings

There are a number of advanced settings available that you may need to utilize in certain circumstances.

Preset

This setting allows you to take a reading of the color temperature from your subject. You need a neutral gray or white reference point that is in exactly the same lighting conditions as your subject from which to take a measurement.

An 18% gray card that is normally used for metering from makes an ideal reference point for this technique. You need to fill the frame with this card, and take a white balance reading from it that you can then set on the camera to give you exactly the right color.

Kelvin input

Some digital cameras have the option of setting a specific white balance in degrees Kelvin. This is useful when you know the precise color temperature of your light source, such as when you are using studio lights. Used in conjunction with a color temperature meter, this gives the most accurate results, although it is not a convenient option for general photography.

By setting the correct white balance for this sunset, the colors are technically correct, but they do not match our expectations. All of the warmth has been st, resulting in a very cold-looking image.

Using the Cloudy white balance setting has added extra warmth to the image. Although not the "right" setting for the color temperature of the light, it gives result much closer to how I remembered e scene.

Creative White Balance

So far we have dealt with getting the white balance correct by matching it exactly to the color temperature of the lighting. That is only part of the story, however, as the "correct" white balance does not always give the desired result.

Producing a neutral result does not always give you the effect that you want. There are many times when a warmer image looks much more pleasing than a neutral or cool one. You can achieve this easily by selecting a white balance with a higher color temperature than your light source. So, in direct sunlight, rather than using the correct 5,500K setting, you can use the Cloudy (6,000K) program setting. This gives your image a subtle warming effect similar to using a warm-up filter on daylight color film.

There are also occasions when producing a neutral-colored result looks completely wrong. A classic example is when shooting a sunrise or sunset. Selecting a white balance to match the color temperature would completely destroy the warm glow that most people want to preserve or even enhance in these shots. Again, you can retain this warmth by setting a Daylight white balance on your camera, or enhance the effect by setting a Cloudy or Shade white balance.

RAW Files

Because the white balance is applied during the processing of an image, shooting in RAW file format allows the setting to be changed when you process your images in most RAW conversion software. Just like in camera, you can choose from automatic settings, from a range of presets, or by color temperature. Many programs also offer a useful extra option; as long as your image contains a white or neutral gray area, you can click on this using an Eyedropper tool to obtain an exact setting for the white balance.

Color Filters

Unlike digital, film is balanced to a single type of light source, so shooting under any other type of light will give a color cast. On daylight-balanced film, this can range from the strong orange or red results from household light bulbs to a slight cool tone in shady conditions. There are two main types of color filters in common use: color-conversion, and color-balancing.

Color-conversion Filters

The stronger color-conversion filters are most commonly used when the color temperature of the light source varies widely from the type of film that you are using. The most common is the 80 series for shooting with daylig film under incandescent lights. You have to match the strength of the filte for the type of lighting you are using (see table below).

Filter	Approximate Kelvin shift	Effect
80A	+2,300	cooling
80B	+2,100	cooling
80C	+1,700	cooling
80D	+1,300	cooling
85	−2,100	warming
85B	−2,300	warming
85C	−1,700	warming

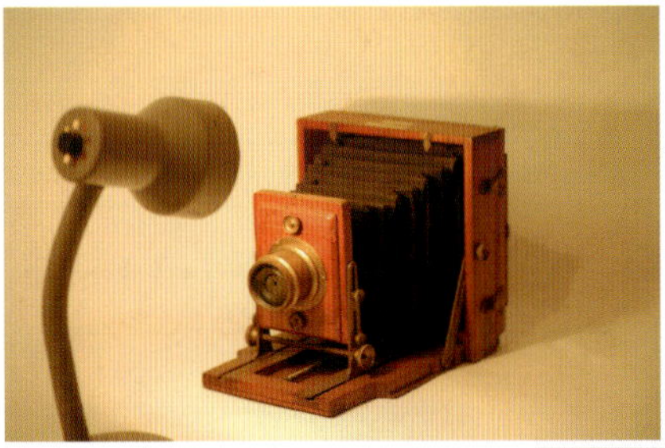

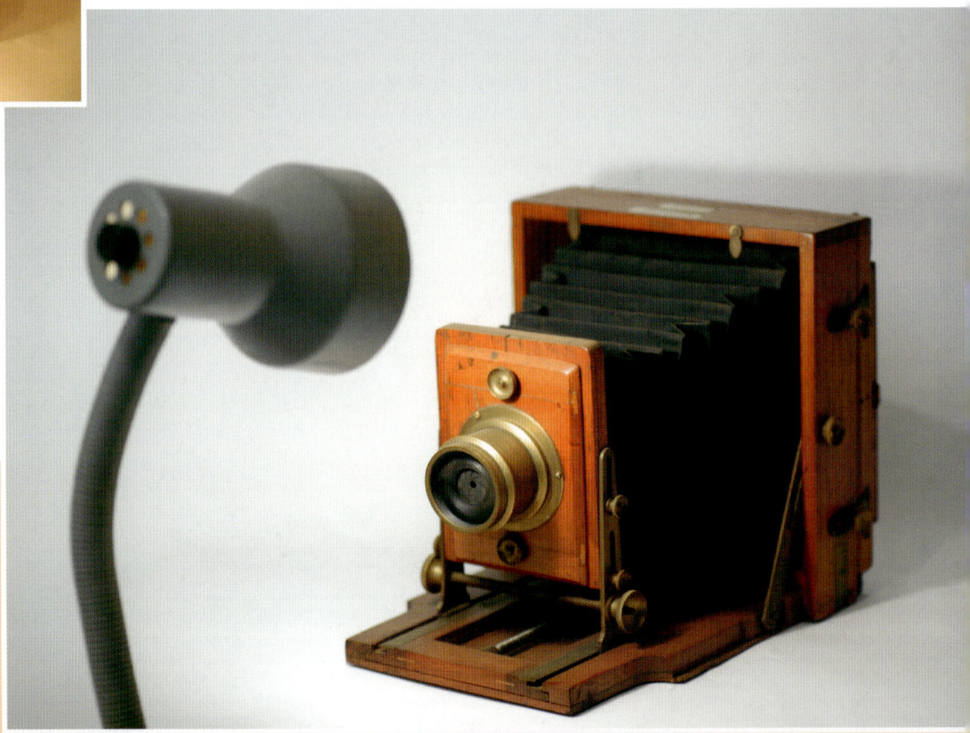

An 80B filter corrects the orange color cast that occurs when shooting under normal household lighting on daylight film.

:olor-balancing Filters

echnically, these filters are designed) make small color corrections etween the light source and the /pe of film you are using. Because ur vision is poor at judging subtle olor casts, for critical applications ıch as industrial and architectural hotography you really need to use a olor temperature meter to use these lters effectively.

Although these filters were eveloped to correct the color for ifferent light sources, like the white alance on a digital camera, they can so be used for creative effect. Many hotographers use an 81 or 81A filter give their images a warmer look. nis is particularly useful on portraits nd landscapes, when the "true" color an often look too cold.

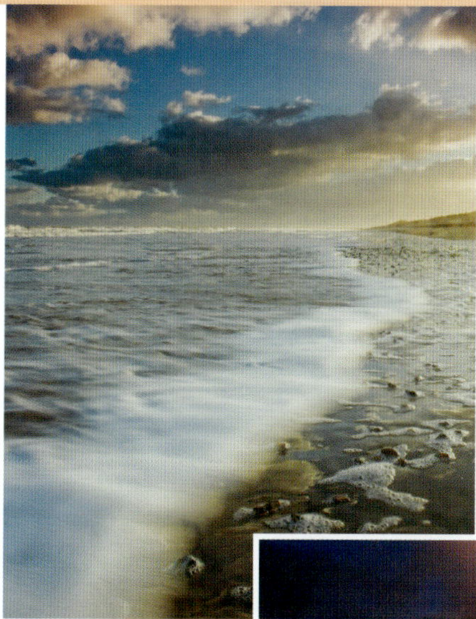

The most common use for an 81A filter is to add extra warmth to your images. Without the filter attached, this sunrise shot lacks the impact that we wanted to create. Adding the filter has enhanced the colors in the original scene.

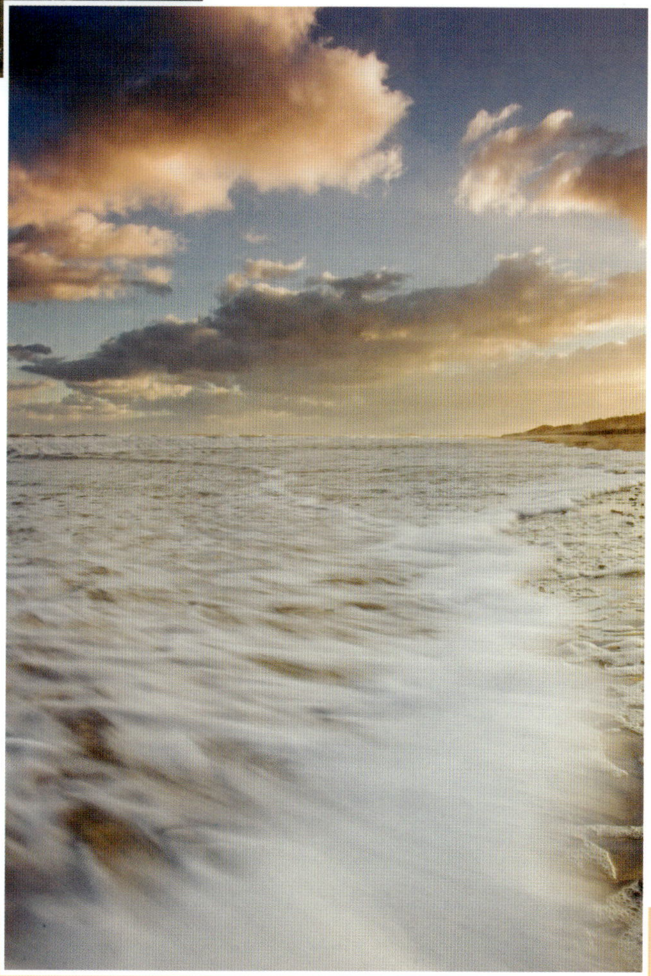

lter	Approximate Kelvin shift	Effect
2	+100	cooling
2A	+200	cooling
2B	+300	cooling
2C	+400	cooling
1	−100	warming
1A	−200	warming
1B	−300	warming
1C	−400	warming
1D	−500	warming
1EF	−650	warming

Tip

Color filters can be used on digital cameras, but you must ensure that the white balance setting is taken off the automatic setting as this will try to "correct" the effect of the filter. To maintain the effect of the filter, simply select the white balance of the type of film you would normally use (most commonly Daylight or Flash) and you will obtain the result you want.

Color-enhancement Filters

Although the effect of colored filters can easily be replicated in-camera or with adjustments in software, there is one filter that still has a place in every photographer's kit bag: the polarizer. This filter has a two-fold effect that can alter the colors in your image. The first is darkening blue skies, and the second is cutting out reflections off nonmetallic surfaces. Both of these properties help to add extra color to your images that would otherwise be lost.

Polarizing filters are supplied in rotating mounts, as the effect varies according to the orientation of the filter. With the filter placed in front of the lens, slowly rotating it allows you to see the image change, with reflections disappearing or the blue sky darkening.

The overall effect of polarizing filters is to increase the color saturation of your images, although the result will depend on the nature of the light that you are shooting in. These filters can also have a slight cooling effect, so there are models available that incorporate a warm-up filter to compensate for this.

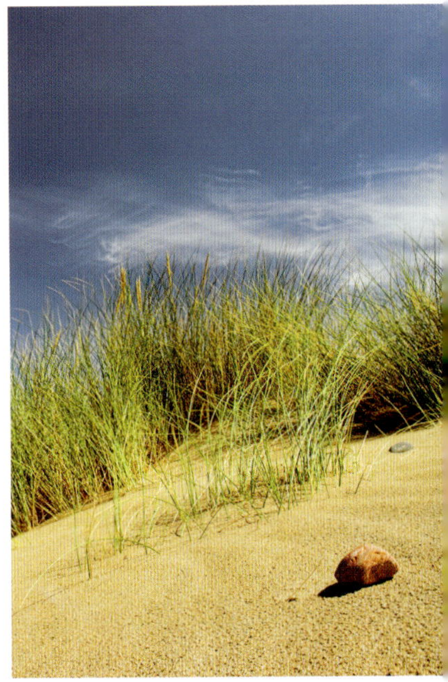

These with and without shots show how a polarizing filter can add extra color saturation to your images. The blue sky in the unfiltered image above, is much less colorful than in the image with the filter attached, right.

How Polarizers Work

Polarizers rely on the wave nature of light. Imagine holding a piece of string that is attached to a point at the opposite end. Shaking this string will produce a series of waves traveling along the string. However, unlike this simplified model, normal light waves vibrate randomly in all directions perpendicular to the direction of travel. The waves in polarized light vibrate only in a single plane.

This is what happens when light is reflected off any nonmetallic surface, with most of the reflected light vibrating in the same plane. A polarizing filter only lets light through that is vibrating in a particular plane, stopping all other light from getting through.

.inear and Circular ›olarizers

•espite their names, linear and circular olarizers look exactly the same. The ames refer to the way that they olarize light, rather than their shape. inear polarizers only let light waves ırough in a single plane. That is, all ıe waves are traveling parallel to each ther. This type of light is not suitable for the sensors used for the modern metering and focusing systems incorporated in most cameras, however. Consequently, a new type of filter has been developed so that, while it is still polarized, the light waves passing through are "twisted" so that they do not appear invisible to these sensors.

If your camera has automatic focus, spot, or multi-pattern metering, you need to use a circular polarizer. Cameras without any of these features can use either linear or circular types—the final results will be the same.

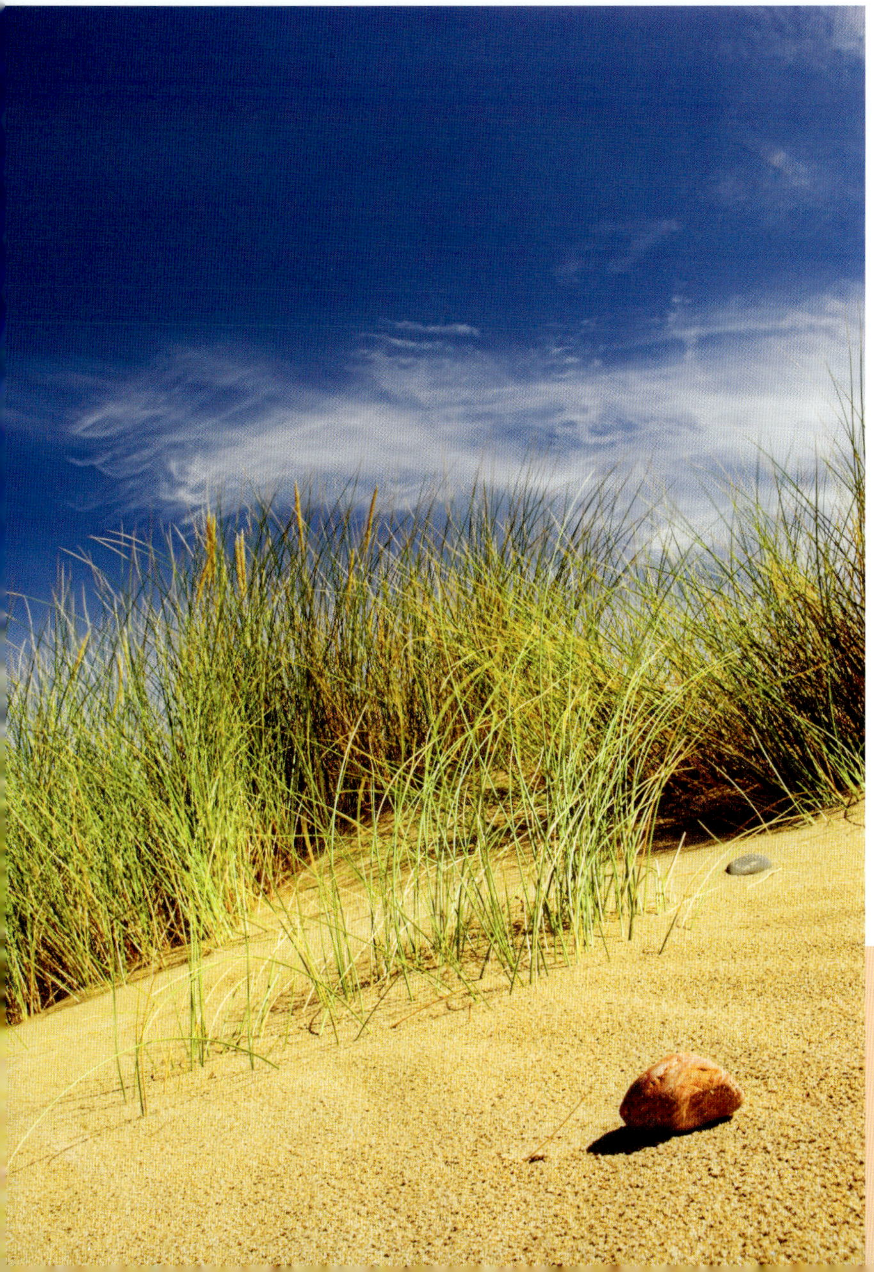

Other Filters to Consider

In addition to polarizing filters, there are a number of other enhancement filters to consider.

Colored graduates
You can use a colored graduated filter to add color to one part of the image and not others. This filter is particularly useful in landscape or architectural photography to impart color to an otherwise bland sky.

Enhancement
This filter is made from glass blended with rare elements to selectively absorb and transmit specific wavelengths of light. The most common type enhances reds, oranges, and yellows, and is particularly useful for capturing the colors of fall leaves and sunsets. These are not to be confused with the warming effect of color-correction filters, as the effect is not uniform across the spectrum. Although these filters are useful, they are very expensive.

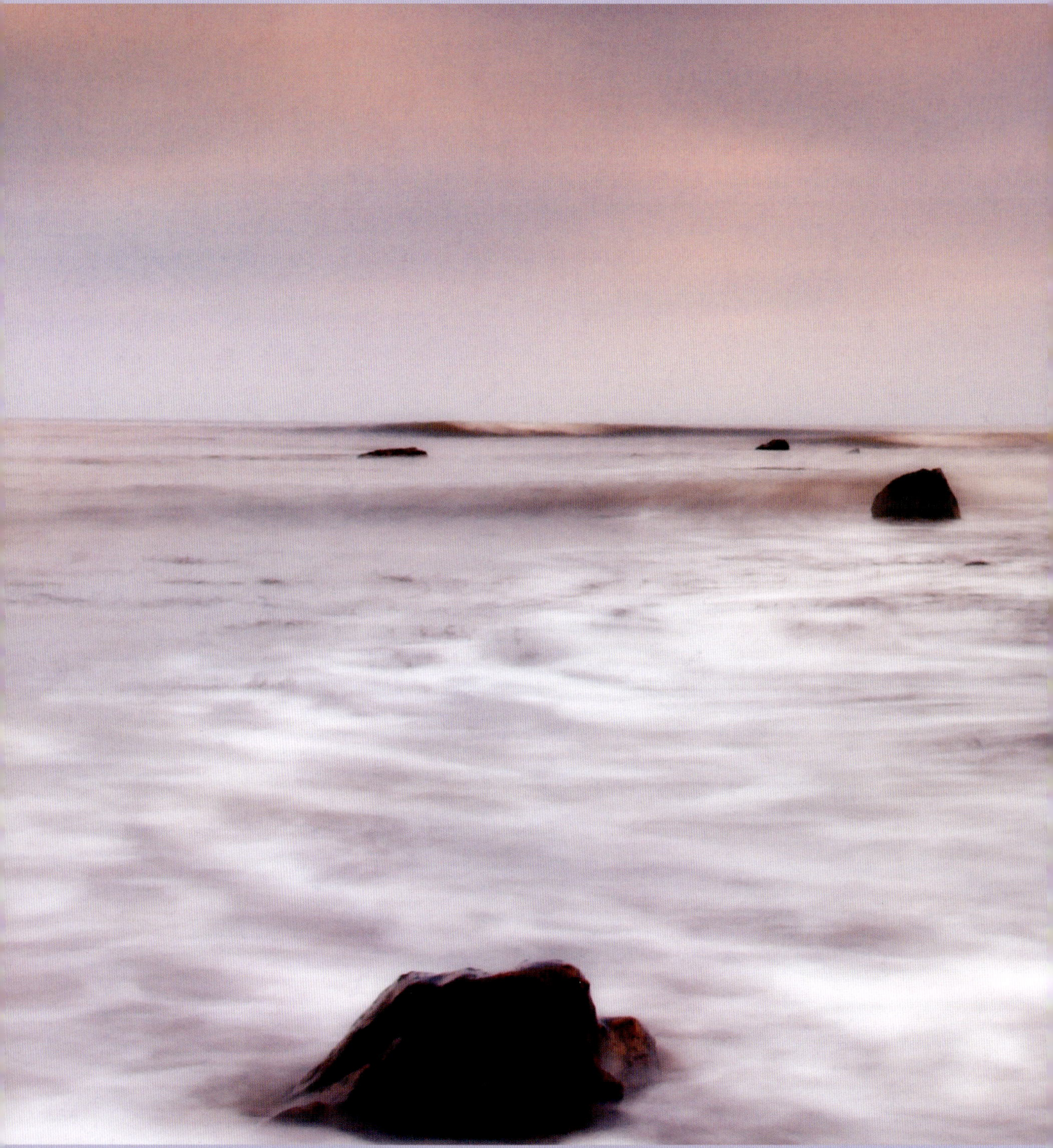

Digital Considerations

04

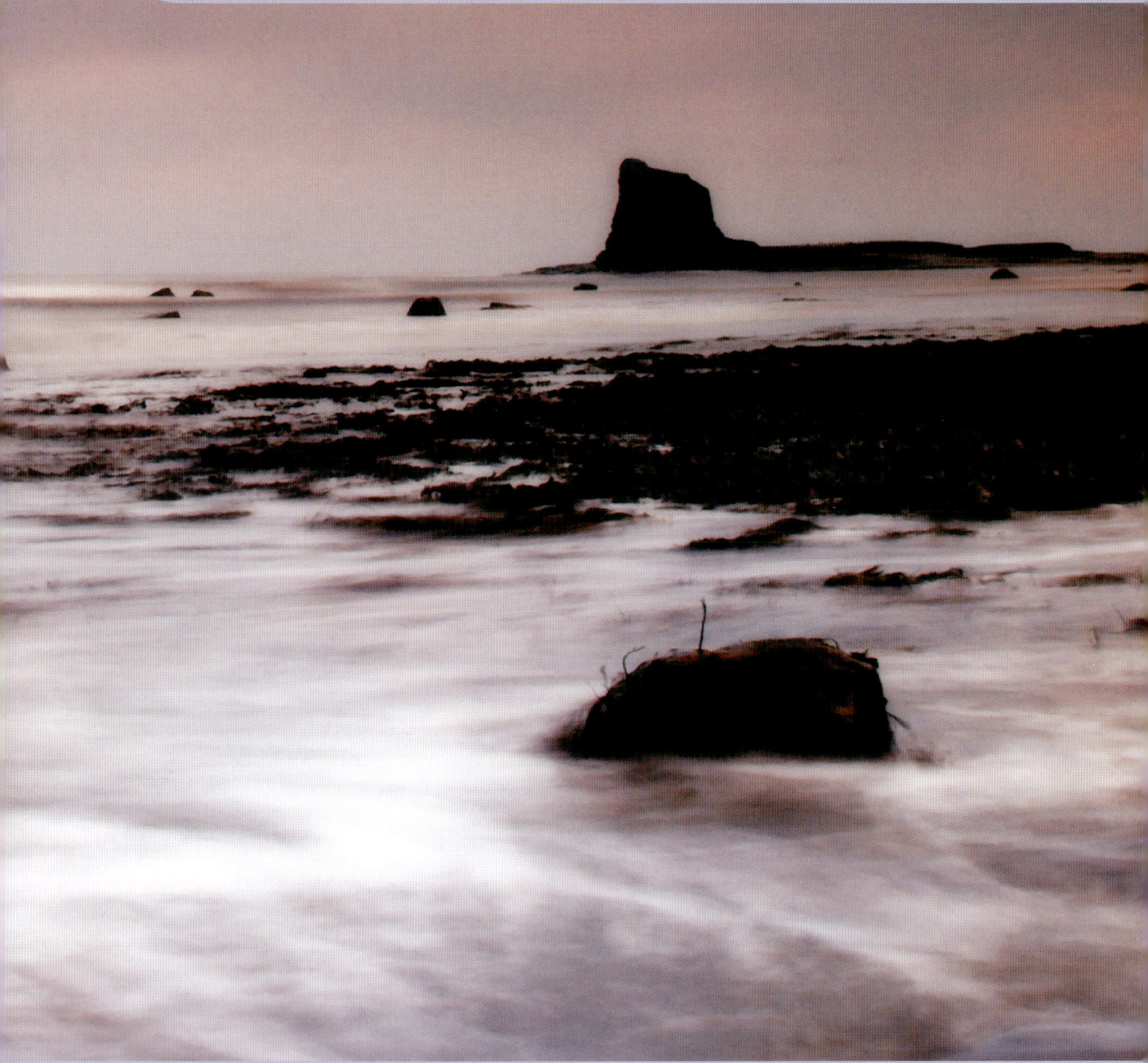

Color Space

Despite being technically inferior to Adode 1998, the sRGB color space (see image below) gives more punchy and saturated colors, so it is a better choice for those looking to print directly from their camera.

Digital photography involves using a host of different devices, from the camera used to capture the image, to the monitor and the printer. All of these use very different technologies to produce their images, and “see” or reproduce colors differently.

To counter this, a number of international standards have been established to avoid changes in color when an image is shared or transferre between these devices. These standard are known as ICC (International Color Convention) profiles.

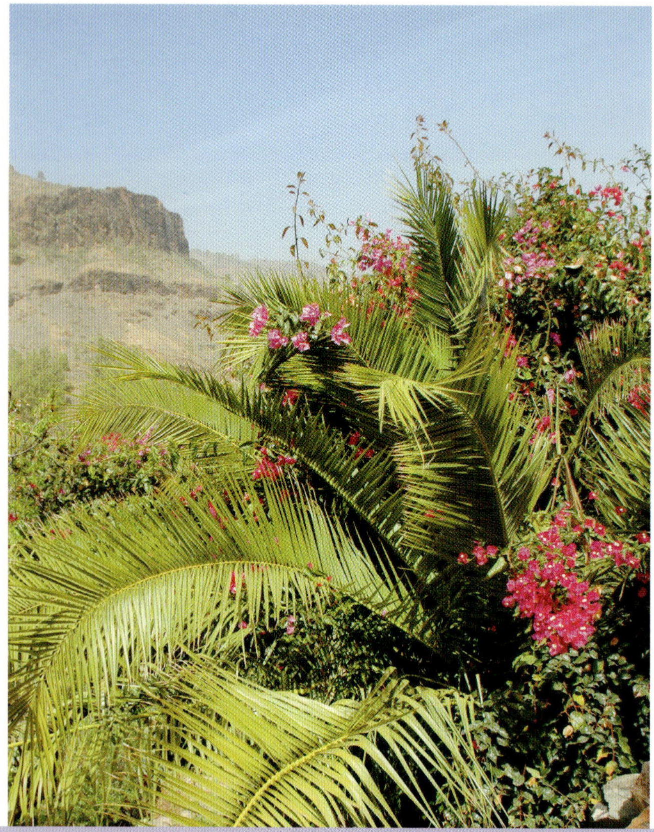

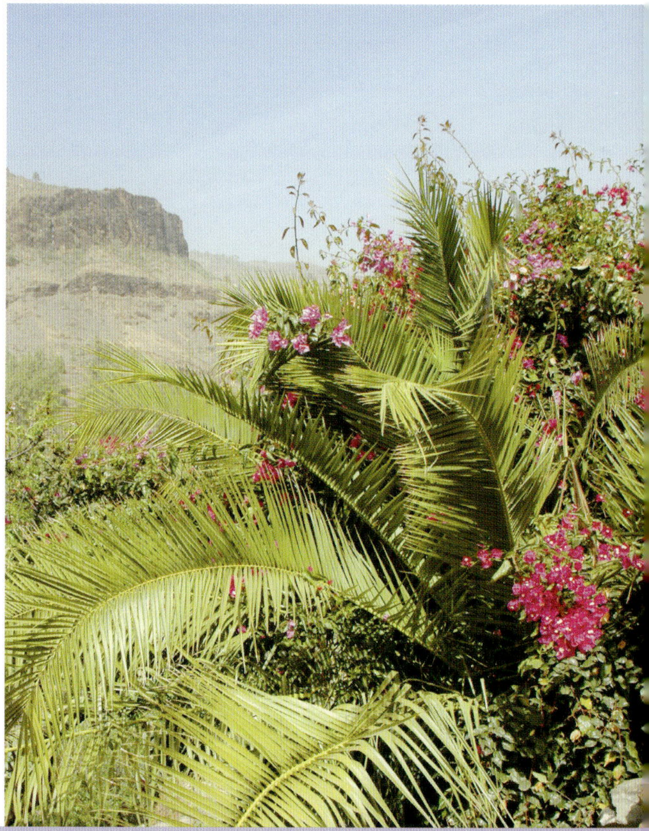

Tip

The key to using color space is consistency. As long as all the devices you are using share the same color profile, you can obtain good results. If one or more are using a different profile, the results are at best unpredictable. Unless you need the extra colors and versatility of Adobe 1998 you should use sRGB as your color space. Ensure that your camera, monitor, software, and printer are all set to sRGB and you will achieve the best results.

he color space is like a map used) define the colors produced by any evice. It also defines the values for ny particular color and the range f colors that can be "seen" or eproduced by that piece of equipment. hink of it like a "paint by numbers" alette of colors, where every color vailable to the painter is given a umber. As long as two people have ne same range of colors available and ne same numbering system, they can oth produce the same images. Change ither of these criteria, however, and ne results will never match.

There are a bewildering number of olor profiles listed by the ICC, but only vo main types are commonly used in hotography: sRGB and Adobe 1998. nce this data is saved with an image, can be reproduced accurately by any evice that uses the same color profile.

Although Adobe 1998 can record a wider range of colors, the results can look flat without some manipulation (see image on left).

sRGB

The choice between the two options comes down to how your images are going to be used or reproduced. For the home user producing prints on their own printer or at a commercial laboratory, sRGB is the best option. It offers a smaller range of colors than Adobe 1998, but is designed to produce the best results straight from the camera.

Many digital cameras also offer a choice of two sRGB options. sRGB 1 offers natural-looking colors. It is usually used for portraits as it produces the best skin tones. The sRGB 2 option gives more saturated colors that are more suitable for landscapes or nature images.

Advantages of sRGB

- You get great results straight from the camera.
- It is the default profile for most home printers and monitors.
- It is the best option for producing images solely for Internet and screen.

Disadvantages of sRGB

- It has a small color range compared to Adobe 1998.
- The picture quality can suffer when an image is manipulated on your computer.

Adobe 1998

Adobe 1998 is the standard profile for most commercial applications. It offers a wider range of colors than sRGB, so is technically a better option. Because of the wider color range it is also the preferred option for those who want to manipulate their images heavily on the computer, as more adjustments can be made before the quality of the image suffers. Despite these technical advantages, it is not necessarily the best option for many, however. Without any adjustments, prints made directly from Adobe 1998 images can look flat and lack punch compared to sRGB images, so they are unsuitable for direct printing or sharing straight out of the camera.

Advantages of Adobe 1998

- This system captures the widest range of colors from your camera.
- It is the standard used by most publishing and commercial users.
- The wider color range means that images can be manipulated more heavily before image quality suffers.

Disadvantages of Adobe 1998

- Results can look flat straight out of the camera.
- It is not suitable for direct printing or on-screen viewing without adjustment.

Bit Depth

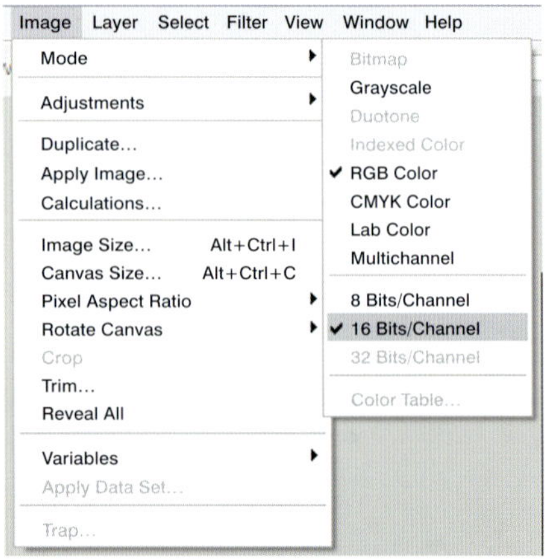

The bit depth of your image can be found in the Image › Mode menu in Photoshop.

The pixels that make up every digital image are individually assigned a number that tells the computer the color and tonal information. This is stored as a binary code, in the form of bits (binary digits). At its simplest, each pixel in a 2-bit image would have one of only two values, and would be either white or black (0 or 1).

The number of these bits of data is known as the bit depth, and is expressed in terms of 2 to the power c 2, 3, 4, and so on. This means that a 4 bit image contains 2 to the power of 4 tonal values. This gives 2 x 2 x 2 x 2, o 16 tones per pixel.

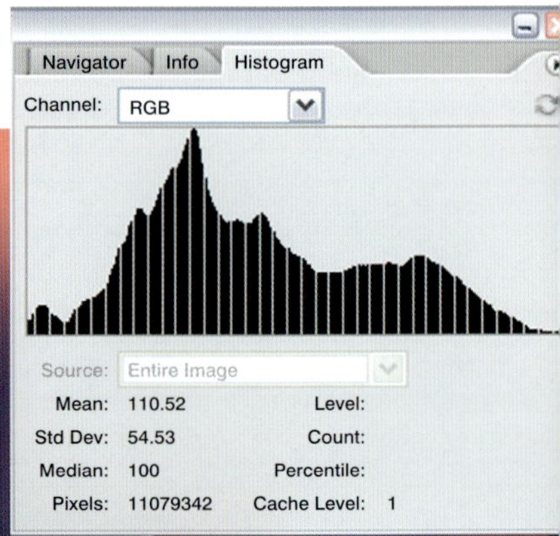

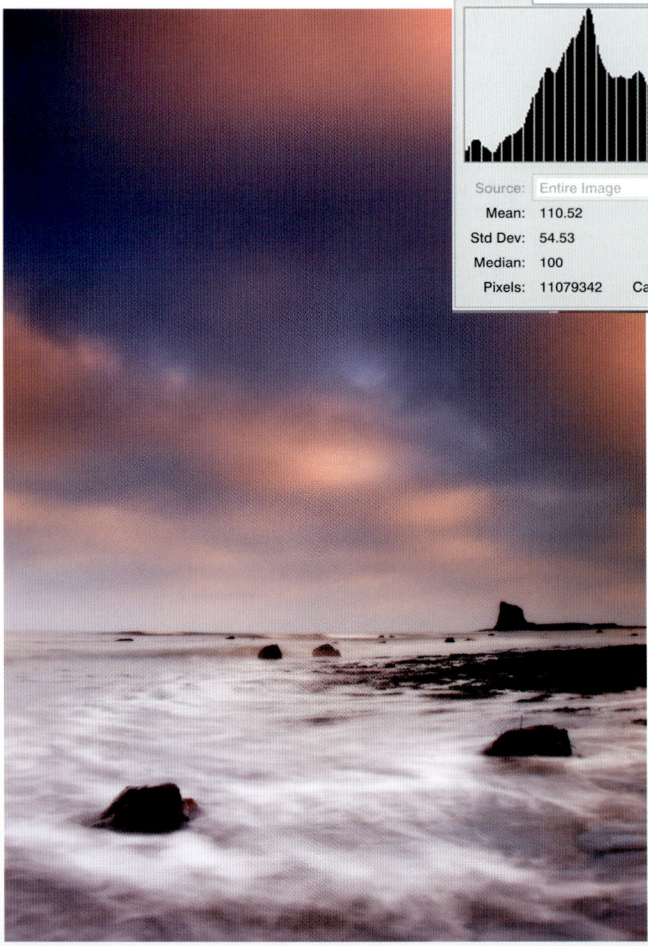

When you apply adjustments such as Curves or Levels to an 8-bit image, the histogram of the image reveals that there are gaps present in the tones of the final image (notice the white lines in the "mountain range" of the histogram). This lost tonal information can cause smooth tones in the image to appear stepped or blocky.

3-bit and 16-bit Files

lthough this would be enough) give a recognizable image, most hotographic images use either - or 16-bit files to produce a much moother image. Larger amounts of ata allow pixels to show a range f tones between these two xtremes, and this is how a simple lack and white, or grayscale, nage is constructed.

Color images are made up from three eparate scales for the red, green, and lue color channels. When viewed, the ombination of the three colors makes p the full color image.

Technically, when working in color, an 8-bit image is actually 24-bit, as there are three channels of 8-bit data. This gives an amazing 16.7 million levels of data—enough to give a smooth-looking image. However, this is still commonly called 8-bit in most situations.

It is possible for some cameras and scanners to record in 16-bit mode (36-bit color). For viewing or printing, these images will have to be converted to 8-bit, however, as most output devices support only this bit depth.

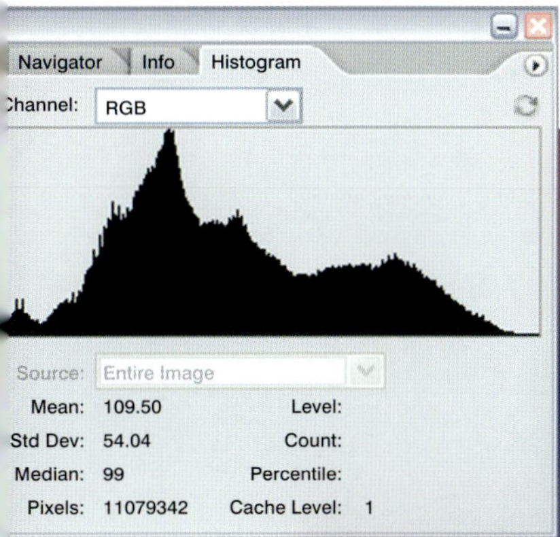

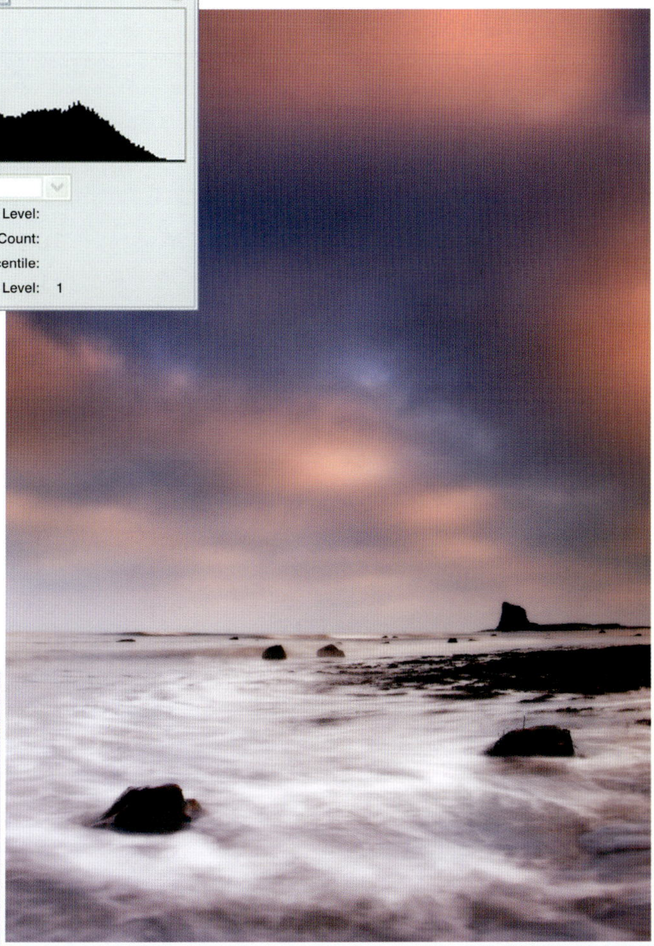

The Advantages of 16-bit Images

Although much of the extra information available in 16-bit images is lost when printed, it is still worth using for images that are going to be manipulated on your computer. Using adjustments such as Levels or Curves means that the software has to throw away some of the tonal information stored in the image. If you are working on an 8-bit image, this means that you can end up with visible "blocking" of tones, rather than the continuous smooth look you want. Although a 16-bit image will still lose information, the end result will be smoother because of the much greater range available, even after converting back to 8-bit for the final image.

Not all image manipulations or adjustments available in your imaging software will work with 16-bit images. Photoshop CS2 offers a much greater range of tools and adjustments than previous versions. Keep the image in 16-bit mode for as long as possible during the working process, only converting to 8-bit when absolutely necessary, or when all adjustments have been made.

Bit depth and tones

1-bit = 2 tones
2-bit = 4 tones
4-bit = 16 tones
8-bit = 256 tones
16-bit = 65,536 tones

« **With a 16-bit image, the histogram is much smoother after applying image adjustments, giving smoother tones and a greater scope for image manipulation.**

Gamut

From cameras to monitors and printers, each piece of equipment in digital imaging can only display, reproduce, or record a certain range of colors. This range is related to the color space used by the device and is known as the color gamut. It is easiest to think of a color gamut like an artist's palette. The greater number of colors the device can choose from, the nearer the result will be to the original.

It is best to record your images with the widest color gamut available. However, if your aim is to produce ink-jet prints, you may find that your images on paper do not look anything like what you saw on your monitor. This is due to the very different ways in which these two devices produce color—the screen is able to display far richer colors than are available from the inks used in the printer. We will deal with matching your monitor and printer in greater depth later (see pp.76–79), but before you start trying to get the two to match you need to ensure that the colors in your images can be reproduced by your printer. This is because the printer is usually the device with the most limited color gamut.

It is easy to add too much saturation to the colors of your image in Photoshop just because they look better on screen, without knowing that your printer will not be able to produce the color accurately. There is a safeguard function within the software to stop this happening called the Gamut Warning.

Using the Gamut Warning

For a visual indication that the colors in your image remain within the color gamut of most printers, you need to switch on the Gamut Warning function. You will find this in the View dropdown menu. Once this is enabled, the colors outside the gamut are shown as gray on your screen.

Switch on the Gamut Warning

1: Once you have opened your image, go to View › Gamut Warning. Any colors in the image that are too intense will be covered by a gray mask; this indicates that they are outside the printer's ability to reproduce.

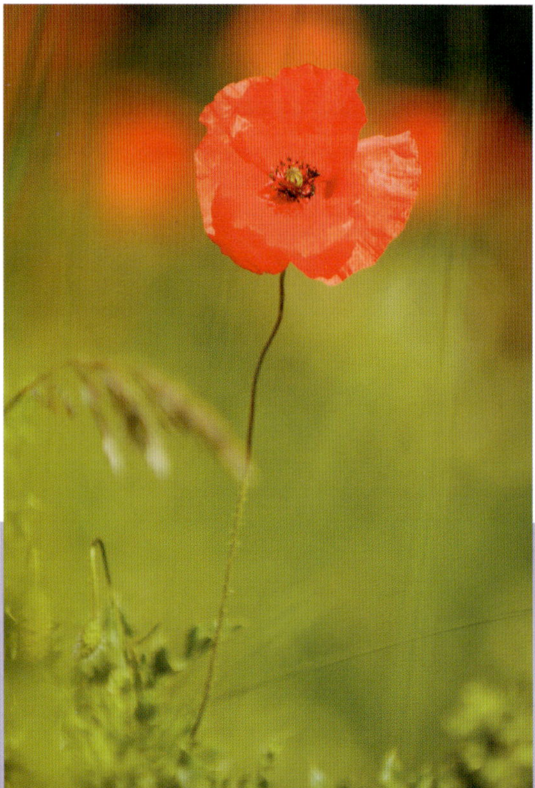

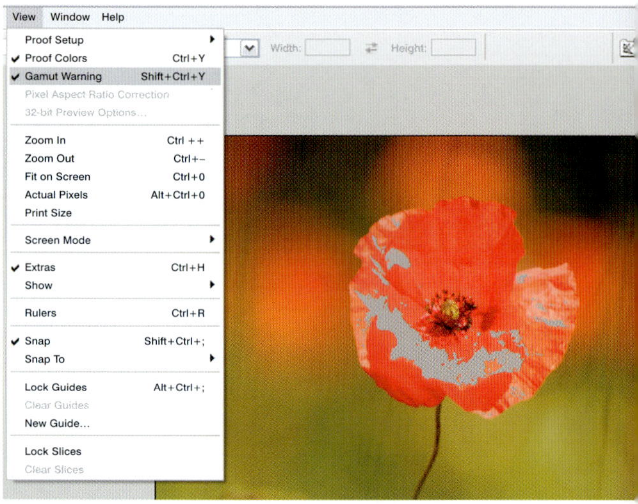

« **Although they may look fine on screen, it is very easy for saturated colors to be outside of the gamut of the printer, leading to a loss of detail.**

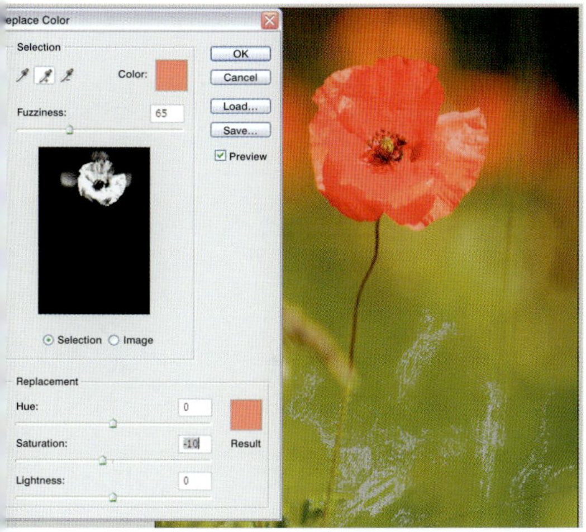

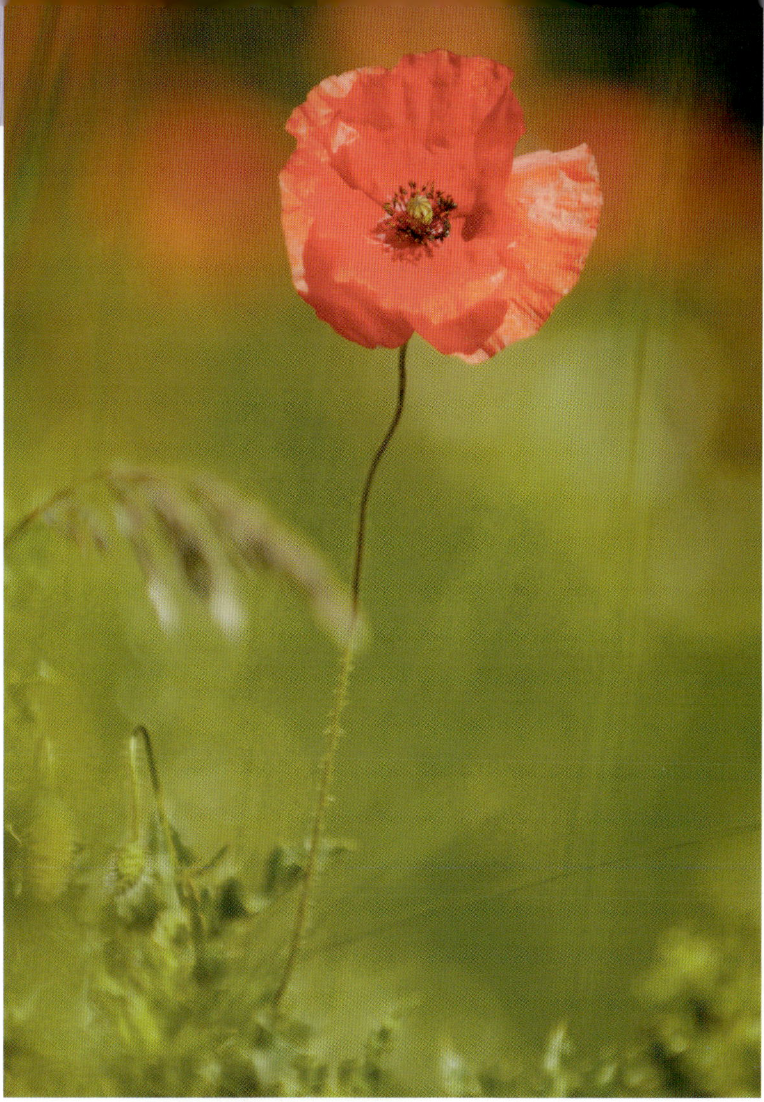

se the Replace Color command
: With the colors that are going to ause problems highlighted, you ow need to reduce these colors sing the Replace Color dialog box. his is opened by going to Image › djustments › Replace Color. Ensure ıe Selection option is enabled in ıe preview window. Then, using ıe dropper tool, click on one of the rayed-out areas on your image. Now djust the Fuzziness slider until the election preview closely matches the ray area on your original image (you ill find this easiest if the dialog is to ne side of the image).

djust the saturation
: Once you are happy with your election, adjust the Saturation slider) the left until the gray warning isappears on your image. It is easiest deal with each color in turn, so you ay need to repeat steps 2 and 3, sing the dropper to select the olors in turn.

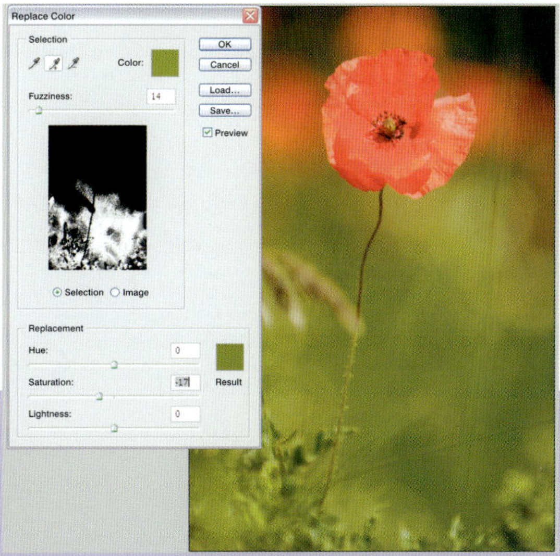

By selectively adjusting the saturation, small areas of color can be reduced so the detail is retained.

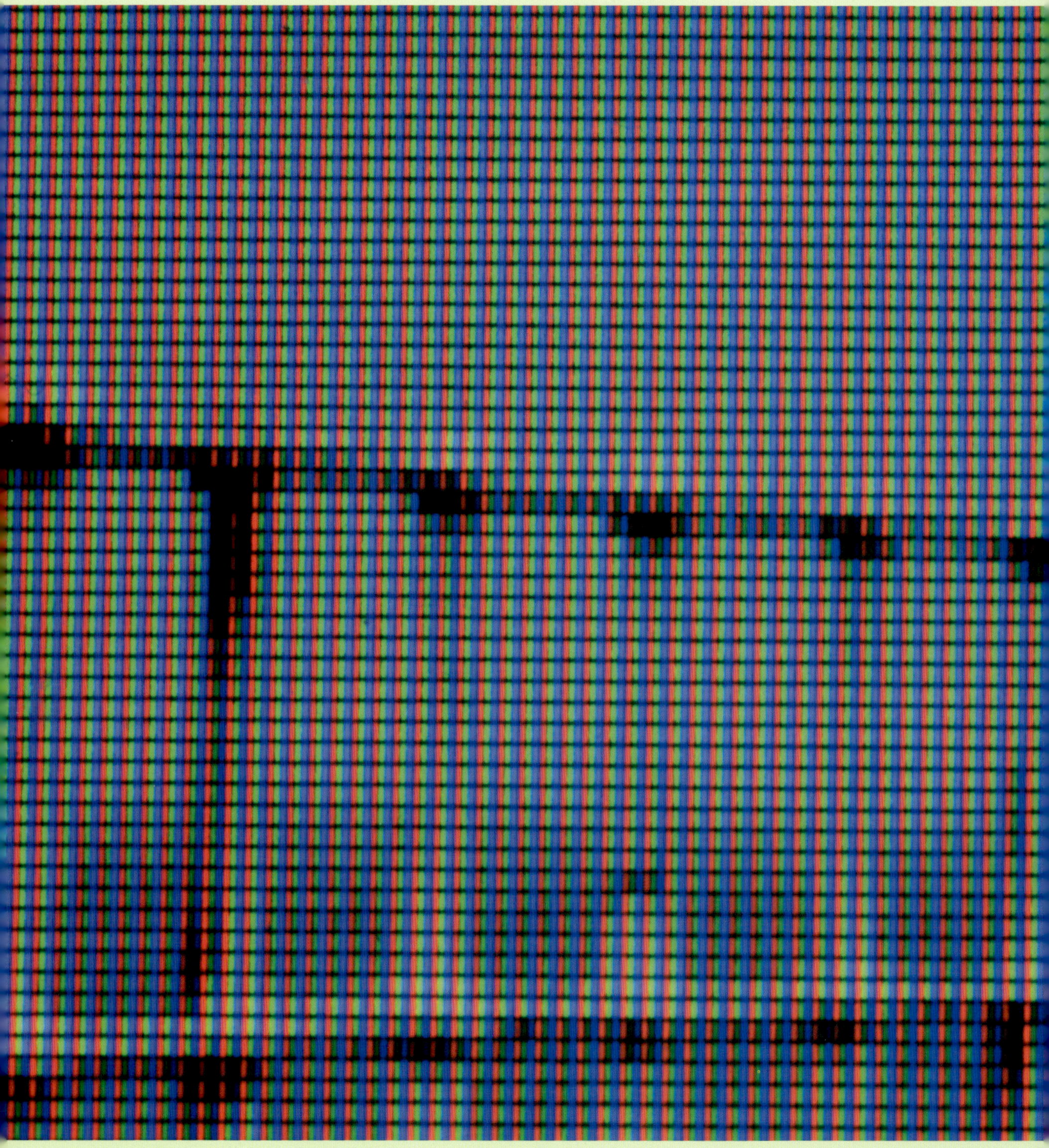

The Digital Darkroom

05

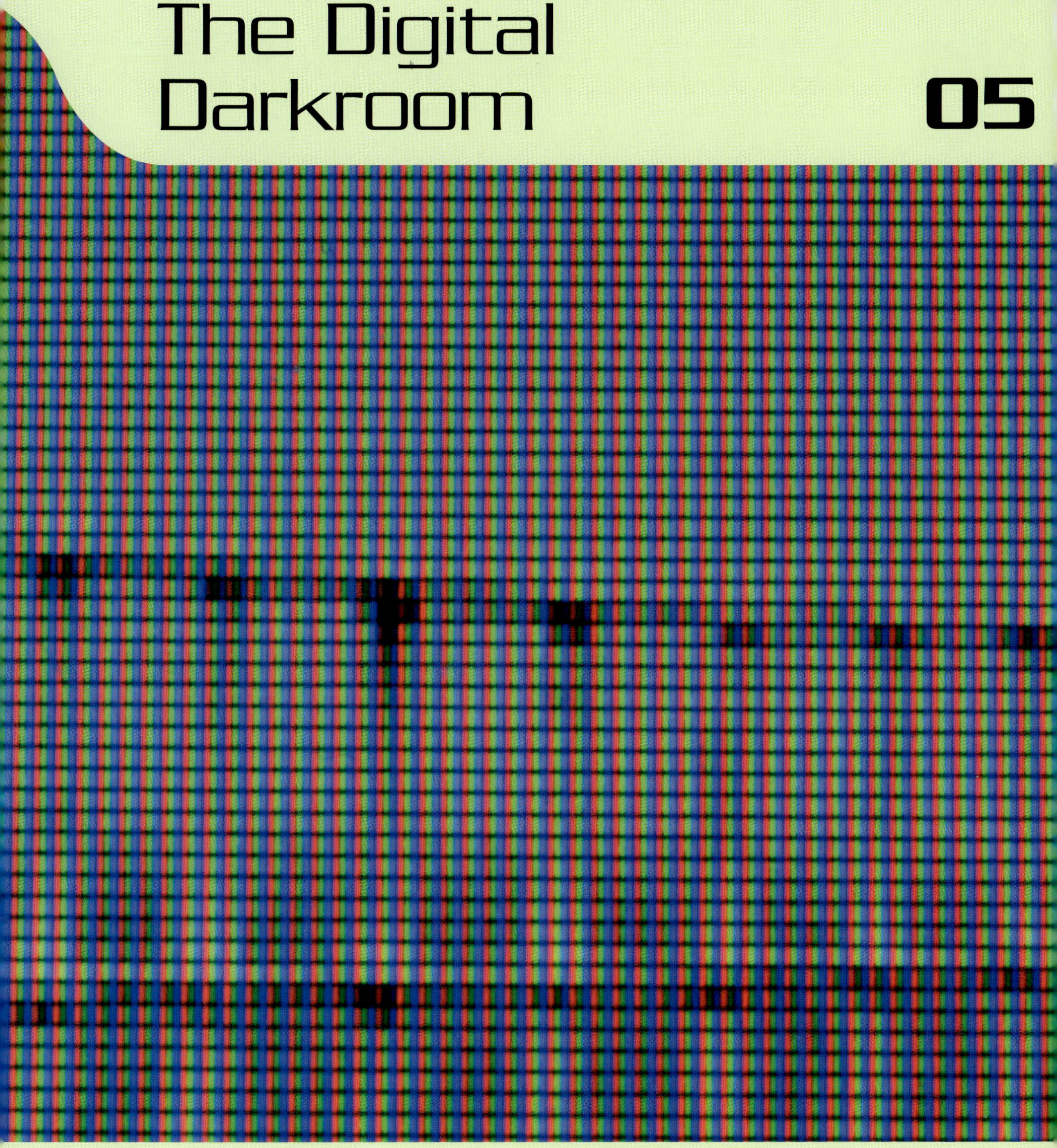

How Monitors Display Color

The quality and consistency of your monitor is key to producing accurate colors in digital images.

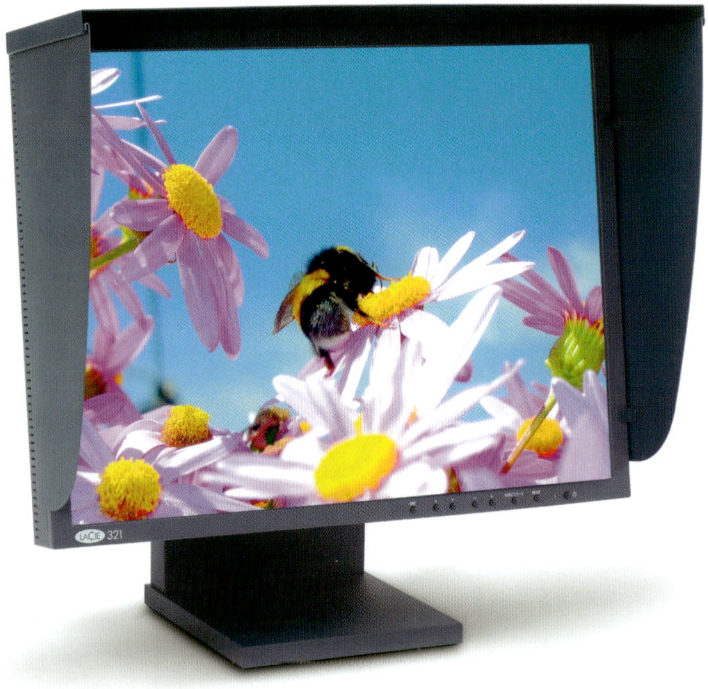

The creativity and control that digital imaging offers has opened up a whole new world of possibilities for almost every photographer. The ability to control the precise color and tones of your images is one of the most welcome aspects of this technology. Along with this extra creativity there is a less welcome, but equally important area: that of color management.

These two words can strike fear into many photographers, but it does not need to be a scary or difficult subject. For most photographers, taking a few simple steps ensures that the color of your images will be more consistent and predictable, whether you are producing prints yourself on a home ink-jet printer or producing images for publication.

Color management involves ensuring that each device in your system, or those outside that you may use, are talking the same language when it comes to colors. How far down the color-management route you need to go largely depends on how you use your images. A closed system, such as simply matching your monitor to your printer, can be established without spending a fortune on extra equipment. People who want to share images outside of their own system need a more absolute and measurable way of ensuring that what they see is the same as what the person or device at the other end sees; this requires a little more effort. But whatever you are using your images for, time spent setting up your digital darkroom in the beginning could save you hours trying to correct problems that occur as your photography expands. So rather than viewing color management as a complicated matter, it is just a case of ensuring that the devices you are going to use to view and print your images are working together.

No matter how you are using your images there is one device that is crucial to get right: your monitor.

'he Monitor

ne monitor on which you view ɔur images lies at the heart of any igital darkroom. It is your main oint of reference when adjusting r manipulating your images; if ne monitor display is wrong, you ill struggle to obtain the results ɔu want.

Before you start trying to adjust e colors of your monitor, you need consider the display and the ositioning. First, ensure that the ackground and desktop of your reen are a simple gray. Do not e tempted to use bright, colorful atterns or images as your desktop ackground. Psychologically strong olors could influence how you see e colors onscreen; for example, a bright red background will make your images appear warmer, making it impossible to adjust either the monitor or your pictures accurately.

The second thing to think about is the lighting conditions around your monitor. Although our vision adapts to changing lighting, these adaptations will influence the colors you see on the monitor. Try to position your monitor away from strong light sources, and ensure that you cannot see reflections from windows or artificial lights on the screen. It also pays to use an area that is a neutral color, as even a brightly colored wall behind the monitor can cause problems when it comes to seeing the colors of your monitor accurately.

To minimize these problems, many professional monitors can be fitted with shades to shield the screen from stray light. These are worth thinking about for critical applications, but for most people the simple steps above will be enough to ensure that the monitor gives the most accurate colors possible.

All monitors use a series of tiny dots to make up the final image. These display red, green, and blue to combine colors together to give the appearance of the original file. Balancing these three colors is the key to getting the monitor settings correct.

The smaller size makes LED monitors a popular choice for most digital photographers.

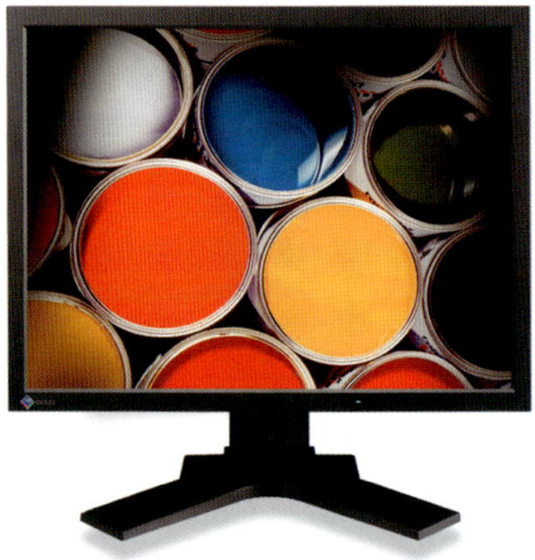

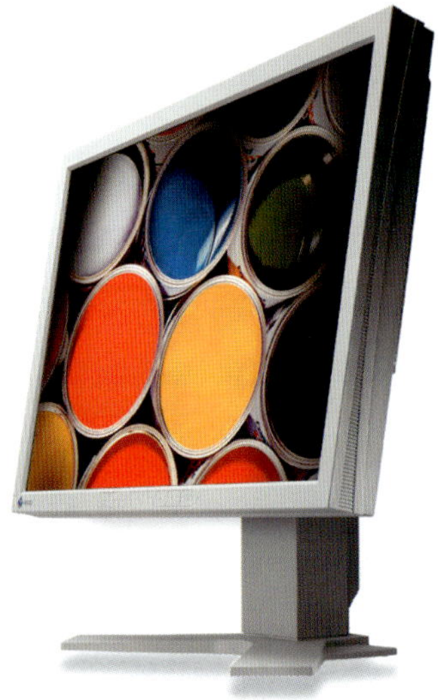

LCD or CRT Screen?

The smaller size and increased affordability of the LCD screen over the traditional CRT monitors makes them a more attractive option for most digital imaging. The choice is largely down to your budget and space considerations, as, despite the fall in price of LCD screens, CRT monitors are a cheaper option. Despite this, LCD screens are becoming the more common option, and this is likely to be the case for the foreseeable future.

Like all technology, things are moving quickly in the world of monitors, but here are a few pros and cons of both systems.

Advantages of LCD

- They are much smaller and more compact than CRT monitors.
- They need less warm-up time compared to CRT monitors.
- They emit very little heat in use.
- The viewable area of the screen is often larger for the same sized screen compared to CRT monitors.
- They have a flat screen as standard.
- The colors stay more consistent over time.

Disadvantages of LCD

- They can be more prone to reflections than CRT models.
- The surface coating is more vulnerable to damage.
- It is more expensive for a high-quality screen.

Advantages of CRT

- They are usually cheaper than similarly specified LCD screens.
- They are not as prone to surface damage as LCD screens.

Disdvantages of CRT

- The large screens are very bulky and heavy.
- The colors can change over time, needing more frequent calibration.
- They need around 30 minutes to warm up before color is consistent.

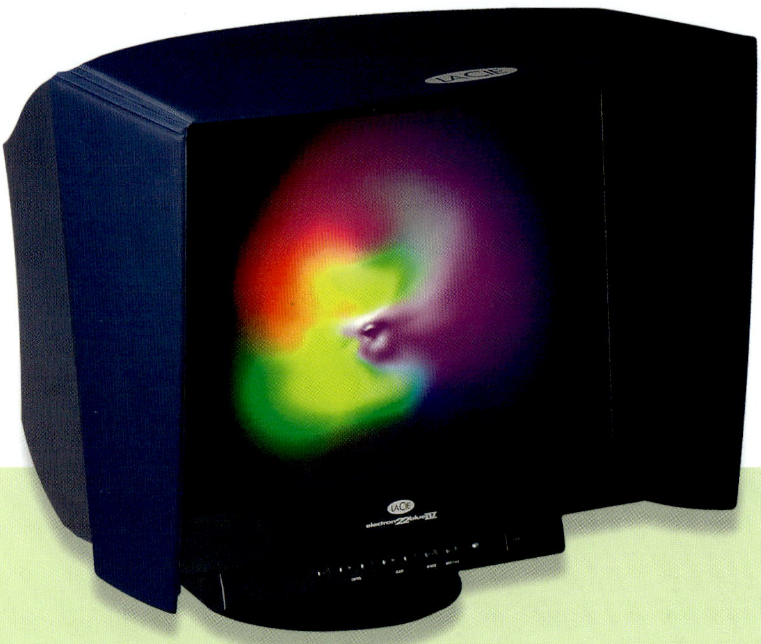

The bulky CRT monitor can still be a good choice for digital photography.

;imple Monitor :alibration

›nce you have decided on your ıonitor and its positioning, you re ready to look at the colors of ıe monitor itself. This is the key rea in getting the colors of your nages correct, so it pays to spend me on this before thinking about ny other device in your system.

There are two main routes to alibrating your monitor. The first is oftware-based and involves following set of on-screen steps to allow you) adjust the monitor settings. The ıain advantage of the software-only olution is cost. The tools you need re probably already installed on your omputer. The main downside with ıis option is that it relies on your ıdgment and ability to adjust the ettings correctly.

The second option uses both ardware and software to accurately ıeasure the colors produced by your ıonitor. This usually involves applying ome basic settings to the monitor, ıen connecting a device to your omputer and running the supplied oftware. Because this method does ot rely on your judgment, it is a ıore reliable and consistent way of alibrating your monitor.

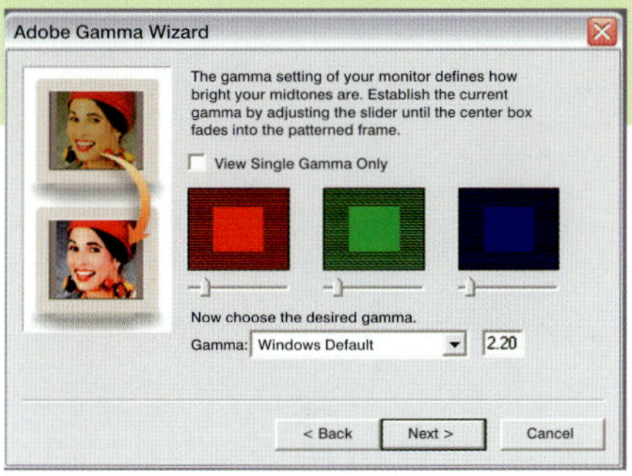

Software Calibration

There are many software-only solutions available, but the most common is Adobe Gamma. This is supplied free with Photoshop and offers a simple step-by-step procedure for setting the contrast and brightness, along with the gamma and white point.

The system works by displaying a sequence of images on-screen that you adjust until the result best matches the optimum option given. When you have finished the setup, you save this setting as a new monitor profile. As long as this is set as the default monitor profile it will be referenced by your software as the one to use, so you do not have to carry out any further adjustments.

Hardware Solutions

There is a range of hardware-based systems on the market, varying greatly in cost. Generally, the more expensive it is, the more adjustments and settings are measured and calibrated by the system, making it more accurate.

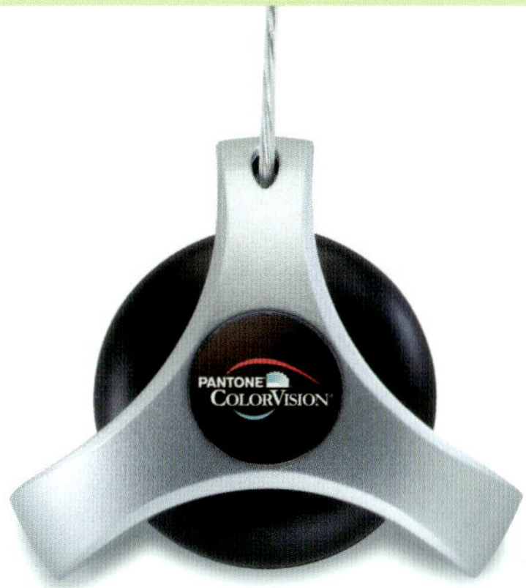

A hardware-based monitor calibration device is a much more reliable and accurate way of ensuring that the colors you see are correct.

All of these systems use a measuring device called a colorimeter that you place on your screen. The software supplied will then run through the setup of the device and usually requires very little input from the user. The device automatically measures the red, green, and blue colors of the monitor and creates a new profile based on the adjustments it has made to the settings. This profile is then loaded as the default for your system. You will be given the opportunity to give it a name so that you can easily identify it.

Before you start any monitor calibration there are two settings that you should ensure are set correctly: gamma and white point. Unless you are directed to use different values, here are the best settings to use for the most accurate colors.

Gamma

This is the relationship between the signal fed from the computer and the brightness of the image on the monitor. This value varies between PC (2.2 gamma) and Apple Macintosh (1.8 gamma) applications. Modern software and computers will account for this difference, so if you specify the correct value for your system it will be displayed correctly.

White point

This is similar to white balance in capture, and defines the color of the light source of the monitor. Although it would seem obvious that you should set this to a daylight (5,000K) setting, the best value for calibrating your monitor is generally agreed to be 6,500K (D65).

Printers

Choosing the right printer will ensure that your prints closely match the vibrancy and colors that you saw in the original scene.

Although viewing your digital images on your computer and being able to share them over the Internet is one of the attractions of digital photography, it does not take away the joy of producing prints from your pictures.

For those wanting to produce high-quality prints from their images, the choice of printer is one of the most crucial decisions for their digital darkroom. For producing prints at home, there are several different types of ink-jet printer on the market, as well as color laser and dye-sublimation models to choose from.

Among these choices, the photo-quality ink-jet printer is the best option for most photographers. They offer the versatility of being able to print on to many different papers and other materials, can produce stunning results, and can be inexpensive to buy.

Ink-jet Printers

All ink-jet printers use the same basic principles to produce their images. Inside the print head of the machine there are at least three separate colored inks (cyan, magenta, and yellow) and one black ink. These print heads take the data from your image and spray the ink onto the paper in tiny dots, which combine to make the final image.

Basic ink-jet printers can be purchased very cheaply, but their suitability for producing good photographs is debatable—although all ink-jets use similar principles, there are many different techniques and technologies used by different models that will affect the quality and permanence of the finished print. As with most technology, you get what you pay for, with more expensive models offering the promise of higher quality and faster printing. Here we discuss the features to look out for when choosing an ink-jet printer.

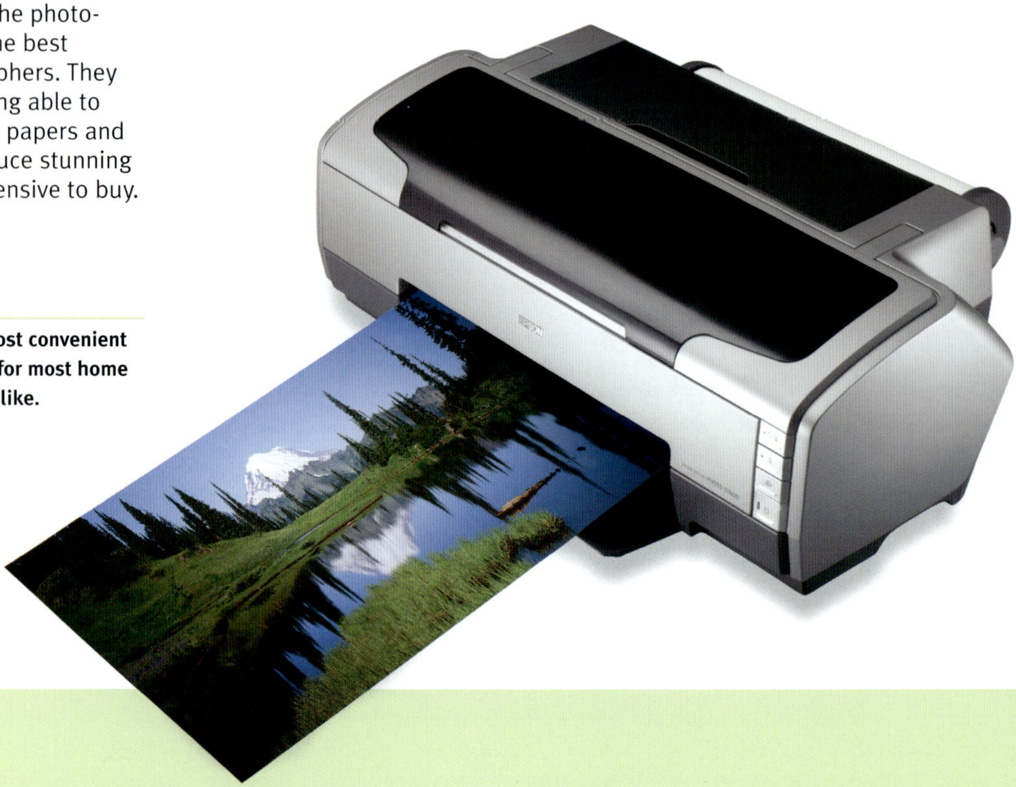

Ink-jet printers are the most convenient and cost-effective option for most home users and professionals alike.

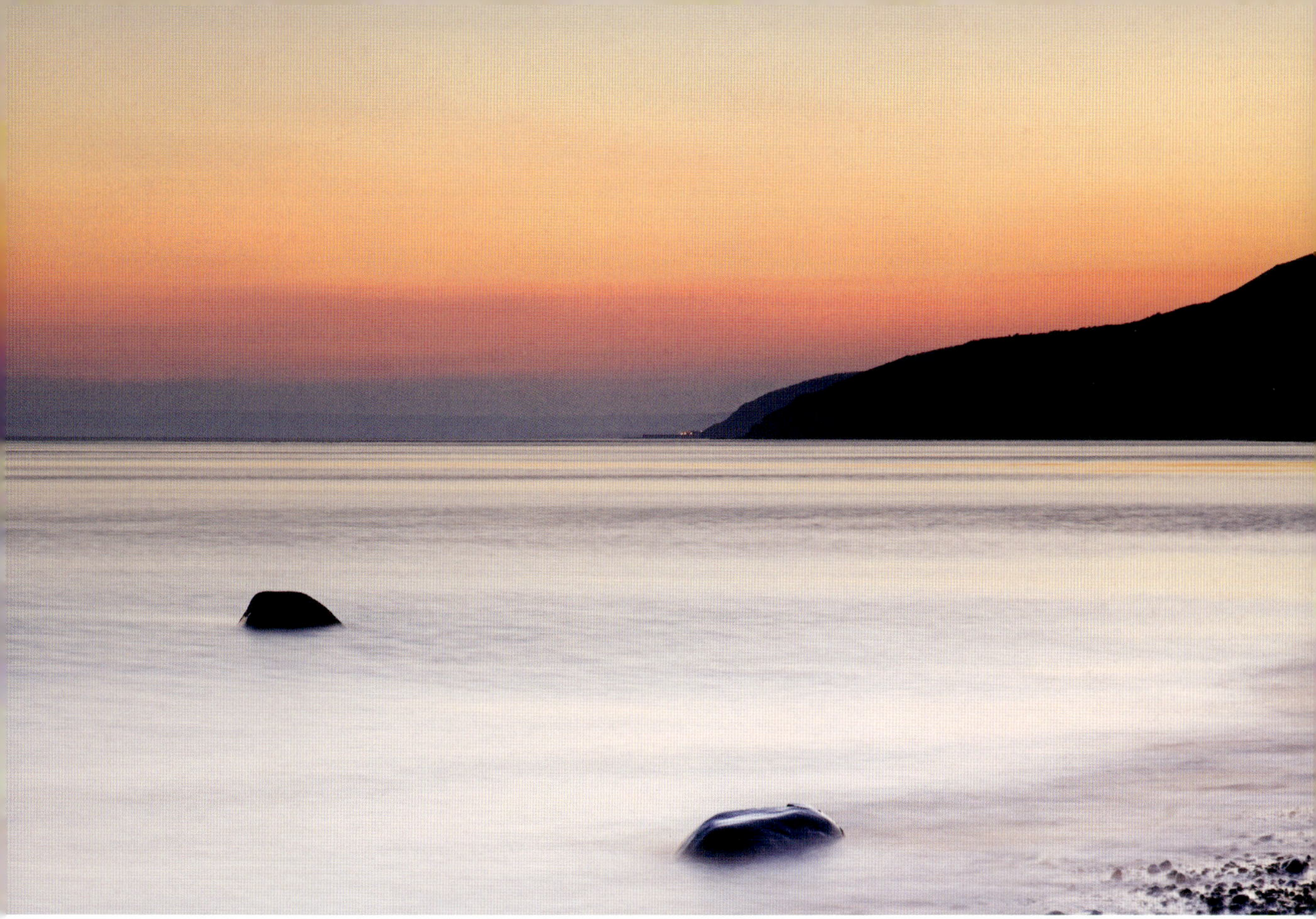

umber of inks

lthough it is possible to make all of he major colors from a simple four-olored ink system, such a system will truggle to reproduce the more subtle olors present in many digital images. o help the printer produce these olors, a photo-quality ink-jet printer ill usually employ at least six colors. hese are the four standard ones yan, magenta, yellow, and black), lus additional light cyan and light agenta inks to give much better olor gradients and skin tones.

Some of the better professional ink-jet printers have taken this principle even further, adding red, blue, and green inks to the printer. These extra colors are generally used to extend the color gamut (range of colors) that the printer is able to produce, rather than improve the rendition of subtle tones. Generally, the greater the number of inks used by the printer, the wider the range of tones and colors it will be able to produce.

The more colored inks provided, the wider the color gamut possible from your ink-jet printer.

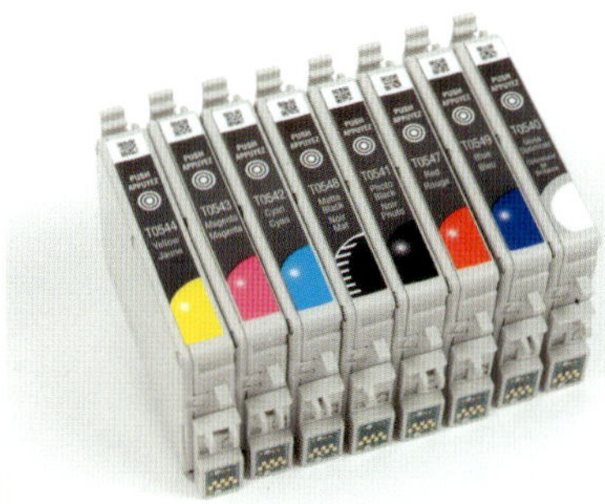

Types of ink

There are two main types of ink used in ink-jet printers: dye-based and pigment-based. Dye-based inks are the most common for general-purpose ink-jet printers and the cheaper photo-quality models. They offer bright and vivid colors, but have given rise to one of the greatest problems associated with home ink-jet printers—impermanence. The colors from cheap dye-based inks can fade very quickly, especially when the print is exposed to sunlight.

This anxiety has led many manufacturers to introduce models that use the more permanent pigment inks. These inks can offer light-fastness similar to traditional photographic papers, and are the best choice for those looking to produce prints for sale or as a permanent record of their images. Traditionally, pigment inks offer lower color saturation than dye-based equivalents, so their use was limited to a small number of printers and specialist monochrome inks. This situation is rapidly changing, however, with the latest generation of pigment-ink printers using a greater range of colors and even an extra gloss "ink" to given them a color gamut similar to dye-based models. All this technology comes at a premium, so if you only need a print as a temporary reference you may be better off with the cheaper dye-based option.

Resolution

This is not to be confused with the image resolution of the file you are trying to print. The resolution of ink-jet printers depends on the tiny droplets of ink that they use to make up the image, rather than the digital image. Simple blocks of a single color can be printed using very low printer resolutions, but the complex tones of a photograph require the ink to be applied precisely. For photo-quality prints, the printer should be able to print at least 1,440 dots per inch (dpi), although many printers offer much greater resolution than this. The highe the resolution of the printer, the bette it will be at producing subtle colors, as this is where the greater accuracy is required.

Ink droplet size

Connected to the resolution of the printer is the actual size of the droplet it produces. Many cheap ink-jet model produce only a single size of ink droplet, which will affect their ability to produce fine detail and subtle color even if the printer offers a very high resolution. The better photo-quality models use a variable droplet size to tailor the ink to the type of detail it is trying to produce. For light and subtle tones, it uses a very fine droplet size; for simple blocks of darker color, it uses larger droplets.

Print Media

The results you can achieve from your ink-jet printer will depend as much on the paper or media that you choose to print on as the printer itself. There is an amazing range of options available to choose from, which would take an entire book to explain, but there are some simple guidelines to help you to choose the right paper for your prints.

- Glossy photo-quality papers: These offer the closest results to traditional gloss photographic prints. They give the brightest, most saturated colors from your printer.

- Luster or semi-matte photo-quality papers: These give a lower color saturation than gloss papers, but have a "softer" look that can suit portraits and subjects with more subtle colors well.

- Watercolor or fine-art papers: Without the benefit of the special coatings used in photo-quality papers, these tend to produce very flat-looking images. They are great for black and white prints, where the contrast and tonality of the image can be easily adjusted to give great results, but for color they are best used for producing "art" prints rather than photographic images for reference or color proofing.

Whichever type of paper you choose, it pays to buy the best you can afford. Once you are happy with the results, stick with a particular paper. As we will see later on, changing either the ink or the paper in your machine can have knock-on effects for any color management or profiles that you have put in place.

Jye-sublimation Printing

his printing technology uses a ribbon ontaining at least three colored yes (cyan, magenta, and yellow). he ribbon is passed over a heated rint head to transfer the image o the paper. The paper is passed nrough the machine once for each f the three colors, and then a final loss coating is applied to the whole nage. Because it does not rely on ny droplets of sprayed ink, it can ffer better rendition of subtle tones nan some ink-jet printers, although ne results tend to be less saturated.

Dye-sublimation printers offer some benefits over their ink-jet counterparts, but the cost and limited paper choice make them a less popular option for home printing.

These printers are also generally more expensive to buy than similarly specified ink-jet models, and can only print on special media, rather than the myriad of options available for ink-jets. Dye-sublimation printers do offer more durable prints than most ink-jets, however, and look and feel more like traditional photographic prints.

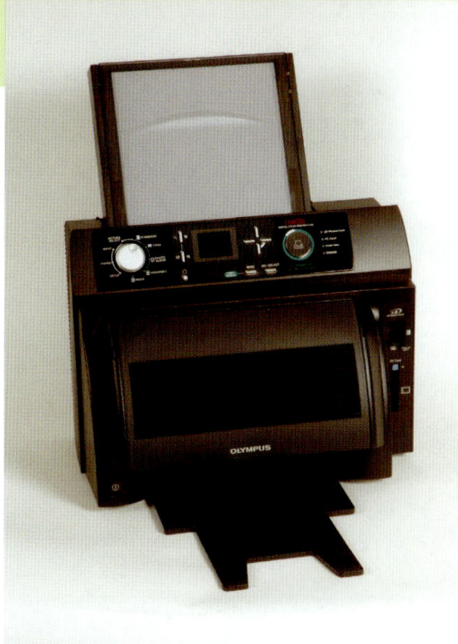

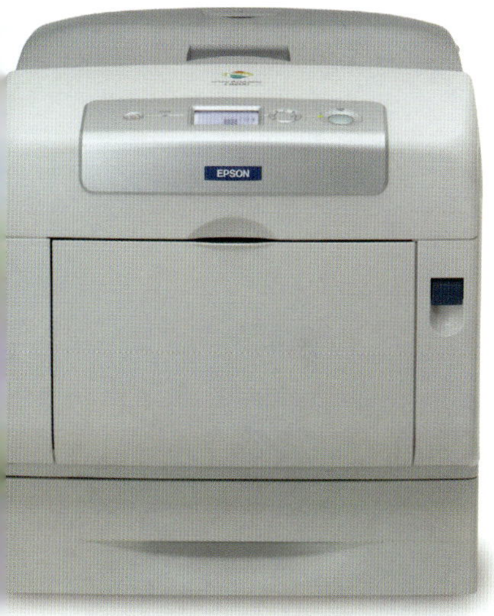

Color Laser Printers

Although they offer superb speed and superior network connectivity, color laser printers still cannot match the quality or versatility of ink-jet printers. They are useful for designers and those simply looking for high-volume output, at the expense of quality, but their suitability for photographic output is limited.

Color laser printers are not generally suitable for high-quality photographic printing.

Direct Printing

There has recently been a trend among printer manufacturers to produce models that can print directly from digital cameras or memory cards. These devices offer great convenience for many photographers, but there are some pitfalls to this route.

The images have to be print-ready straight out of the camera, so sRGB color space should be used. Using the wider color gamut of Adobe RGB can result in flat-looking images. While some models do offer limited adjustments to the color, saturation, and contrast of your images, without the aid of a proper monitor they are difficult to use accurately. Having said this, they are a useful proofing device for use on location, either for checking the lighting ratios, or for giving clients reference images to take away with them.

Color Management

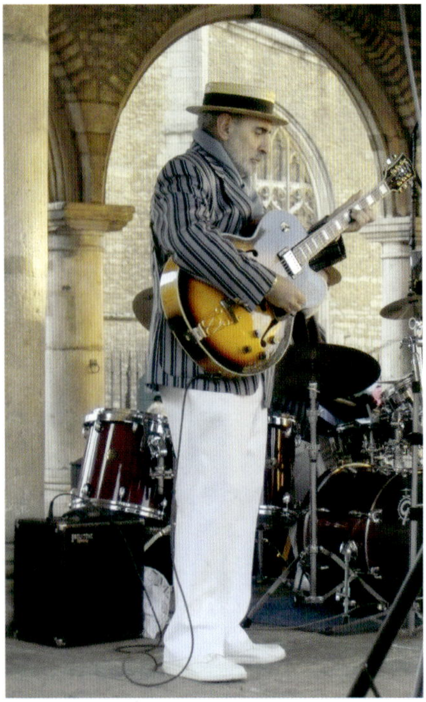

Even if you have calibrated your monitor as discussed previously, this deals only with the colors that you see onscreen. Although these may be correct, there is still no guarantee that they will be the same when you output your images onto different devices. To achieve this, you have to tackle the issue of color management. Although it is often seen as hugely complicated, color management has a simple principle at its heart—to maintain the same colors in an image as it is transferred between the different devices you use.

Problems occur when the colors of the image are converted by the software or hardware into a different set of colors that bears little resemblance to the original image. To stop this happening, most software and hardware has a set of tools that manages how this conversion occurs. This is where color management

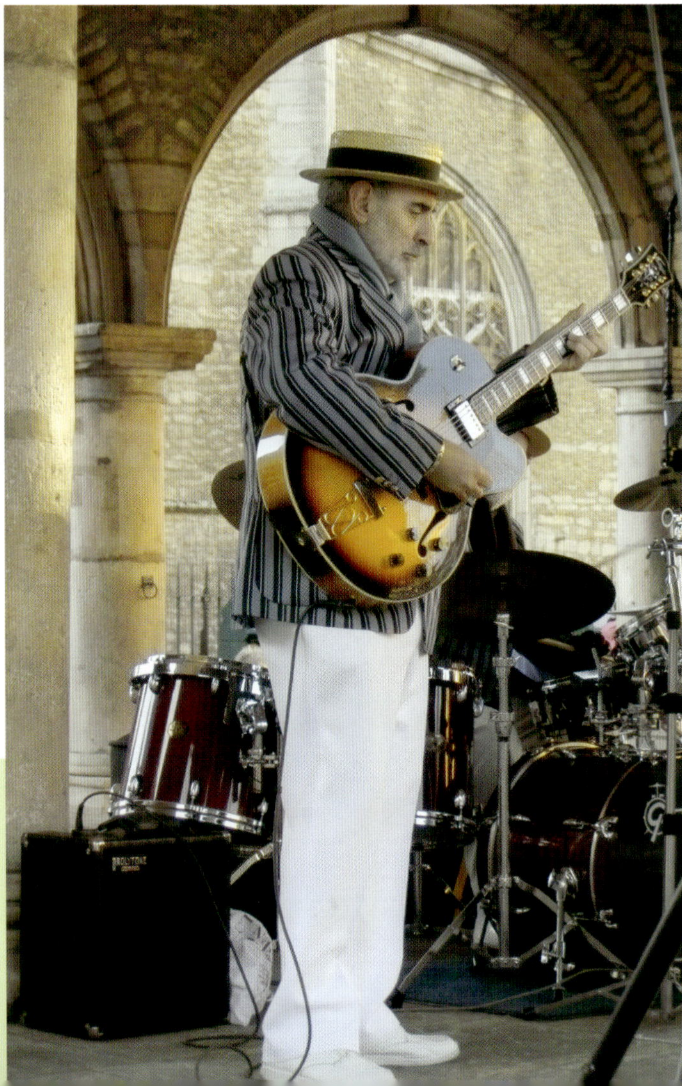

Ensuring that the information contained in your image is interpreted correctly by your software and hardware will ensure that your results will be printed and viewed as you intended. Without some basic color management in place, the colors can be converted with disastrous results. Notice how the skin tones on the non-color-managed image on the right have a strong yellow cast.

omes in—by assigning different profiles” to the devices in the chain, ou can control how the color is andled by them, and so ensure that he colors do not change.

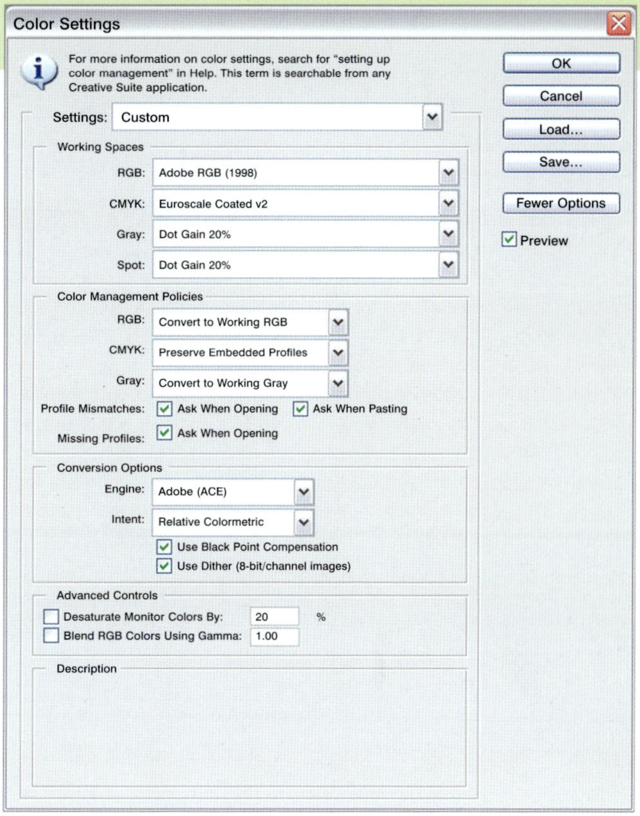

Photoshop Color Settings

nce you have decided on the color pace that you are going to use, ne first step is to ensure that your naging software is set to use it as the efault working value. You will find the olor Settings in Photoshop by going) Edit › Color Settings.

In the dialog window, choose ustom in the Settings dropdown nenu. This will allow you to choose ne settings that suit your setup. he Working Spaces area allows you) choose the color space that will ecome the default for the software. ritical users should choose Adobe RGB 1998 for the widest color gamut, although sRGB could be used for a simple closed system. This is selected using the RGB dropdown menu.

The next set of choices involves whether you want to convert images to the working space or not. In the Color Management Policies area, choose Convert to Working RGB from the RGB dropdown menu to ensure that the color space remains the same for every image that is opened in the software. The set of three tick boxes below this tells the software to flag up any images that have a different or no color space attached. The best option is to tick all three boxes so you receive a warning whenever a conversion is going to take place.

The final choice at this point involves the Conversion Options at the bottom of the window. This selects the Color Management Engine or Module (CME or CMM) that is used to convert the colors that do not match the Working Space. Adobe ACE is generally recognized to be the best CME at this conversion, so select this option.

Embedding the Color Profile

There is no point in changing the color settings in your software unless you apply this color space to the image when you save it. When you come to save the image, choose the File › Save As command, and ensure that at the bottom of the dialog window the Embed Color Profile box is ticked. This will ensure that the image has the working color space attached, meaning that it can be interpreted correctly throughout the system.

There are essentially two types of color management needed for the different requirements of the photographer. The first is the user who sees the ink-jet print that they are producing as the final result. This type of user needs only to match their monitor to their printer to achieve the right results. This approach is reasonably simple and, as the system is a closed loop, these users do not necessarily need to worry about how their images would be interpreted by devices outside of their own setup.

The second type is for those who need to be sure that the images they produce can be accurately printed and interpreted by other people's devices. This area includes anyone who has their pictures printed by a commercial laboratory, or who is producing images for publication. This route is a little more difficult, and may involve spending some extra money, as the settings and profiles need to be transferable between the various devices used along the way.

Whichever user type you fall into, the most important aspect of color management is that you choose a color space that suits your workflow, and then stick to it. Whether you choose the Adobe 1998 or the sRGB color space will largely be down to how you want to use your images. Professional photographers or anyone supplying images for editorial or commercial printing have little choice, as Adobe 1998 is almost universally used in these applications. Ensure that your choice is used as the workin color space in every application that you are likely to use, from RAW conversion software to image-editing and printing. If you are the first type o user and need only control the colors within your own system, this simple step may well be enough. Although the various devices are not matched, the differences will be more consisten and predictable, allowing you to fine-tune your image adjustments with much more confidence.

Once you have taken this step, you are ready to progress further into color management (which we cover in the following pages), but try this solution first before spending money on expensive solutions to your color problems.

For those who are supplying images to a third party for printing, try to find out the color profile or color space preferred by the system used at your destination. This will allow you to tailc your color settings to suit it and have at least a fighting chance of getting consistent colors.

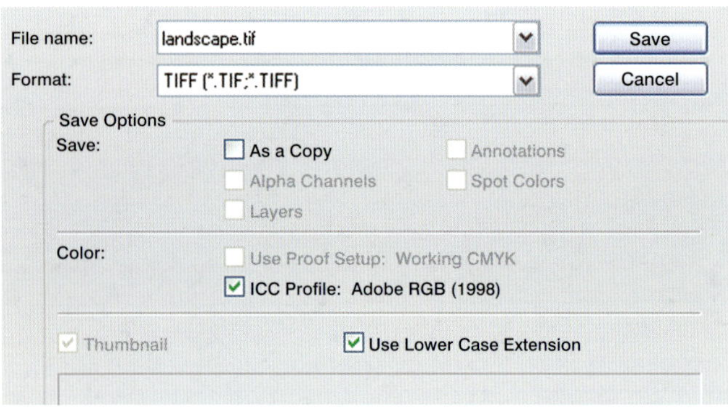

To ensure the color profile remains with your image, tick the Embed Color Profile box in the Save As dialog window.

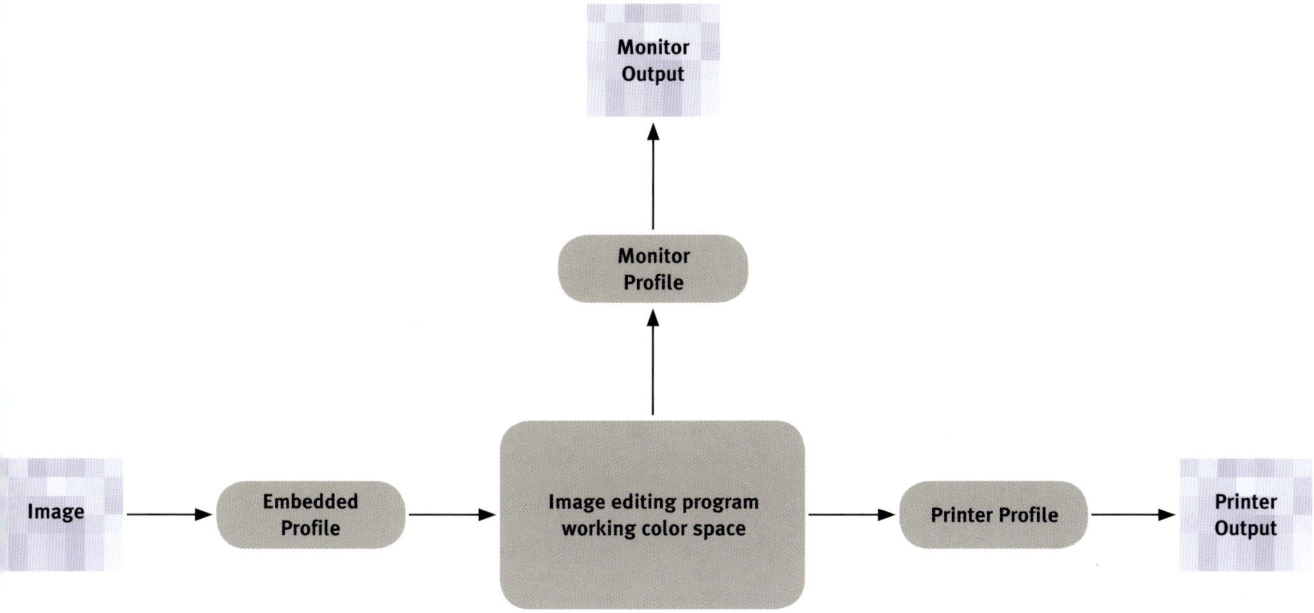

Color management can appear complex to most photographers. This simplified diagram shows the basic elements needed to ensure that the colors of your images are maintained throughout your system. ne important aspects are the choice of a working space at gives you the best results and profiles for your onitor and printer to allow your system to interpret the lors in the image correctly. We will cover this in more etail in the section on color profiles.

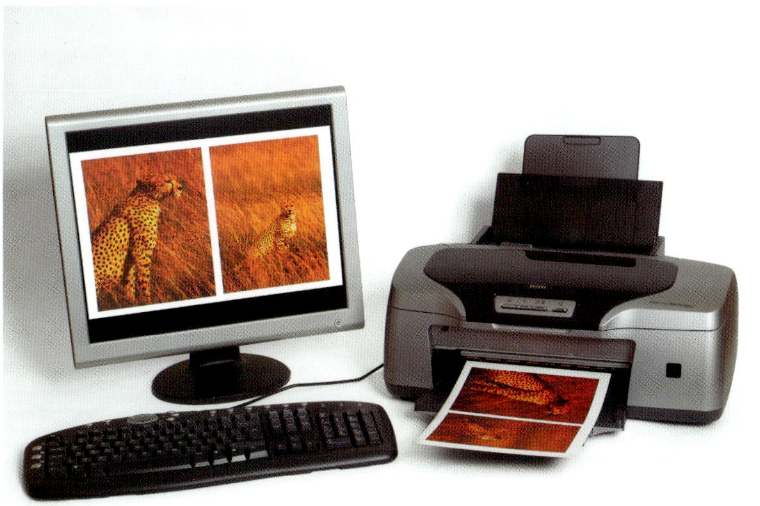

Even a simple home computer setup will benefit from basic color management.

Matching Your Monitor and Printer

For most photographers using a digital darkroom, getting their prints to match the results they see on their monitor is the single most important task. This is the holy grail of many photographers producing ink-jet prints on their computer, and—as with any aspect of color management—you need to go about it in a logical way. There is no point changing the settings on your printer if the colors you see on your monitor or the colors in your image are wrong. First ensure that your monitor is accurate; then make sure that the color space and profiles that you use are consistent. Only then should you look at your final prints.

Before we investigate how to do this, we need to establish one thing—no matter how hard you try, the image on your monitor and your print will never match exactly. The different color gamuts and the way that the devices produce color mean that it is not possible for a print and a monitor to look exactly the same. Having said this, what you can do is obtain results that are close enough so that you will be able to accurately predict the results from your printer by the image you see onscreen. That is all you can ask.

Despite these problems, don't despair: the actual process of printer profiling is fairly simple. There are two main ways of producing more consistent prints, depending on your needs. The first, and easiest, option is to ask a specialist lab to produce a custom profile for you. This means they will do all the hard work of measuring the colors. However, this method can be expensive, especially if you like to use a range of papers.

The second, "homemade," approach takes a little more time and effort on your part, but will produce good results providing the rest of your system is consistent (see p.79 for more information).

Principles of Printer Profiling

Profiling your home printer need not be difficult, but it does rely on a few simple principles in order for it to work successfully:

- You need to produce separate profiles for each type of paper that you use.

- If you change ink type, you need to produce a whole new set of profiles for the different papers.

- Even when replacing ink cartridges with new ones of the same brand these can vary in color, so do not expect a single profile to apply forever. Whenever you change inks, produce a test print to ensure that the results are consistent.

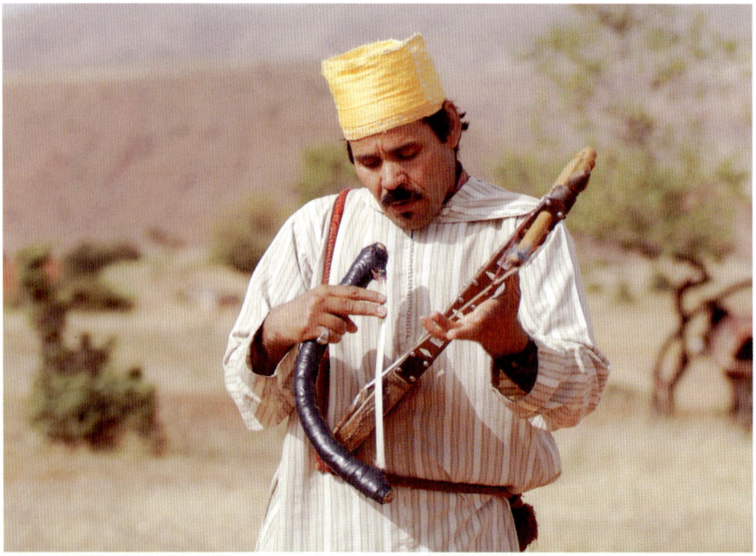

Without matching your monitor and printer, color casts are almost inevitable.

By matching your monitor and printer, you can produce accurate and consistent results.

ʼrint Viewing

ʼne apparent color of the inks used ɔ produce ink-jet prints is greatly ɪfluenced by the color of the light you se to view them under. This effect, ılled metamorism, means that you ıust use a consistent light source for ssessing your test prints.

The most commonly accepted ɔlor temperature for print viewing 5,000K, also known as D50. There ʼe dedicated print-viewing booths vailable, at a price, but acceptable ʼsults can be obtained by using a ɹorescent light source calibrated this color temperature.

Custom Profiles

There are a number of companies that will take away some of the hard work involved in producing accurate prints. This method works by supplying a color chart that you print out using your preferred ink and paper. You send this print off to the lab for them to measure the colors using a spectrometer. This is a device that accurately assesses the color of each swatch and compares them to the original file. The lab then produces a profile based on these readings, which is sent or e-mailed to you. This profile is placed in your computer's Color Sync (Macintosh) or Color Folder (PC), and is used as the profile associated with this printer.

Over time, you may need to adjust the colors of your image, and if you start to use different inks or paper you will need to have another profile produced for this combination.

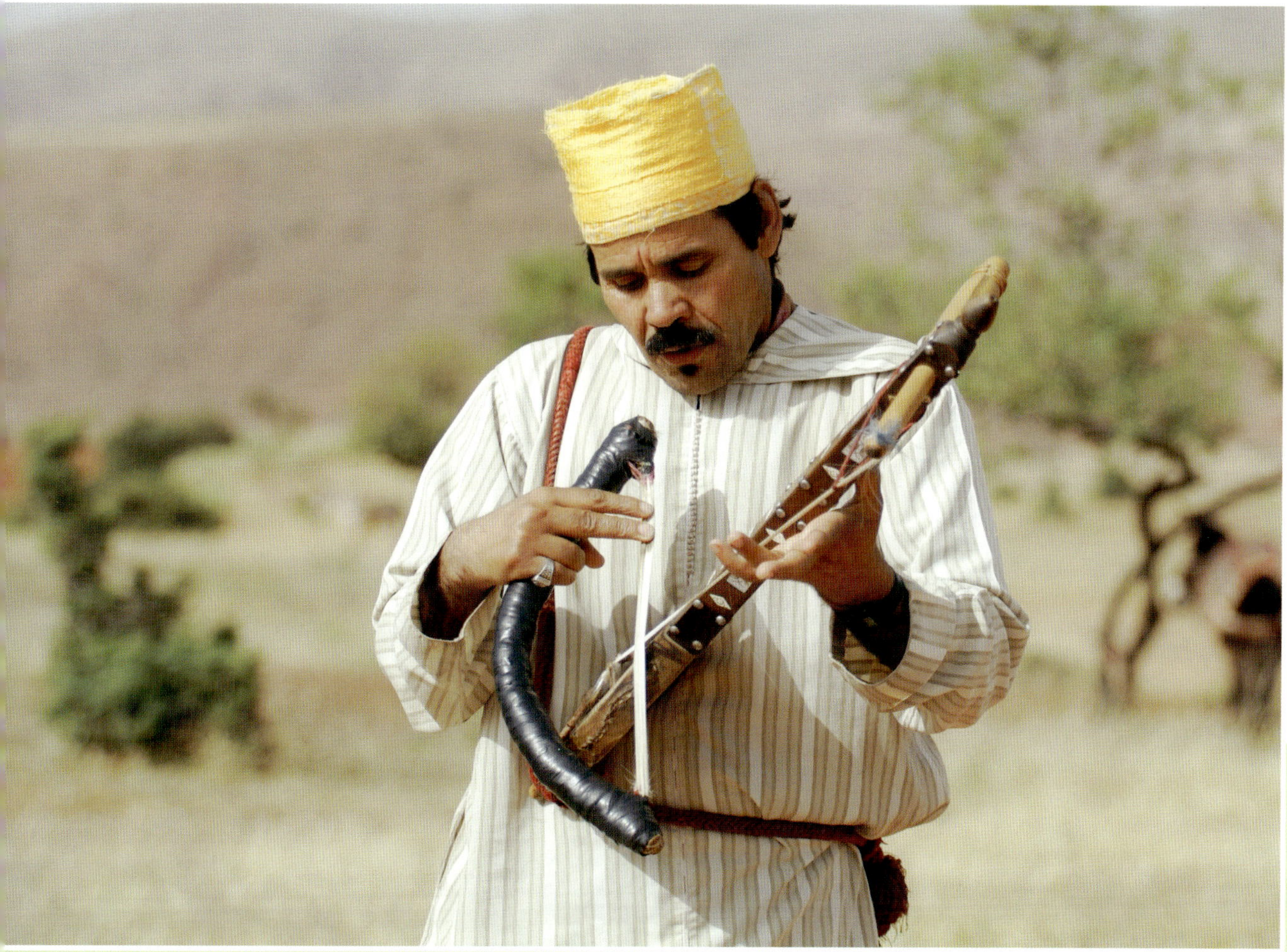

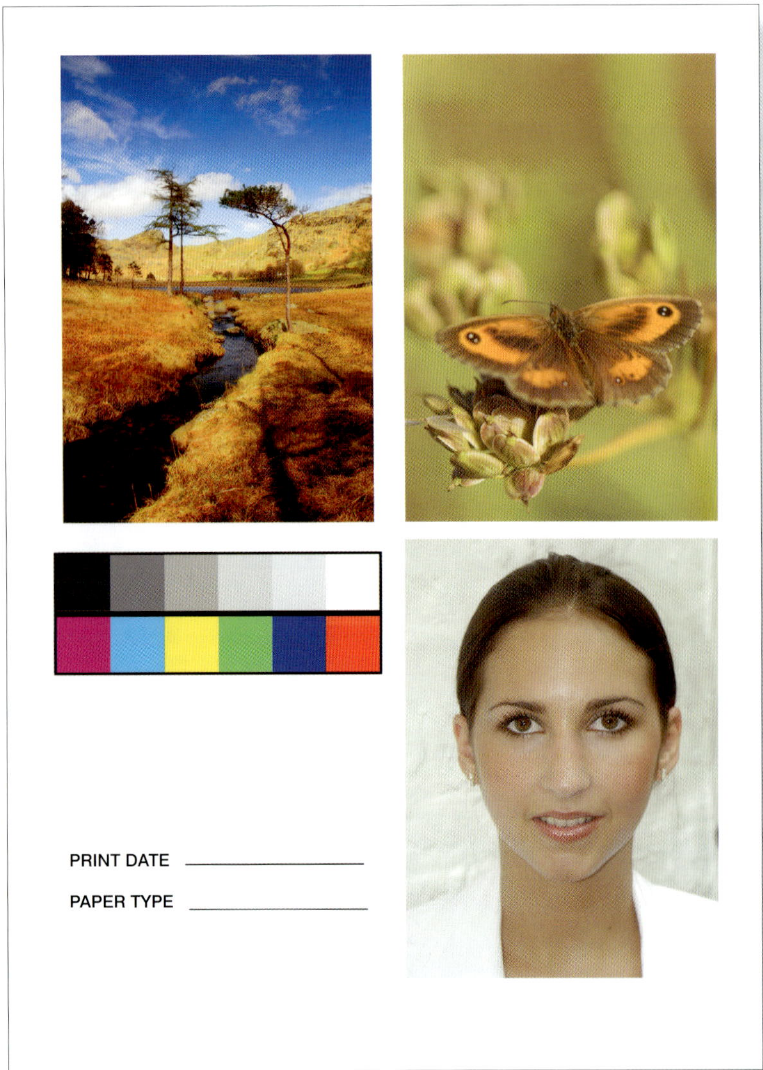

Producing your own test print is a simple way of calibrating your printer. The test print should include at least two of your own typical images, along with a grayscale and primary color swatches.

The Homemade Option

You do not need to go to the expense of having a profile produced; you can make one yourself. Be warned that producing your own settings relies on your own ability to judge and correct colors successfully. This solution may take plenty of time and materials to perfect, so do not assume that it is necessarily the cheapest option.

The first thing you need is a test image to assess the colors produced by your printer. You can produce your own, like the one illustrated, by simply using three images with different colors for reference. It is also much easier to accurately assess any color casts by using a grayscale (blocks of neutral tones from black to white) and a series of color swatches of the primary and secondary colors.

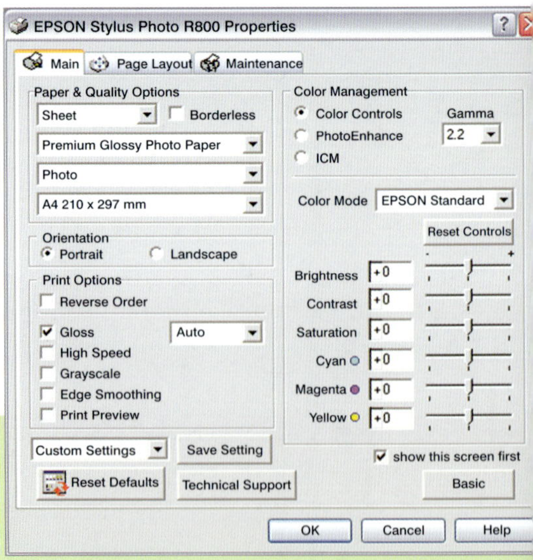

1. To allow you to create your own printer profile, ensure that the color control tools are available in your printer driver—usually found by selecting the Advanced options.

nce you have produced this image, ou need to print it out with any djustments in the printer driver. ost printer drivers offer the option f showing color adjustments, often y clicking on an Advanced option. his brings up a number of sliders for rightness, contrast, and saturation, ogether with cyan, magenta, and ellow color adjustments.

Having produced your initial print, ou need to compare it with the test nage on your monitor. Adjust the ettings available in the printer driver correct any differences between the print and the original image, then produce another print. You will probably need to do this several times to match the two accurately.

Once you are happy with the result, use the Save Settings option in the printer driver. You may find it easiest to name this profile with the type of paper used, as this makes it easier to remember which media was used for the print. The next time you want to print on that type of paper, simply choose it from the dropdown menu and it will reproduce the settings that you applied to your test print.

Adjusting Settings From Your Test Print

Color casts are easiest to see in the grayscale area of the test print, while the images and color swatches are there to allow you to adjust the brightness, contrast, and saturation sliders.

As a starting point for correcting color casts, here are the adjustments needed for the most common types. The amount needed is arrived at by trial and error.

Color cast	Adjustment
Blue	Increase yellow
Red	Increase cyan
Green	Increase magenta
Cyan	Decrease cyan
Magenta	Decrease magenta
Yellow	Decrease yellow

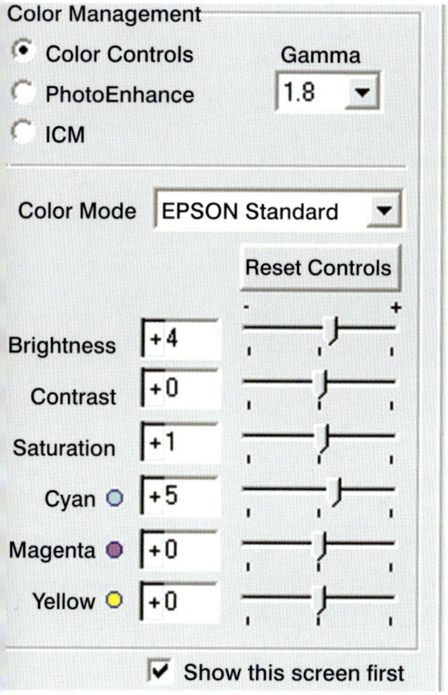

2. Adjust the color controls until you obtain the colors correct in your test print.

3. When you are happy with the result, you can save these settings to use whenever you print on the same paper.

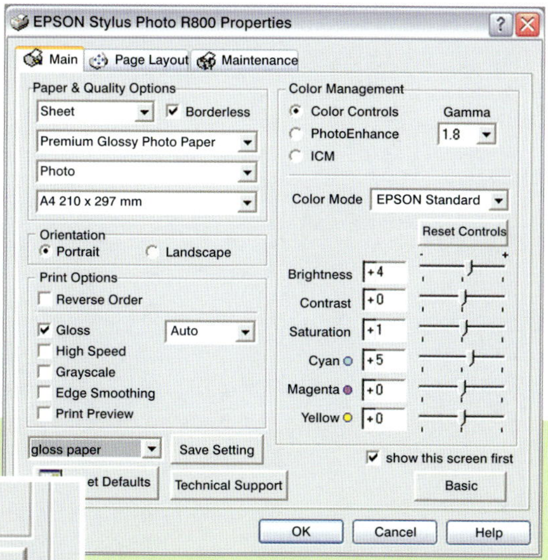

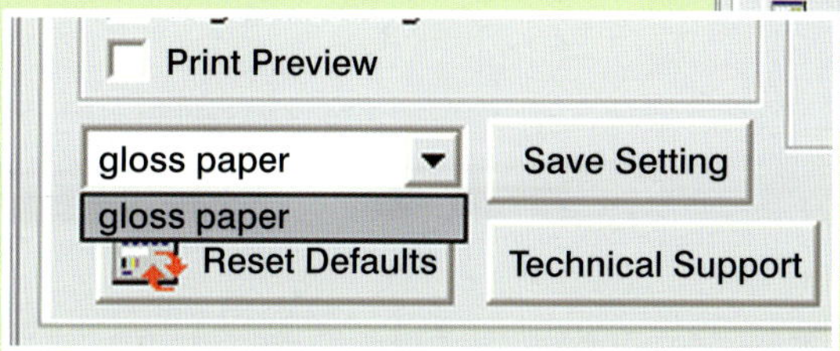

Device Profiles

Despite its apparent complexity, color management centers on a simple theory—maintaining consistent colors as your image is transferred between different devices. As we have seen, the difficulty is that each device captures, displays, or outputs colors in a different way.

The key to color management lies in characterizing the color response of each device and image file so that the software knows how to interpret the colors and translate them effectively between devices. In a color-managed system, this is done by attaching something known as an ICC profile to each device and image file so that it can be easily identified and interpreted. These ICC profiles define the color space and gamut available from the device or image file. You need to ensure that everything in your system has one attached or associated with it.

The first step in any profiling should be your monitor (see p.64). Those serious about consistent profiling should invest in a monitor-calibration device for the most consistent results.

In a studio environment, using a color target such as the GretagMacbeth ColorChecker™ allows you to calibrate the camera accurately and set up a profile to ensure consistent colors.

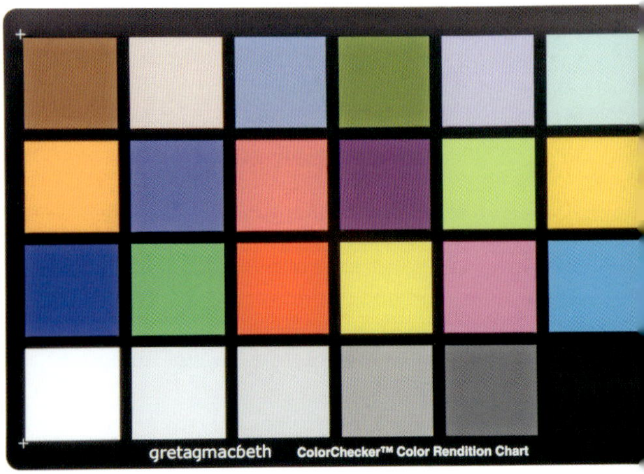

Scanner or Camera Profiling

Profiling your input device will not solve every issue with color casts or incorrect exposure. However, it can help to introduce greater consistency within your workflow, so you know how to deal with color problems.

Simple profiling involves shooting or scanning a target containing standard colors that can be measured as it is transferred through your system. The image produced by your camera or scanner can then be adjusted so that the colors are accurate in your imaging software. These adjustments are saved and can be applied to other images to produce an accurate result.

Profiling digital cameras is difficult, as you need to create a profile for every lighting condition you shoot in—something that is not really practical for most photographers. The one area where this can be done successfully is in the studio, where the lighting is consistent and controllable.

Profiling scanners is easier and more useful than profiling digital cameras, as the light source of the scanner is consistent. Profiling needs to be done for each type of film you use, as the color rendition varies between emulsions.

The changing lighting and conditions means that it is not possible to create an accurate profile for most outdoor situations. In these cases, it is best to rely on the generic camera profile supplied with most cameras.

)igital Camera 'rofiling

s discussed above, profiling your igital camera is not practical for many eople, although studio photographers 'ho use the same lighting setup will enefit from profiling their cameras) save time and effort adjusting ıdividual images. Using your normal nooting settings and lighting, you eed to shoot a color target such as ıe GretagMacbeth ColorChecker to ive you an image to measure the olors from.

Opening this in your editing oftware, you then need to make ıre that the exposure is accurate by ensuring that the full range of the grayscale is recorded. Then apply image adjustments to match the colors on the monitor as closely as possible to the colors on the original target. This can be done by eye, although for more accurate results profiling software can be used that measures the colors of the image and the target values and applies the correct adjustments. These adjustments are then saved as a profile for the camera and applied to any subsequent images taken in these lighting conditions.

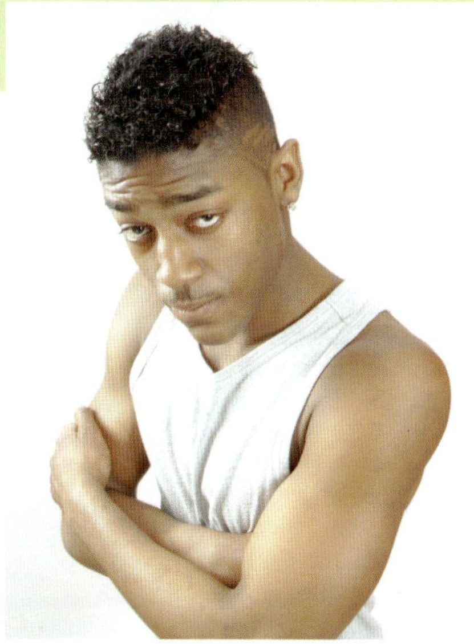

Camera calibration can be useful for the studio photographer, eliminating the need for individual image adjustments. As long as the lighting remains constant, you can calibrate the camera to suit the conditions.

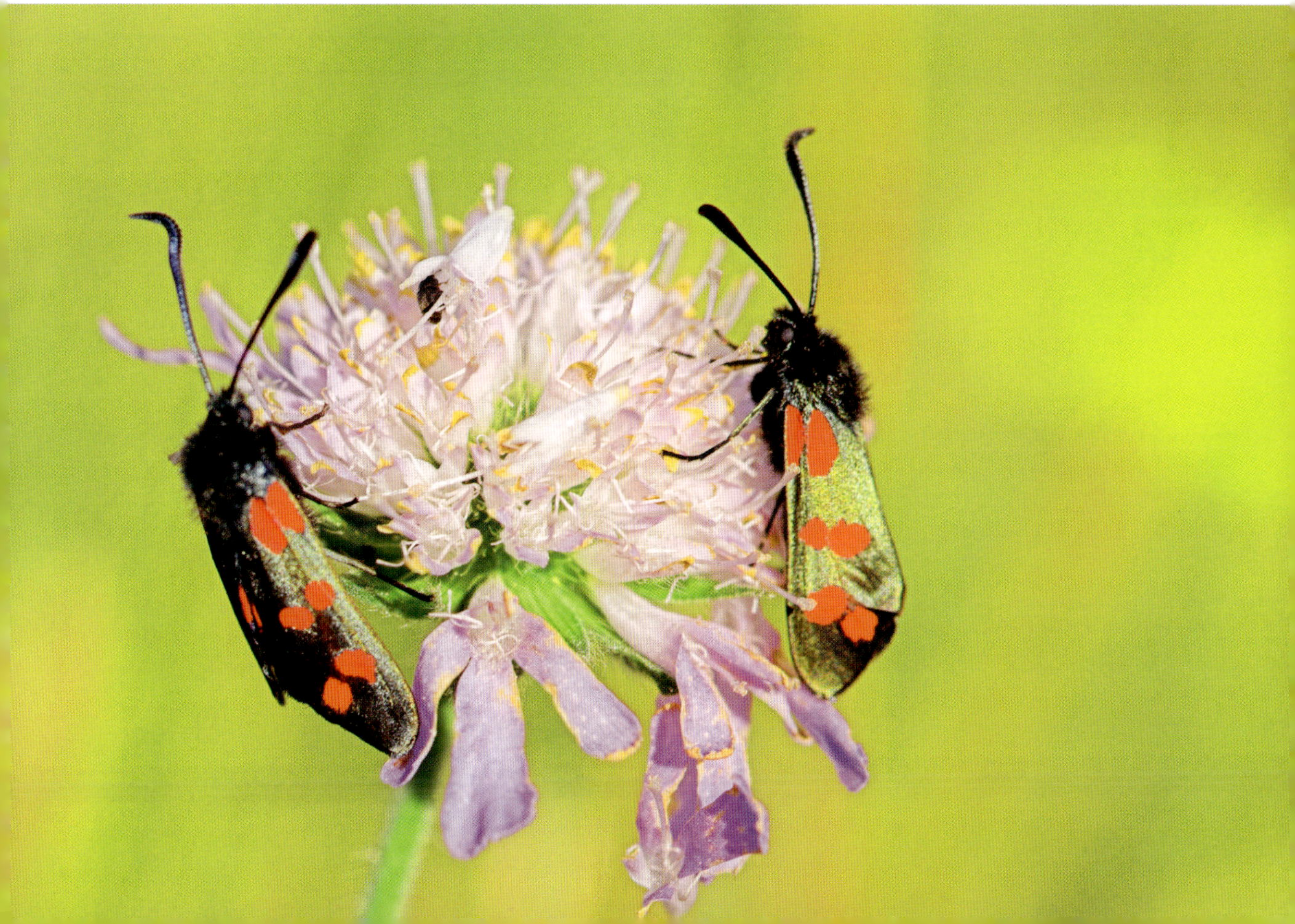

Scanner Profiling

Profiling your film scanner is much more practical than profiling digital cameras as the profile does not vary with the light source of the original subject, only that of the scanner itself and the film type you are using. This means that you need to produce a separate profile for each film that you use, but once this is done you can use it whenever you use this film to produce accurate results. A word of warning, though: scanner profiling will not cure color casts from different lighting on the original scene; it only gives you an accurate reproduction of the original image. If your original image has a color cast, you will still need to correct it manually.

To profile your scanner, you need to purchase an image of a color target on the film that you are going to use. The most common is the IT-8 color target, which is available in a variety of film and photographic paper formats. Some scanner-profiling programs use their own color targets, so check before you invest in a particular product.

This standard image is scanned and inspected for scratches, dust, and rogue pixels to ensure consistent colors over the swatches. The result is opened in the profiling software; then you locate each color in turn for the software to compare it to the original values. This information is used to create a color profile for the scanner and can be used when scanning this particular type of film.

Strictly, this procedure only applies to color slide film, as color negatives do not contain the original colors of the image. In practice, however, you can get targets shot on color negative film and use the same procedure to calibrate the scanner by converting it to a positive image using the scanner software. Although it is not quite as accurate as color slide profiling, this produces acceptable results from most applications.

Film scanners can be calibrated to ensure that the results are consistent when scanning a particular emulsion type.

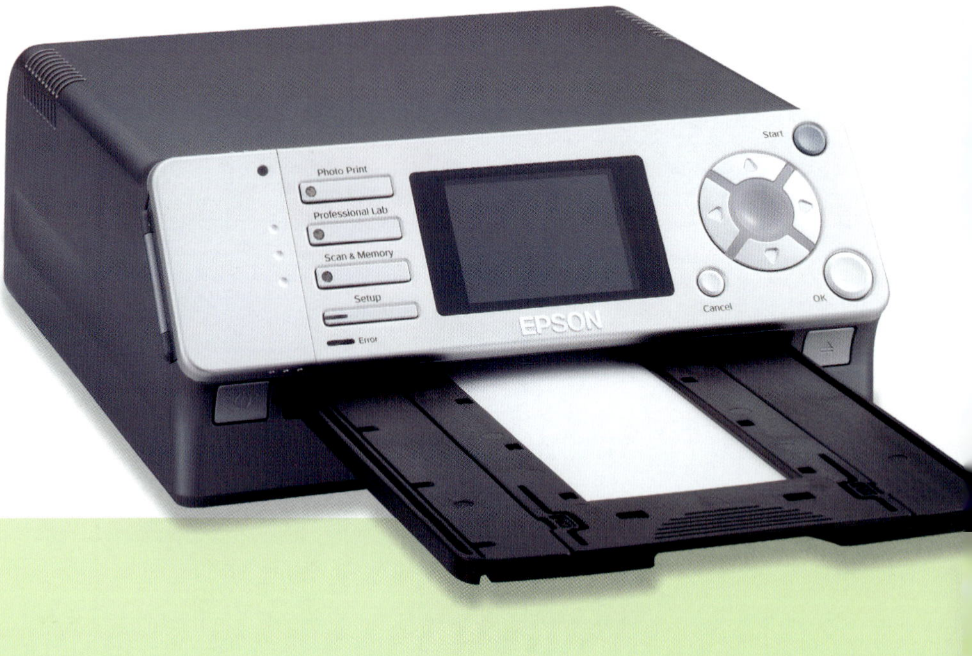

The IT-8 calibration target is one of the most commonly used to calibrate scanners. These are available on a vide range of film stocks to llow you to set up your scanner or each type of film.

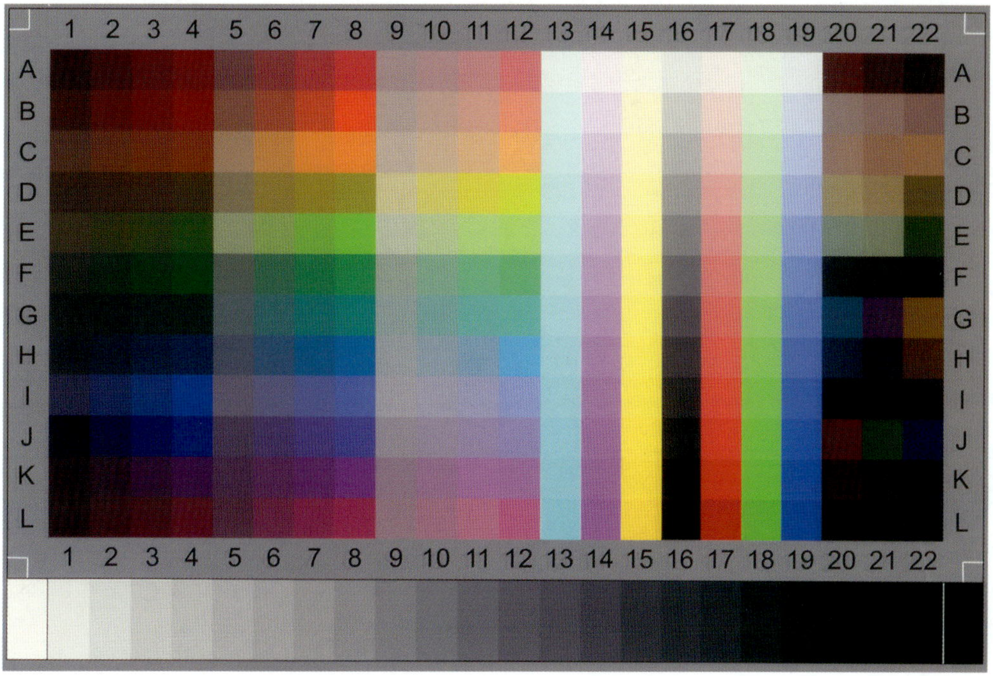

Ising commercial color-profiling oftware, the results from either ameras or scanners are saved as an CC profile that is used to define the olors from that device. Like all color-nanagement methods, this relies on ou ensuring that this profile is ssigned in any settings available in our imaging software.

The homemade route of applying djustments to the visual image does ot create an ICC profile, but should be saved as an action and applied to your images manually. But is it worth all this effort?

Whether or not you go to the trouble of profiling your scanner will largely be down to how often you use the same settings or scan the same type of film. For large-volume users in a commercial environment, the values of profiling can be tremendous; it saves a lot of time in adjusting individual images. For less demanding users, or those who shoot digitally in a wide range of lighting, the benefits are less obvious. These users are probably best off simply ensuring that they use consistent color spaces and use the generic device profiles offered by their software.

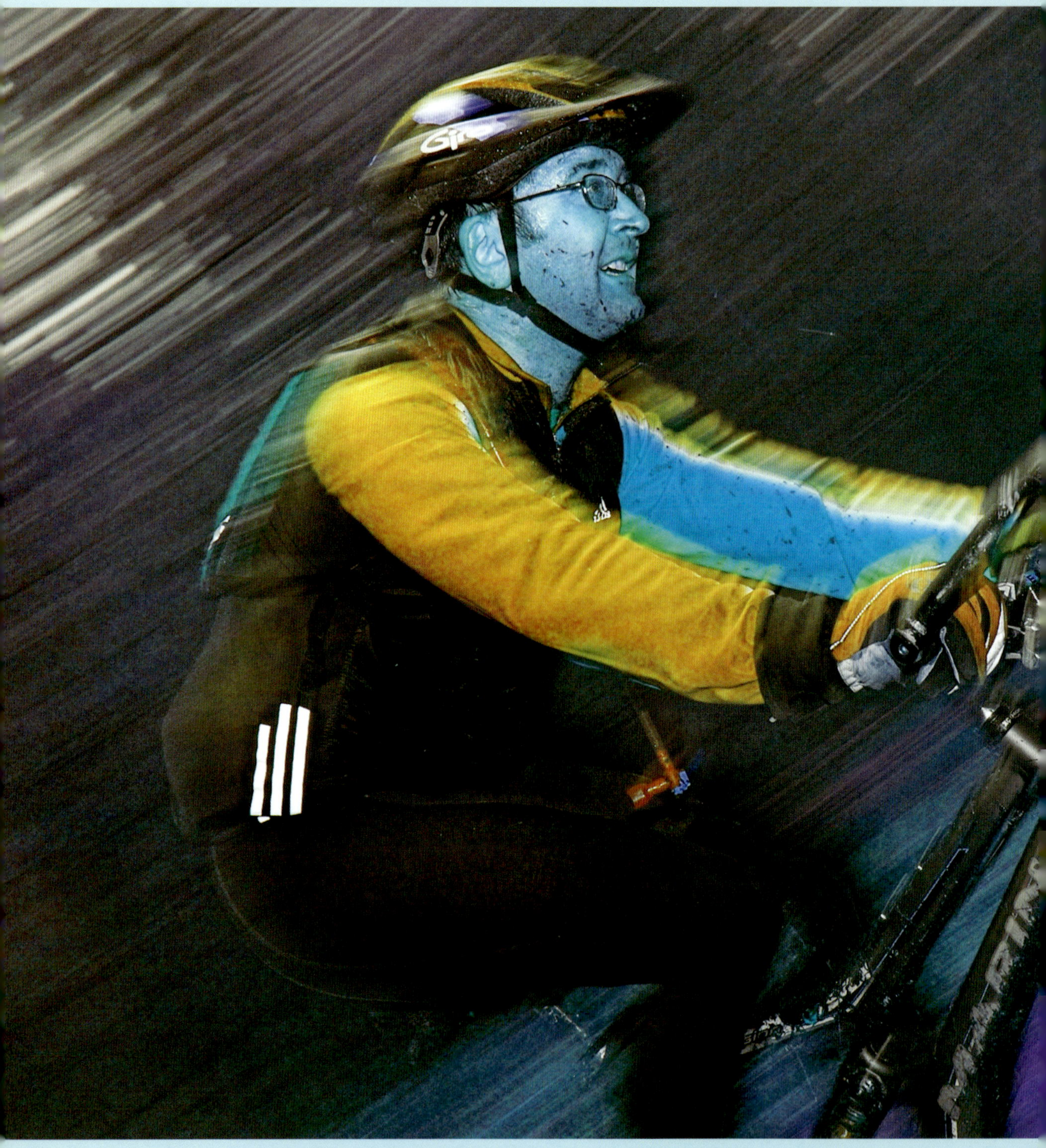

Software

06

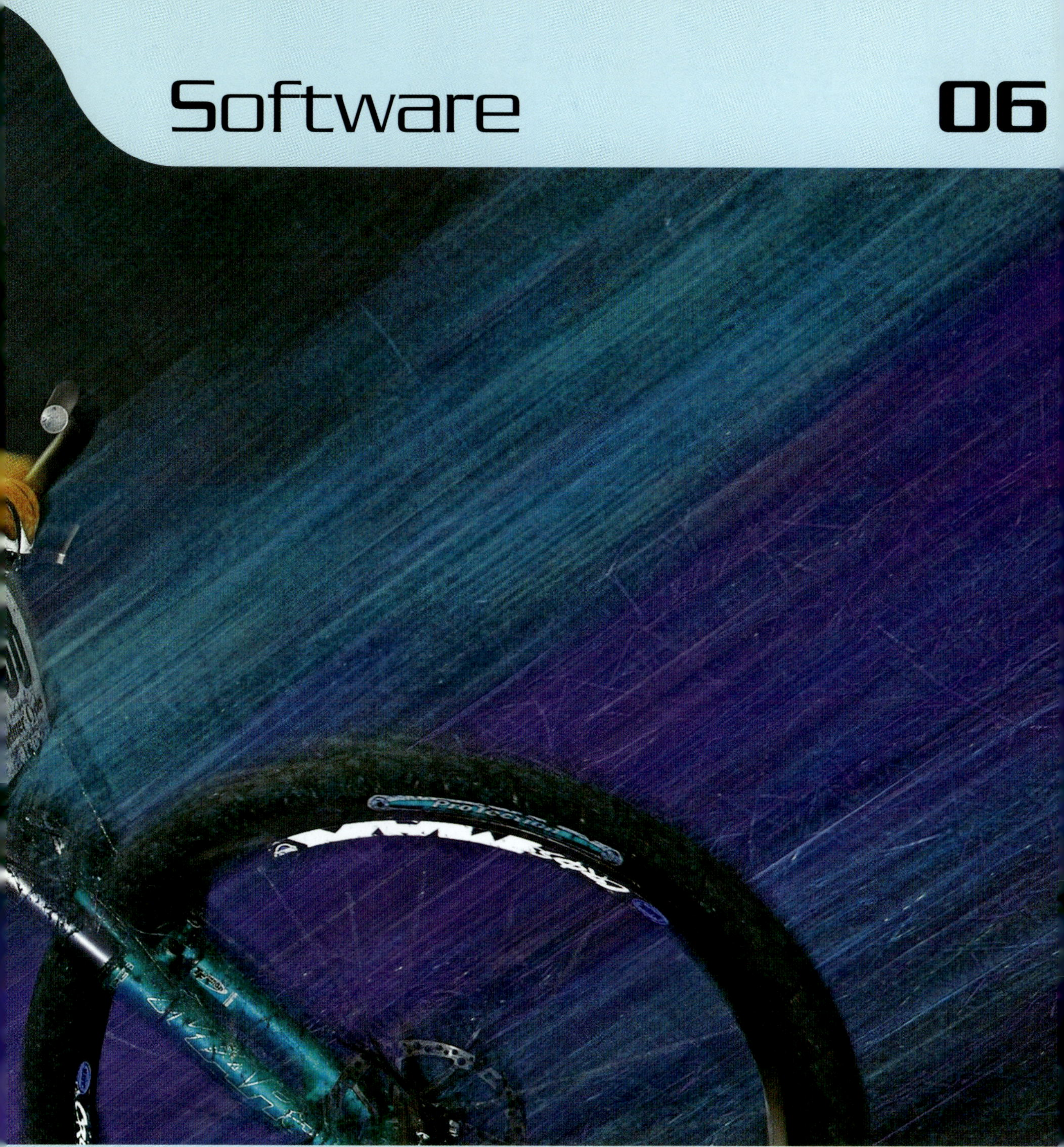

Hue/Saturation

Image-editing software offers a huge range of features for you to exploit. Although most of you will be familiar with image-editing programs such as Photoshop, let us look at the basic controls and tools that we will be using before delving into the complexities of adjusting, enhancing, and manipulating colors. Some of these tools directly affect the colors of your images; others deal primarily with tonality and contrast. Even these have a huge effect on how the colors appear in the final result, so even the more experienced image editor should take a moment to familiarize themselves with these tools. There is always something new to learn, no matter how much you already know.

Adjusting Hue and Saturation

We will start with one of the tools central to adjusting and controlling the colors of your image—Hue/Saturation. This can be opened by going to Image › Adjustments › Hue/Saturation. This control allows you to adjust the color and saturation of the whole image, or of individual colors by selecting the color channel in the Edit menu.

The dialog box contains three main control sliders: Hue, Saturation, and Lightness.

Hue

This is a means of altering the color of the image. The value displayed refers to the number of degrees of rotation around an RGB color wheel. For example, a +180 degree value would turn a red pixel into a cyan, and a blue to yellow.

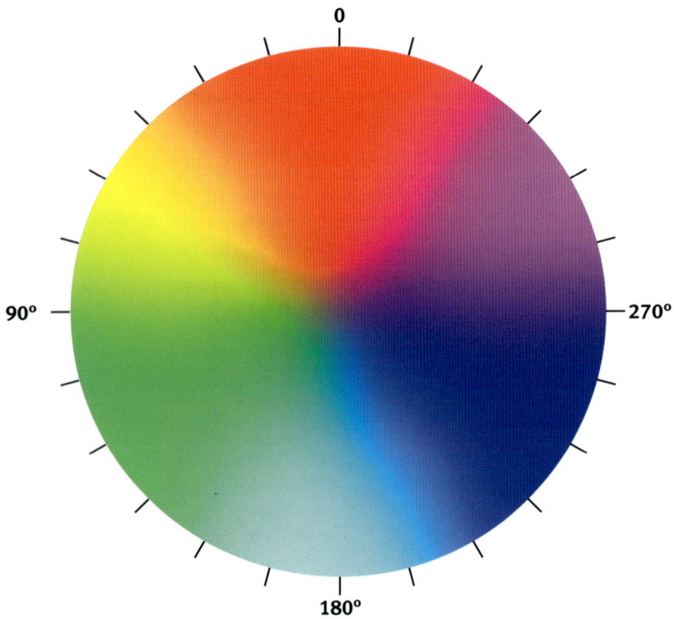

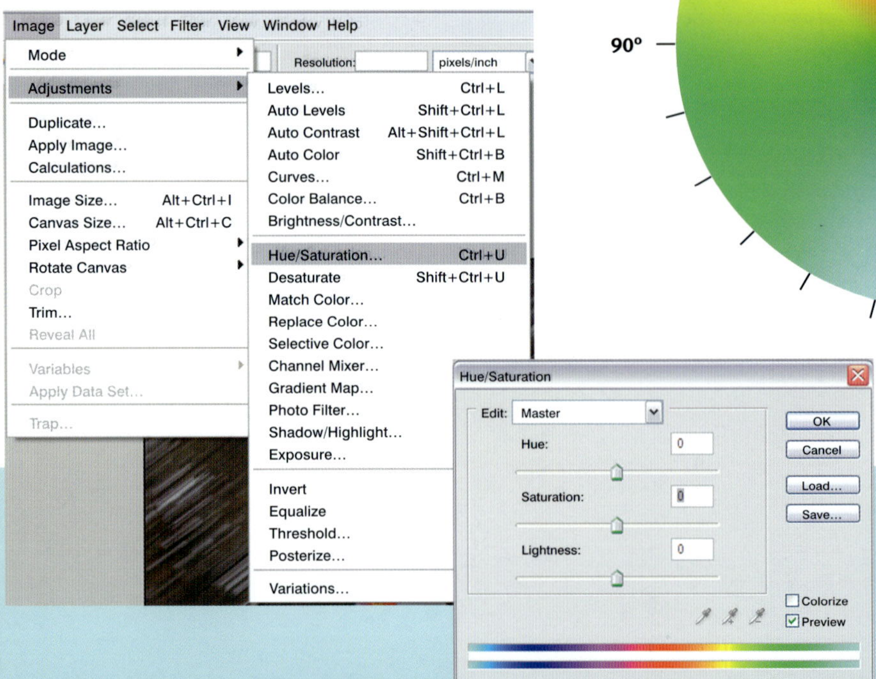

aturation
'his allows you to add saturation to, r subtract it from, your image. Moving he slider left lowers saturation, with he minimum giving a black-and-/hite image.

ightness
his is a crude way of altering the rightness of your image by adding vhite or black. This is rarely used, as evels or Curves offers much greater egrees of control. There is also a ange of extra controls in the Hue/ aturation window.

Edit
This dropdown menu allows you to apply the adjustments selected in the other controls to all of the colors in the image, or selectively to individual colors.

Colorize
This enables you to add a color or hue to a grayscale image, and is used to replicate the toning effects of black-and-white images.

Preview
This allows you to see the effect of the adjustments in your image before they are applied.

Eyedropper tools
These tools enable you to select the colors that will be affected by clicking on the relevant part of your image. The +Eyedropper is used to add extra colors to the selection and the –Eyedropper will remove them.

Color bars
There are also two color spectrums along the bottom of the window. The top one indicates the colors in the original image; the lower shows the corresponding modified colors after any adjustments you make.

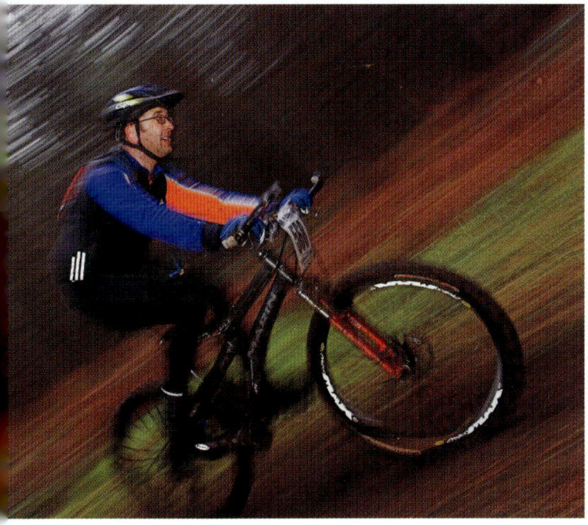

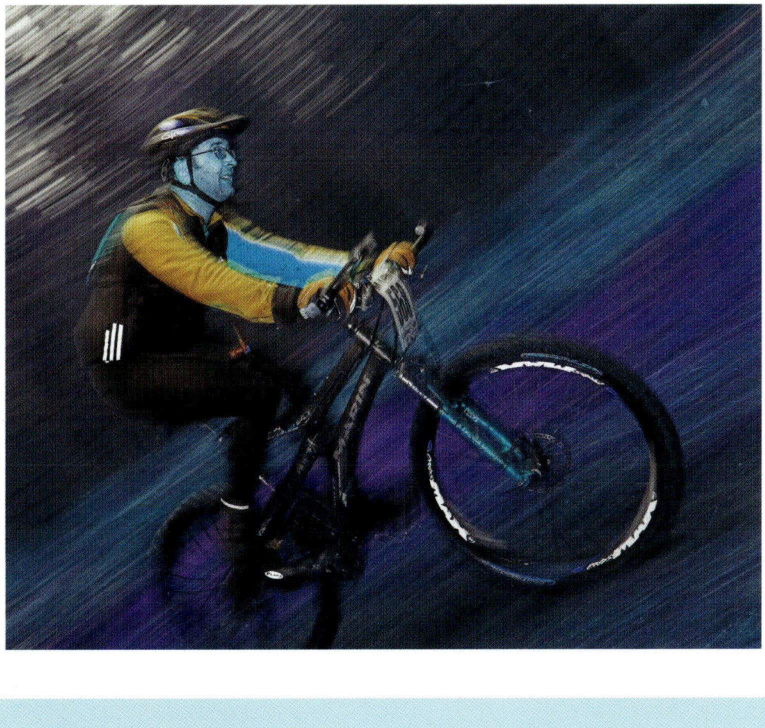

The Hue control allows you to transform the original colors of an image radically. In this image, with the Hue set to +180, every color has been transformed into the color opposite it on the color wheel. The reen foliage has become magenta, while the red and lue of the cyclist's jacket are now cyan and yellow.

Levels

Before you can start to judge the color of your images successfully, you need to ensure that the exposure is accurate. Even the most sophisticated modern exposure systems built into digital cameras do not always get it right every time. For the highest-quality results, it pays to get the exposure right when you shoot your images, although Photoshop gives you the ability to alter the exposures very simply.

On opening the Levels dialog box, the distribution of the tones in your image is shown in the form of a graph known as a histogram. This is found in Image › Adjustments › Levels. The main area to be aware of is a graph that looks like a mountain range. For a well-exposed image, the area of the graph would extend right across the horizontal axis. In practice, you often find that the distribution is quite uneven, indicating that the image does not contain tones right across the range from shadows to highlights.

For most subjects, the key to using the Levels feature is to get the histogram "mountain range" to fill this axis. You do this by dragging the small triangles along the bottom of the horizontal axis so that they meet the slope of the histogram. The central triangle gives you control of the midtone of the image. Dragging this to the left darkens the midtones; dragging them to the right lightens them.

In normal use, these adjustments will affect all of the colors in the image; for more advanced adjustments, you can select individual colors using the Channel dropdown menu at the top of the window. This is particularly useful for color balancing as it allows the tonal range of the red, green, and blue channels to be adjusted independently. We will find out how to use this on p.138.

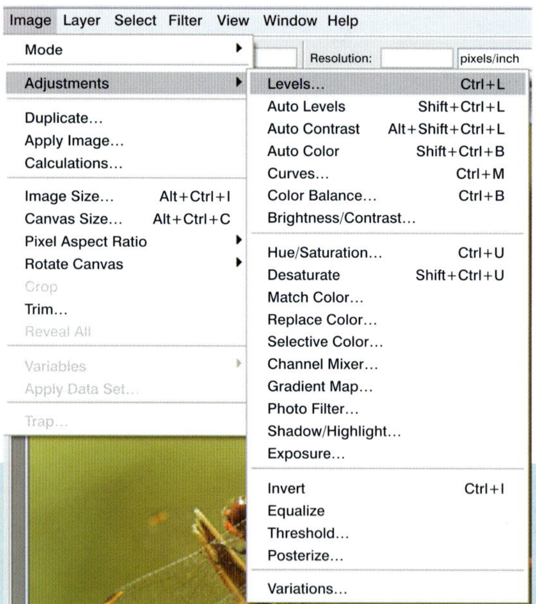

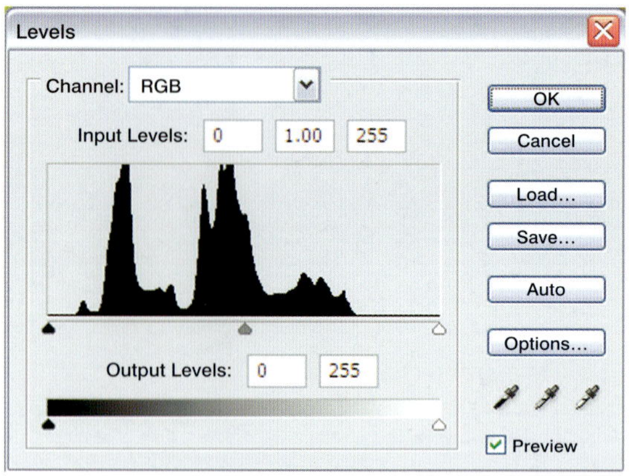

Tip

Digital images are much better at retrieving information from the shadows than from the highlights. Therefore, it pays to underexpose slightly to ensure that you do not lose highlight detail. Do not overdo this, however, because retrieving shadow detail is likely to cause an increase in noise levels, especially in the darker tones.

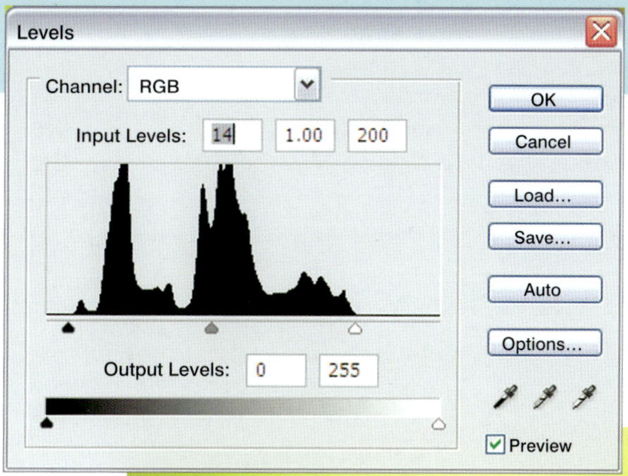

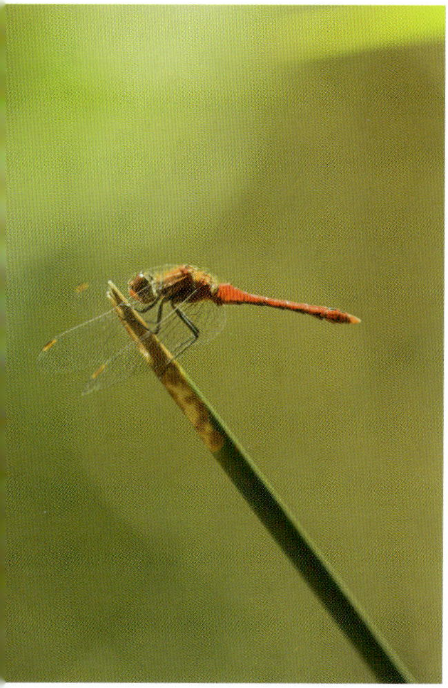

For this shot, I did not have time to get the exposure exact before the dragonfly took flight. The resulting image is flat and lacks both bright highlights and shadows.

Brightness and Contrast

While these controls would seem more obvious choices for adjusting the exposure of your images, they are not the best tools for the job. These controls apply the same amount of change to the whole of the image, so you can lose information in both the highlight and the shadow areas. These controls are thus best avoided for all image adjustments.

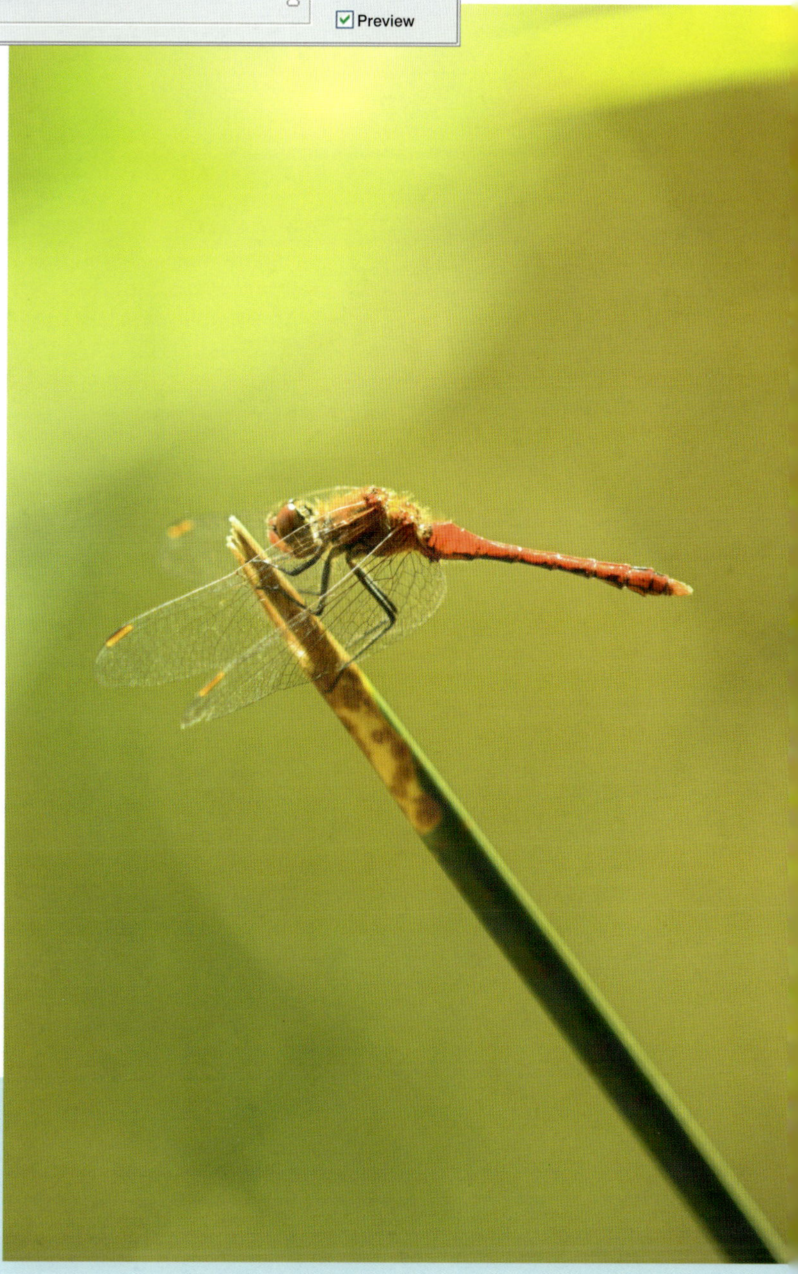

Dragging the left and right triangles to the base of the histogram makes an immediate improvement to the contrast of the image. This increase in contrast also helps to improve the colors of the image, making em appear both brighter and more saturated.

Curves

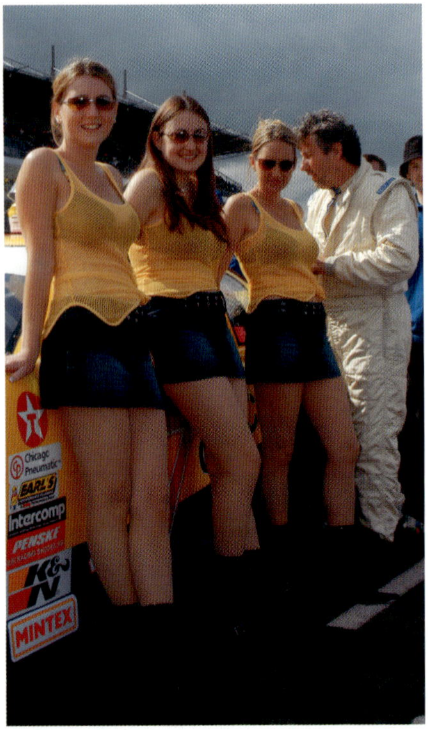

Lightening shadow detail is beyond the scope of simple Levels adjustment. For this shot taken against the light, most of the faces are in shadow, so skin tones look dull and flat.

Along with the Levels control, the Curves control in Photoshop allows you to adjust the range of tones in your image. While Levels allows you to adjust only three points within the tonal range, the Curves control offers the ability to fine-tune the placing of almost any point from the shadows to the highlights.

When you first open the Curves dialog box, the linear graph shows a straight, diagonal line from the bottom left to the top right. The bottom left of this graph represents the shadows; the top right represents the highlights.

You can move any point of this line by clicking and dragging it to adjust the tonality of the image. Moving a point up and down lightens or darken the density; moving it left or right adjusts the contrast. The steeper the angle of the line, the higher the contrast will be.

Normally, the curve is applied acros all of the colors of the image, indicate by RGB in the Channel menu at the to of the window. You can adjust the curv of individual color channels as well by clicking on the relevant color channel in the dropdown menu.

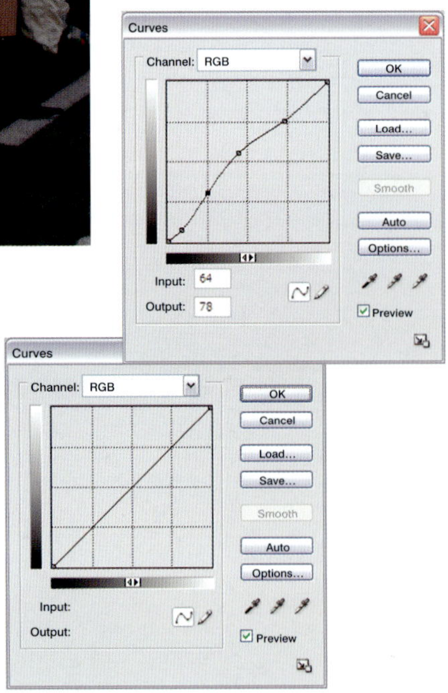

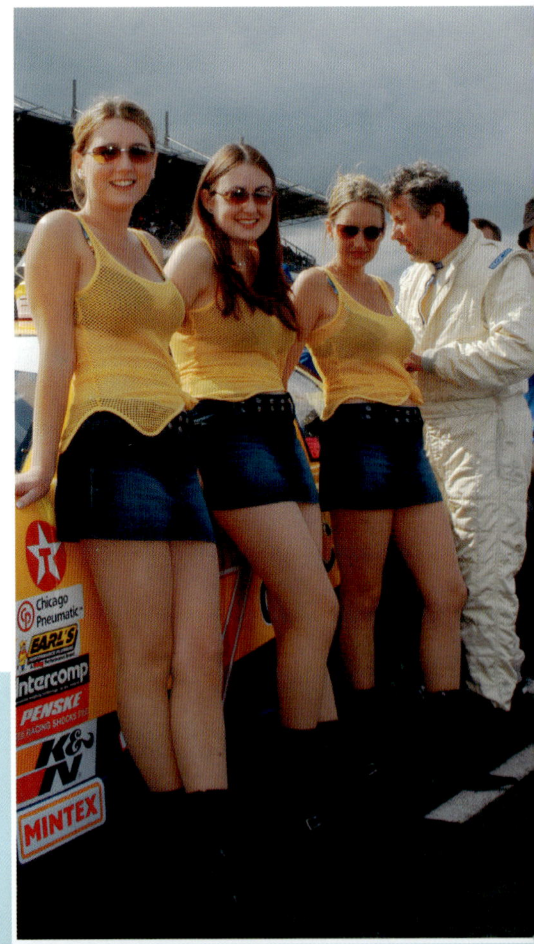

Applying a simple Curves adjustment by raising the left-hand side of the graph lightens the shadow density.

‹hadow/Highlight

ften overlooked by advanced users :customed to manipulating tones ‹ith the Curves control, this feature is much simpler option for many users. s the name implies, it allows you ‹ adjust the density of the shadows ıd highlights using simple sliders, ‹ther than having to get just the right ljustment points on the graph of the ırves adjustment.

This feature is found in Image › ljustments › Shadow/Highlight, and ffers you three adjustment sliders: ıadows, Highlights, and Midtones. ıe most useful is the Shadows ›ntrol, which allows you to reveal etail in areas that would otherwise ›pear too dark. For most images eeding adjustment, this should be ›oved to between 10% and 30%; any ore can result in large increases in ›ise and make the image appear ›orse than the original.

The Highlight control should be sed with caution: it is very easy r adjustments here to result in e highlights looking solarized or versed, as the software is having ‹ invent information to fill in e highlights.

The final slider controls the midtone ›ntrast. After you have adjusted the ıadows, you may need to raise this der to retain some punch in the image, but only add the minimum amount necessary to get the results you want.

For more advanced users, there is a Show More Options tick box at the bottom of the window to allow you to fine-tune your adjustments. This allows you to control the range of tones and area that the shadow and highlight sliders affect.

There is also a Color Correction slider that allows you to increase or decrease the colors in the image. Although useful as a quick fix, it is usually best to adjust the colors separately.

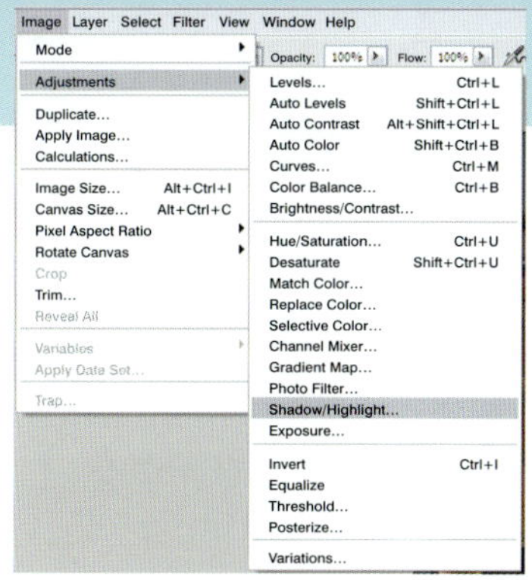

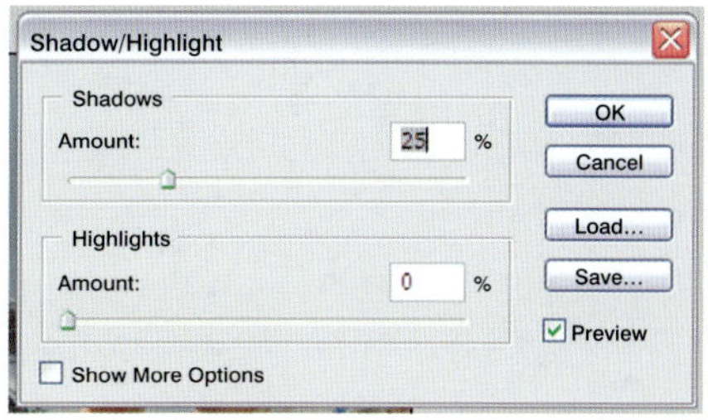

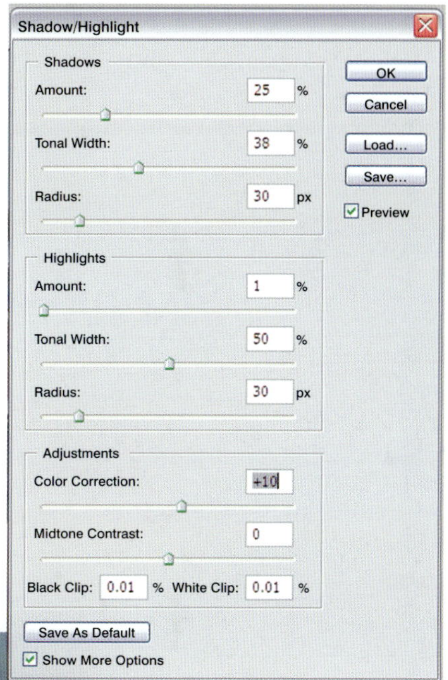

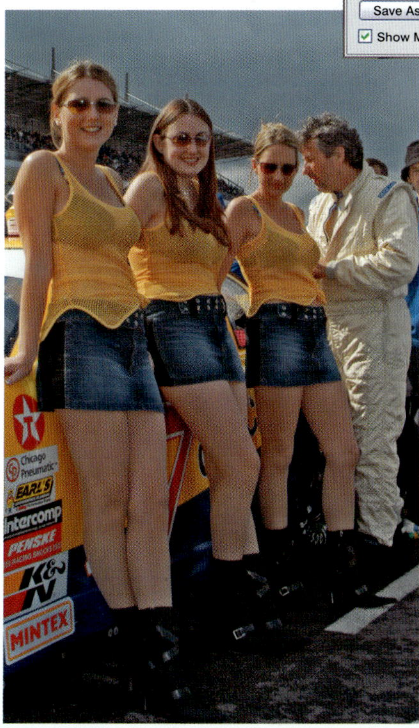

Using the Shadow/Highlight adjustment allows you to brighten shadow detail simply and easily.

Tip

One major advantage of using the Shadow/Highlight control is that it retains a wider range of tones in the shadows than a Curves adjustment. This is especially useful with 8-bit images that have fewer tonal values to work with, so can suffer from contrast and tone adjustments more than 16-bit images.

Color Channels

Red channel

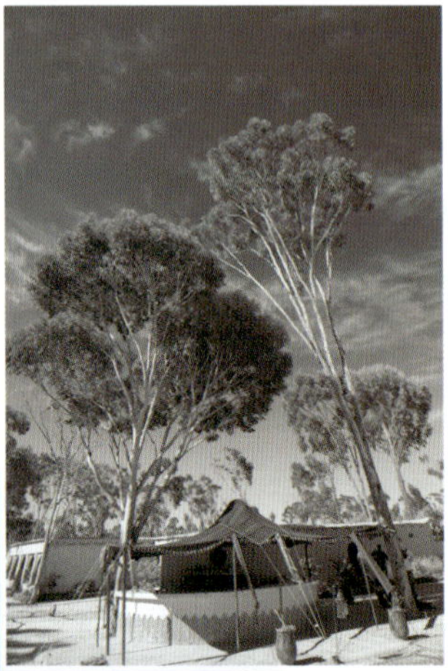

Green channel

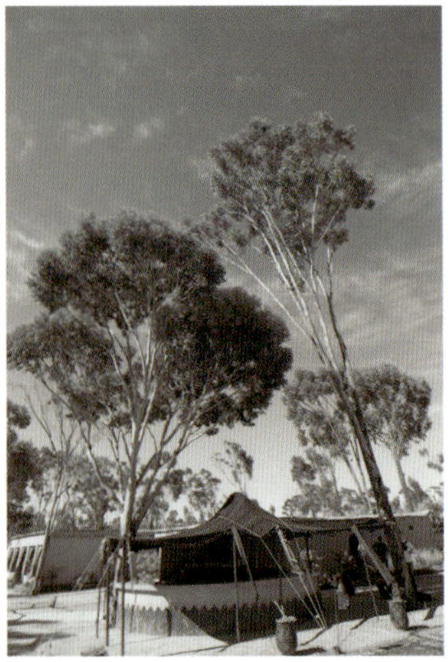

Blue channel

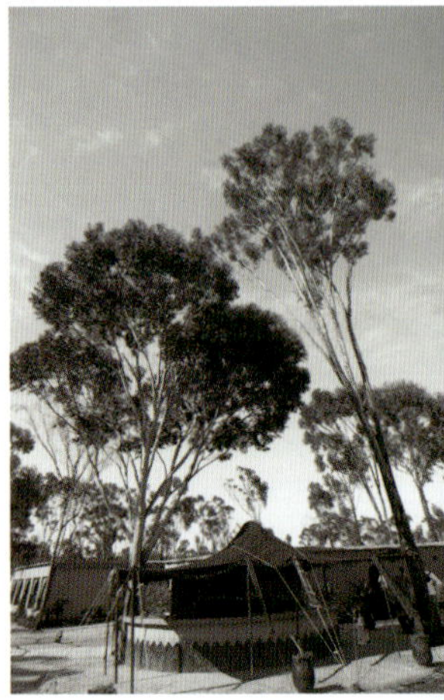

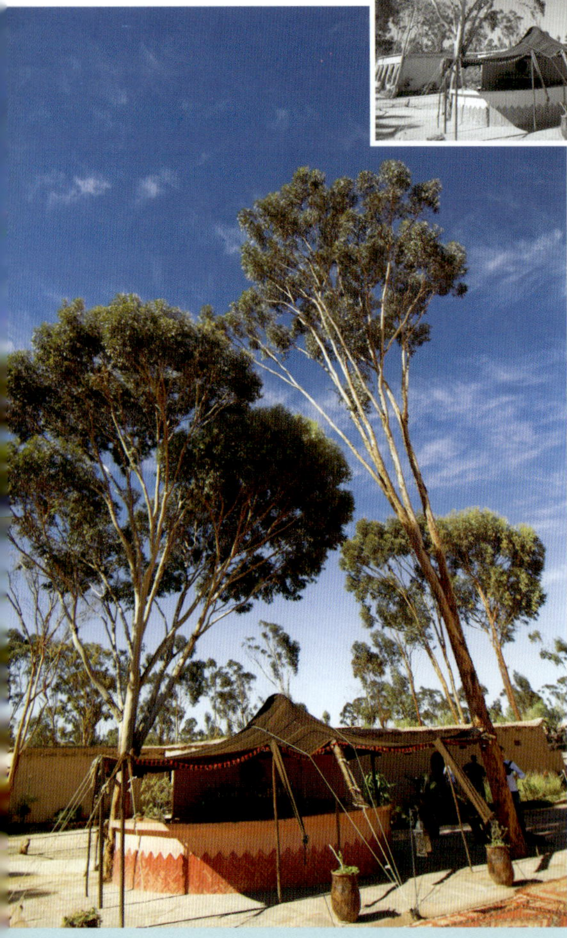

This RGB color picture is made up from three grayscale images. The three channels contain information that can be translated into the relevant colors to achieve the final color result. Notice how the blue sky is very dark in the red channel image, but very light in the blue channel.

It may come as a surprise, but your color digital images do not actually contain any color at all. A digital image is made up of a series of grayscale images that are combined together to make the color image that you finally see. As we have seen in earlier chapters, the basic RGB digital image is made up from red, green, and blue components. These three grayscale images are known as the color channels.

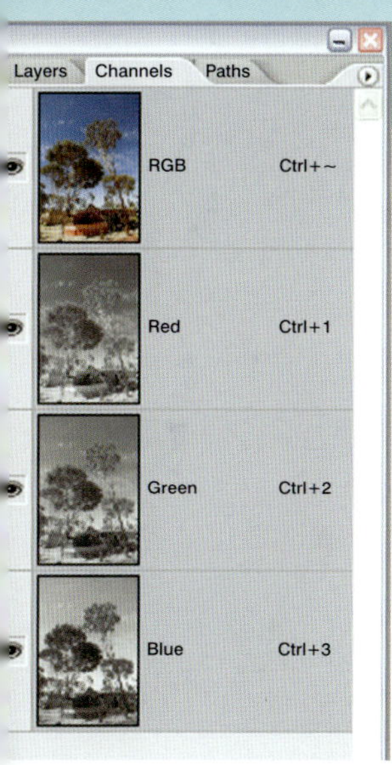

Displaying Color Channel Information

You can easily view the grayscale images that make up your image by going to Window › Channels, which will bring up the Channels palette. This shows the full RGB image and the color channels.

You can select each channel individually by clicking on each one in the palette. You can also hide the color channel by clicking on the eye symbol to the left.

ayers

ne of the most misunderstood, ıd most powerful, tools available Photoshop is the ability to work layers. This function allows you to ɔply adjustments to images that are ·parate from the original, making it ɔssible to experiment with effects ithout affecting the original.

To understand how layers work, ıagine your image as a print with yers of transparent sheets laid over Each of these sheets can contain formation or images that are then ·en over the original image. Each yer can be individually added or moved from the image, and the way at they interact with the main image ın be adjusted.

These layers have countless uses, ıt the main one is to allow any ljustments to be made on a copy of e original image, leaving the original ıtouched. Once you are familiar with them, I would suggest that you use them at almost every stage of your image adjustments and manipulations. Even simple color or saturation adjustments are safer and more versatile when they are made on a separate layer.

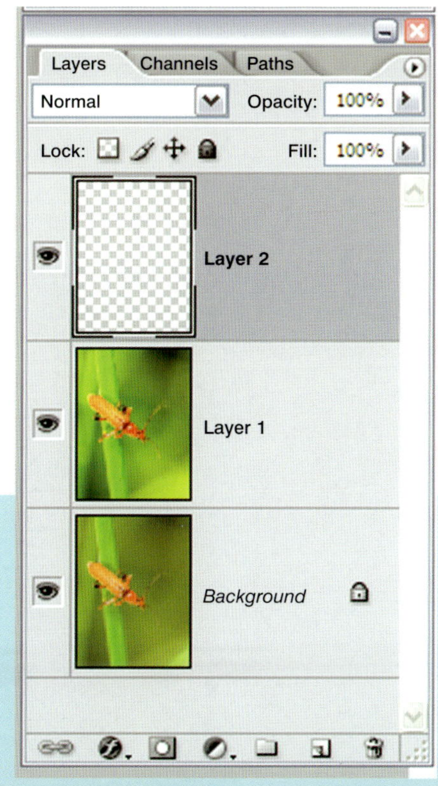

Channel Mixer

The easiest way to adjust the color of individual color channels is to use the Channel Mixer. This is found in the main menu by going to Image › Adjustments › Channel Mixer. You can adjust the color and brightness of individual color channels by selecting the color from the dropdown menu at the top of the window. The red, green, and blue sliders adjust the color of each channel; the Constant slider adjusts the brightness.

Although the Channel Mixer is most commonly used for black-and-white conversions, it is also a useful tool for color balancing that we will explore on p.138.

The color channels will vary according to which color mode your image uses. For CMYK, the image is made up of cyan, magenta, yellow, and black channels.

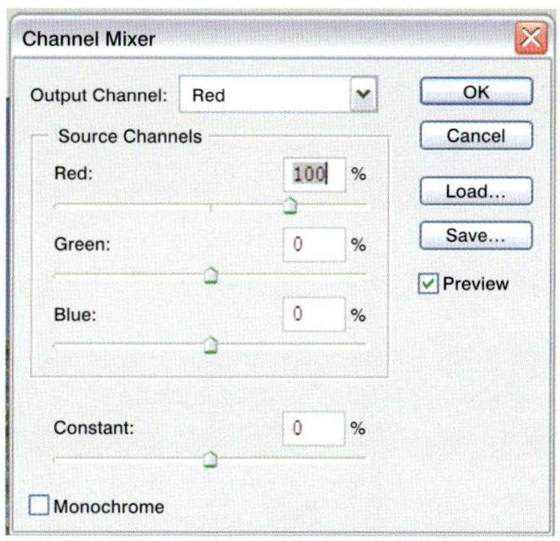

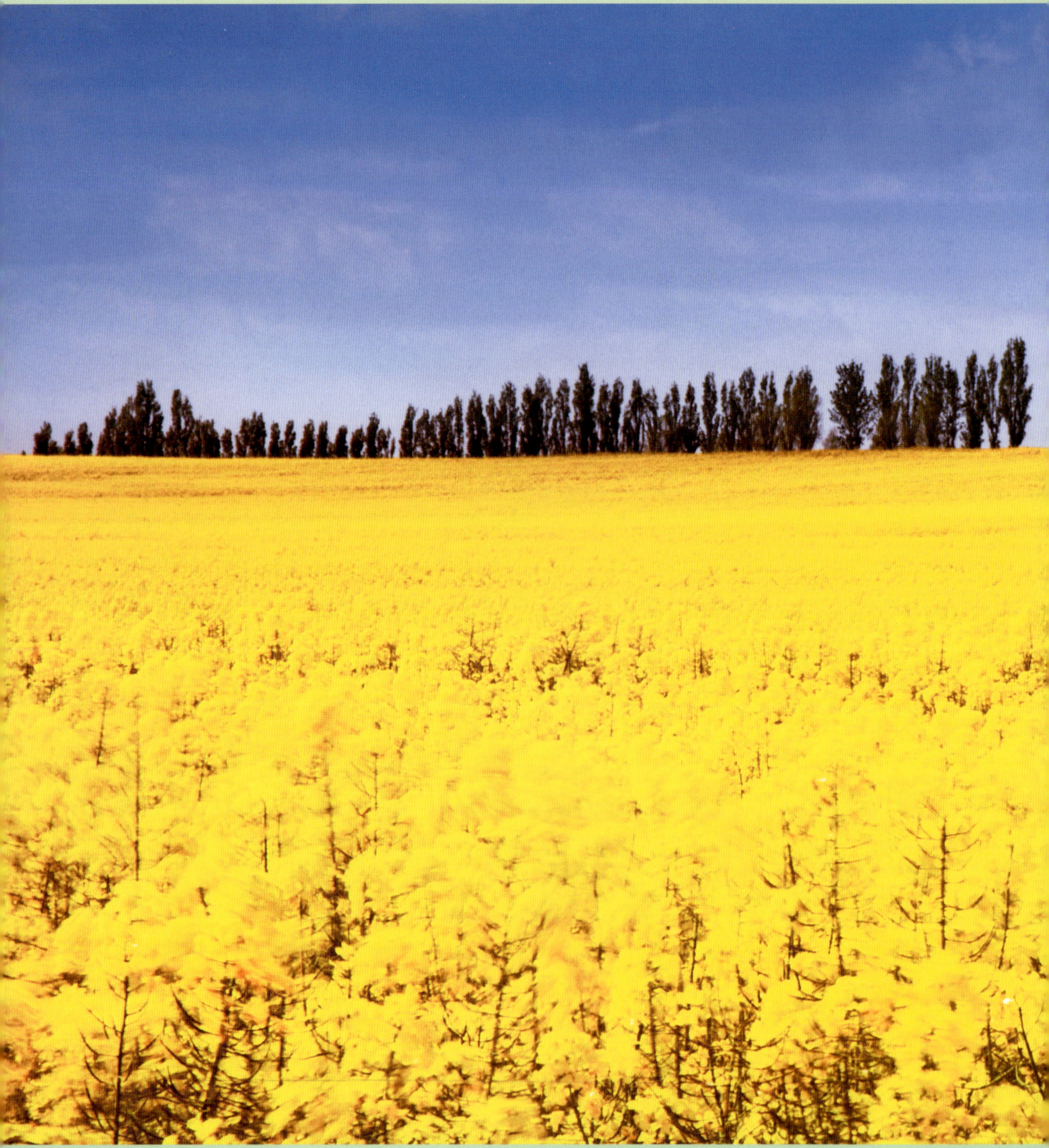

Practical Techniques

07

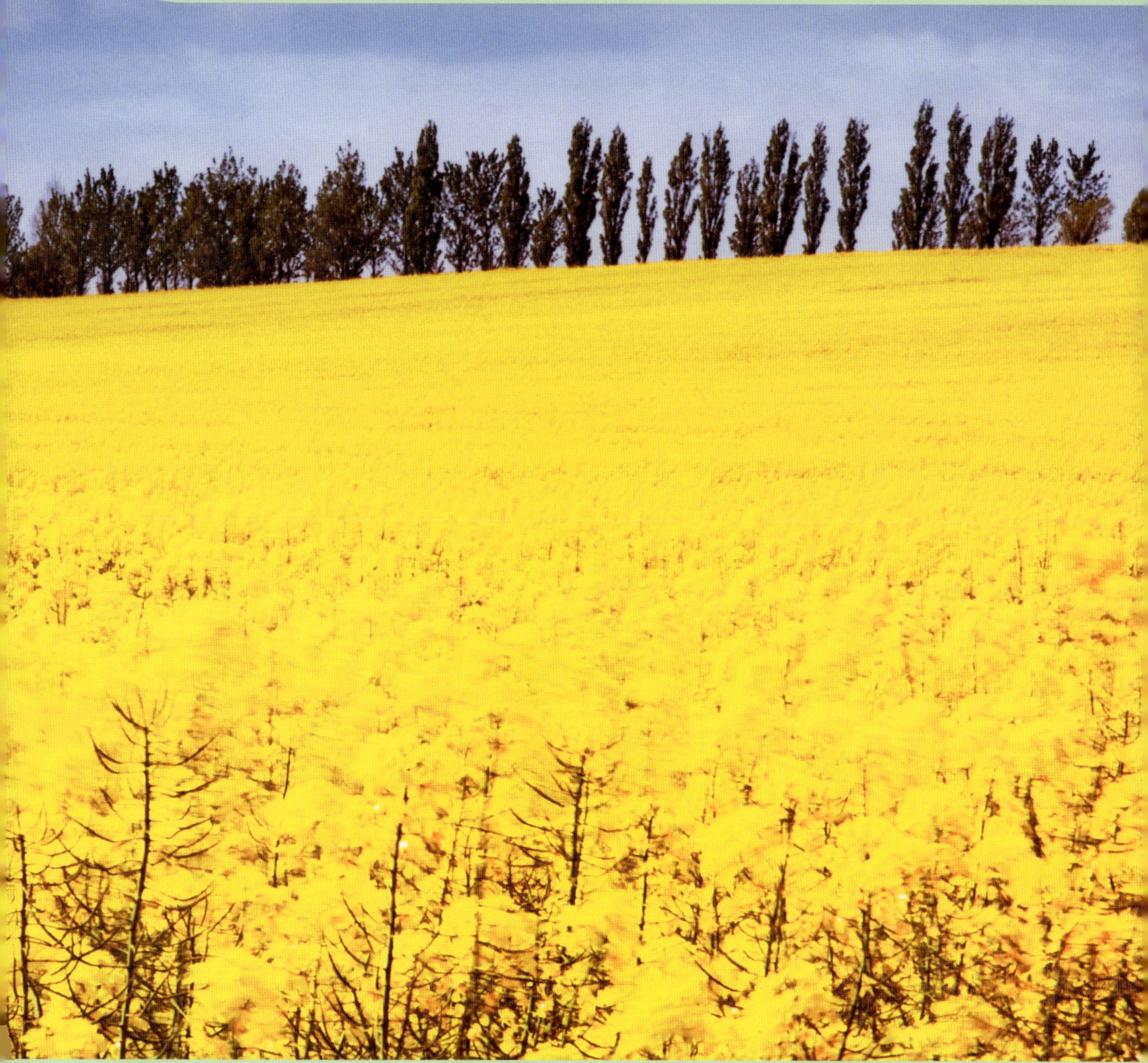

Harmonious Colors

Using pastel colors that are close to each other on the color wheel produces harmonious and tranquil-looking images. This is especially true when using cooler colors, such as the magenta in this image.

Learning the theory behind how colors work together and why certain color combinations are attractive is all very well, but how do you put this into practice in your photography? This chapter deals with the practical aspects of spotting potential in your subject and capturing the scene successfully.

Over the following pages, we will also discover how you can use the colors that nature offers, the seasonal changes that you may have to contend with, and how to create either an accurate rendition or your own interpretation of the colors.

Let's start with harmonious colors. Harmonious colors often work without you noticing them; they combine so naturally and easily that the effect is much less obvious than the bolder effect of complementary colors, which we will explore next.

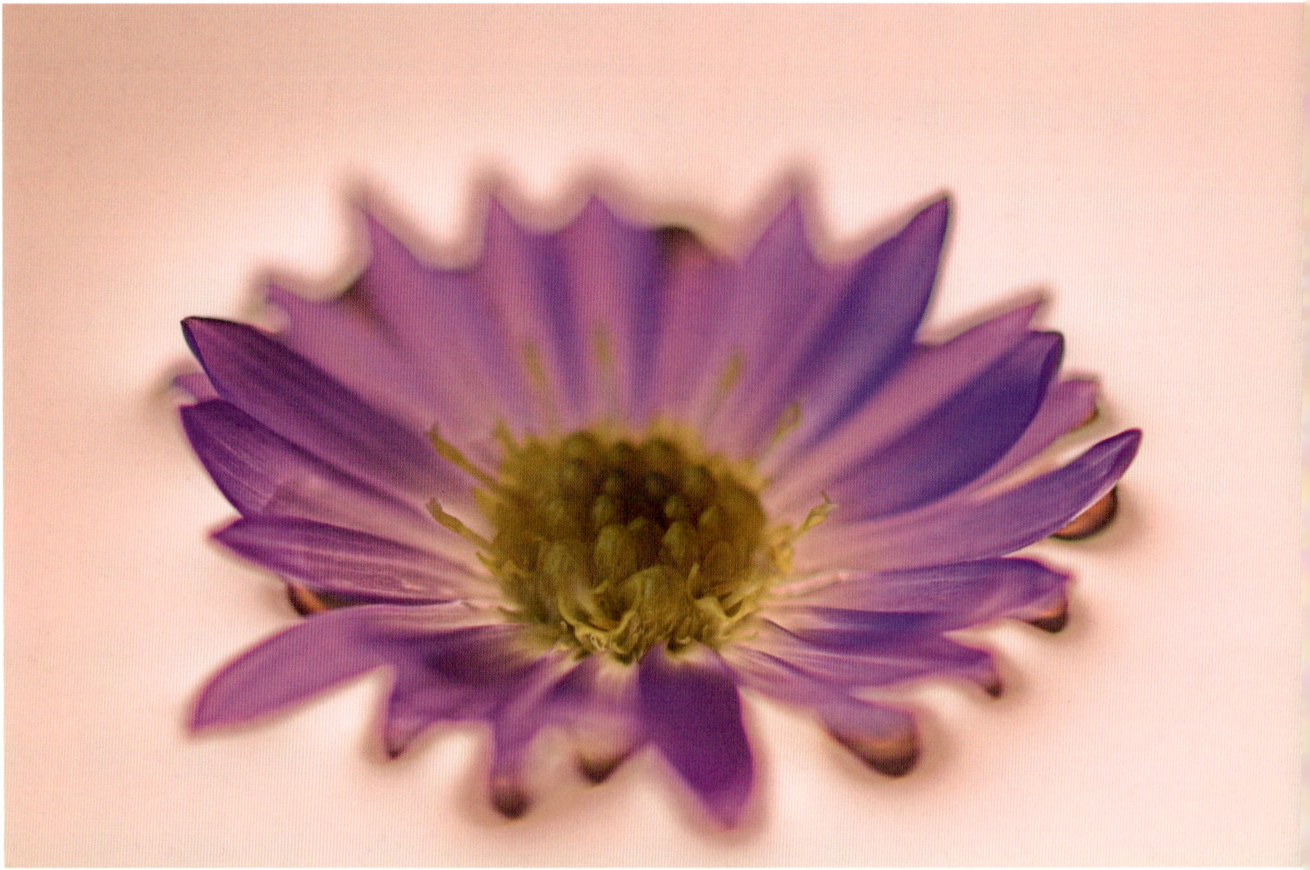

:xploring Harmonious :olors

oing back to the color wheel, armonious colors are those that lie ose to each other. Because these olors naturally work together, they e very easy on the eye. Images ontaining only these colors usually roduce the most restful and beautiful sults. These colors appear natural hen viewed together and do not ash, so they are effective at filling e entire image with color without e end result looking too busy or verwhelming to the viewer.

Even when working with colors next each other on the color wheel, ome colors still tend to stand out ore than others. The more dominant olors such as yellow and red grab our tention more than blues and greens, need to be used with care. This oes not mean that you cannot use ese colors, however—two dominant olors can work, as long as they are of similar brightness.

The calm, restful feel of images at contain harmonious colors can e enhanced by using muted colors. astel shades work particularly ell as color harmonies, as they do ot dominate an image like more turated colors. That is not to say that turated colors cannot be used as lor harmonies, but it is something be aware of when exploring color rmonies in your photography.

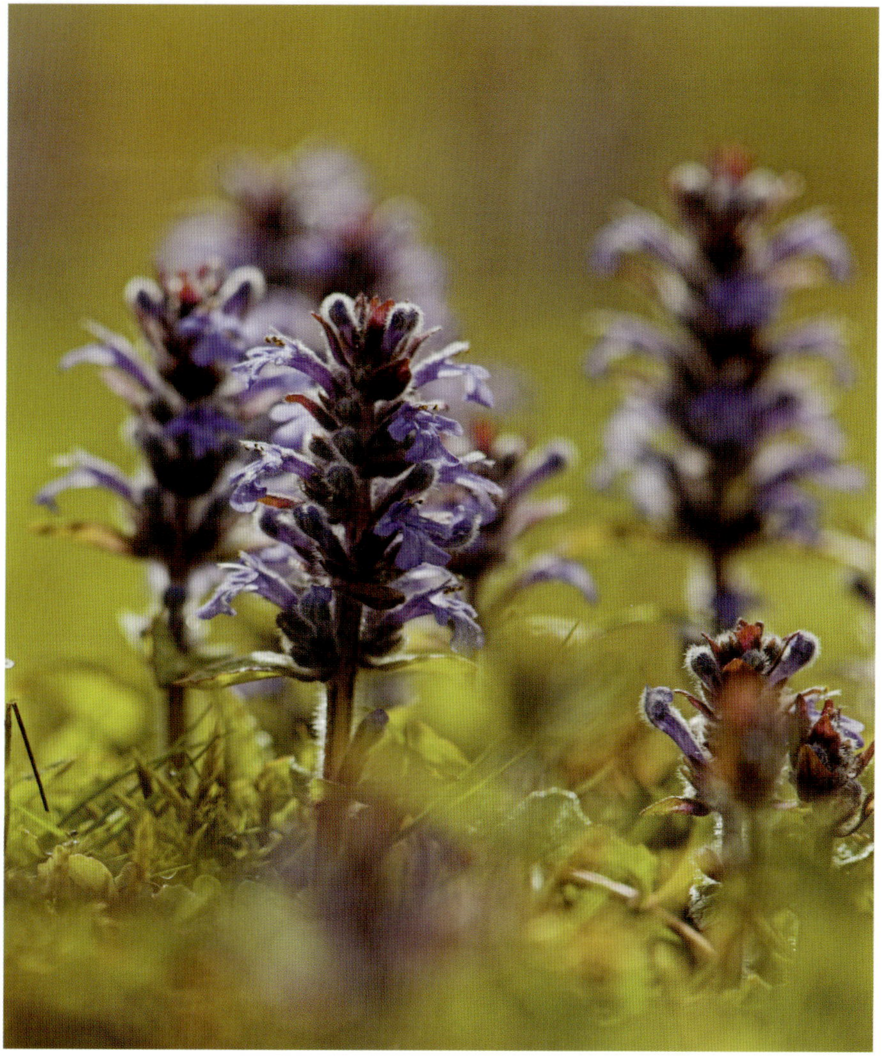

Nature is full of colors that work well together; here, the green background of grass is the perfect complement for the blue flowers.

Tip

Both color harmonies and contrasts work best if you limit the number of colors you include. The most powerful combinations involve just two basic colors—although this can include different shades of the two. As soon as you introduce more colors, the effect is often diminished, as more colors will compete for attention.

Colors in Nature

One of the best places to learn about harmonious colors is in nature. The color of many plants and animals has evolved over millions of years so they blend into their environment. Spotting these harmonies is often more difficult than finding color contrasts, because they have evolved to not grab our attention. Take a fresh look at the world around you and the way that the colors work together; here are some of the more common color harmonies that you will find.

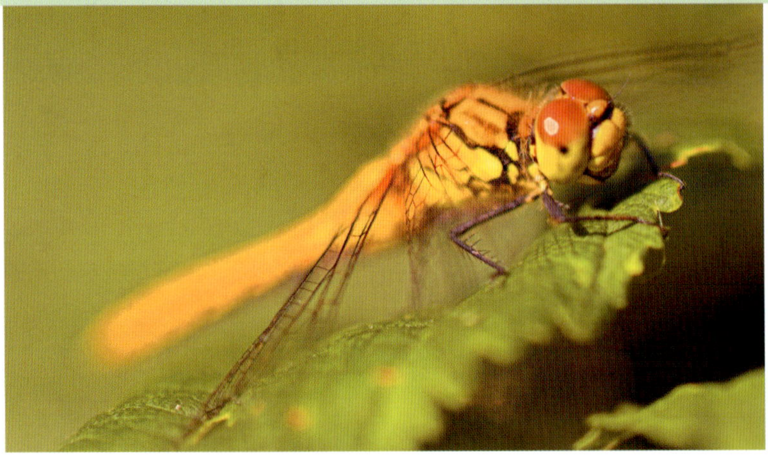

Green/yellow
Yellow is one of the brightest colors so tends to stand out strongly in isolation or against a contrasting color. Combine it with green, however, and the effect is much less obvious. Because the two colors work well together and are a familiar sight in nature, yellow becomes a less dominant color, although it is still the color that grabs attention.

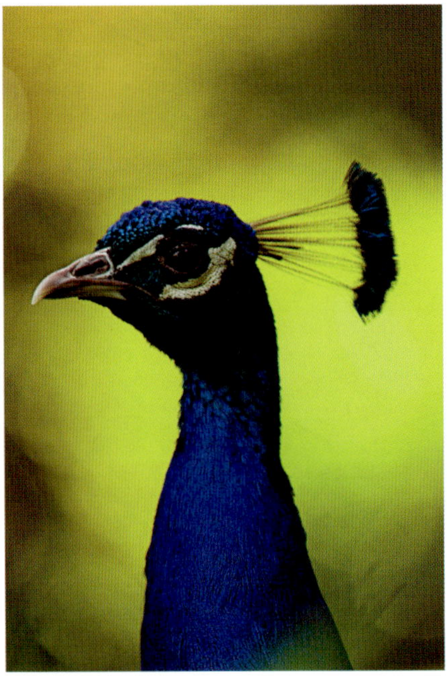

Blue/green
The combination of green foliage and blue sky means that these two colors are such a familiar sight that it is easy to overlook them. Although both colors are saturated, cooler colors tend to work more naturally together as they do not attract our attention as much as the more dominant reds and yellows.

Yellow/red
The combination of these two bright and warm colors can produce very vibrant images if the colors are highly saturated. The more muted tones of these fall leaves creates a more harmonious image, however, giving it a peaceful feel. This is the key to using more dominant colors harmoniously: look out for the more subtle hues that combine well together rather than the brighter, more vivid colors.

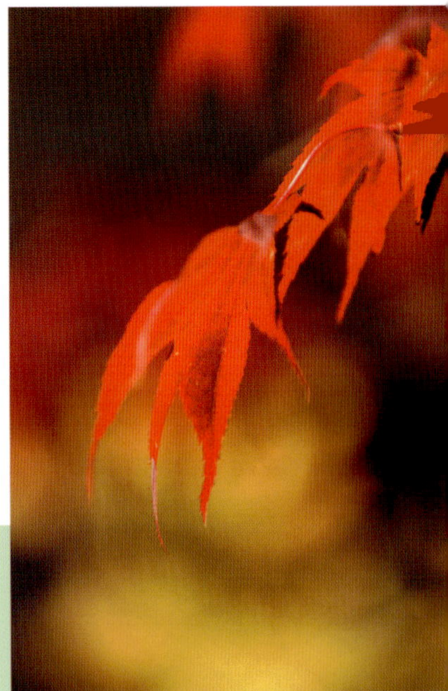

Red/orange
Similar to yellow and red, this combination produces a warm-looking image. Care is needed when working with red, as even when working with harmonious colors it tends to dominate the image. In this picture, the red kite takes up a very small area of the frame, but it still commands our attention.

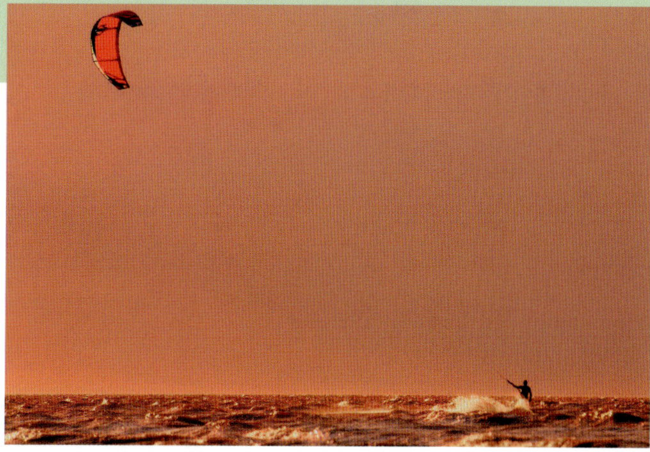

lagenta/red
his combination of a cool magenta nd the much warmer red can produce color contrast if the hues are widely paced on the color wheel. Here the agenta and red hues are closely matched, so produce a harmonious result. This harmony is enhanced by the muted colors involved; more saturated colors would destroy the way the colors work together.

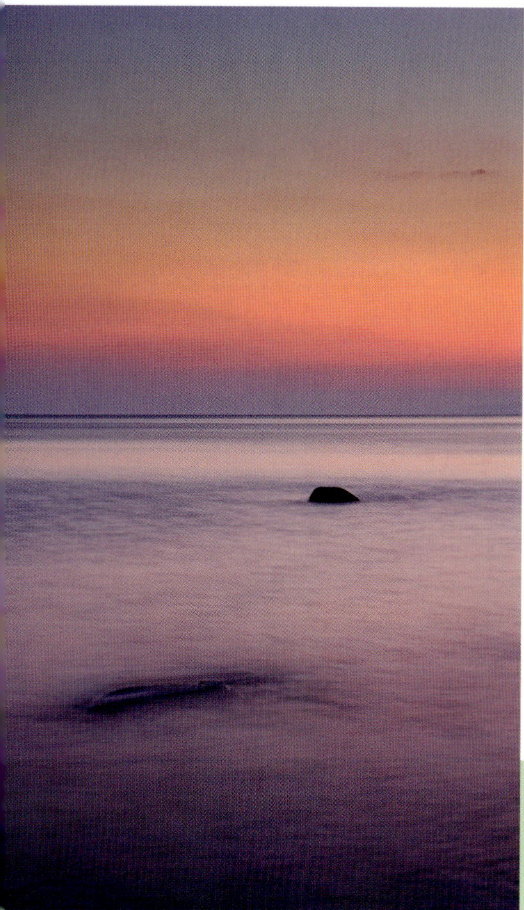

Camouflage

The colors used for camouflage do not necessarily need to be an exact match for their surroundings; as long as the colors are harmonious, the object will not stand out from the background. While camouflage is great for the safety of the animals that use it, it can be a nightmare for the nature photographer. When faced with animals that are camouflaged, try to fill the frame as much as possible with the main subject, otherwise it will disappear into the background.

On the plus side, learning how to use camouflage yourself can make it possible to get closer to your subject, and is a key element in the fieldcraft needed for a budding wildlife photographer. Think about the color of the clothes that you wear when out shooting wildlife—wearing colors that are harmonious with your environment will allow you to blend in.

Tip

The type of lighting can also influence the harmony of the image. Harsh, high-contrast light naturally creates a more dynamic image, so can work against harmonious colors by creating very dark shadows and bright highlights. The limited brightness range created by soft lighting enhances the sense of calm with harmonious colors. A more limited range of tones in the images helps to emphasize the effect of harmonious colors.

Complementary Colors

Have you ever wondered why objects in an image sometimes seem to "pop" out at you? It is often not simply the color itself, but how it combines with those around it that makes a particular hue stand out. This technique of using complementary (or contrasting) colors works by combining colors that are on opposite sides of the color wheel. Using contrasting colors is one of the most powerful tools in your color armory, as the combinations usually produce particularly eye-catching and effective images.

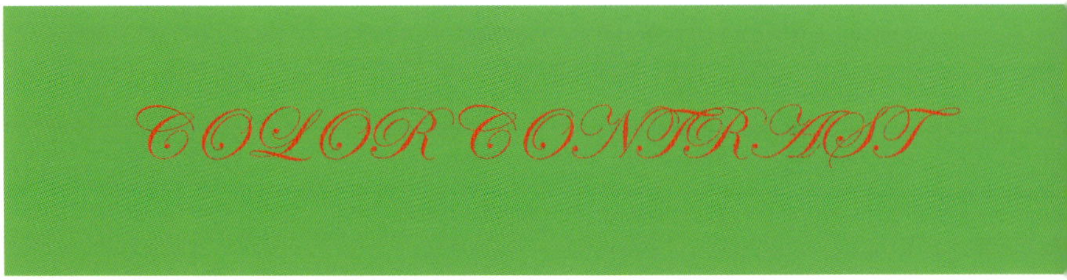

Using Complementary Colors

Combinations of bright, primary colors as contrasts will give your images the most impact, as the saturated colors are naturally more dominant than more muted hues. This technique is commonly used by advertisers looking to grab consumers' attention. Take a look at the packaging and advertising around you and you will find color combinations such as red/blue or blue/yellow that leap out at you.

Although in theory the colors should be exactly opposite on the color whee for maximum contrast, combining two of the primary colors such as red and green can produce striking contrasts. This is largely because red is a naturally dominant color, so it contrasts well with any color that is more recessive.

Not all color contrasts work, howeve and working with complementary color often requires more effort to make them succeed than when you are usin harmonious colors. It is all too easy for the color contrasts produced by complementary colors to clash rather than produce the impact that you want

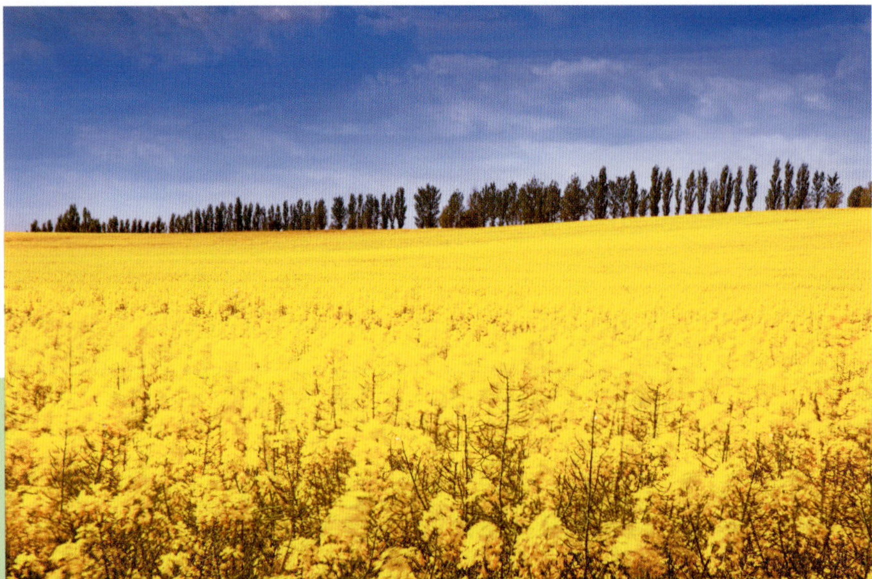

Strong complementary colors such as yellow and blue create vibrant images full of impact. Including the blue sky on this shot enhances the vibrancy of the yellow oilseed plants.

Composition

When shooting color contrasts, do not be afraid to be bold with your composition and the placing of colors. A classic compositional technique is to use the rule of thirds when positioning the strongest-colored object. To use this, imagine dividing the frame into nine equal areas by drawing two dividing lines along the horizontal and vertical. The points where these lines intersect are where to place the subject. Putting your strongest subject on these points creates a well-balanced composition.

When working with color contrasts, the relative size of the objects in the frame also influences the impact of the color. A strong color such as red naturally appears more dominant than more recessive green or blue. If they are given equal areas of the frame, the stronger color takes all of your attention, so you are less aware of the contrast between the colors.

Strangely, the best way of maximizing the impact of the strongest color is by using less of it in the image rather than more. This ratio of colors takes some experimentation to get right, as there are many variables, but as a general rule the more dominant the color, the less you need to use.

When strong color contrasts are combined with complex images or text, the result can lessen the impact of both the olor and the message.

'or example, red and green usually vorks well in nature, as it is a ombination that is a common sight n many flowers. These are two such trong colors that they both draw 'our attention and rely on a simple omposition and easily recognizable cene to work effectively. This same airing used in text or a complex esign can be very unsettling, owever, as your brain has difficulty n deciding which is more important—he color or the message contained n the image.

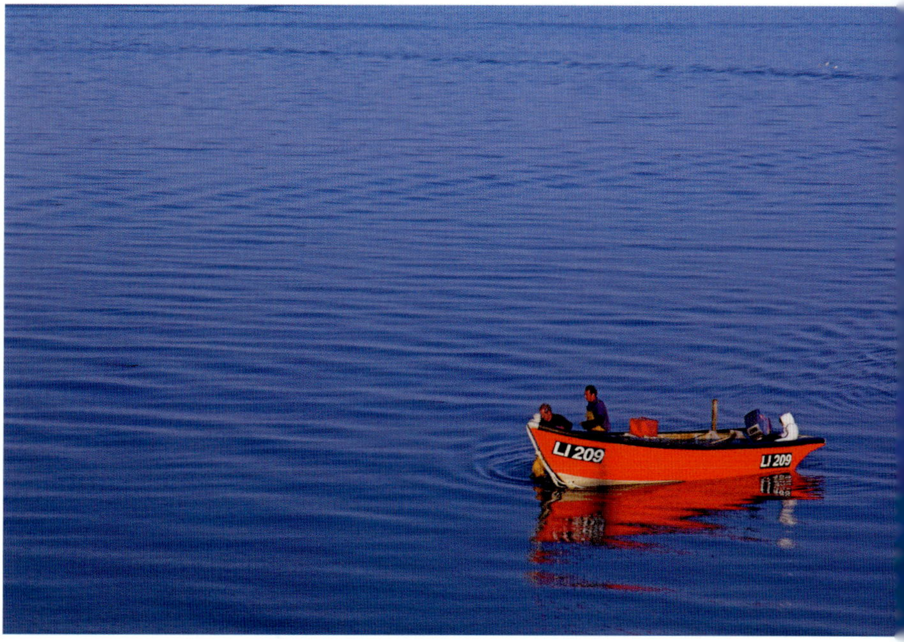

The visual impact of the dominant color of the red boat against the blue sea is enhanced by placing it on an intersection of the lines used in the rule of thirds. Notice that, although it is only small in the frame, your eye is immediately drawn to the boat.

Making the most of color contrasts is often about simplicity. If the image is too busy, the contrast can be lost because your mind spends too much time trying to work out what is going on in the image. By keeping to the fewest number of elements, you will increase the impact of the most dominant subject in the frame.

Like most rules, however, this one is there to be broken; using color contrasts in very busy images can be effective at producing unsettling images, as the various elements jostle for attention.

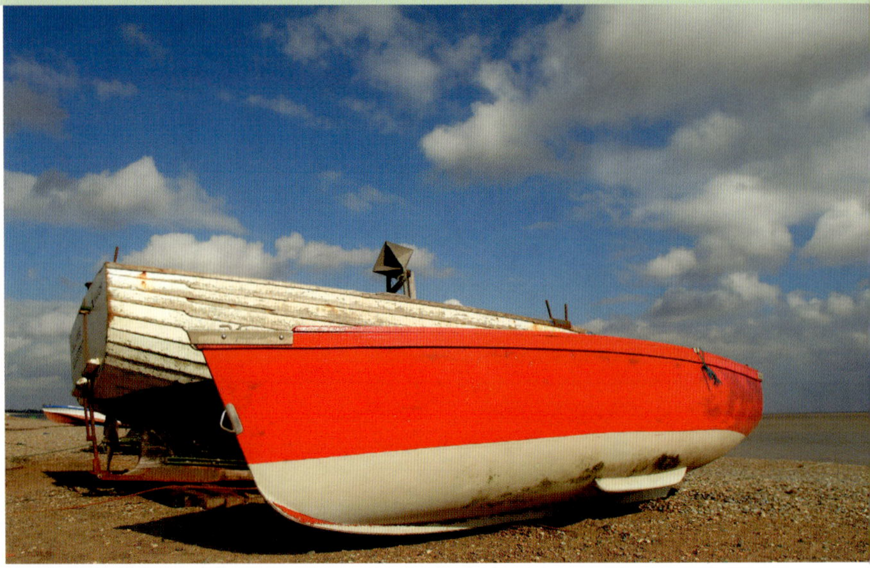

Common Color Contrasts

In this section let's explore some of the most effective color contrasts that you can exploit in your photography.

Red/blue

While these two colors are not precisely opposite on the color wheel, they naturally contrast well when used together. This is because they are at the extremes of our color perception. Red is a very dominant color, and blue is one of the most recessive. We associate them with very different moods and feelings, so a slight sense of unease is created when they are both included in an image. In this image, it is the red of the boat that grabs all of the attention, although the blue plays its part by adding to the impact. If the sky behind were a complementary color to red the image would not have the same impact.

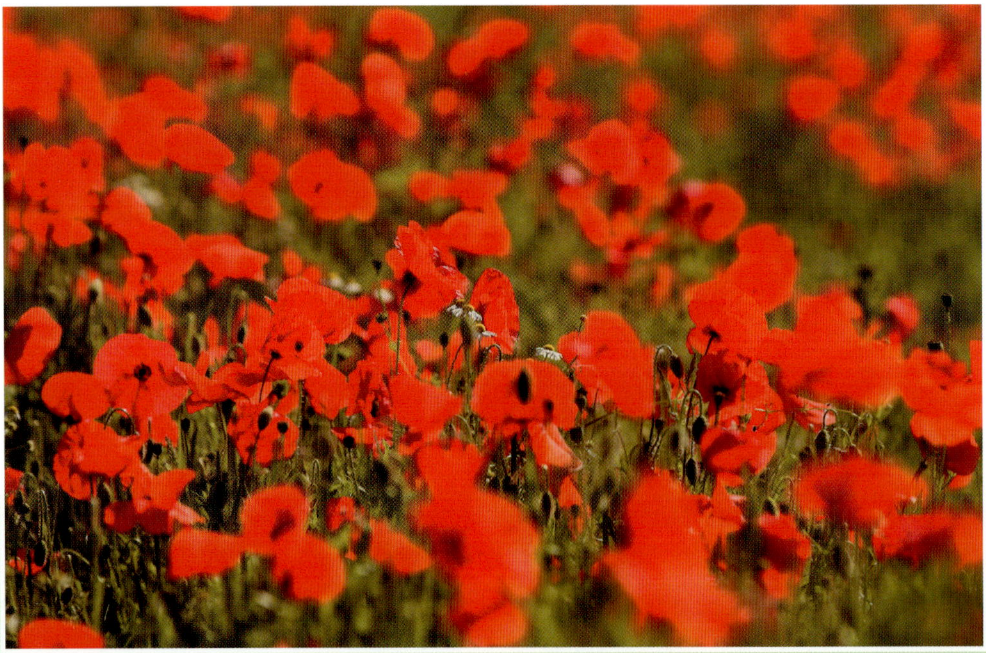

The contrast between the red poppies and the green creates a very vibrant image However, because there are so many areas that are shouting for attention, it is difficult for your eye to rest on any single area of the image.

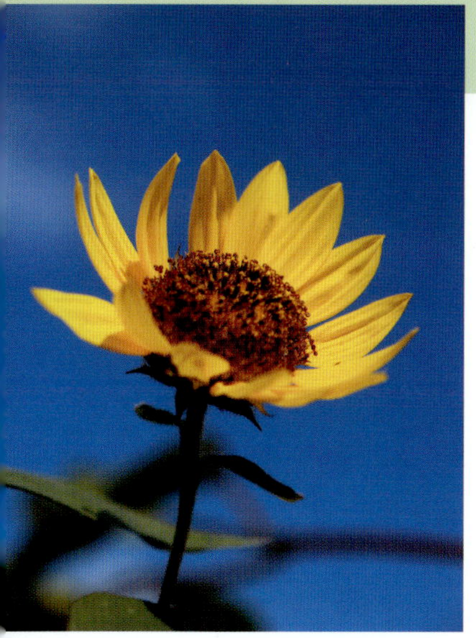

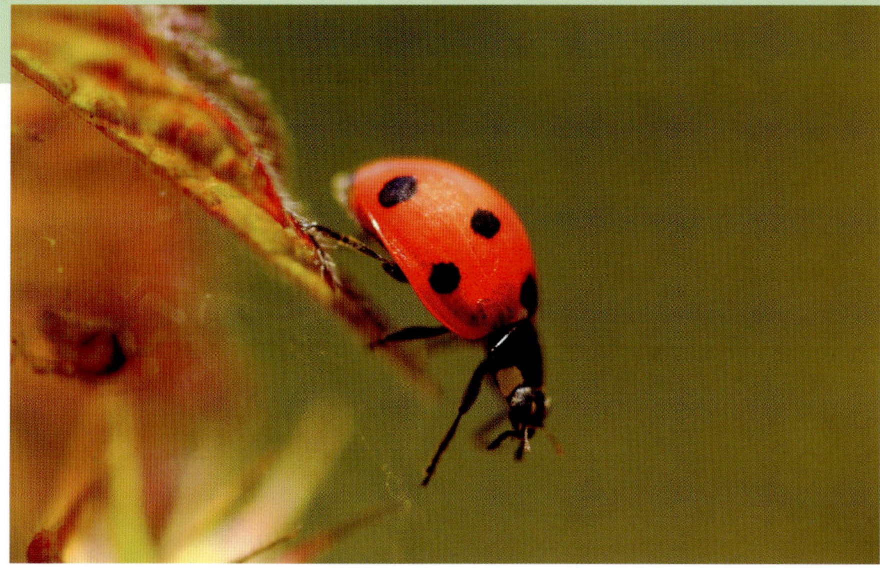

ellow/blue

his shot illustrates a classic way of naking your subject stand out from ne background by placing it against complementary color. The yellow of nis sunflower is made to look brighter nd more colorful by using the blue ky as a background. This combination eels bright and cheerful; these are two olors that we associate with sunny ays, and the image therefore looks ery welcoming. This is a favorite color ombination for advertisers seeking to romote the natural and fresh appeal f their product.

Red/green

When dealing with red subjects, green is an excellent choice for a contrasting background. The combination is one used by many plants and animals to stand out from their surroundings and attract attention. Similar to using blue as a contrast to red, green is a much more recessive color and enhances the perceived vibrancy of the more dominant color.

Magenta/green

These two colors are directly opposite on the color wheel, so the contrast between them is high. Magenta (or purple) is quite a cool color, though, so although the flower stands out well from the green background the effect is not as pronounced as some contrasts. Compared to the red/green combination, the contrast actually appears less, despite the fact that these colors should give a greater contrast according to the color wheel. This is because red is such a dominant color that it can contrast well with the other primary colors.

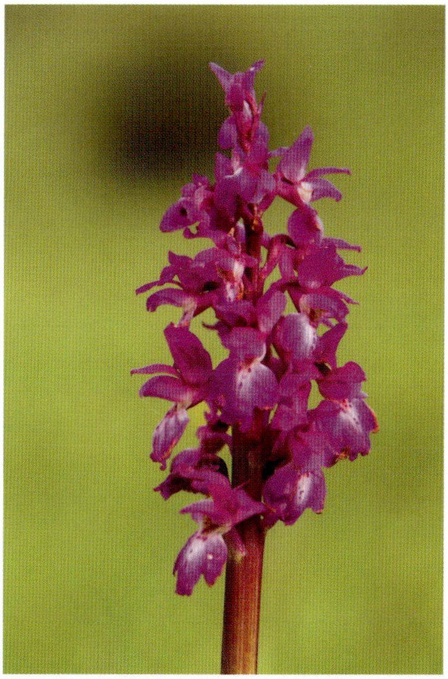

Skin Tones

Despite the almost infinite range of tones and colors around the world, most people still spot a poor skin tone immediately. We are so used to seeing healthy-looking people in photographs that even slight inaccuracies can give the subject in your portraits an unhealthy appearance.

Obtaining Accurate Skin Tones

In order to obtain accurate skin tones, the first thing to consider is the type of light that you are shooting in. In general, soft lighting creates the most natural-looking skin tones. The harsh shadows and bright highlights of high-contrast light such as direct sunlight can make it very difficult to obtain a consistent skin tone across the whole contrast range.

One thing to watch out for is colors reflected by brightly colored objects near your subject. Stand your model next to bright green foliage and you will find that their skin can take on an unwelcome green tinge, especially in the shadows. This can also be true of clothing, although this may be more difficult to change, as not everyone will welcome you criticizing their clothes. Try to persuade them that the problem is solely because of the reflection and you may succeed.

There are two ways to help reduce this problem, both of which also help to lower the contrast. The first is to use a white or silver reflector to add light to the shadow areas. Position it opposite the main light source and vary the angle until you get the light reflected just where you want it. A white reflector gives natural-looking, soft light bounced back into the shadows. A silver one gives a much brighter reflection and can be over-the-top for most portraits. The downside with this solution is that you will probably need an assistant to hold the reflector, although a range of methods can be tried to support it in position if necessary.

A more self-contained solution is to use a burst of flash to add light to the shadows. This technique is known as fill-in, or fill, flash, and is one of the most useful that you can learn. For natural-looking results, the trick lies in not adding too much flash so that it becomes the main light source. Most cameras have a small built-in flash that is ideal for this technique for individual portraits, as it does not require a large, powerful flash unit to add enough light. If your camera has a fill-in flash setting use this, although, depending on the model, you may find that it adds too much flash to the exposure. Many cameras allow you to adjust the flash exposure independently of the main exposure. If you find that the flash is too bright, reduce the setting by –1 or –2 stops. Apart from balancing the exposure, the main problem with this technique is the white balance. If the color temperature of the main light source is different from the 5,000K of most flash units, you could run into the problem of dealing with mixed lighting. We discuss this in more detail on p.108.

Even when you are dealing with only a single light source, white balance still has a huge part to play in obtaining accurate skin tones. For accurate colors, ensure that the

It is very tempting to increase the saturation on digital images to give them more impact. This can be very effective for many subjects, but it can cause problems with portraits. Simply adding saturation can emphasize skin blemishes and give your subject a very unhealthy-looking glow. The default setting on many digital cameras gives more than enough saturation for most portraits.

Tip

If you are shooting JPEG images using an sRGB color space, there are usually two versions to choose from. For portraits, use the sRGB 1 (sometimes called portrait) option. Although it produces less saturated images than sRGB 2, it is much better at giving accurate skin tones.

ɿhite balance you use is correct ɔr the light falling on the subject. ˈ your subject is in shadow but the ackground is sunny (or vice versa), is unlikely that an automatic white alance setting will give the correct olor. For critical shots, try to take a ɿhite balance reading from a piece of ɿhite or gray card in the same lighting s the subject and use the preset ıcility to lock the white balance.

Many people prefer slightly warmer kin tones than is strictly accurate. his tends to make most subjects ɔok healthier, but take care not to verdo it. Even switching between the aylight and Cloudy settings in sunlit ɔnditions can often be too much for ıost skin tones.

Case Study 1

Shooting portraits outdoors does not come much more nerve-wracking than wedding photography. The range of tones and colors you have to deal with can make the job of capturing this special day particularly demanding. For this image, I was asked to shoot some portraits after the ceremony. Although the garden location was very scenic, it posed a number of problems for obtaining accurate skin tones. The only suitable location meant shooting with the sun behind the happy couple, meaning that their faces were in shadow. The green reflections from the foliage gave a very unflattering cast on their faces, and I knew that the only solution would be to use fill-in flash. I set the exposure compensation on the flash to $-1\frac{1}{2}$ stops to ensure that the flash did not overpower the main exposure. The white balance was set to Daylight, as both the natural light and flash were approximately the same color temperature.

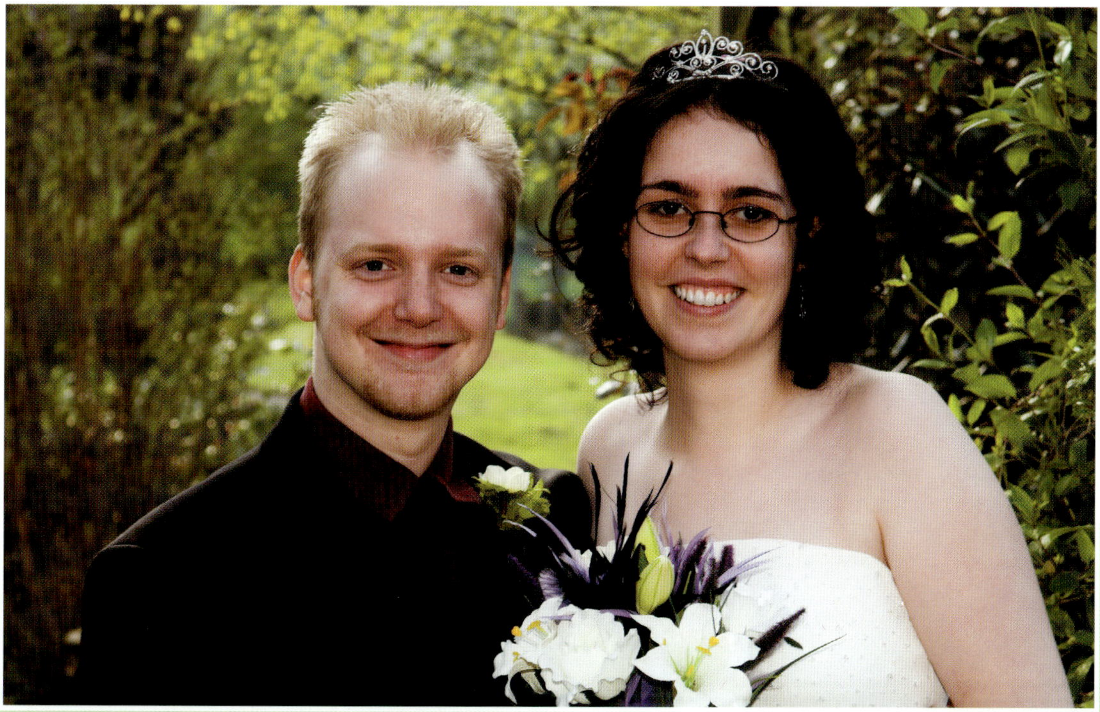

In the controlled environment of the studio, ensuring that both background and clothes are neutral can help you to get the skin tones accurate.

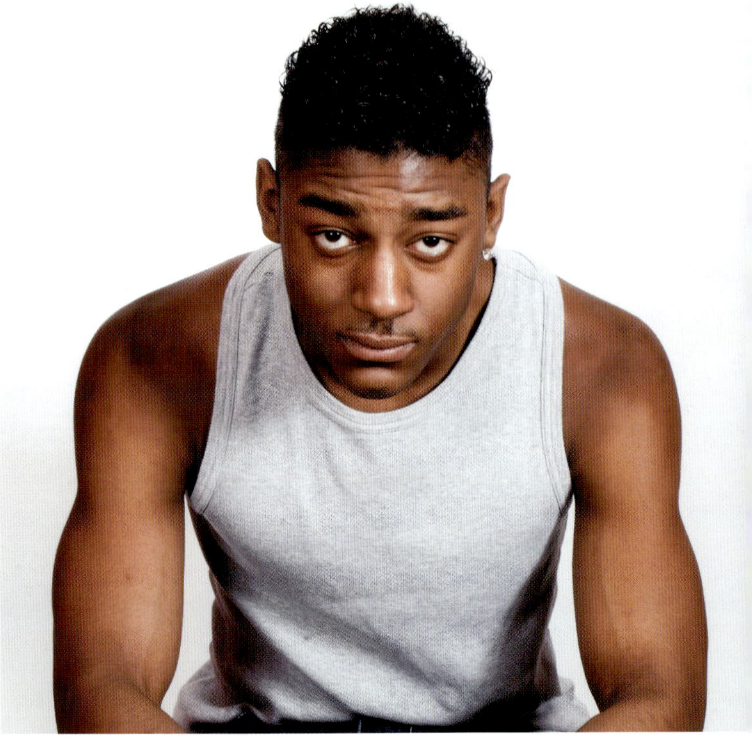

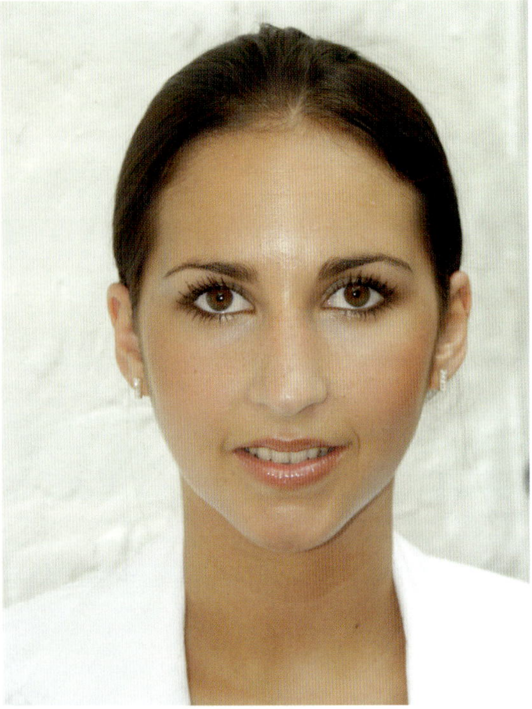

Shooting in diffuse daylight produces very flattering skin tones. For this image, I took a white balance reading from the white jacket the model was wearing to ensure the colors were accurate.

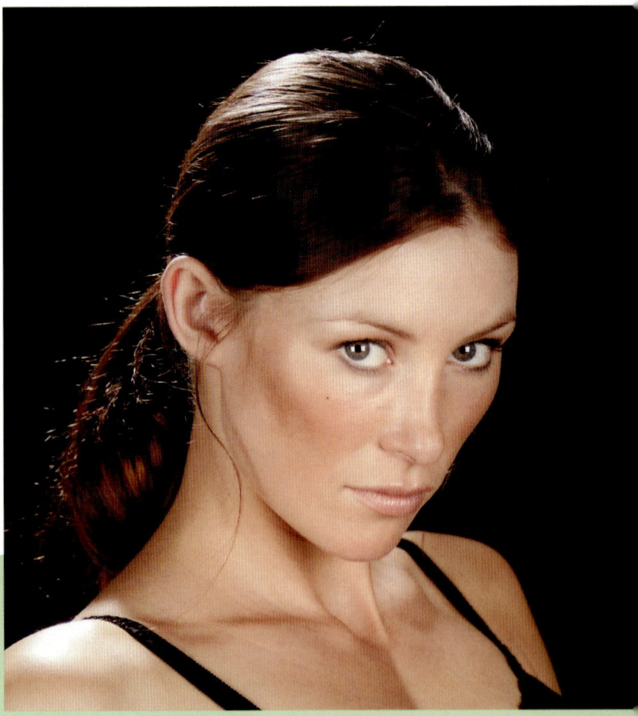

Using studio flash gives much more control over the lighting and color in your portraits. For this image, using two flash heads with softboxes attached meant that the white balance could be set to the flash setting to give the correct colors.

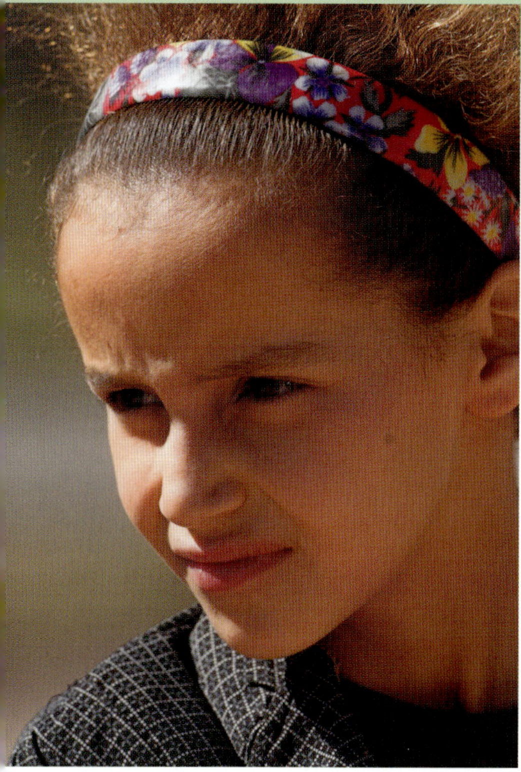

Because you do not have any control over the lighting, candid portraits are best shot on automatic white balance.

Many outdoor portraits benefit from a burst of fill-in flash to help eliminate unsightly shadows and make the subject stand out from the background.

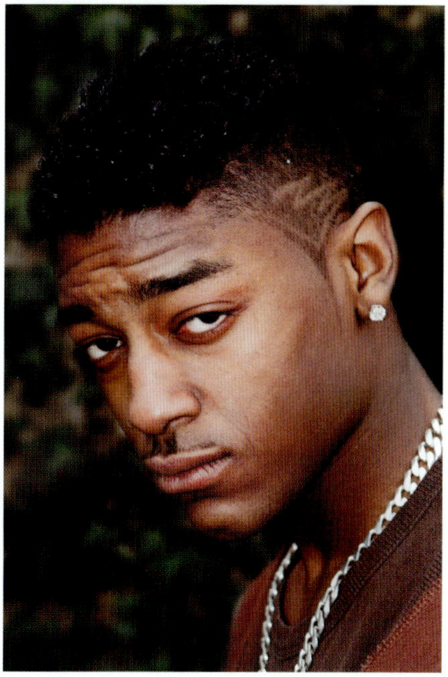

ase Study 2

though still important, getting :curate skin tones in action and orts images is less critical than most her portrait images. You can be faced th all sorts of lighting, and with fast-moving subjects you will not have time to adjust the settings on your camera for individual shots. The best solution here is to shoot in RAW mode and adjust the white balance when you process the images in your conversion software. For this boxing image, the camera was set to automatic white balance, as the lighting varied considerably depending on where the boxers were in the ring. When processing the image, a reading was taken from the white areas on the clothes to give an accurate white balance.

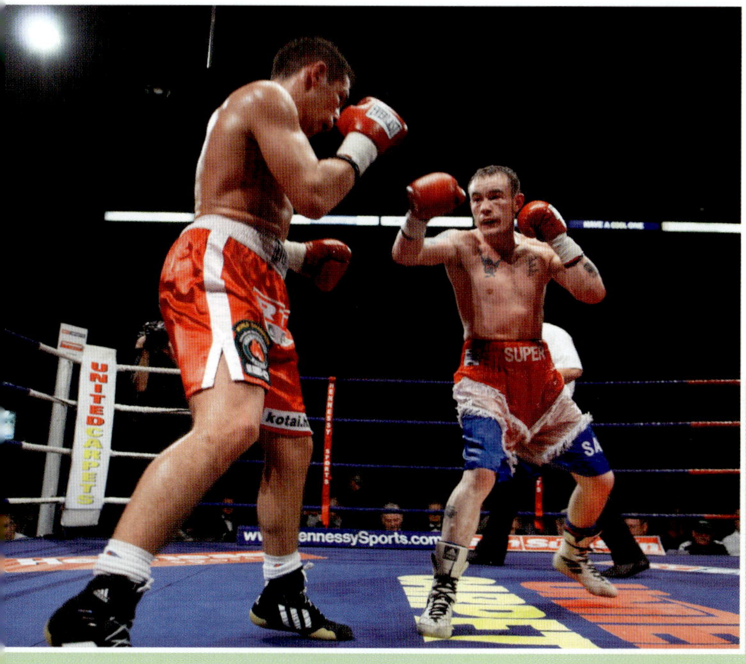

Mixed Lighting

Obtaining the correct colors when your subject is lit by more than one type of lighting can be one of the greatest challenges in photography. Even by adjusting the white balance on a digital camera, with two or more color temperatures to deal with you are still going to end up with color casts on different areas of your image.

Dealing With Mixed Lighting

There are no hard-and-fast rules when it comes to dealing with mixed lighting, as the variations are almost endless. The task can be made simpler by assessing what type of mixed lighting you are faced with. These situations can broadly be divided into two categories. The first is when you introduce your own light source, such as flash, to illuminate your main subject. The second is when you are shooting in an environment that contains more than one light source, such as an interior with both daylight and artificial lighting. Both situations demand slightly different solutions—although be prepared for some compromise when it comes to certain areas and colors in the subject.

For the first situation, where you have control over one of the light sources, the solution is relatively simple. Putting a filter or lighting gel over the light that you have introduce so that its color temperature matches the existing light source means that you will have only one color temperature to deal with (see the panel opposite for more information).

When the light sources are out of your control, the problem is more difficult. The simplest solution is to decide on the most important area of the subject and concentrate on getting the correct colors in this alone For example, you could be shooting a portrait with the person in different lighting to the background. In this situation, forget about the backgroun and set the white balance to suit the color temperature of the light on your subject. The background colors will be technically incorrect, but that is fa better than having the wrong colors c the main subject.

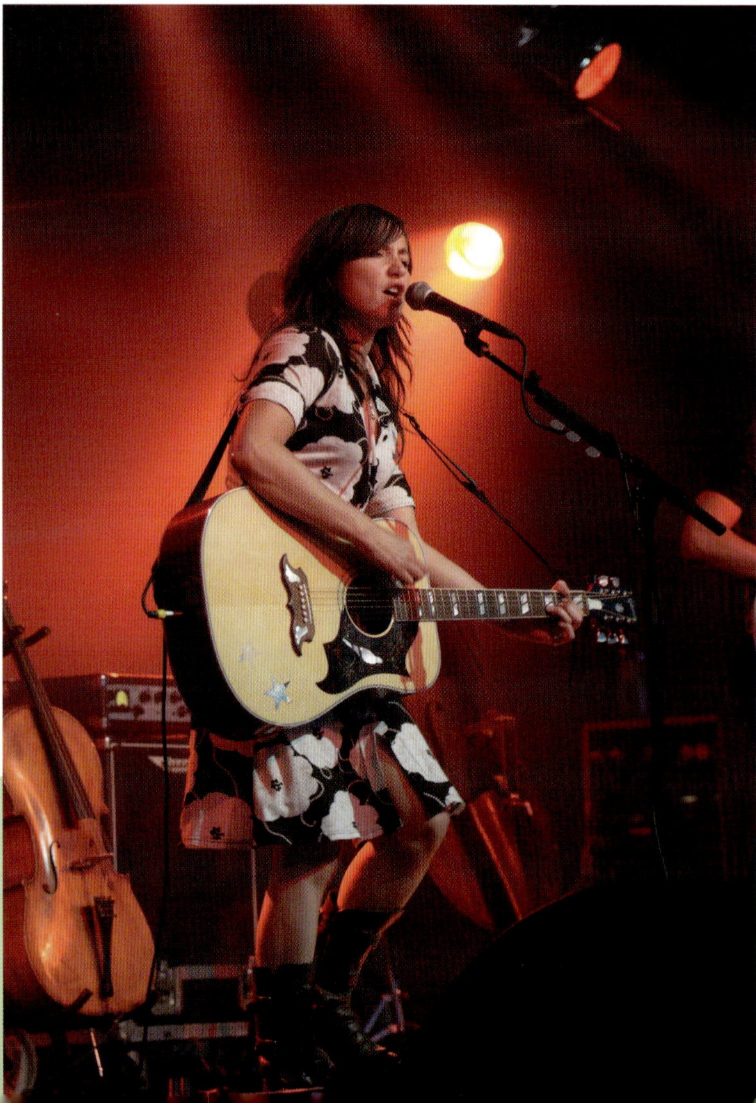

« When the lighting is completely out of your control, you will have to compromise on the accuracy of the colors. For this image, we concentrated on getting the skin tones as realistic as possible by adjusting the white balance of the RAW image.

Filtering the Light Source

For these shots, the background was lit by a normal household lamp, with a flash lighting the statue. The background should be white, while the statue is a neutral gray.

- By setting the white balance to flash, the statue is correct, but the background has a yellow color cast.
- Using an incandescent white balance corrects the background, but the statue takes on a strong blue color.
- Placing a tungsten-balancing filter over the flash means that both light sources have a similar white balance, allowing both the statue and background to remain neutral.

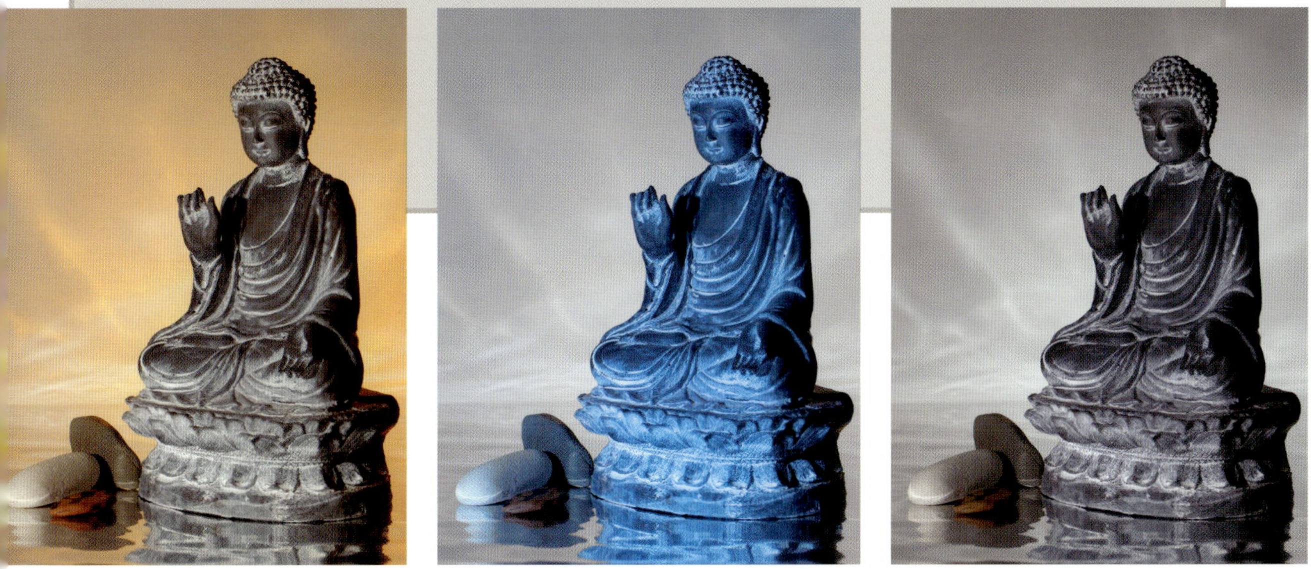

AW Capture

ooting RAW images gives you e opportunity to adjust the white lance setting when you process the ages in your conversion software. is is much easier than trying to get e exact settings right when you are shooting in mixed lighting. Most RAW software allows you to take a white balance reading from the image.
To do this successfully, you need a neutral area to measure from. If your subject does not include one, try to take a shot in the same lighting of a neutral object. The ideal solution is to use a gray card, which would normally be used for exposure measurement, and place it in the scene for a measurement to be taken.

Tip

For architecture and interior photographers, mixed lighting is often a fact of life. If you are going to be dealing with it often, you may want to invest in a color temperature meter to accurately measure the light sources. This allows film users to assess the best filtration on either the camera or light source.

Background Colors

While you are shooting images, you naturally concentrate most of your attention on the main subject, and it is all too easy to forget what is going on in the background. This results in mistakes such as trees apparently growing out of people's heads. While these errors can ruin your images, we will take it for granted that you have avoided these simple problems and move on to how the color and tone of your background affects your images.

Dealing with Background Colors

We have already seen how complementary and harmonious colors work together, so if you are working with a subject with a strong color you will need to keep these in mind when dealing with backgrounds. But the color of the background also affects the way we look at the whole picture, and which part of the image takes our attention.

This effect is due to how we perceive the color that is in the background. Some colors are perceived as more dominant than others. Using red or bright yellow as a background color will immediately draw our eye to this rather than the subject, unless the subject is also a dominant color. The opposite is true of recessive colors such as green and blue. These colors work more naturally as backgrounds—these are colors that we normally see around us, so we do not pay them as much attention as the brighter colors. While this covers the primary colors, the hues that you tend to come across in nature are rarely as simple as this. Green foliage in particular often contains a great deal of yellow—especially fresh, new growth. This yellow content makes what should be a recessive color become much more prominent.

The best way around this in the field is to look for areas of shade, because as well as the color, the brightness of the background also plays a part in how it appears. No matter what the color, the darker the background the less the viewer will notice it.

The overall effect of the background can also affect the whole mood of the picture, especially if it occupies a large area of the frame. A blue background, for example, gives the image a cool feel. We will discuss these moods further on p.116.

Green
This is one of the most common color you will find for outdoor photography Green backgrounds tend to lend an image a feeling of calm, and the color does not detract attention too much from the main subject.

Blue
This is one of the most recessive colo so is one of the most useful for focusir attention on your subject. Blue can impart a cold, analytical feel, especiall when combined with a neutral subjec

Yellow
A bright, fresh color like yellow makes the image appear very uplifting and energetic. This brightness does take attention away from the subject, however, so yellow should be used with care.

Red
The overpowering effect of red takes all the attention away from the subje The overall feel of the image is quite unsettling because red is usually a signal for danger.

How Background Colors Affect a Neutral-colored Subject

Shooting this neutral-colored statue against different colored backgrounds affects both how we feel about the image and how much attention we pay to the statue. Even though the statue is exactly the same size in each image, it can appear to be smaller or larger in the frame because of the color of the background.

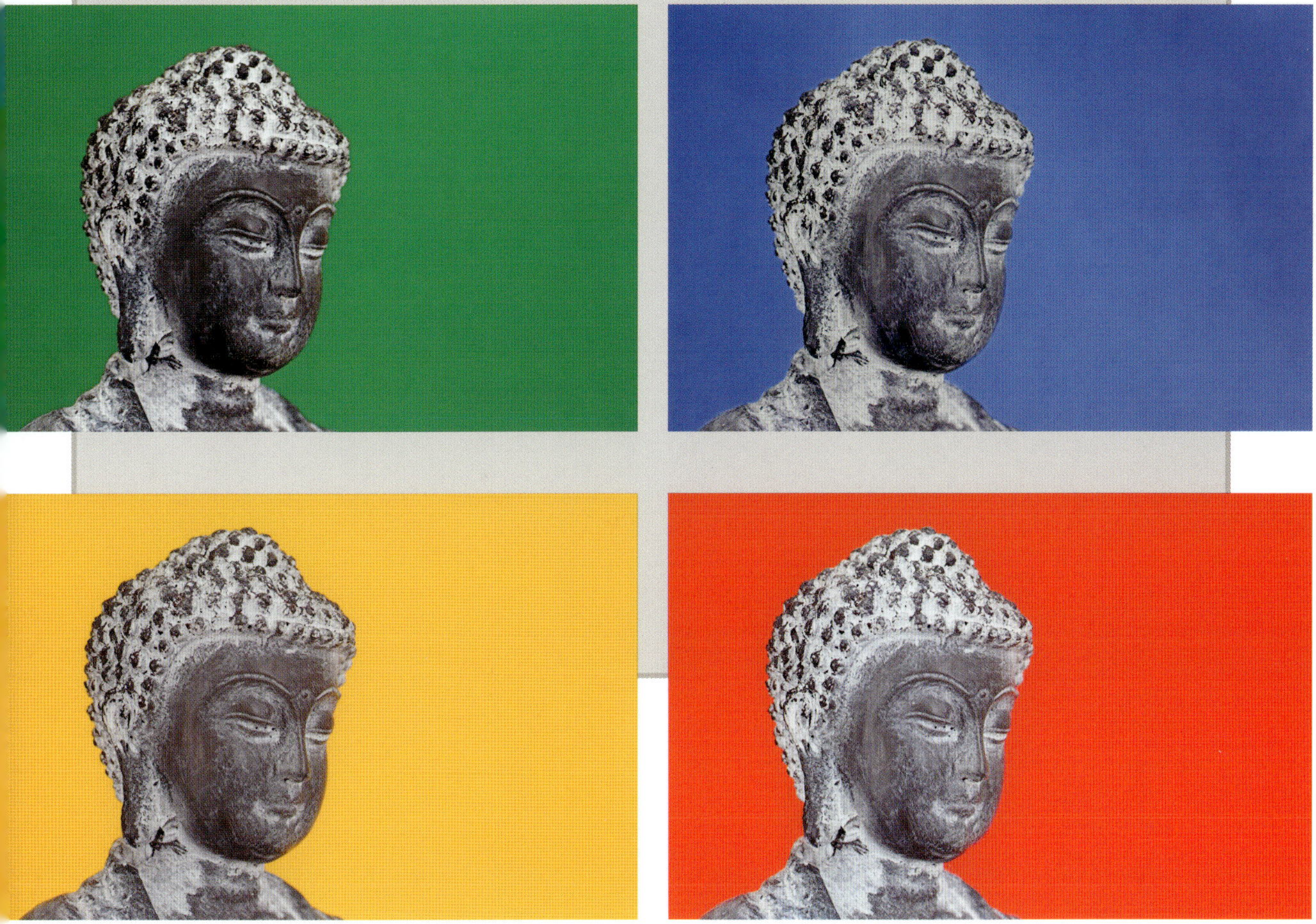

Adjusting Background Color and Brightness

While you should do everything possible to control the background color at the time of shooting, there is a simple way you can adjust background color in Photoshop. This technique is best used on simple, single-colored backgrounds to make the final image as believable as possible.

Open the Replace Color window by going to Image › Adjustments › Replace Color and make sure that the Selection option is highlighted under the preview image. Now, using the main Eyedropper tool, click on the background color that you want to adjust. Then move the Fuzziness slider until the whole of the background is selected in the preview window but your main subject is still visible.

Once you are happy with this selection, you can adjust the Hue, Saturation, and Lightness sliders to produce the effect you require. You can keep a check on the effect on your image by ticking the Preview option in the Replace Color window. Once you are happy with the result, click OK.

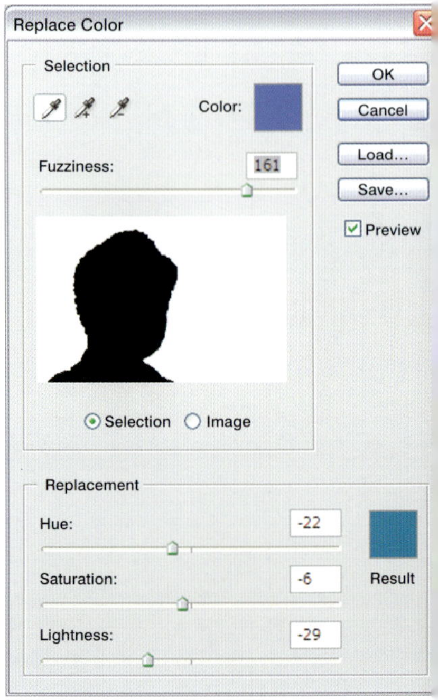

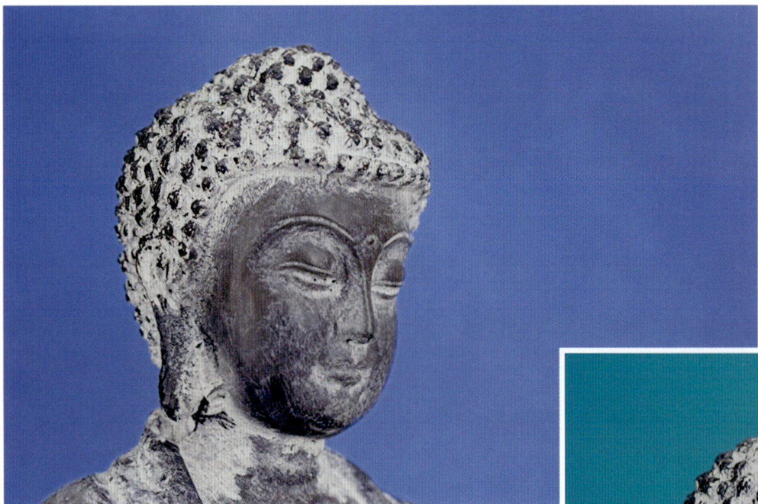

Using the Replace Color function allows you to change background colors simply and easily. Here we have used it to adjust the bright blue background to a less saturated, darker cyan.

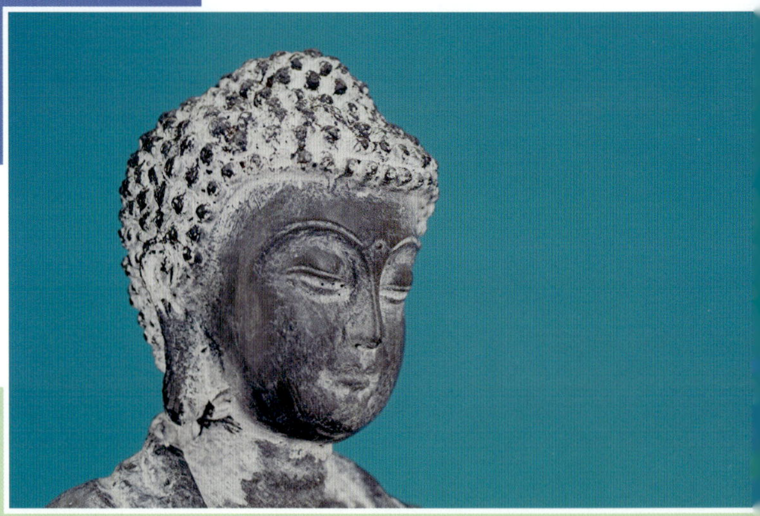

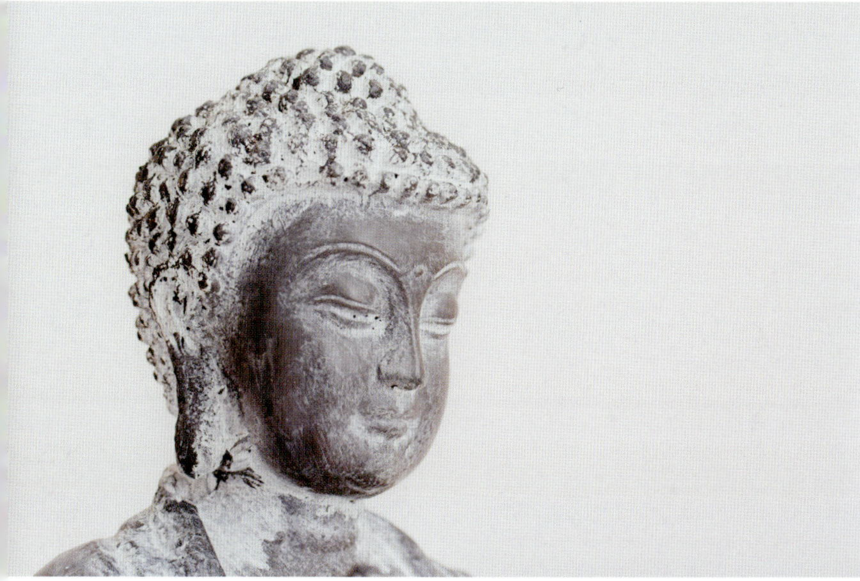

Using white backgrounds gives the image a very pure feeling. The brightness of the background draws attention to the figure, unlike when shooting against a color. This is great for portraits if you do not want the background to detract from the main subject.

As well as giving a solemn feel to the picture, with a black background this image has an air of mystery and intrigue. This is largely because, as we re inquisitive, we naturally look for detail the background. So despite the fact that e should not focus on a black background, the subject is neutral it does not hold our tention. The opposite is true with colored bjects, especially red, as the color is bright ough to take all of our attention, so we pay uch less regard to the background.

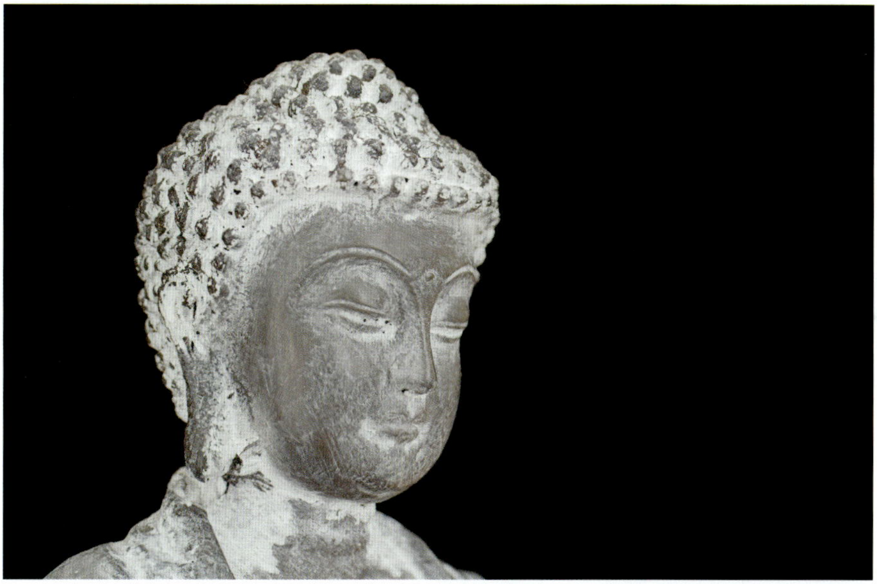

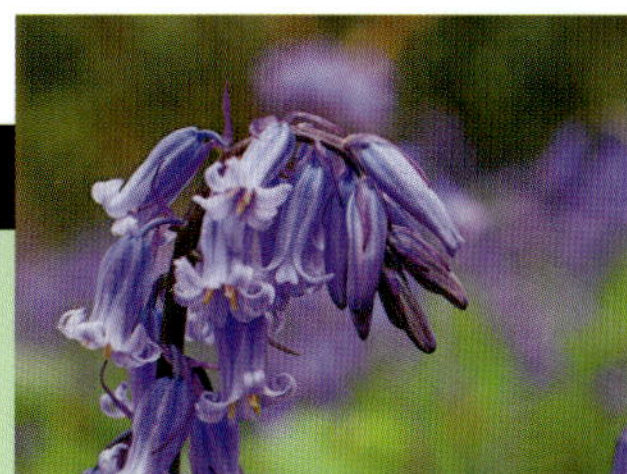

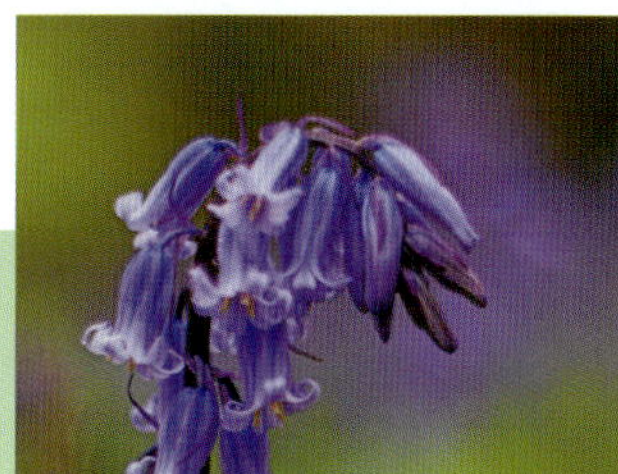

Tip

A handy technique for making the most of background colors is to use limited depth of field to throw the background out of focus. By doing this you can get rid of detail that would detract attention from the main subject and create a more uniform tone as a backdrop. This effect is achieved by using a wide aperture such as f/2.8 or f/4 so that only the main subject is sharp.

Limited Color Palette

Traditionally when we talk about monochrome images we think of black and white, but that is not really what the phrase means. Monochrome literally means "one color," and limiting your images to variations of a single color can produce stunning images.

Exploiting Limited Colors

This technique is all about choosing your subject carefully so that there is only a single color visible in the frame. It requires careful choice of subject, as the predominance of one color means that you need variations in the tones or brightness, or to include areas of a neutral color to prevent your images looking too flat.

Look out for natural highlights or brighter areas of the subject to give your images a focal point, while darker areas tend to recede into the background. Take care not to include any clashing colors, as this will give your images a completely different feel. Simply including a tiny area of red in a predominantly green image, for instance, will draw the viewer's attention immediately, destroying the feeling of calm that the rest of the image has.

In nature, shooting foliage is one of the most common ways of limiting the colors in a scene. There are almos unlimited opportunities for using this technique in close-up or macro photography. Getting in close to your subject allows you to concentrate on filling the frame with small areas of color.

With only one color filling the frame white balance is best set to a preset value according to the lighting, as the automatic system will try to adjust the colors to produce a neutral result.

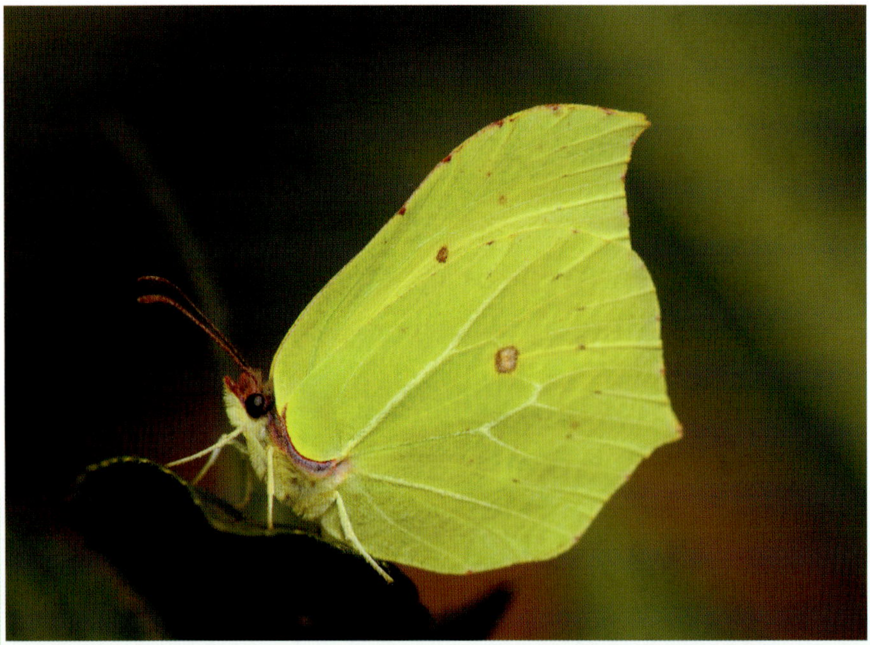

Case Study 1

With a color designed to camouflage i against foliage, this butterfly is hard t make stand out from the background. The solution was to carefully move th camera position until the light green of the butterfly contrasted against the darker foliage. Because the eye is naturally drawn toward the lighter tone, the butterfly is a strong focal point, despite the similar colors. To retain the green hues of the image, the white balance was set to suit the shady conditions I was shooting in.

Tip

Using a telephoto lens to isolate small areas of the scene is a great way to achieve images with a limited color palette. Rather than shooting the wider landscape, look for details that contain only a single color. You can include some neutral tones in the frame, but ensure that they do not detract from the overall color of the subject.

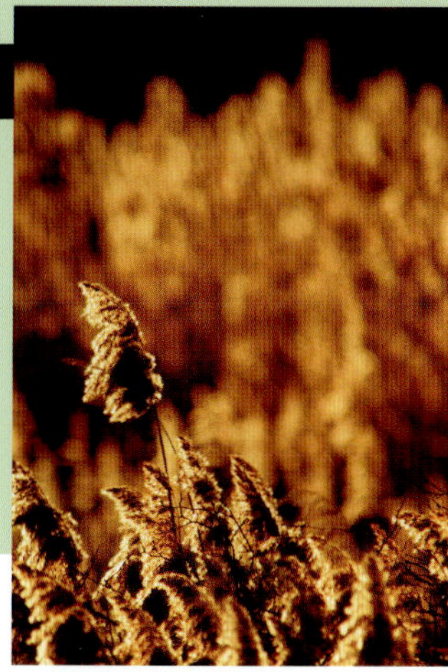

» Selecting areas that contain a single color is much easier with a telephoto lens.

:ase Study 2

/hile the basic subjects in these two nages are similar, the conditions and olors present in the original scene nean that they create very different nages. The bright green plants in ne water in the first image produce a unchy, vibrant photograph that really aps out at you. To make the most f these, I used a polarizing filter to liminate the reflections on the water nd maximize the color. The image was not in bright, sunny conditions that nade the colors even more vibrant. ne more muted tones of the second nage produce an image that looks nore like a toned black-and-white nage than a color one. It was shot n heavy shade, so there was a very mited range of colors in the scene.

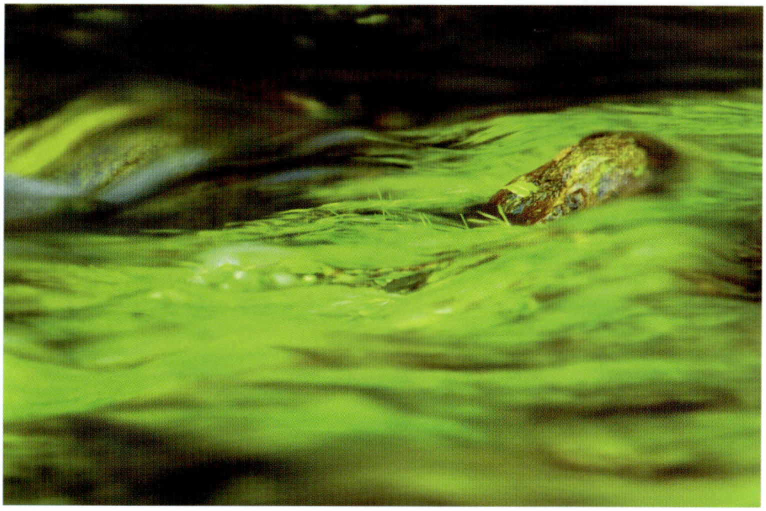

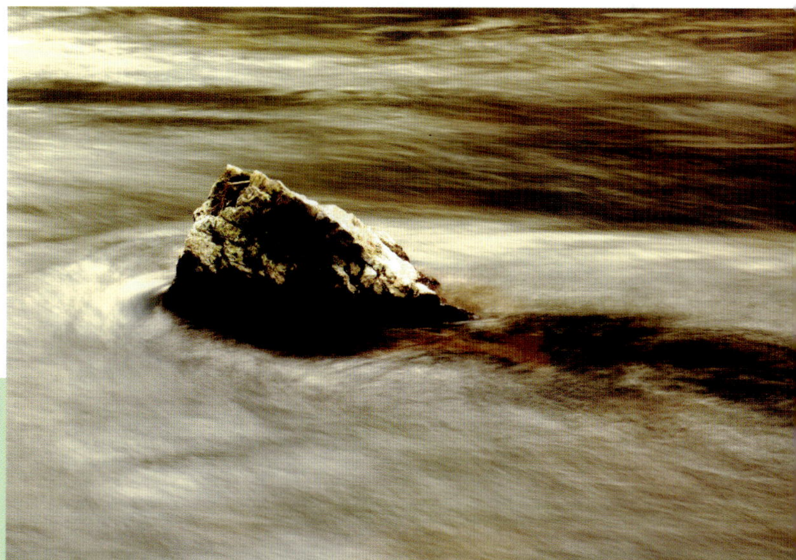

Tip

When using studio flash, use either Flash or Daylight white balance, as the short duration of the flash is likely to give inconsistent results with the automatic setting.

Color Moods

Although color theory is very good at dealing with how colors work together, it does not really cover the emotional reaction that colors can evoke. How we react to different colors can be influenced by our cultural history, personal experience, or simply by association with a particular object or feeling. There are many variables when it comes to our individual color associations, but there are some general moods that particular colors or tones generate in most people. In this section, let's deal with how to impart a particular mood to a picture through using similar tones, and how you can capture or enhance these feelings.

As a photographer, you need to have some feeling for how the color looks. Although I can give you advice, do not ignore your own emotions. Just because a certain subject would normally be given a warm or cold look, don't think that this is the only solution.

One of the greatest benefits of digital photography is the ability to experiment with different settings and treatments of your subject without the extra expense involved in shooting film. This freedom means that if you are in any doubt as to how the scene should look, you can shoot plenty of frames using different white balance settings. Alternatively, if you shoot RAW files, you can simply change these when you process the images. From control of the photographic studio, where you can create the mood and tonality of an image from scratch, to working outdoors, where the mood is often dictated to you by the subject and the lighting conditions, being able to recognize and use color moods is one of the most effective means for you to create your own interpretation of the world.

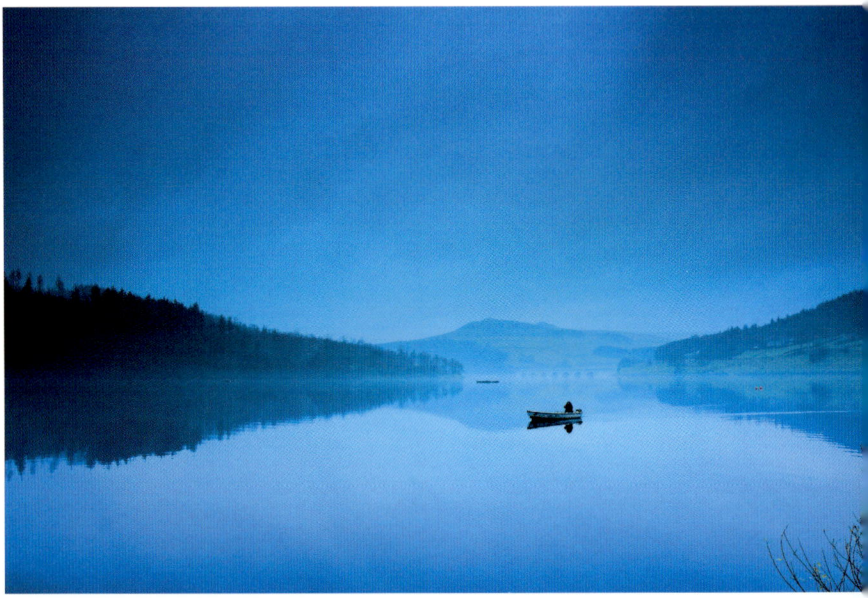

Simply changing the white balance setting has given this image three completely different effects. Cool: Setting the white balance to Incandescent (3,000K) has given the image a very cold feel. It is an extremely effective look for conveying a sense of isolation and space, but makes the scene appear uninviting.

Tip

The simplest way to change the overall mood of images is to use the white balance setting on your digital camera, or to use color filters. When shooting JPEG images, you should use the setting to give the effect that you want at the time of shooting. Shooting RAW, you can change this setting later on, but it can be difficult to visualize the effect. To allow you to see the effect when you review your images on the rear LCD, set the white balance at the time of shooting and use the versatility of changing the setting later on to fine-tune the color.

Tip

Using colors to convey mood does not mean that the whole scene has to be a single color, although this certainly makes it easier. Even the inclusion of red in an otherwise cool scene does not destroy the overall feel of the image. In fact, just like using complementary colors, this contrast can add impact to your images.

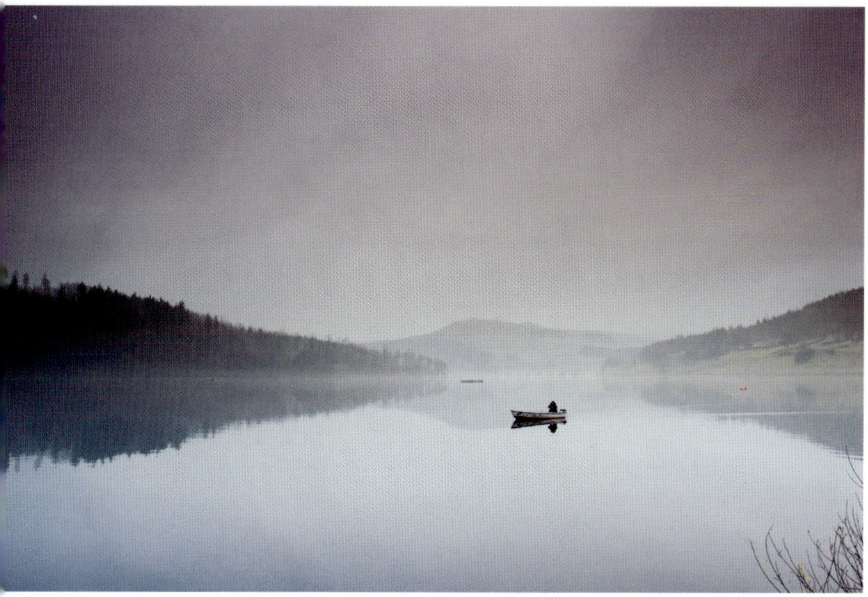

As the permutations of these mood options are almost endless, we will deal with the three main moods you can create using warm, cool, and neutral colors. Once you have mastered these you will have the building blocks to go and create your own images, and even to see the world in new ways.

Neutral: Because of the lack of color in the actual scene, using the "correct" Cloudy (6,000K) setting still gives quite a stark image. But this is an accurate ndition of what we saw, and the neutral ne gives an almost black-and-white look the image.

Warm: Setting the white balance to Shade (7,000K) gives a much warmer feel to the shot. It results in a much more welcoming scene, and compared to the her images, it is the one that most people ould choose as their favorite.

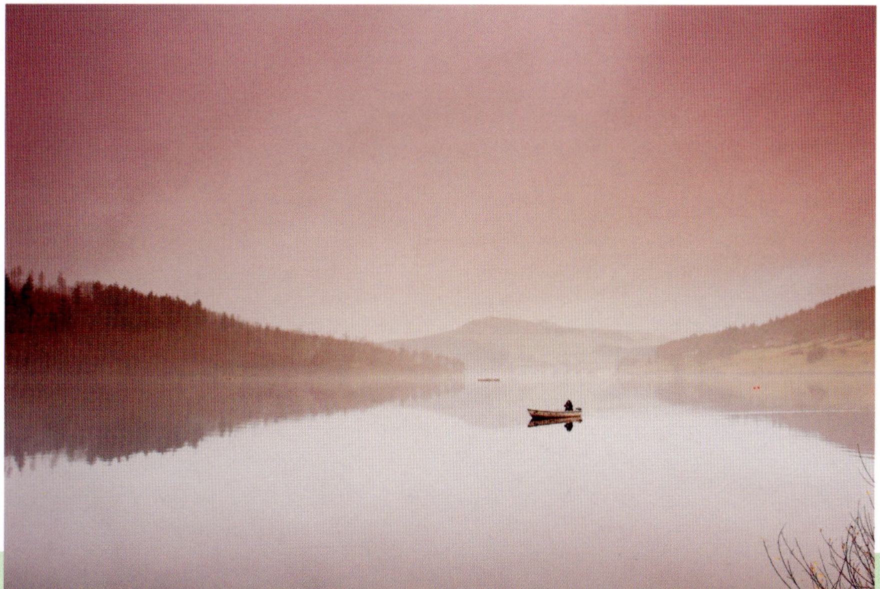

Warm Colors

Most people prefer images that have a warm overall color. These colors make us feel more comfortable, evoke emotions of safety, and generally make us happy. Landscape and portrait photographers have for years used the trick of adding warmth to make their images more appealing.

Adding subtle warmth to your images is quite simple. For example, shooting when the sun is low in the sky tends to produce warmer light than during the middle of the day. Using a white balance setting with a color temperature higher than the ambient light (such as a Cloudy 6,000K setting in Daylight 5,500K) will give your image a warmer tone.

Case Study

When shooting this flower from a wider view, much of the intensity of the bright orange petals was lost, so I excluded everything around it and filled the frame with these warm hues. The result looks as if it were shot using a colored filter, but the colors are an accurate representation of the subject. Using a wide (f/4) aperture and focusing on the water droplets meant that the background petals became blurred and indistinct. This allows the image to convey the color without drawing too much attention away from the main point of focus, which is important when dealing with such vibrant colors.

Finding a subject with a naturally warm color produces images that are more appealing than cooler colors.

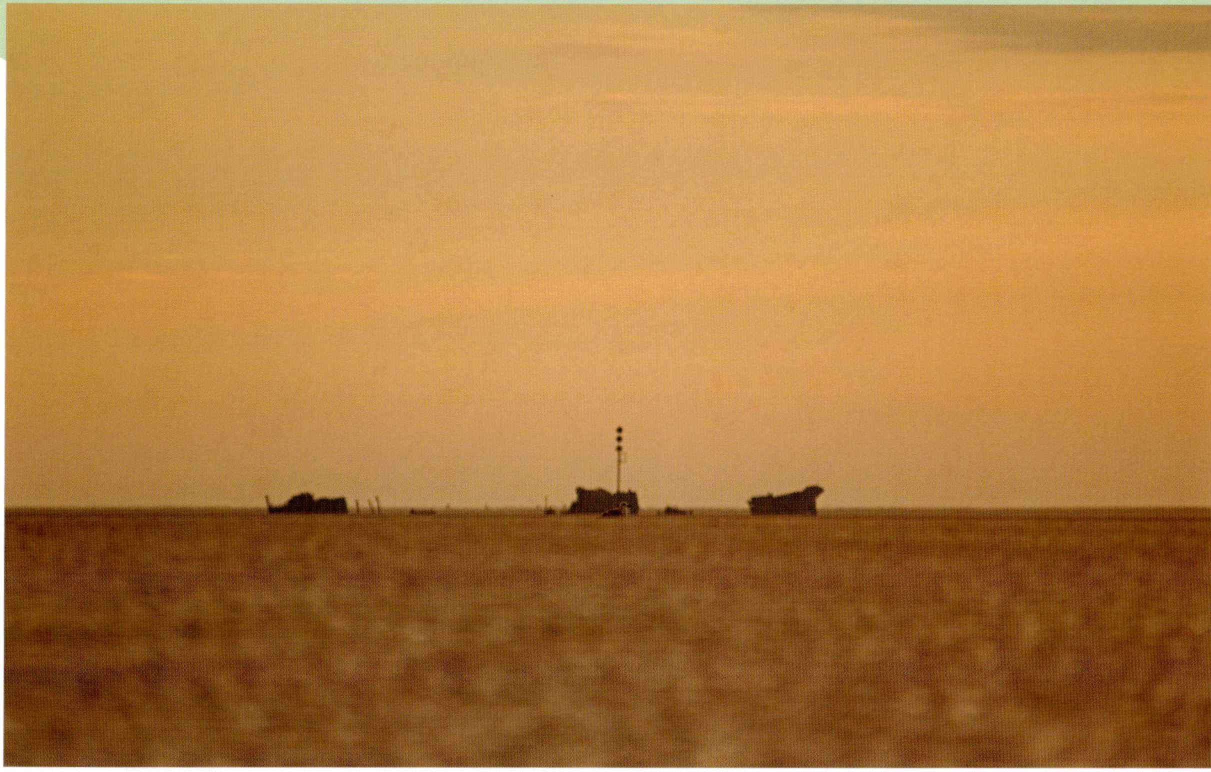

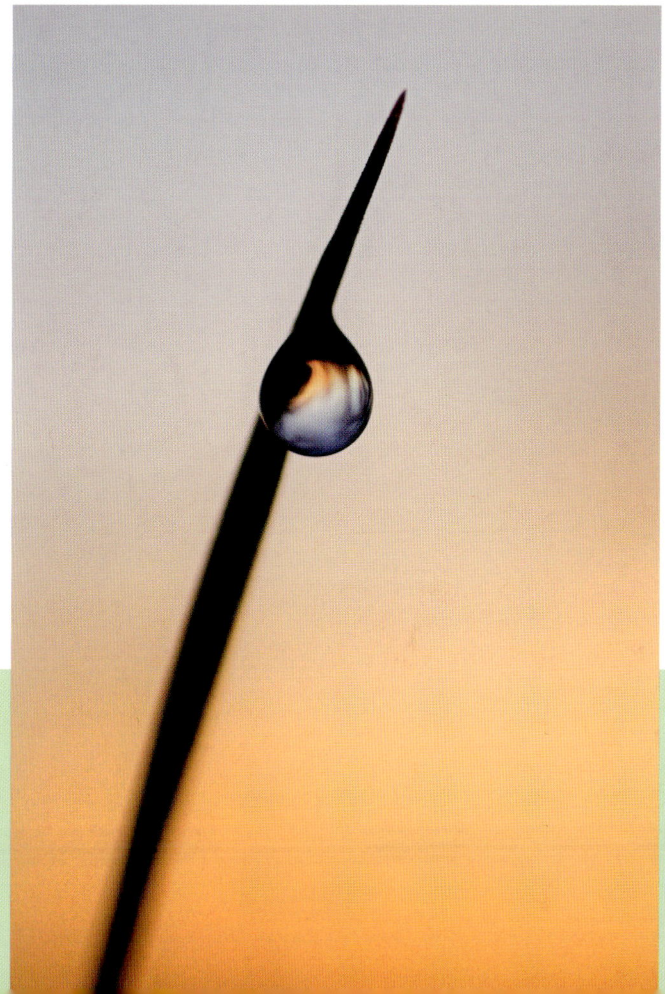

A more traditional use of a warm color mood, this image of stranded boats on a beach against the sunset belies the fact that it was actually very cold and bleak when I shot the image.

Using the warm tones of the sky at sunrise as a background adds a warm look to this image of dew on a blade of grass.

Cool Colors

The look and feel of cold images are generally less appealing than neutral or warm tones. Most people feel slightly uncomfortable when faced with a cool-looking image, and this is especially true of portraits. Cool-looking skin tones are associated with ill-health, or even death, so they are best avoided for many images. This does not mean that you should ignore the power that cool tones can have in your images, however.

Conveying a feeling of cold and isolation in a bleak landscape is a classic use of cool-tones. Shooting before dawn or after dusk can produce the most startling results, as the lack of direct sunlight can give an otherworldly feel to your shot. Alternatively, use this technique in heavy fog or mist for a really stark look.

To give your image a cool tone, use a white balance setting with a color temperature lower than the light that you are shooting in (in daylight 5,500K, use an Incandescent 3,000K setting, for example).

Case Study

This image was taken on a deserted beach just before dawn on a cold, bleak winter's day. This cold scene called out for a treatment that would emphasize the sense of isolation and bleakness that I felt at the time. I set the white balance of the camera to Tungsten to ensure that I achieved the cool look that I sought.

The unsettling feel was enhanced by placing the solitary post in the center of the frame, rather than the more conventional positioning to one side for a more balanced composition. This may not be a common approach for most landscapes, but with the right subject using cool tones can produce attention-grabbing images.

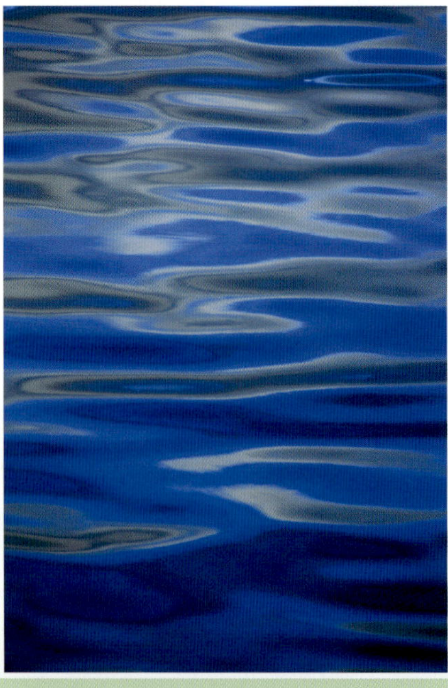

Water is a natural subject for using cool tones. Using the reflection of a pure blue sky in the water enhances the impression of simplicity in this image.

This is not a welcoming image, but using cool tones can enhance the feeling of space in landscape photographs.

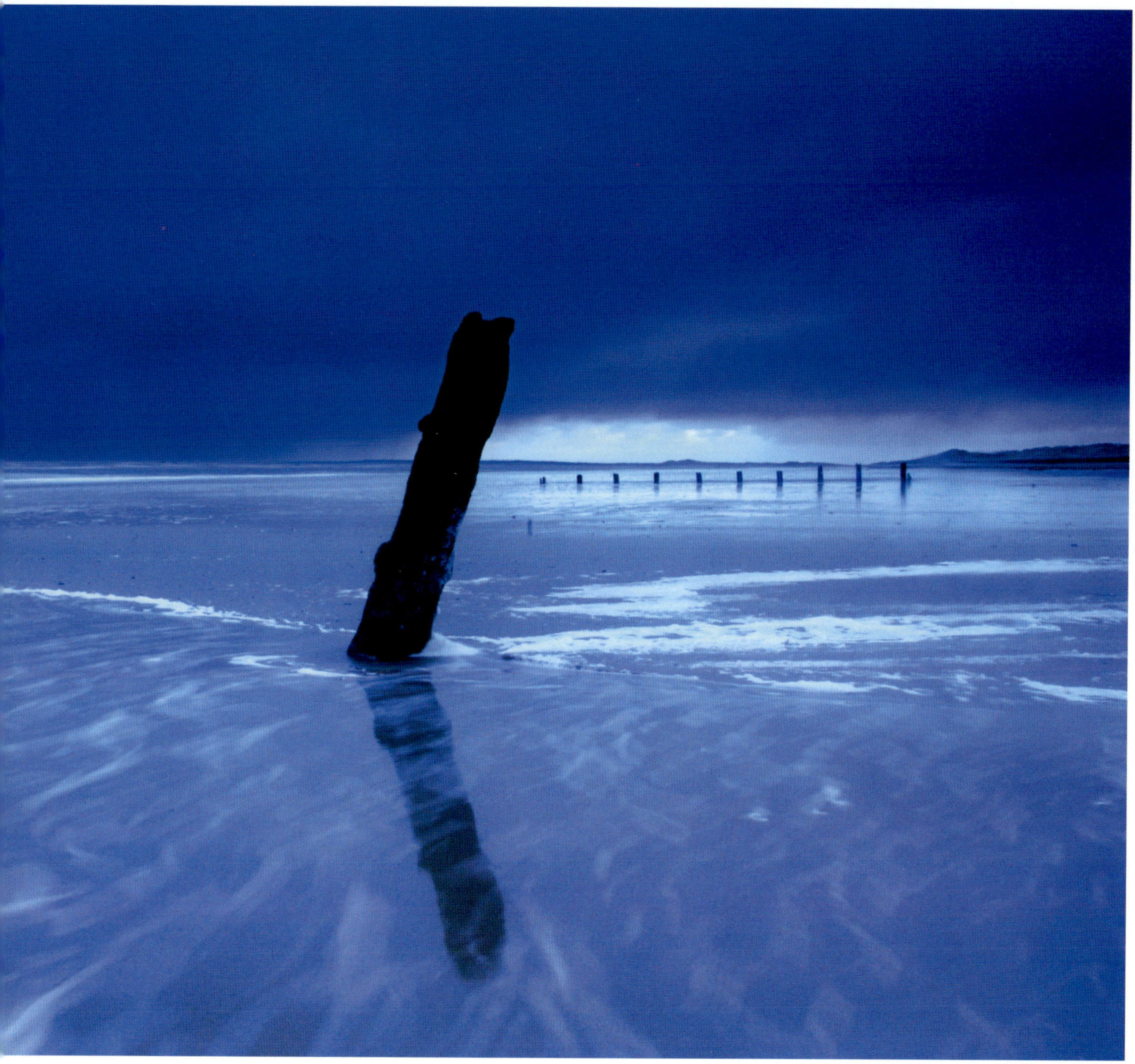

Finding subjects without color can prove difficult, but it's certainly not impossible. This flowing stream in heavy shade produced an image that was almost pure black and white without any adjustments to the saturation.

Neutral Colors

It may seem odd to include a section that relies on the absence of color in this book, but this can be just as powerful as the most vibrant and colorful image. Neutral colors can be used to impart an air of simplicity and purity to your images, such as shooting a portrait against a pure white background. Although there may be some color in the subject, it is the overall look of the image that produce a neutral feel. It concentrates all the attention on the main subject, as there are no colors to confuse the viewer.

There are two ways in which you can achieve a neutral look to your images. The first requires similar skills to those needed for black-and-white photography, as it involves removing the colors from a scene by reducing the saturation. This can be most easily achieved by reducing the saturation of your image in imaging software.

The second involves finding subjects or backgrounds that are already a neutral color. In outdoor photography this can be very difficult, as even the most neutral-looking natural objects, such as rocks or mist, tend to have a color or colors present. It is not impossible, though when it comes to using neutral backgrounds your best bet is to use manmade objects. For small subjects, a simple piece of card or paper makes a superb option. Alternatively, full-scale studio backdrops are available for producing simple portraits.

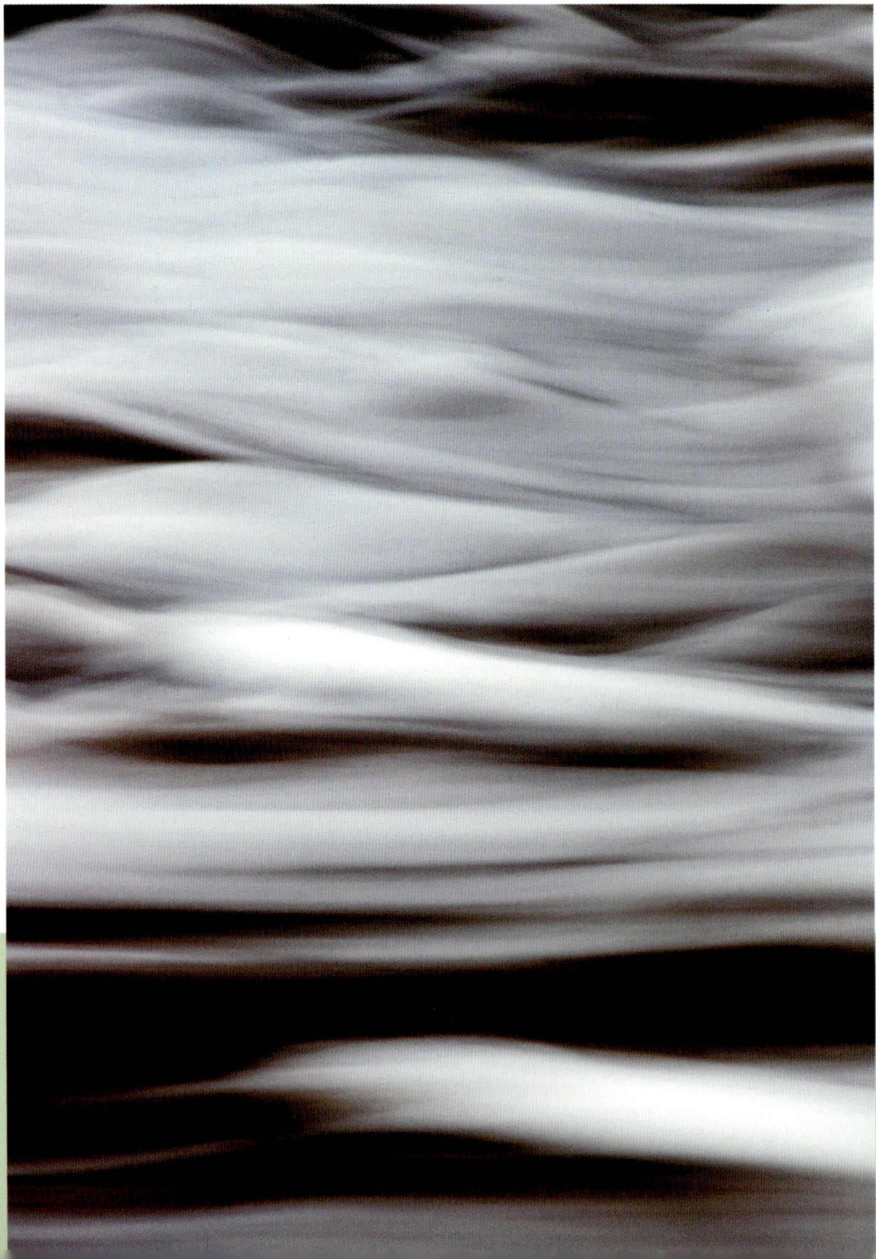

With this backlit plant, I needed to search hard to find an area of deep shadow to use as a black background to eliminate the color of the plants around the subject.

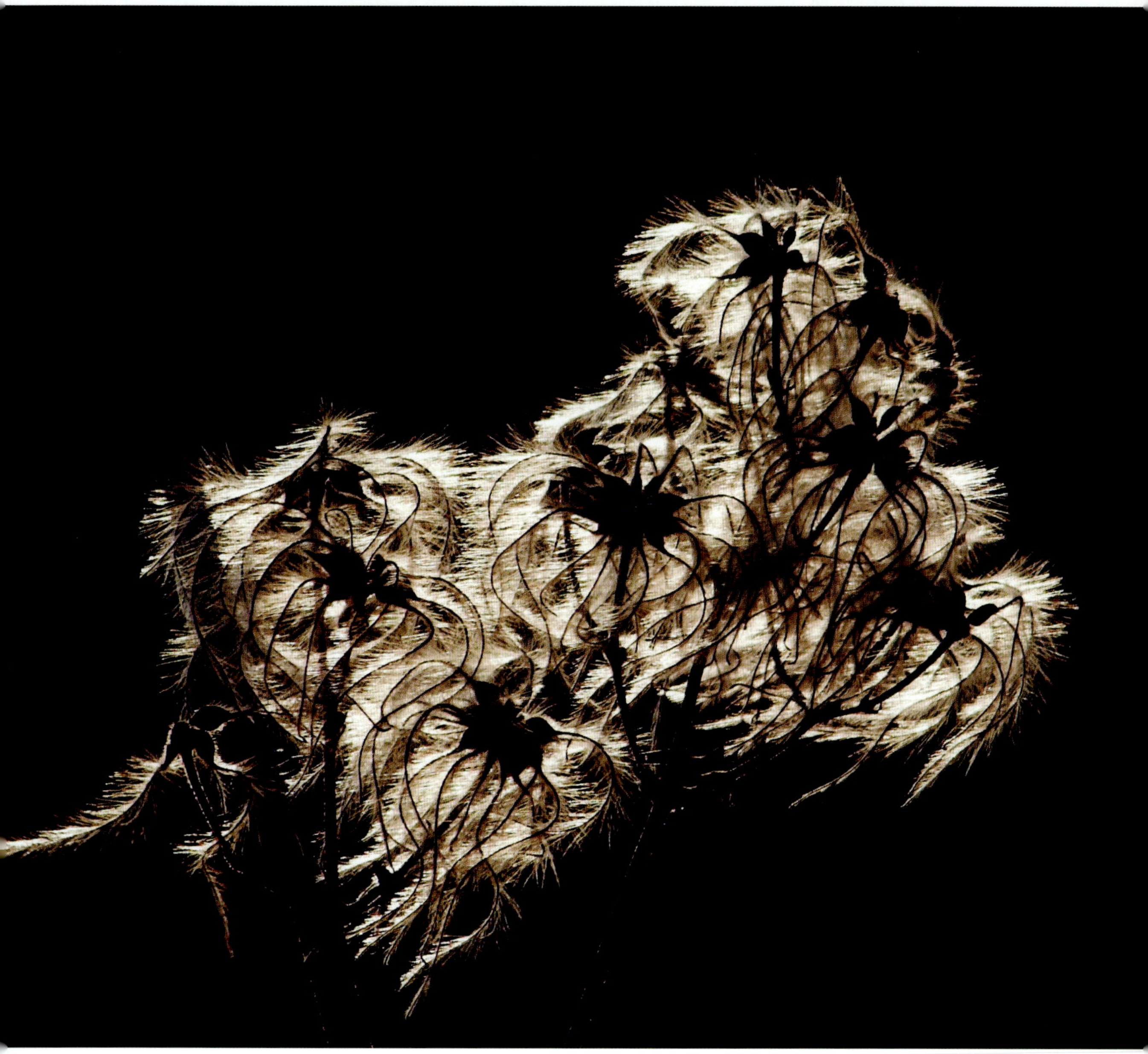

Capturing Seasonal Color

In the modern world, we are increasingly detached from the cycles of nature. With modern houses insulated against the cold of winter and air-conditioned to keep us cool in the summer, it is easy to think that we have tamed nature. But nature and landscape photography are all about being in tune with nature and what is happening in the world outside our homes and offices.

In the following pages, we explore how you can make the most of the colors, lighting, and atmosphere of each of the four seasons. In warmer climates you may not experience really wintry conditions, but the advice for summer will be useful throughout the year.

In temperate climates, the changing seasons bring their own color palettes and photographic challenges. Despite these, it is often the cycle of seasonal changes that brings some of the most spectacular and rewarding photographic experiences.

Whether you are shooting nature, animals, landscapes, or outdoor portraits, the quality of the light plays a massive part in the success or failure of your images. Knowing how to deal with the changing conditions throughout the year will help you to improve the color and impact of your images. Even before you pick up your camera, look at the lighting: is it sunny or cloudy? Is the sun high in the sky or near the horizon? All of these factors will affect your images.

My first advice for this type of photography is to get out and experience as many of the conditions that nature can throw at you. I am not talking about putting yourself in dangerous situations; simply take time to see how the seasons affect the world around you. For me (and most outdoor photographers), photography is a great excuse for getting out into the open away from the pressures of modern life, and capturing some great images too.

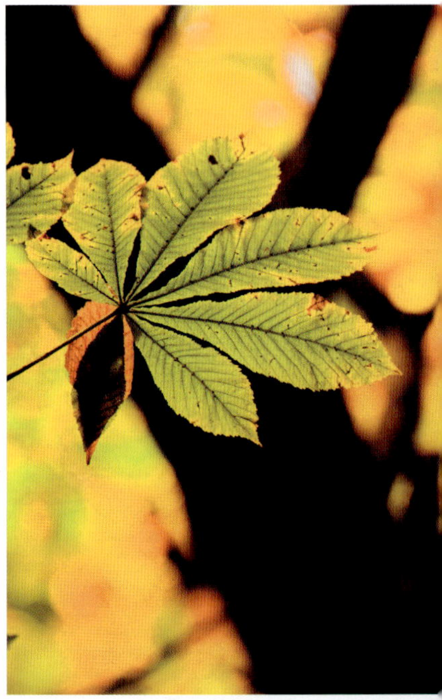

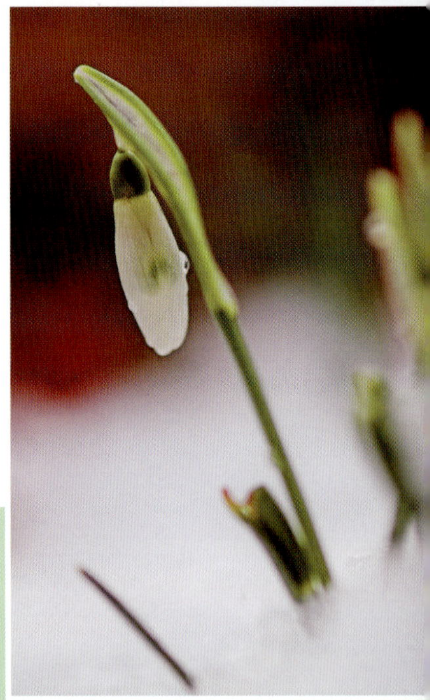

The changing conditions throughout the year can pose unique problems for outdoor photography. How you approach these challenges will make or break your photography. Try to work with nature nd you will be rewarded with images that really apture the moods and colors of each season. Try to go ut in the middle of winter looking for bright, colorful ubjects, for example, and you are likely to come ome disappointed.

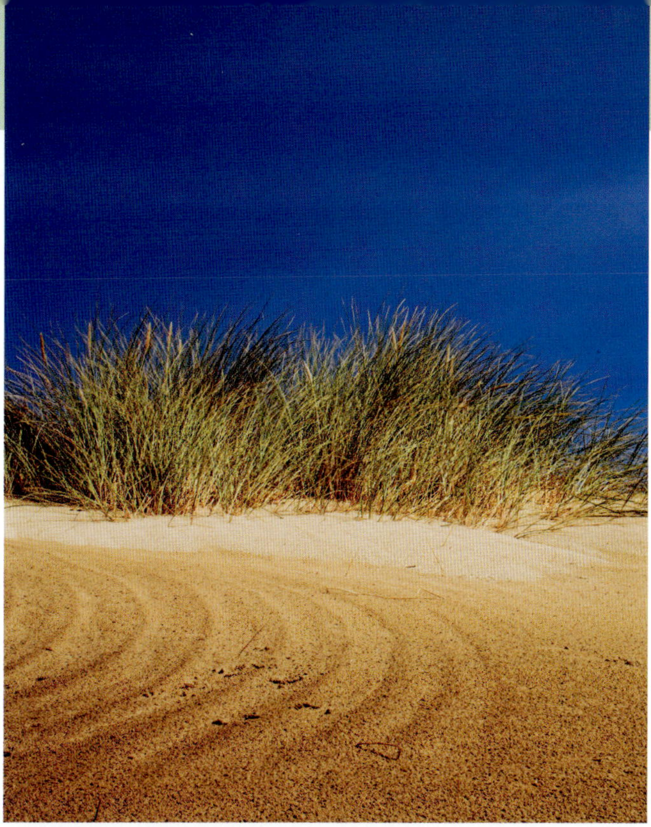

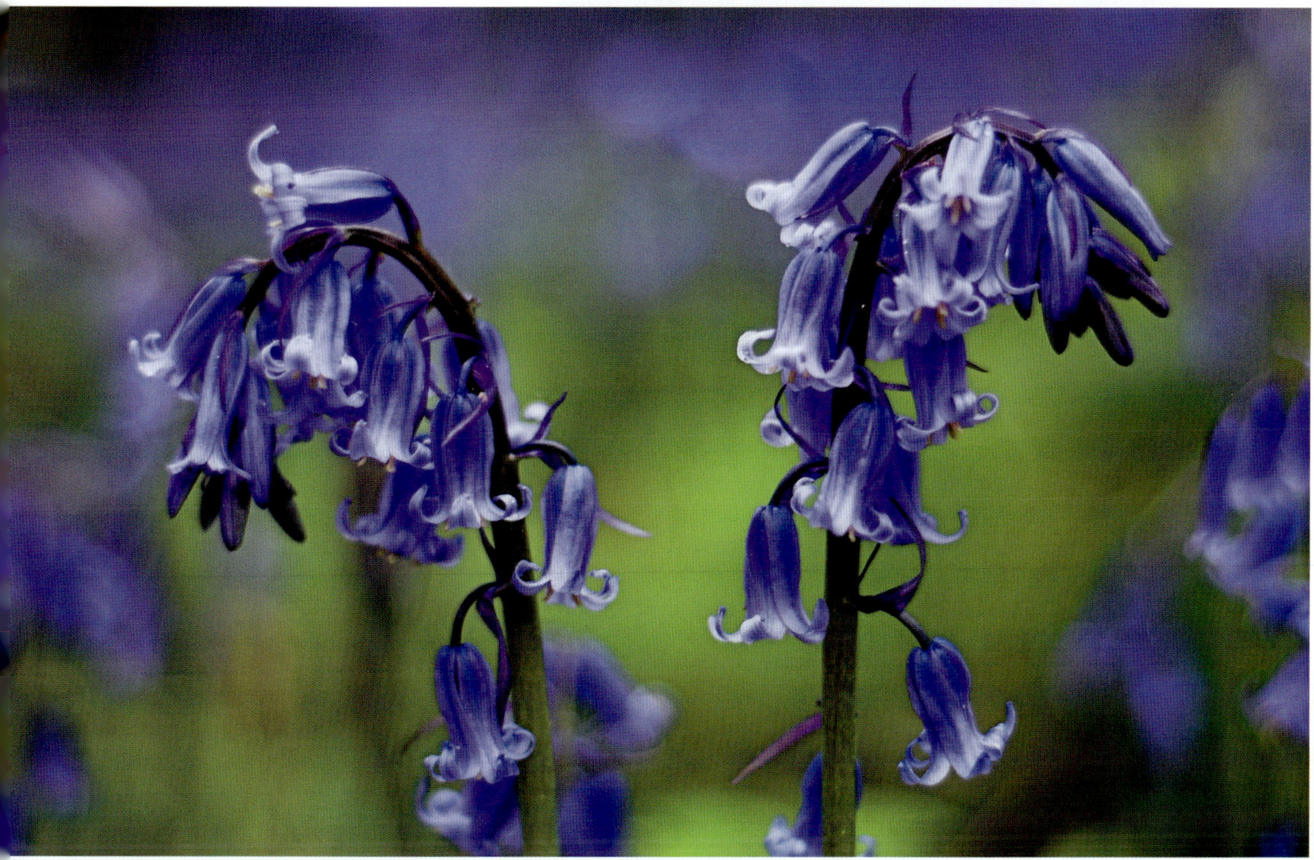

Fall Colors

This season has long been a favorite with poets, artists, and, more recently, photographers. It is the transition from the predominant green of summer to the golden tones of yellows, reds, and browns that makes this season such a fruitful season for photography. As well as the obvious changes in the colors, it is also the quality of the light at this time of year that makes a significant difference. The sun tends to be lower in the sky and is often less harsh than during the summer months.

Shooting early in the morning or late evening will add even more warmth to the color of fall foliage. In these conditions, warm-up filters will prove unnecessary as you can let nature take control. Similarly, on digital cameras setting the white balance to daylight will give your images a subtle warm tone.

When the sun is higher in the sky during the middle of the day the higher color temperature makes your images appear more blue. This cooler light is not the best for capturing fall colors. You can compensate for this by using a Cloudy white balance setting, or by adding an 81A warm-up filter.

Overcast or misty days at this time of year are ideal for capturing waterfalls and details in the landscape. The softer, lower-contrast lighting means that both film and digital can retain much more detail in the highlights and shadows. To make the most of these conditions, use a polarizing filter to cut out any reflections off the foliage and add extra saturation to the colors.

Fall is also a great time for insect photography, especially the vibrant and colorful dragonflies. The cooler weather means that they are less active and more easily approached. Choose a white balance setting to suit the lighting conditions to record the colors as accurately as possible. Although you do not have any direct control over the background, it can make or break this type of image. Look out for background colors that are complementary to the colors of your subject to make them stand out as much as possible. If the insect has red markings, look for some green foliage as a backdrop; for blue, look out for yellow or warm fall colors.

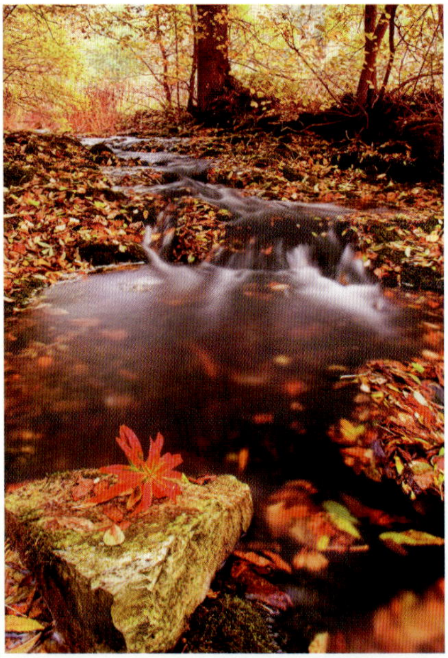

The warm colors in this fall scene were enhanced by using a Cloudy white balance setting on the camera.

Tips for Shooting in Fall

- Shoot in early morning or evening light for warm colors.
- During the middle of the day use a Cloudy white balance setting or 81A warm-up filter to enhance the warm colors.
- Try shooting fall foliage with the light behind the subject to bring out the colors.

Case Study

Woodland is the natural place to head for during the fall months; the colors and tones of the foliage make it one of the most amazing times of the year for photography. Rather than try to capture the whole woodland, I chose this particular tree because of the superb range of colors. However, shooting it from a "normal" horizontal position did not do justice to the scene. By shooting up into the light, the full glory of the foliage was much more evident, so I used the shape of the trunk and branches to create a dynamic diagonal composition. Adding a polarizing filter enhanced the colors even further.

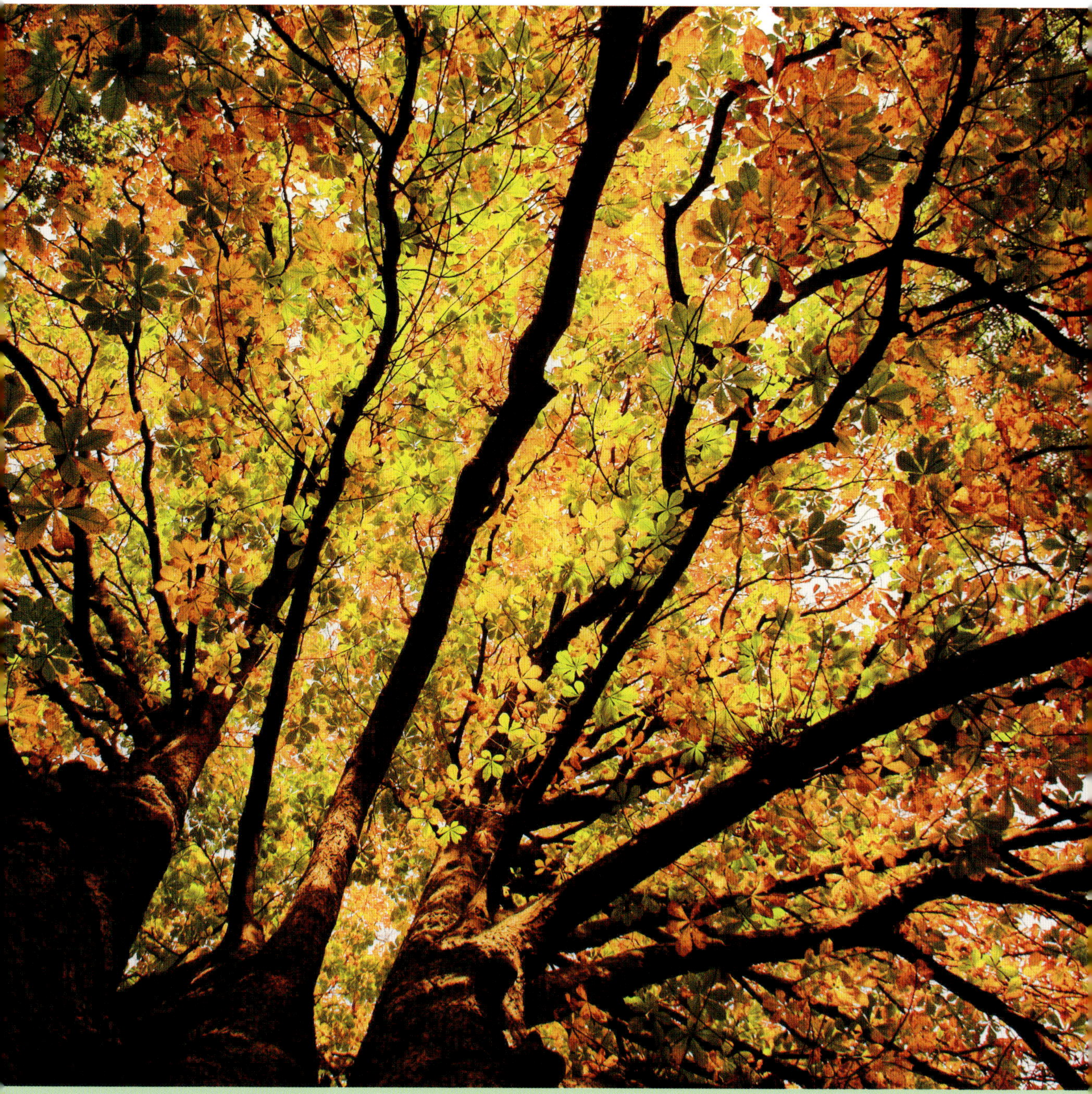

Shooting into the light can enhance the colors of fall foliage.

The drab colors and lack of foliage can be used to your advantage when shooting wildlife images in winter, as they make the few splashes of color that nature does provide easier to spot and photograph.

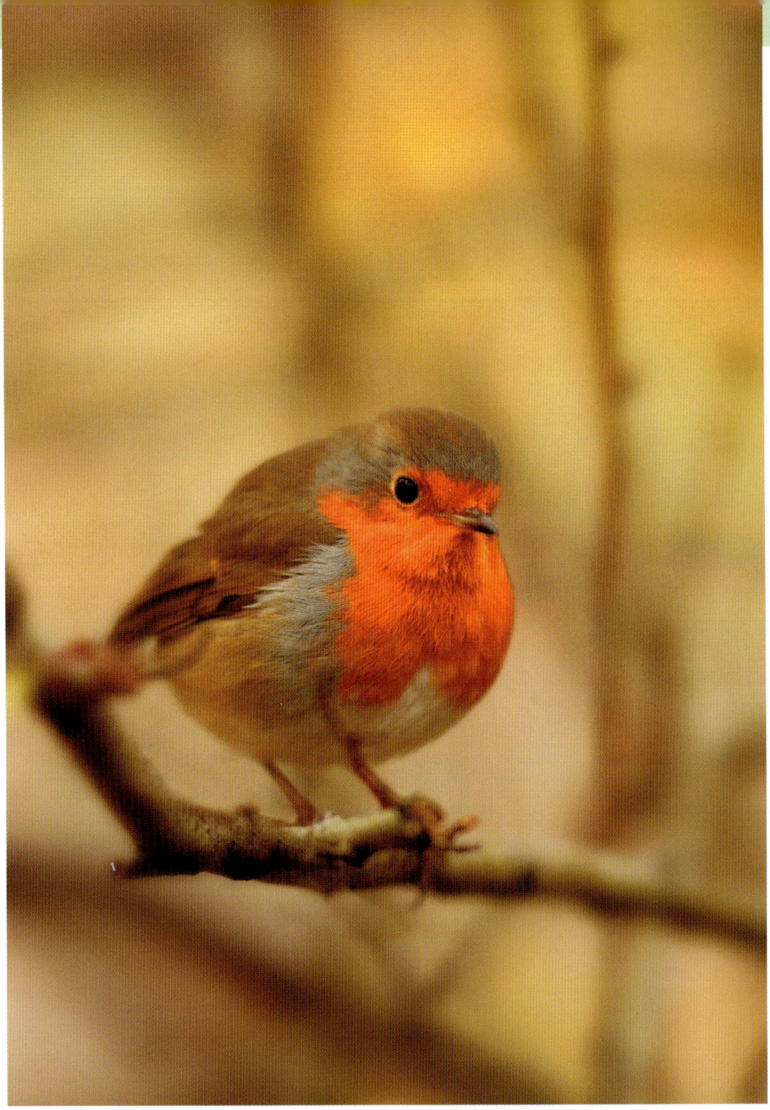

Winter Colors

It is lazy to think of the winter months as a time for putting the camera away and staying indoors. For those willing to put up with the cold there are a host of photographic opportunities that are well worth the effort.

Many of the most colorful plants and animals will be absent, but those that are present are often easier to see or approach at this time of year. The lack of dense foliage makes spotting subjects easier, and the drab colors make the perfect backdrop for maximizing the impact of the main subject.

Snow may turn almost every scene into a picture-postcard view, but photographing it can cause problems. The first is exposure. A predominantly white subject will fool even the most sophisticated metering system, causing the image to be underexposed. This will result in the snow being recorded as a murky gray. The amount of compensation needed will depend on how much snow there is in the frame. For a light covering with some foliage showing through, add an extra stop of exposure compensation; for a heavy covering, try up to 2 stops.

Although we see snow as pure white, this is not necessarily how your camera or film will record it. Unlike most landscape images, this is one subject that will benefit from a cooler white balance than would normally be used. In sunny conditions use the Daylight setting, while you could go for an even cooler look by using the Incandescent lighting setting.

Tips for Shooting in Winter

- When shooting snow scenes set your camera to overexpose by 1 to 2 stops.
- Look out for the few splashes of color that nature provides, and use them.
- Use a cooler white balance setting than normal to enhance the impression of the cold.

Case Study

With snow covering the ground and bright, white clouds in the sky, the metering of the camera struggled to get the right exposure in this winter scene. Without adjusting the camera, the snow was recorded as dull gray, so I used the exposure compensation facility to increase the exposure by $1\frac{1}{2}$ stops to brighten the image. Having taken the shot, I then reviewed the image on the rear LCD of the camera and checked the histogram display to ensure that the highlight detail was still within the limits of the graph. For film capture, it pays to take a series of different exposures (known as bracketing). On slide film, use half-stop increases in exposure for up to 2 stops.

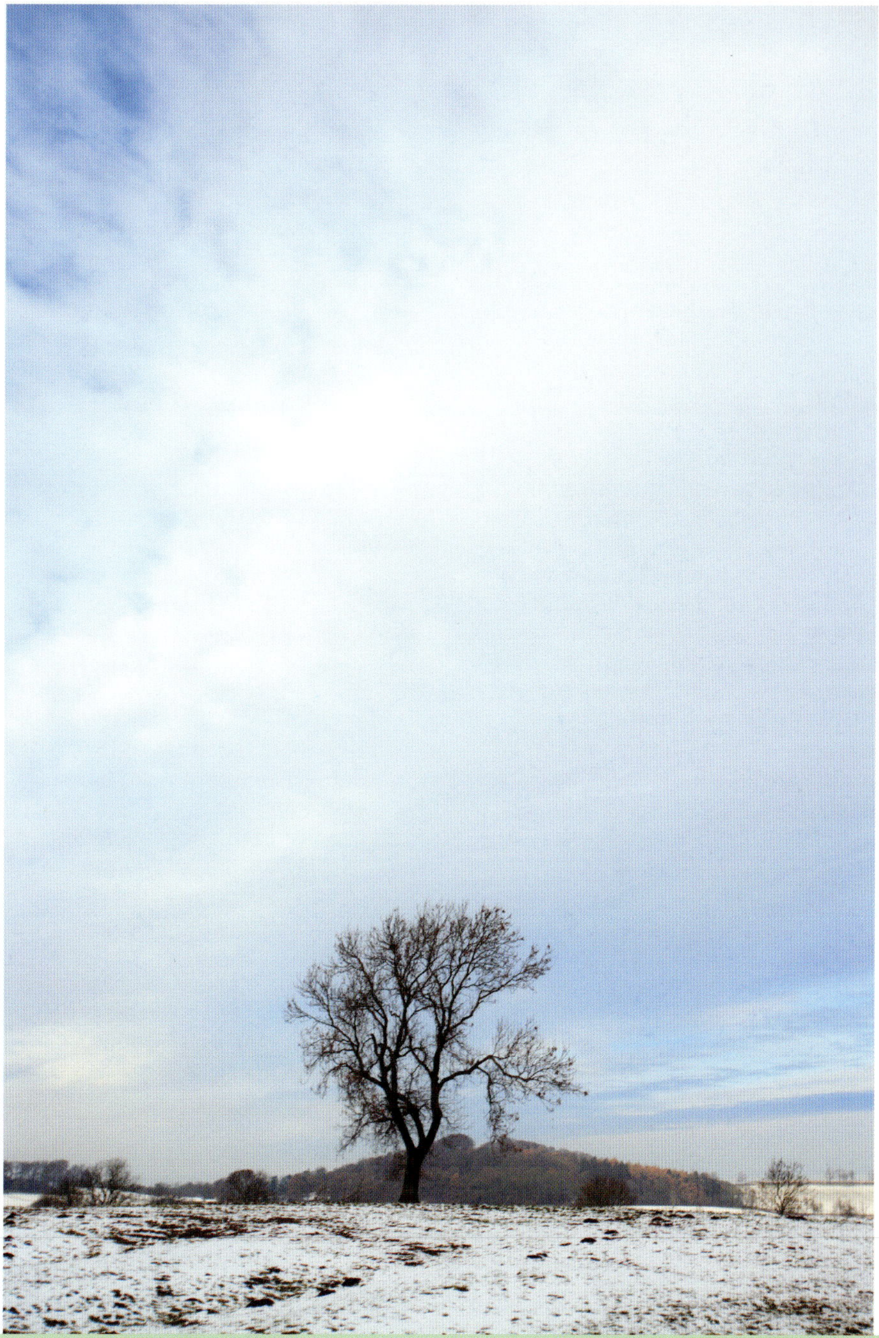

Snow can fool even the most sophisticated exposure systems into under exposing your images.

Spring Colors

When nature finally bursts back into life in the spring, the riot of colors brings a whole range of photographic opportunities. The key to getting great spring images is capturing the fresh colors and crisp light.

Many of the first spring flowers such as snowdrops are mainly white or of muted colors. But even these can prove a great subject. Try contrasting these flowers with the first green shoots for maximum impact. A late snowfall or frost can produce an almost monochrome look in your images. With so much white in the subject, take care to avoid obvious color casts. To record the colors accurately, match the white balance to the lighting conditions. For example, if you are shooting in sunlight, use a Daylight white balance setting.

As the season progresses, you may find more yellow flowers appearing. To capture these flowers with maximum impact, try shooting from a low viewpoint and use the contrast between the yellow bloom against a pure blue sky. A polarizing filter will help to increase the saturation of both flower and sky.

Capturing yellow and green tones poses few problems, but blue flowers can be difficult to record accurately, particularly on film. Shooting blue flowers is best done on bright days with a clear blue sky, but avoid shooting in direct sunlight. Getting the right color on digital is easier. For accuracy, use a manual white balance setting for the lighting conditions (usually daylight) rather than automatic as this can be fooled by the large amount of green and blue within the frame.

Tips for Shooting in Spring

- Try to shoot flower close-ups on bright days, but avoid blooms in direct sunlight.
- Spring is a great time for shooting in woodland, as the foliage tends to be lighter and less dense than in the summer months.
- Use the bright, clear light to shoot landscapes, but avoid using warm-up techniques as this can make the spring colors look dull and muddy.

Case Study

The dappled light streaming through fresh spring foliage can be difficult to capture accurately. Unlike most of my outdoor photography, I wanted to avoid making this scene look too warm, as this would destroy the color of the leaves. Therefore, I set the white balance of the camera to Daylight to retain the fresh greens.

Although the image was an accurate rendition of the scene, it lacked some of the atmosphere that attracted me in the first place. I decided to add a weak soft-focus filter to the camera to soften the highlights and add some sparkle to the image. As a final touch, back at the computer, I added extra saturation to the image in Photoshop to add even more punch to the colors.

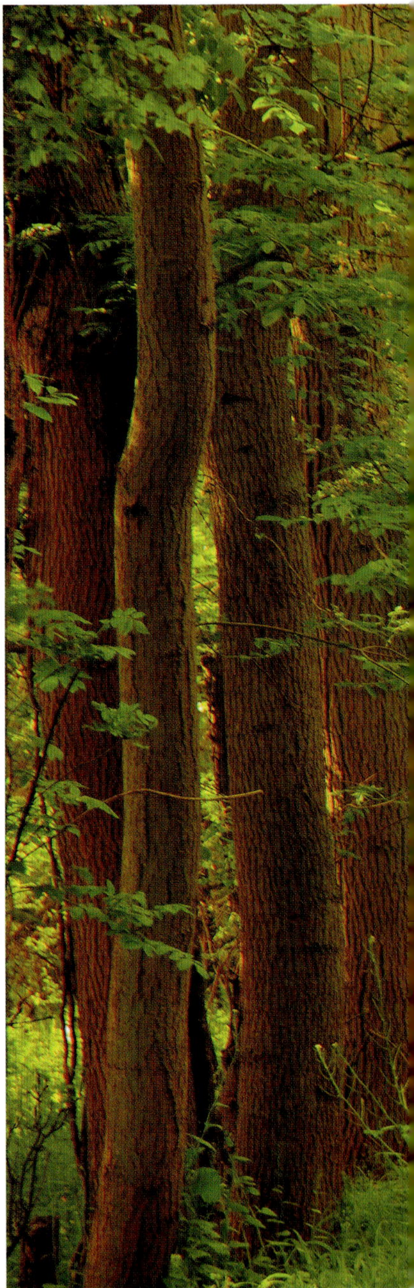

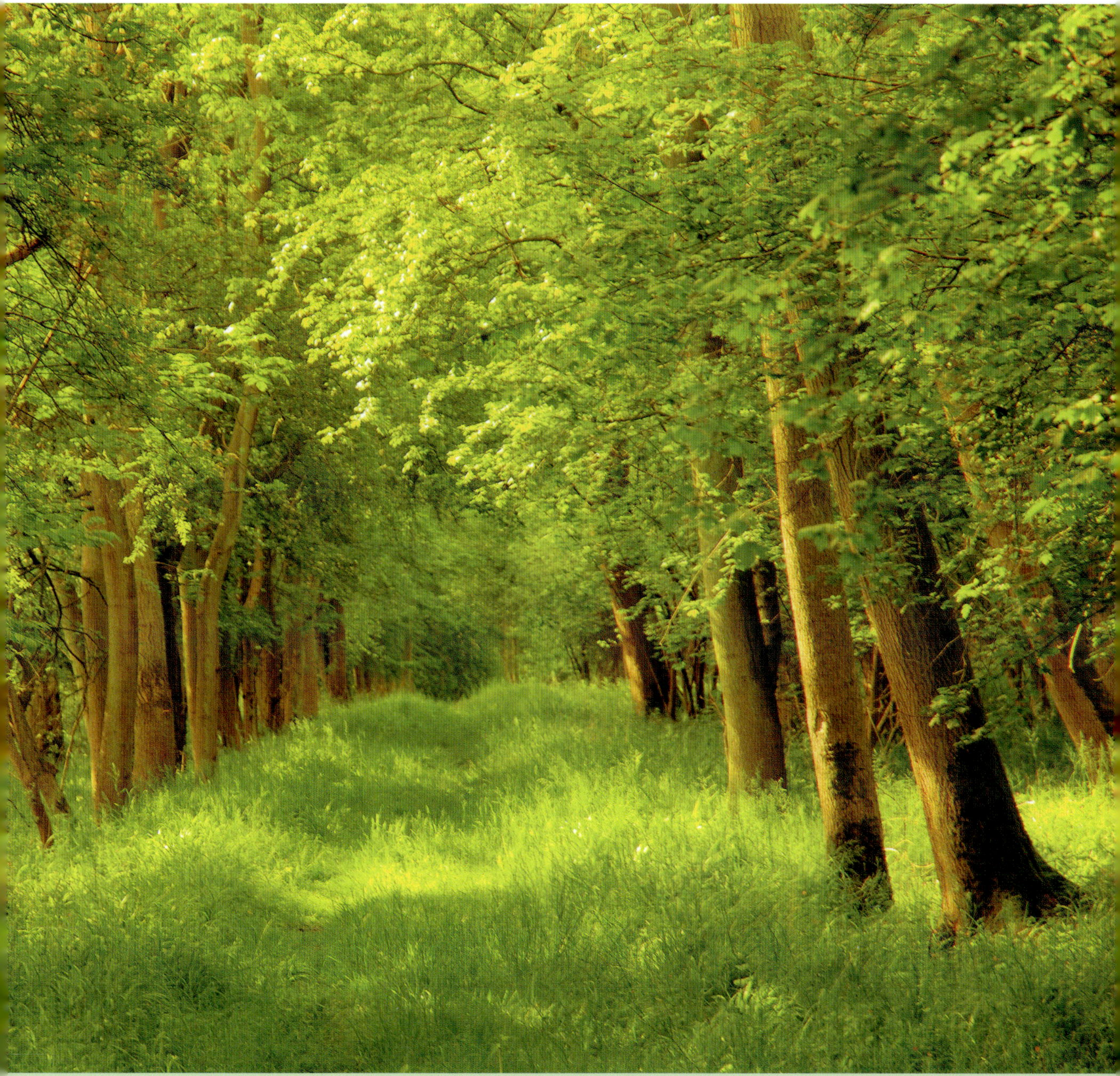

Summer Colors

With plenty of sunshine and nature in full bloom, summer would seem the ideal time for photographing color. The warmer weather can often cause haze to build up in the atmosphere, however, giving flat light and dull skies. In these conditions, look for details rather than shoot the wider landscape. By excluding the sky from your images you can concentrate on finding color contrasts or harmonies that work well together.

When the sky is clear, the sun during the summer months can be very harsh. This high-contrast light produces very dark shadows and bright highlights. Both film and digital cameras struggle to record detail in both, which can produce problems when trying to capture color. In these conditions, it is usually best to expose for the highlight areas for colorful results, as these will be in full sunlight and give the strongest color saturation. A polarizing filter will help cut down the reflections off many subjects and help to increase the color saturation even further.

Like any time of year, much of the best light for photography is just after sunrise and just before sunset. In summer, sunrise can be so early that it is out of the question for all but the most dedicated photographers. The hour or so before sunset is usually the more convenient time to use the low angle and warmer light during the summer, although the problems with haze can still be a challenge, producing very flat-looking results.

Tips for Shooting in Summer

- In bright sunlight use a polarizing filter to help cut down on reflections.
- On bright, hazy days try to exclude dull skies in your images.
- On days with a clear blue sky look for simple graphic images using the sky as a backdrop.

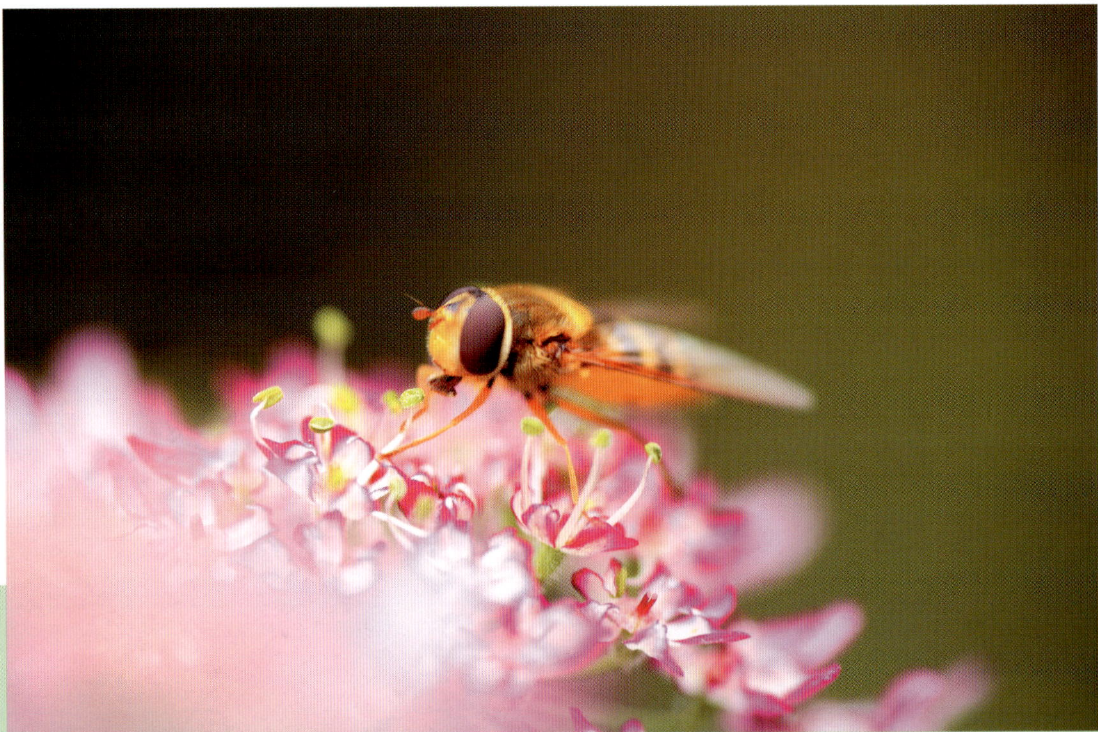

« With nature in full bloom, summer is a great time for shooting details such as flowers and insects. Look out for color contrasts to make your images really stand out.

:ase Study

urprisingly, the height of summer can ctually be one of the most difficult imes of the year for photographing olor. When the sun is high in the ky the lighting is often too harsh or great landscapes, and heat haze uickly builds up to make the sky ull and lacking in color. For this nage of summer poppies, I decided o concentrate on the amazing color f the flower rather than the wider ındscape. Using the dark shadows reated by the bright sunshine as a ackdrop made the red of the poppy lmost jump out of the scene, as lack and red create one of the most owerful color contrasts. Using a wide perture (f/4) on a 200mm lens has ırown the flowers in the background ut of focus, creating just a blur of olor to give the impression of summer reens and reds.

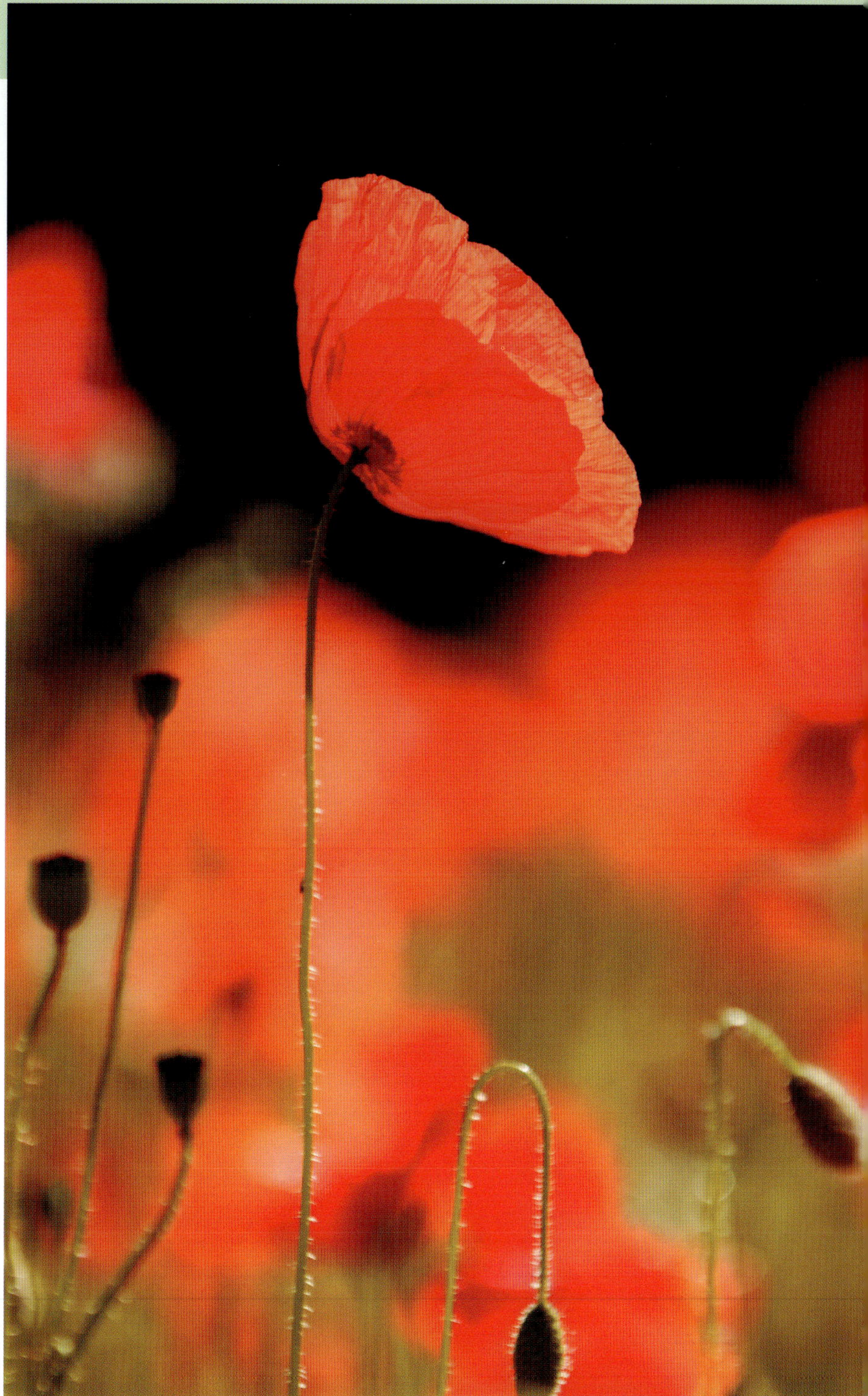

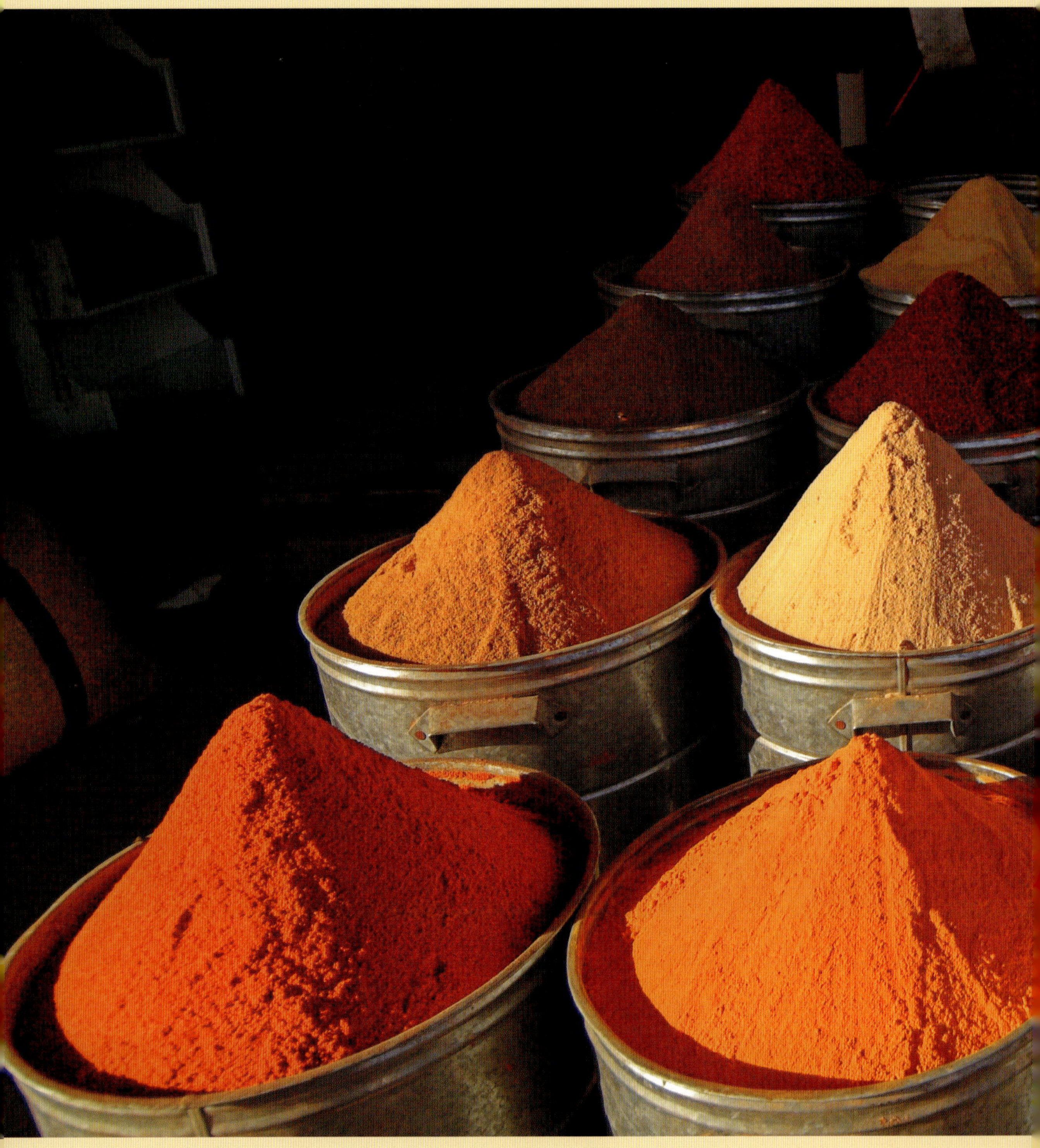

Digital Manipulation

08

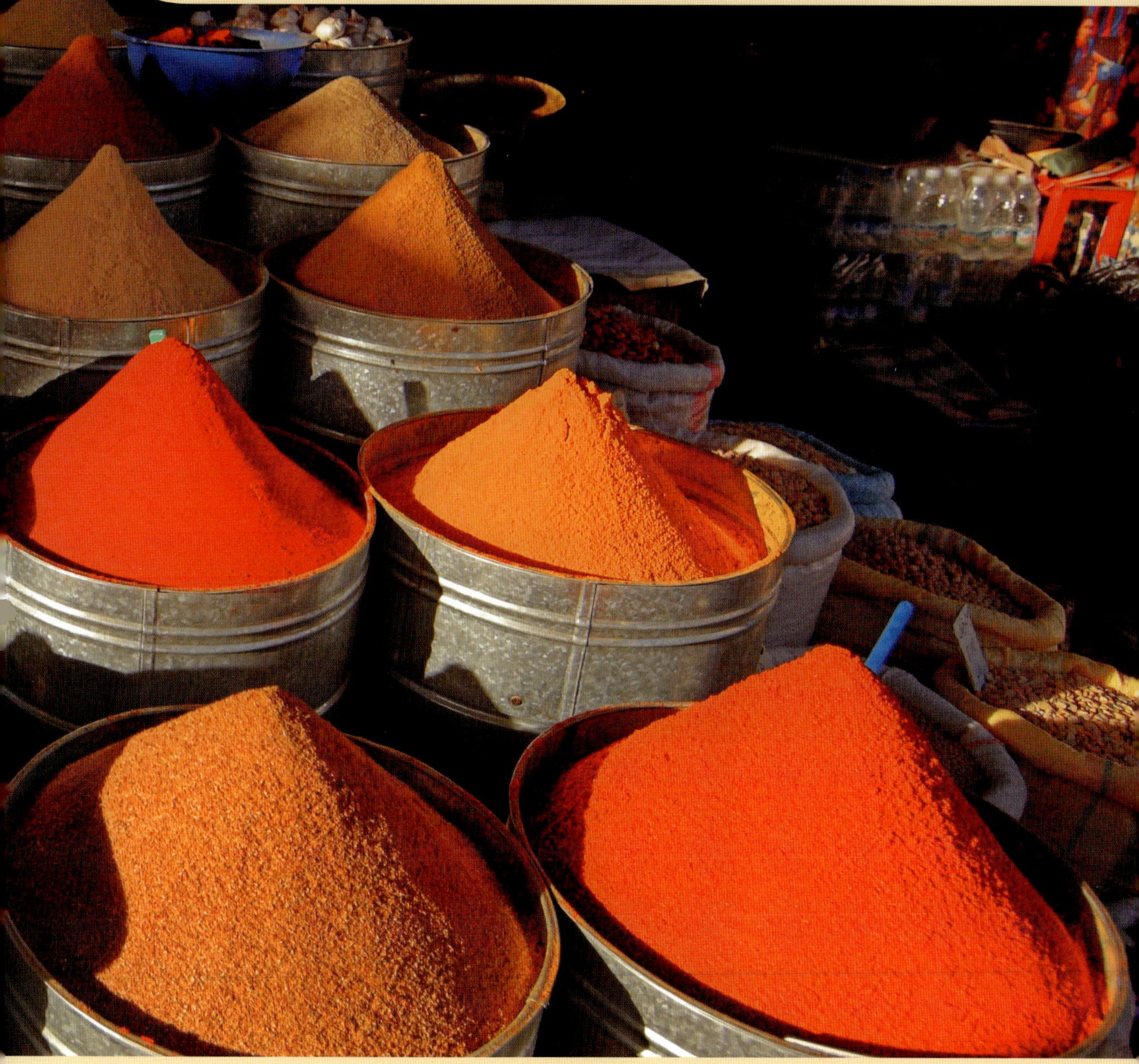

Color Balancing

In this section, we cover the main challenges that you will face in making the most of the powerful tools available in image-editing software—from simple adjustments that can be done in minutes, to more complicated procedures for exploring the full range of color possibilities that the software offers. We start with the method for obtaining the correct colors by using the color-balancing controls.

Color casts are one of the most common problems faced by the digital photographer. These can be as simple as an incorrect white balance setting selected when you shot the photograph (or the automatic white balance getting it wrong), to the more complicated problems encountered when different tonal areas of the image, such as shadows, take on the colors around them.

There are almost endless ways in which color casts can be corrected in Photoshop and similar programs; here are the most useful that I have found when dealing with the most common problems.

Auto Color

This is one of the "forgotten" functions that is a good first resort when you are looking for a quick and easy solution to color-balance problems. It is found under the main menu by going to Image › Adjustments › Auto Color. Like all automatic features, it does not get it right every time, but it can produce great results. However, do not rely on this facility for every situation and color problem that you face.

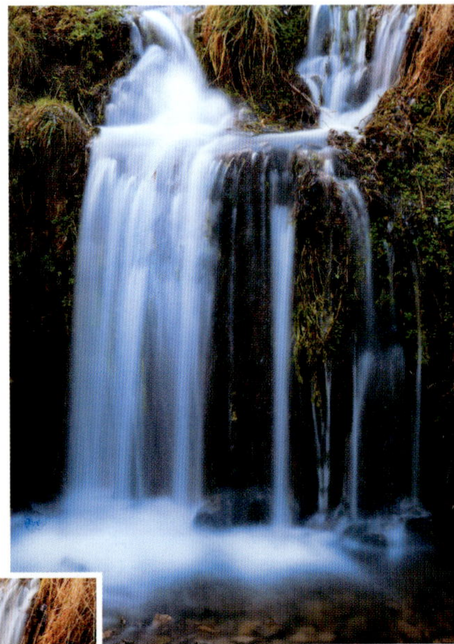

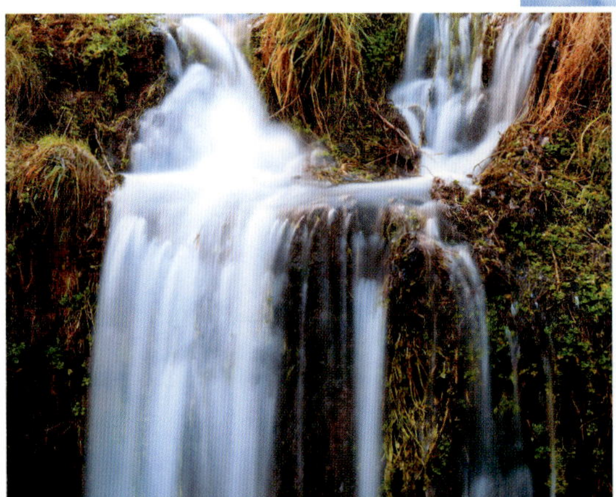

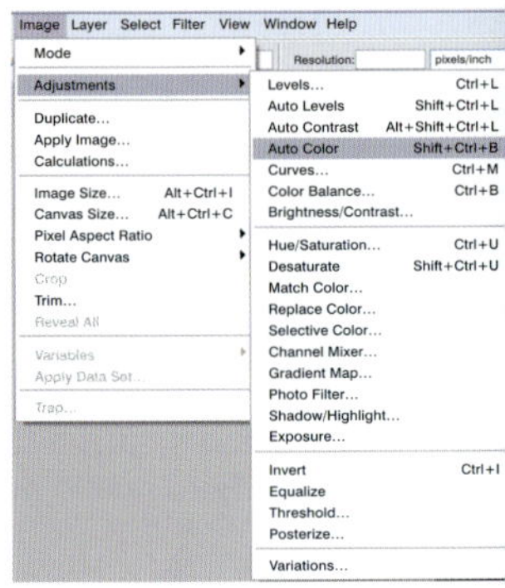

Using Auto Color has produced a more neutral result than the original image above, but it struggles when faced with variations in color such as the blue cast in the water at the bottom of this image.

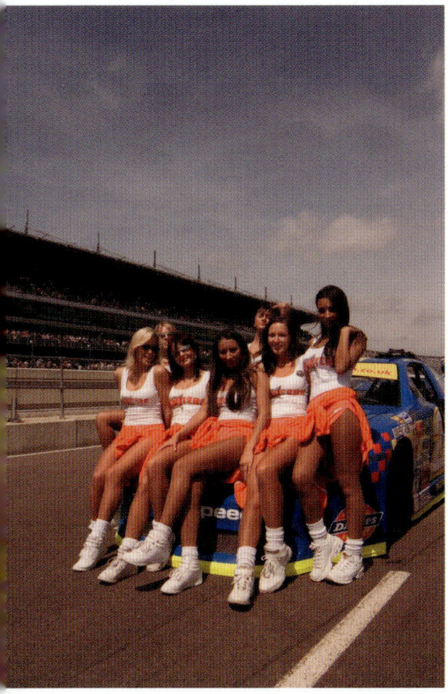

Variations

For simple manual control, the Variations facility is ideal for those new to adjusting the color of their images. By going to Image › Adjustments › Variations you will open a window showing your current image in the center with a range of options around it. The amount of variation in the color is adjusted using the Fine/Coarse slider. For small variations, move this to the left; for greater differences, move it to the right. You will see the images around the current one decrease or increase in color variation.

Above the variations, two images allow you to compare your original image with the adjusted one, while to the right there are three images with brightness variations. For the purposes of color balance, we will concern ourselves solely with the color variations. First decide on the amount of variation on the Fine/Coarse slider. For most images, it is better to use small adjustments and build them up gradually. Now simply click on the variation that looks most neutral to you. Keep an eye on the before and after images at the top of the window to ensure that you are going in the right direction, and keep clicking on the best image until you are happy with the result.

Using Variations successfully relies both on your monitor displaying colors accurately and your ability to choose the correct color. So although this is a good starting point for adjusting colors, it can produce poor results.

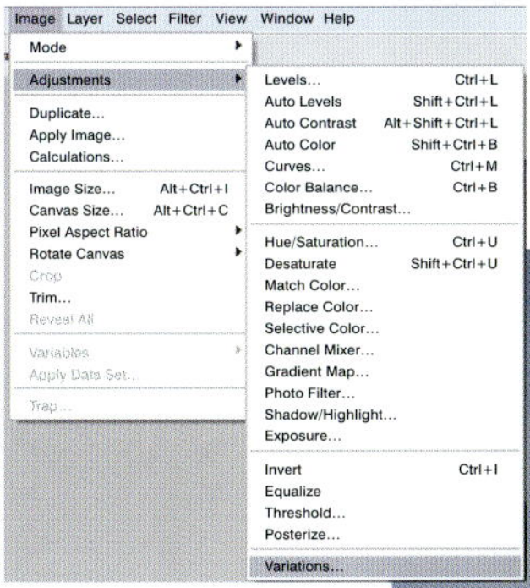

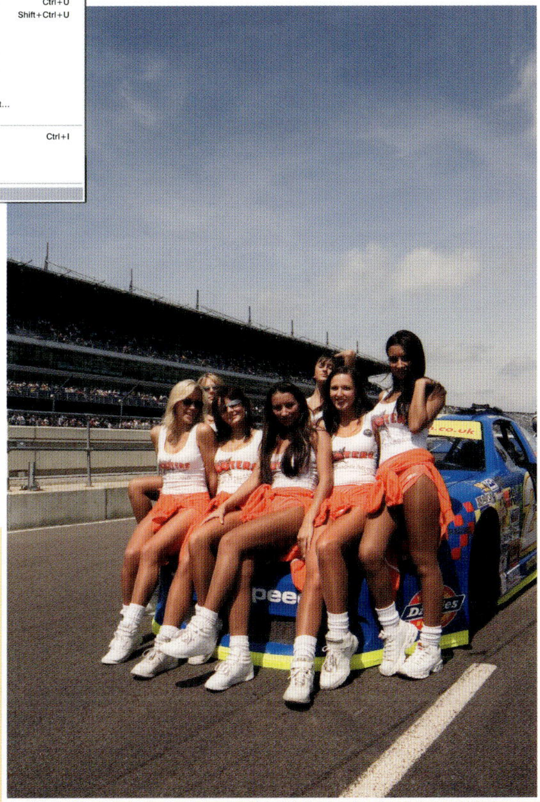

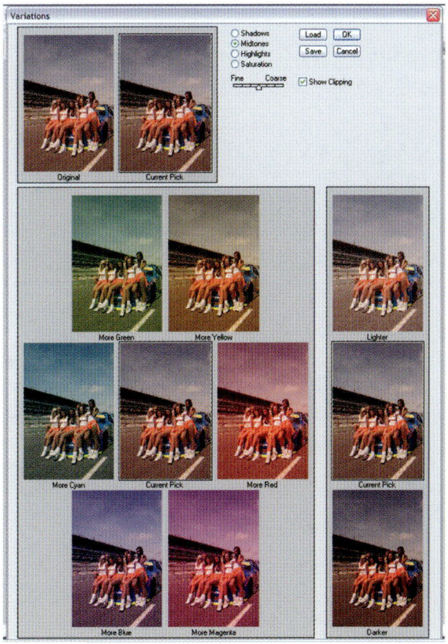

Channel Mixer

Although the Channel Mixer is more usually used for creating dramatic changes in color and black and white conversions, it can also prove a useful tool for color balancing. It is found by going to Image › Adjustments › Channel Mixer. This tool allows you to adjust the three color channels along with the overall brightness of each channel.

The Channel Mixer is best used for bringing out and adjusting one of the three colors without affecting the other two channels. In our image, the color of the sky was much too warm and the image had a slight green cast. While some other methods could have corrected these problems to an extent, the Channel Mixer allowed the blue sky to be enhanced without giving the image an overall blue cast.

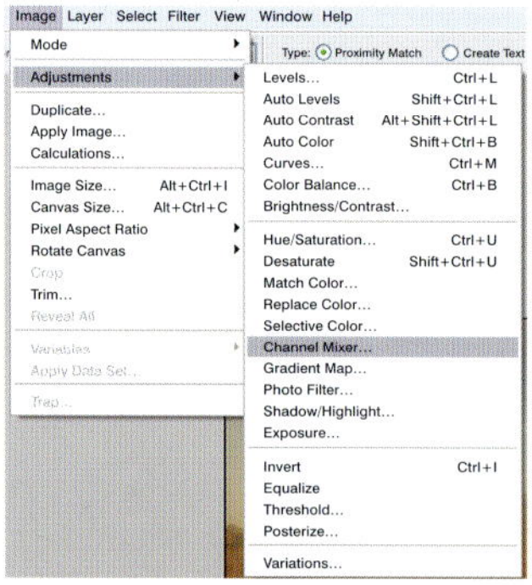

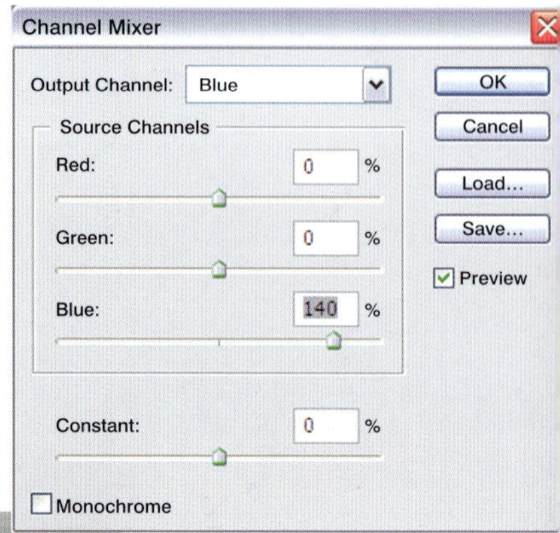

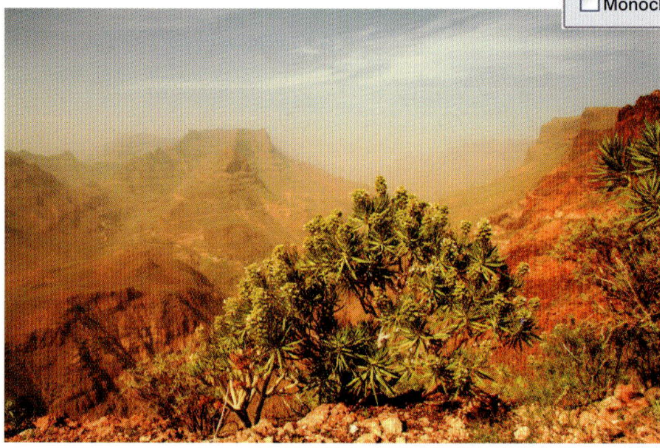

To increase the intensity of the blue sky, we selected blue as the output channel at the top of the window and then dragged the blue slider to give a value of 140%.

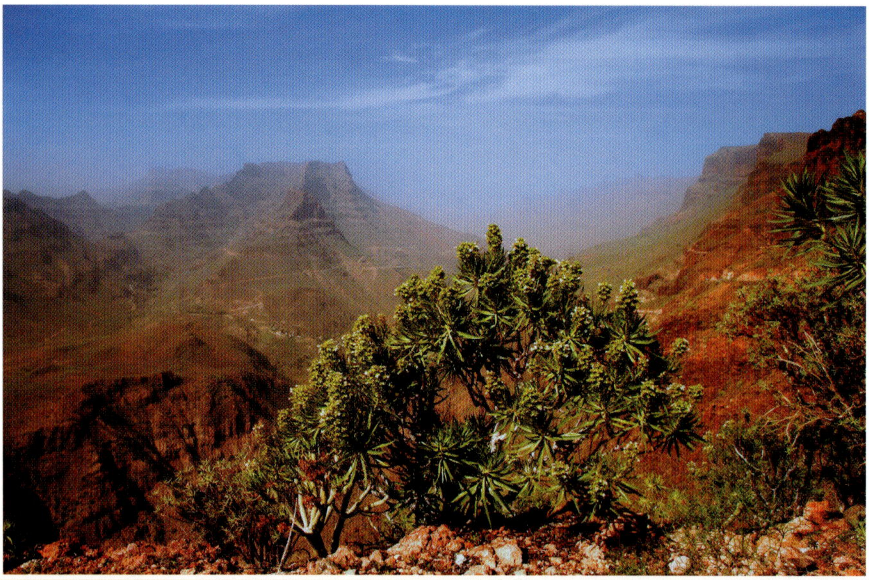

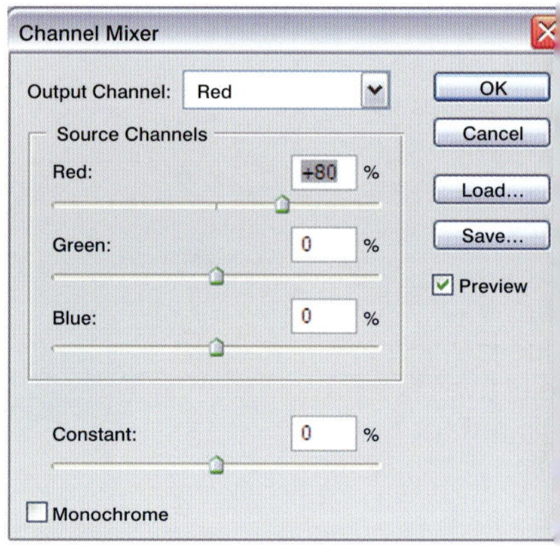

To reduce the overall warm tone of the image, we adjusted the red output channel. Dragging the Red slider back to 80% produced a much more neutral image.

ielective Color

ielective Color is an excellent option vhen your image has small areas of olor that are difficult to pinpoint and orrect with the more general color djustments. You access this feature hrough Image › Adjustments › ielective Color.

Selective Color gives you the ability o target your adjustments to a articular color from the dropdown nenu at the top of the window. These ptions include cyan, magenta, and ellow, as well as red, green, and blue. his enables you to adjust specific roblem colors in your image.

Using these adjustments takes a ttle practice, as you need to be able o recognize which color needs attention n your image. This is why it is best sed for specific color adjustments ather than overall color balancing.

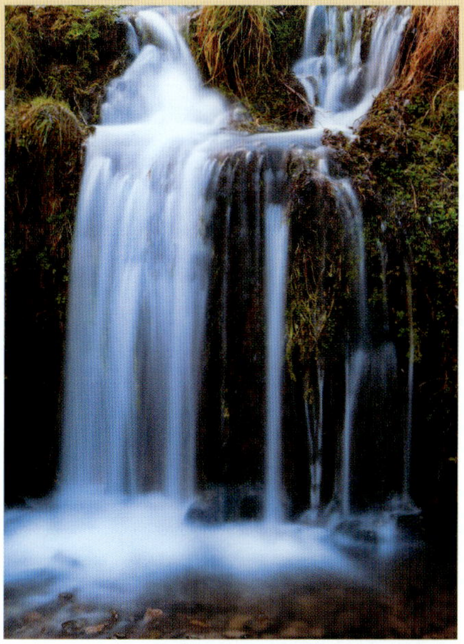

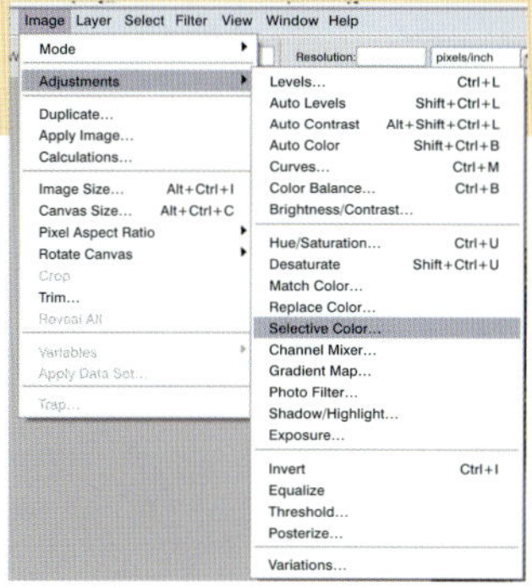

The shadows at the bottom of the frame on this waterfall image have taken on a distinct blue/cyan color cast due to the shot being taken under a clear blue sky. Normal color-balance techniques to remove this resulted in poor color at the top of the frame, which was in direct sunlight. Using Selective Color to remove cyan from the blues provided a means to remove the color cast without inflicting unwanted color casts on the rest of the image.

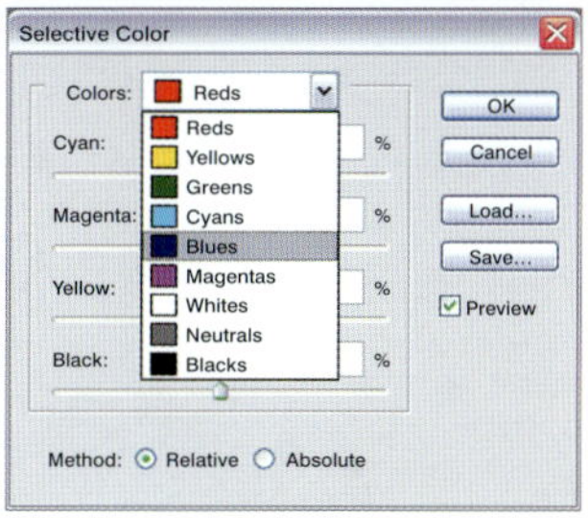

.imitations of ielective Color

ecause Selective Color changes all reas of the image containing the color nat you have chosen to adjust, it can ause problems with some images. , for example, the image we used bove had contained a person in a lue jacket, using the blue channel for elective color would have affected nis part of the frame as well, giving ncorrect colors in the jacket.

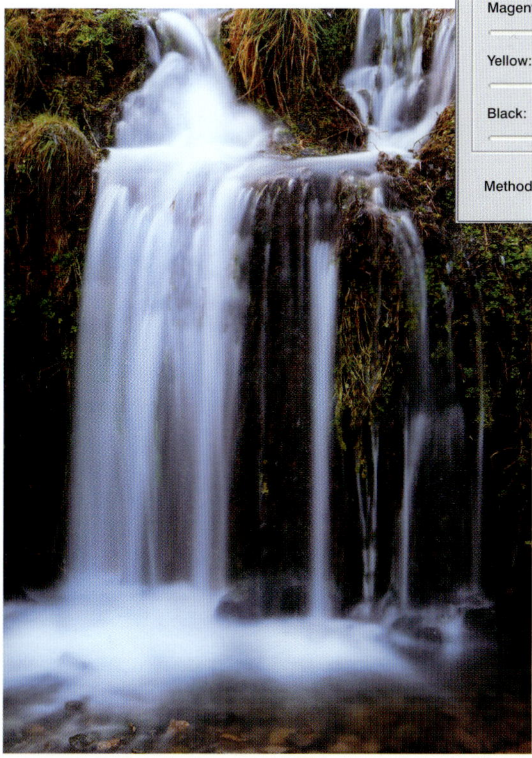

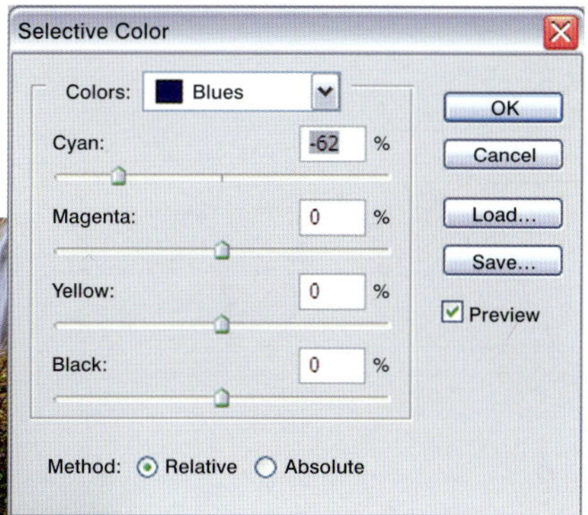

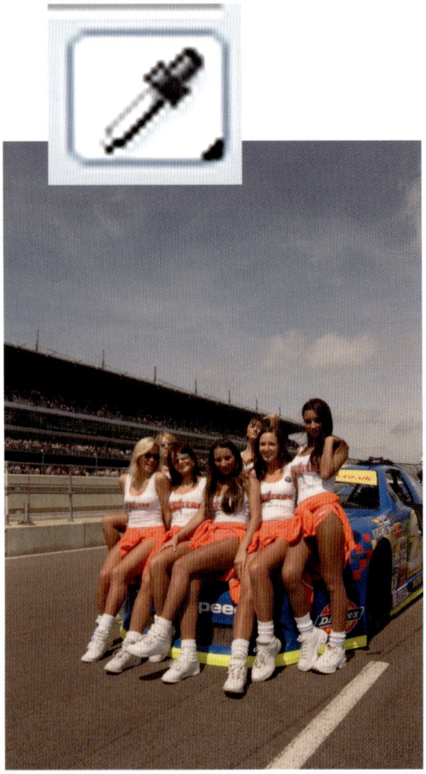

Using Levels and Measured Colors

Adjusting the levels on individual color channels is a great way to correct the colors of your images. You can do this process by eye, but you can also take your technique a step further by using the Eyedropper to sample areas of the image that you know should have a neutral color.

The best and most accurate way of using this method is to include a grayscale or color checker (see panel) in your image, but this is rarely an option for most photographers outside of a studio or full location photo shoot. Luckily, you can still use this method as long as your image contains a white highlight and neutral shadow area. Using an actual measurement of the neutral colors in your image takes away much of the guesswork from color balancing.

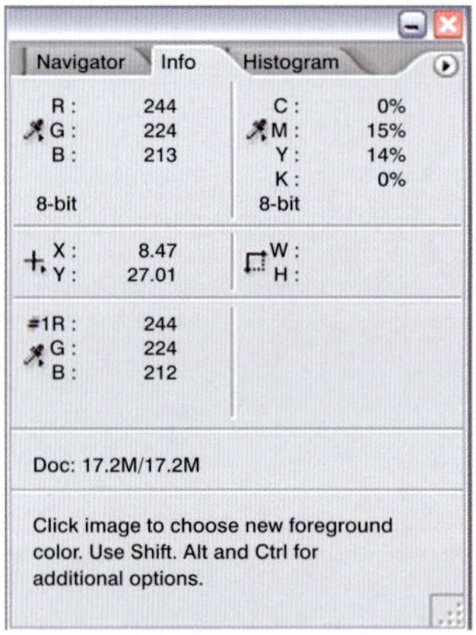

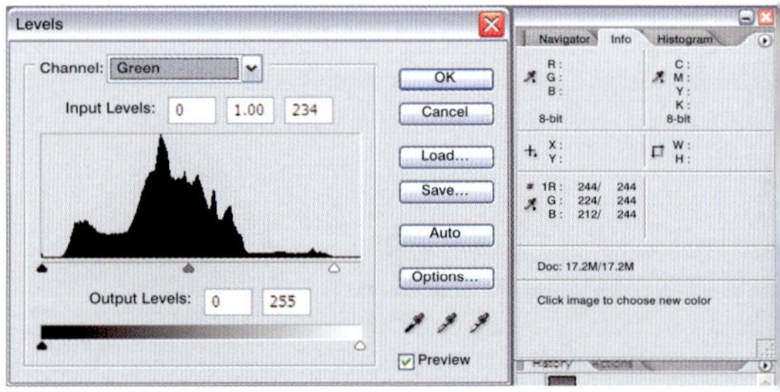

Step 1

Once you have opened the image to be corrected, open the Info palette by going to Window › Info to allow you to view the RGB values of the areas of the image. Then select the Eyedropper tool from the Tools palette on the left of the screen and find the brightest area of white that is present in your image. Look for an area that has a maximum value of around 240 to 250 for any one of the three color values in the Info palette, with all three above 210. For this image, we knew that the T-shirts worn by the models should be white. They gave red 244, green 224, and blue 212 values, although you may find that two values are the same in some images. Holding the Eyedropper over this area, hold down the Ctrl key and click the left mouse button. The values will appear at the bottom of the info panel as a locked value.

Step 2

After measuring the white point, open Levels (Image › Adjustments › Levels) to adjust the colors. A second set of values will now appear next to the locked values at the bottom of the Info palette; these will change when you adjust the image. The channels that you need to adjust are those that are below the highest of the three. Choose these in turn in the Channel menu at the top of the Levels window, and move the right-hand triangle toward the histogram until the value in the info panel matches the highest value. Adjust the second channel in the same way so that all RGB values are the same. Then click OK.

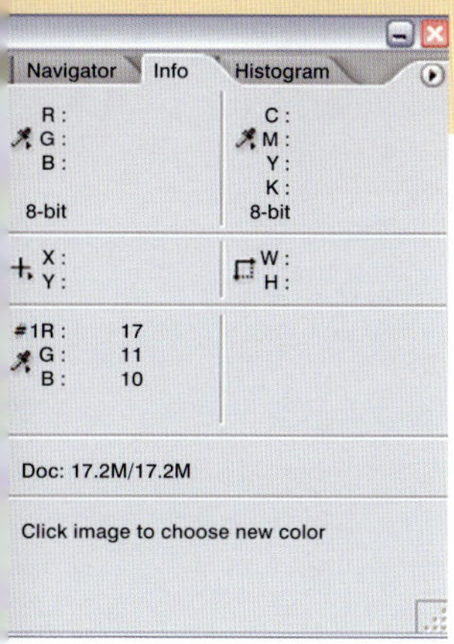

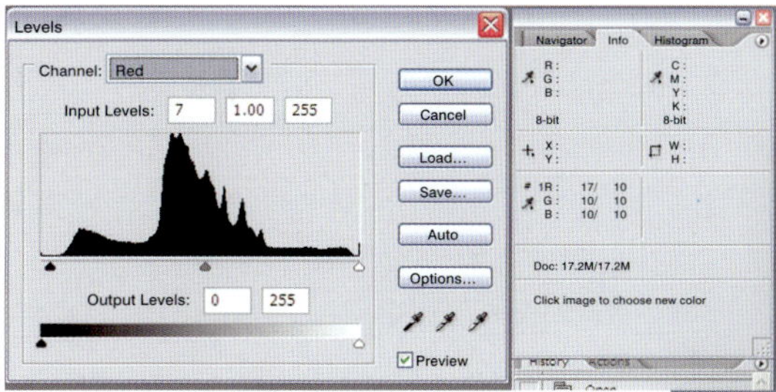

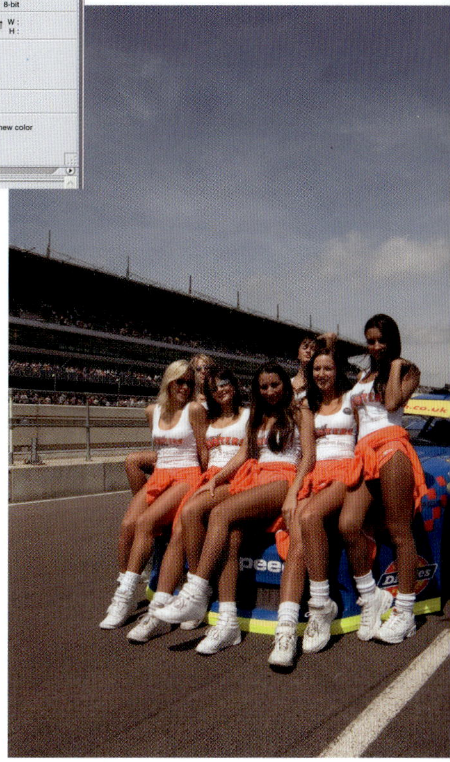

tep 3

ou now need to move the color ampler point to a shadow area to take new color reading. Simply click on he existing point while holding down he Ctrl key to drag it over a shadow rea while checking the RGB values the Info palette. The ideal area will ontain no values above around 25, ith a minimum value of 10 to 15 in ne of the color channels. We found he area inside the wheel arch of the ar to give the best values of red 17, reen 11, and blue 10. As with the hite area selection, the success of his method relies on selecting an area hat should be neutral, so take your me when choosing a suitable point.

Step 4

Once again, open the Levels window (Image › Adjustments › Levels). This time you will be adjusting the left-hand triangle. Choose one or two of the channels in turn that have a value above the lowest of the three. Drag the triangle until the reading alongside the locked value matches the lowest. In our case, the red and green channels were adjusted to give a value of 10. Once all three values match, you have finished. As long as the color sampler points were accurate, your image should be correctly color balanced.

Color Checker

An industry-standard color checker such as this one by GretagMacbeth takes all the guesswork out of making color adjustments. It contains a series of standard colors and a grayscale that allow you to track the color rendition throughout the processing of the image. You need to include it in at least one frame of the images you take in a particular lighting, so it is not usually suitable for outdoor conditions where the light can change. However, in controlled conditions it is invaluable.

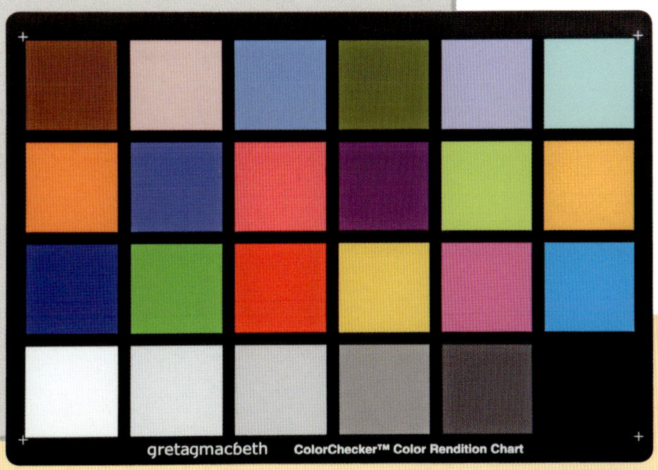

Simple Saturation

One of the easiest and most effective ways to give your images more impact is to add extra saturation to the colors. With film capture you would have to choose the right emulsion, but digital photography offers a quick and simple solution to those wanting more punchy images.

Using Curves for Saturation

The Hue/Saturation control in Photoshop offers many users all they need for basic adjustments to the saturation of their images, and with a little help from the Curves control you can get great results with the minimum of effort. You can use the Hue/Saturation control alone, but adding extra contrast with the Curves control makes the colors appear stronger. Here is a two-step route to adding saturation to your images.

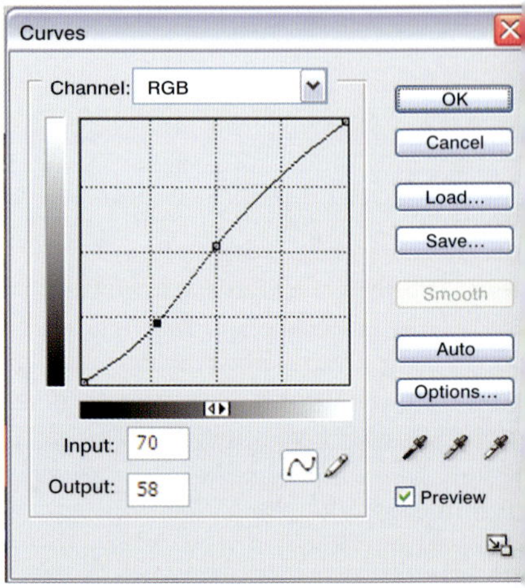

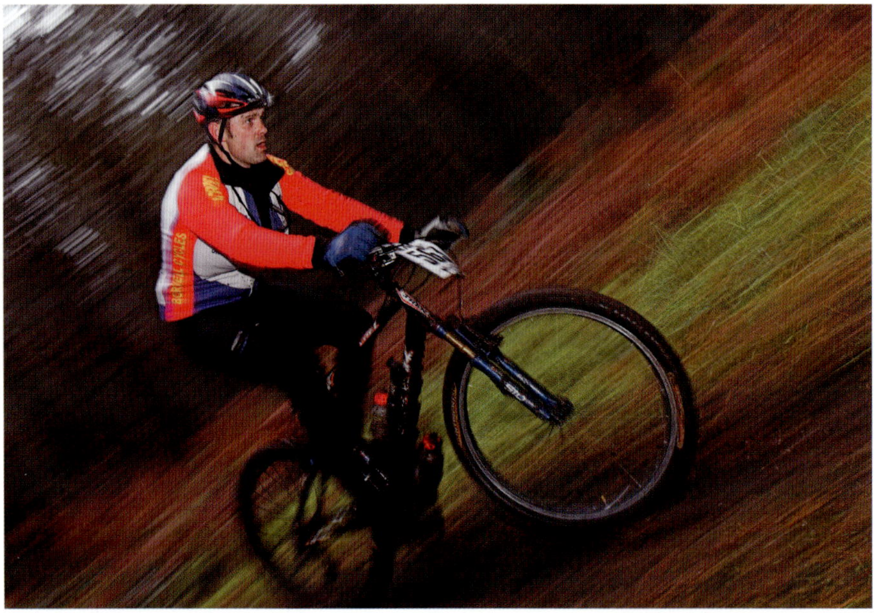

Step 1

The first adjustment to the image is to increase the contrast by using the Curves control (Image › Adjustments › Curves). For most images, a gentle S-shaped curve immediately gives more impact, so click on the middle of the line on the graph once to lock its position. Then drag the bottom half down slightly to darken the shadow areas. The top part will automatically curve upward slightly as a result, brightening the highlights. You may need to take this further by dragging it upward, but take care not to go too far, as you can lose detail in the highlight areas of the image.

This shot of a mountain bike race was shot in very dull, cloudy conditions, and even a burst of fill-in flash failed to give the colors the impact that I wanted.

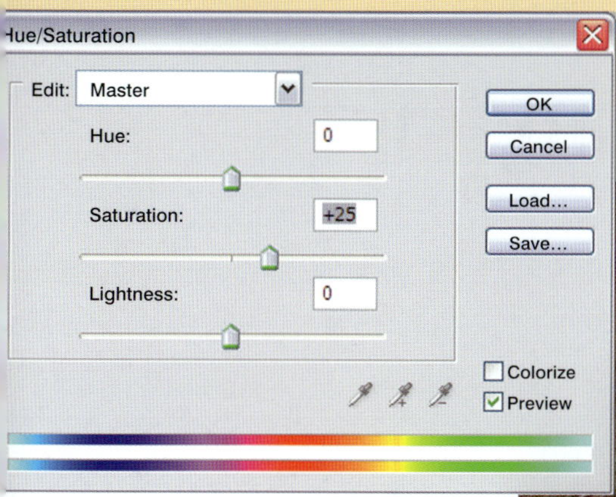

Adding saturation and a Curves adjustment gave the image much more impact and vibrancy.

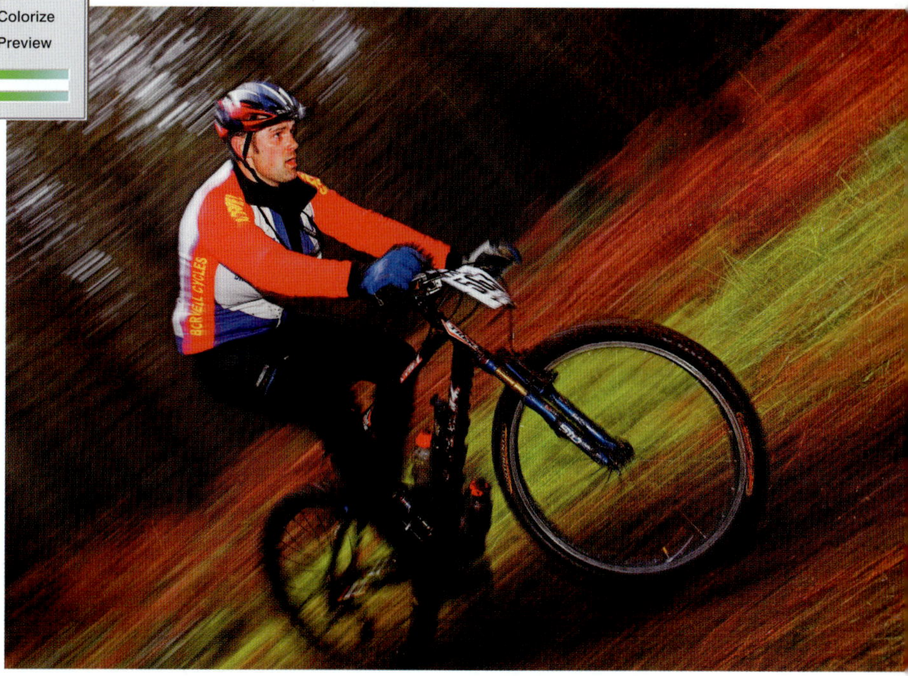

tep 2

ow open the Hue/Saturation indow (Image › Adjustments › Hue/ aturation) and drag the Saturation ider gradually to the right. We used a ılue of +25 for our image. The precise nount that you need will depend on e saturation of your original image, ıt a value between +10 and +30 is sually enough. Once you are happy ith the result, click OK.

imitations of imple Saturation djustments

s with any onscreen adjustments, lding saturation relies on both your onitor displaying colors accurately and ur judgment to get the right increase. ith a little practice the latter is not ırd to do, but it is easy to go overboard ith saturation and produce very brant images. Use the Saturation der with care, as what looks bright nd punchy on screen can often look er-the-top when you produce a print.

When adjusting images for print it is also possible that your printer will not be able to reproduce the saturation that you see on your monitor. This is because monitors can display a greater range of color intensities than printer inks can produce. This is especially true of simple saturation adjustments because they are applied across the whole color range. To get the saturation you want in one color of your image, another color will be increased beyond the limit of the printer. The best way to prevent this is to use the Gamut Warning facility to indicate when the colors in your image are outside your printer's capability (see p.60).

Advanced Saturation

Although simple saturation adjustments are useful for many images, there are times when you want greater control over the individual colors. One use for these more targeted adjustments is when your image contains some vibrant hues and some hues that need a boost. By using a "global" adjustment, you will not be able to get the saturation you want from the duller colors without the others becoming oversaturated, or worse still going out of gamut. Targeting individual colors in this way also allows you to make small adjustments to the hue of individual colors.

Often a less noticeable, but still significant, effect of oversaturating colors is an increase in noise. This is usually most obvious when shooting landscapes with clear blue skies, as the blue channel tends to be the most affected of the three color channels. Balancing the saturation adjustments needed for the sky and the landscape can result in a duller result than you were after, or unacceptable levels of noise in the sky.

When working with individual color controls, it still pays to keep an eye on other areas of the image; they can contain small amounts of the color that you are adjusting which can produce unwanted effects.

Photoshop offers two main ways of targeting these individual colors: the first is the more advanced options in the Hue/Saturation control, and the second, for even more control, is through Selective Color adjustment.

The low color saturation and contrast of this image made it an obvious candidate for a simple saturation adjustment. However, applying the amount of saturation needed for the sand resulted in unacceptable noise levels in the blue sky, so a more sophisticated adjustment was required.

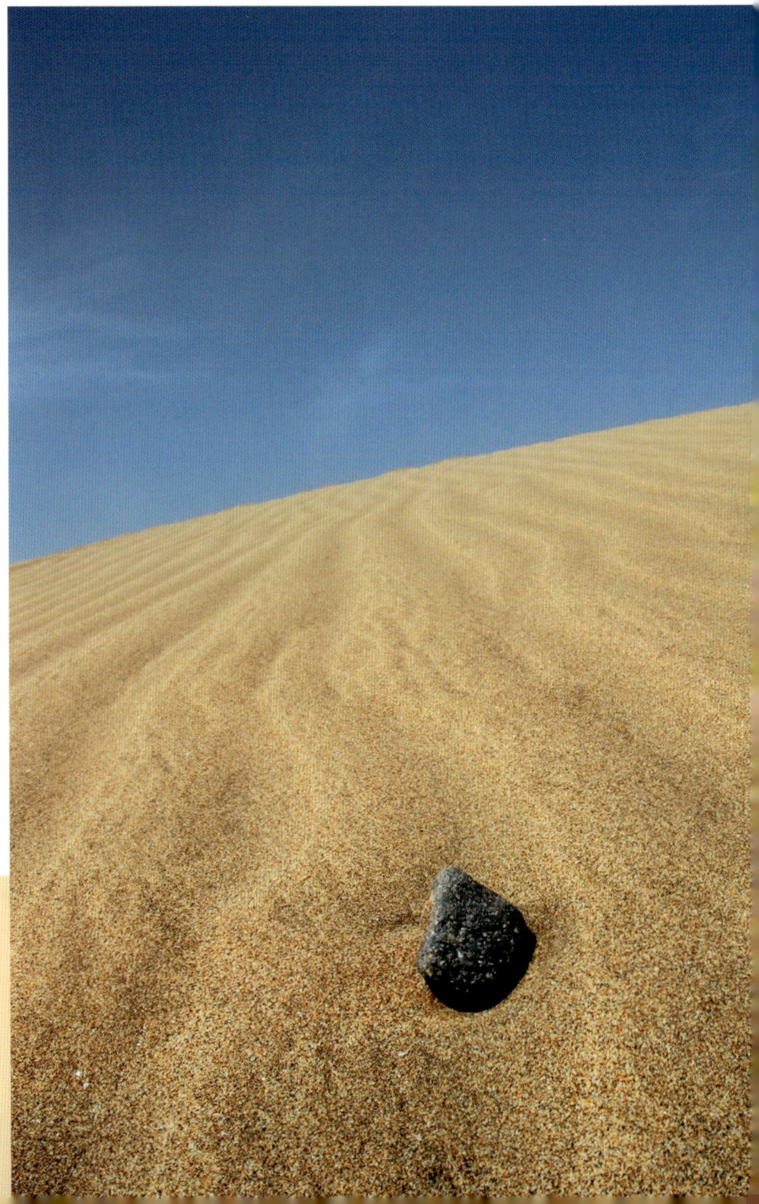

\dvanced
·lue/Saturation
·djustments

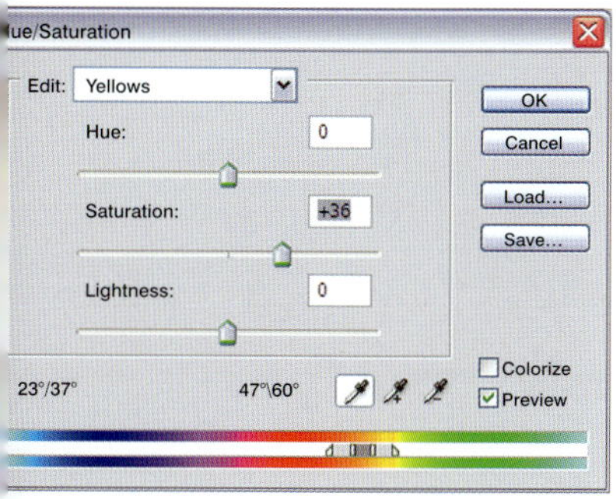

\tep 1

ɔr this image we wanted to adjust ıe blue and yellow areas separately, s a single adjustment did not roduce acceptable results. Opening ıe Hue/Saturation window (Image Adjustments › Hue/Saturation), we rst wanted to adjust the color of the and, so we chose Yellow from the Edit ropdown menu. To narrow the range f colors that would be affected by the djustment, we then clicked on the yedropper icon in the window and icked on the sand to select the exact ne that we wanted to target. The ellows in our image were particularly ull, so we needed to drag the aturation slider up to +36 to give e sand the vibrancy we wanted.

» With both the sky and sand adjusted individually, the final result has much more impact than the original image, without sacrificing quality.

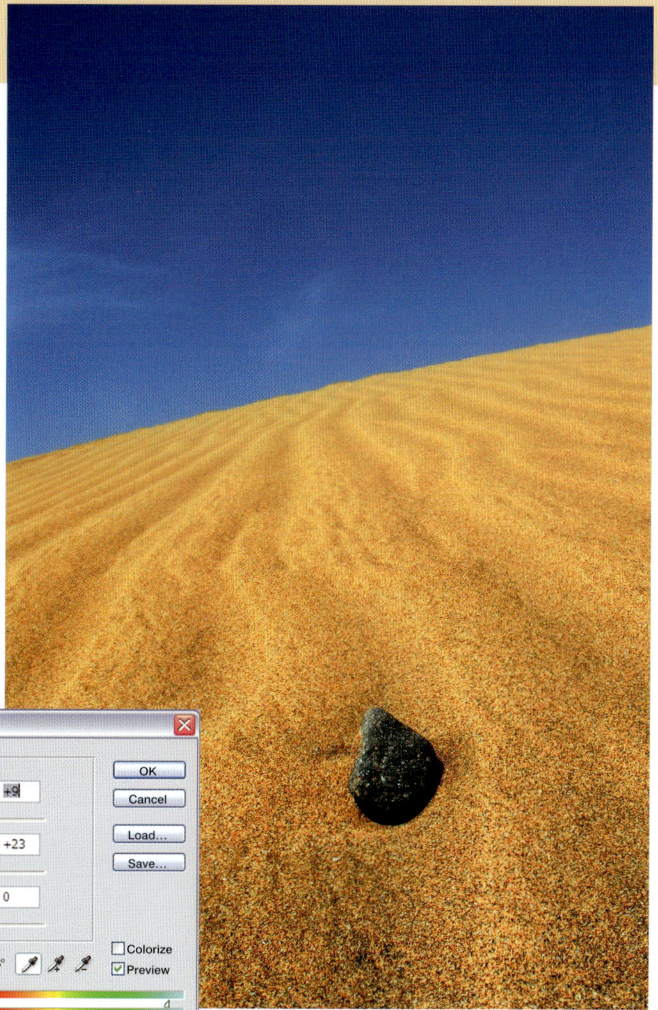

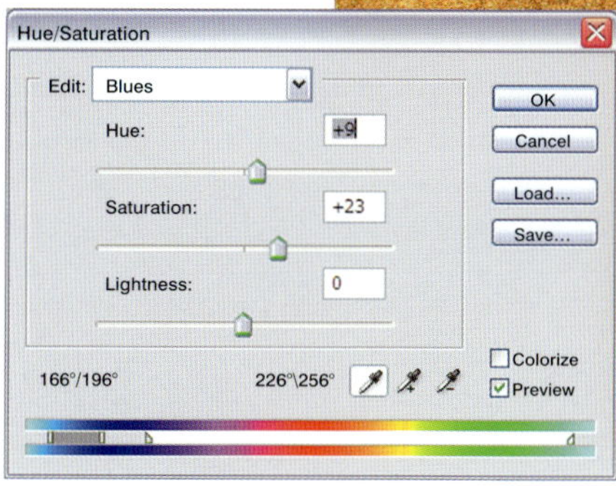

Step 2

With the Hue/Saturation window still open, we turned our attention to the sky by selecting Blue from the dropdown edit menu. Once again, we used the Eyedropper tool to select an area of the sky to ensure we were working on the correct colors. We then dragged the Saturation slider gradually to the right until we were happy with the amount without image noise becoming more visible. We found a value of +26 was the best for our image, although this will vary according to the needs of your original image. As a final adjustment, we dragged the Hue slider to give a +9 shift to make the sky a stronger blue tone. Once happy with the image, we simply clicked OK to apply the adjustments.

Selective Color

Although the individual color adjustments in Hue/Saturation offer a comprehensive range of controls, Photoshop provides an even more advanced tool for controlling individual colors. The Selective Color option allows you to control the precise hues present in any of the primary and secondary colors, as well as the white, black, and neutral tones. This is particularly useful for targeting individual colors in your image and fine-tuning their hue and saturation.

Because the adjustments are made to the cyan, magenta, yellow, and black values of the color, this technique demands that you understand the relationship between the primary and secondary colors. If you want to adjust any of the red, green, and blue primary colors, you will need to adjust the opposite secondary color for the greatest effect. For example, when working on a red color you decrease the amount of cyan to make it more vibrant. The other color sliders will also affect the color, so it is best to start with the opposite secondary color and see if that gives the effect you want, leaving the other colors alone until you have tried this one.

Because of this complication, it is easy for the newcomer to these adjustments to create some pretty awful color shifts in the image. Therefore, it is best to work on a separate copy of the image as a Layer to ensure that any mistakes are easily reversible.

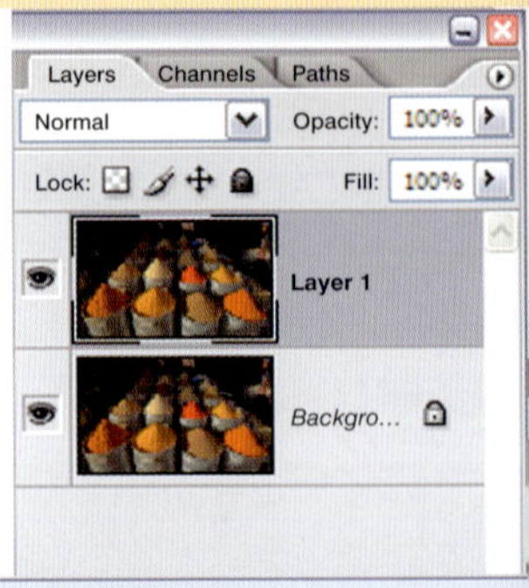

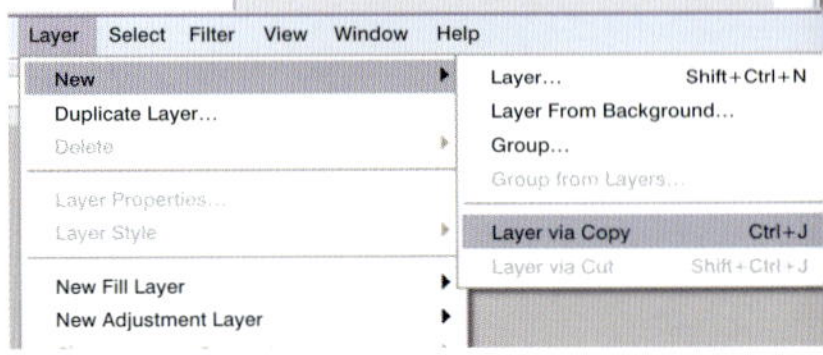

Step 1

Before using complicated image adjustments such as Selective Color, I created a copy of the original image as a new layer by going to Layer › New › Via Copy. To make sure that any adjustments are made to this layer, ensure that the Layers palette is visible on screen. If it is not visible, go to Window › Layers to reveal it and ensure that the top layer in the stack is highlighted.

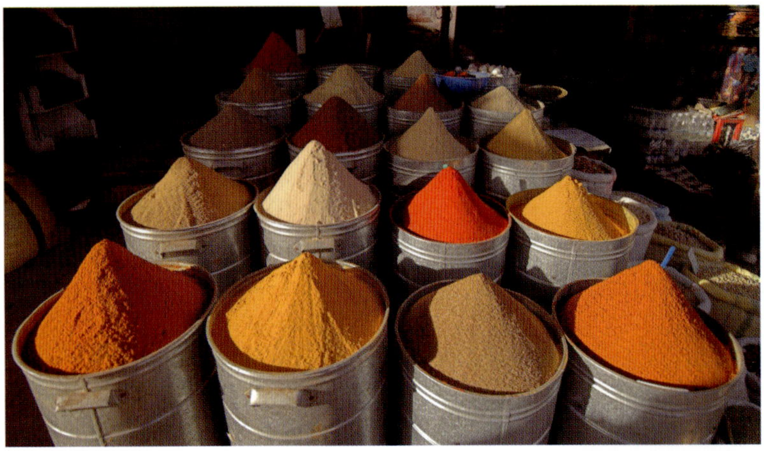

The colors of these spices on a market stall were much less vibrant than they appeared at the time. This was largely due to the difficult lighting conditions of sunlight and various artificial light sources present in the location. I did not have time to make any adjustments at the time of shooting, as it was very much a "grabbed" shot.

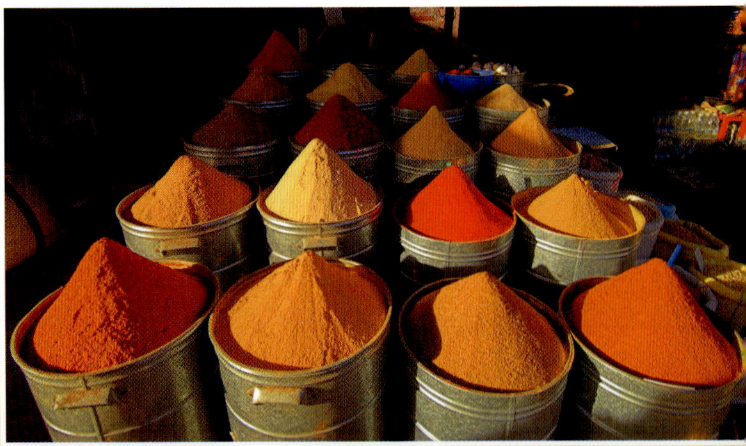

Adjusting the colors in the Hue/Saturation controls improved the colors of the spices. However, even by using individual color adjustments there was still a yellow cast on the metal barrels, and trying to eliminate this with color balancing affected the spices.

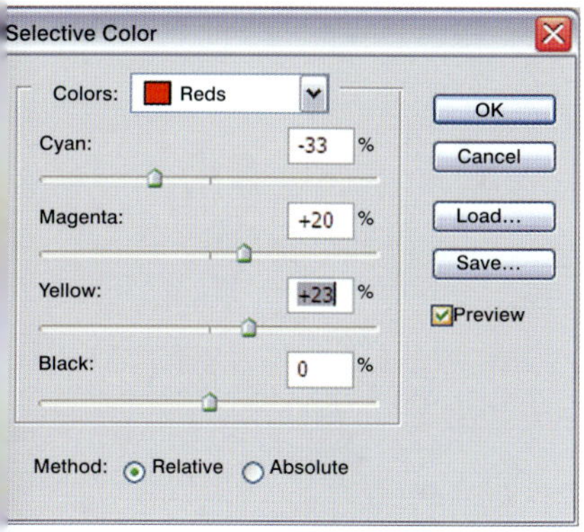

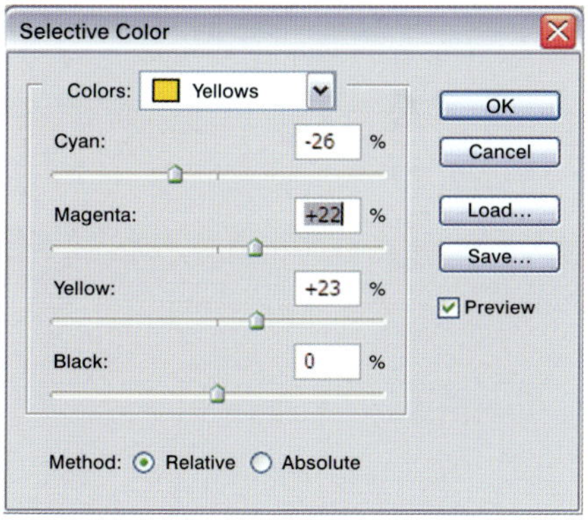

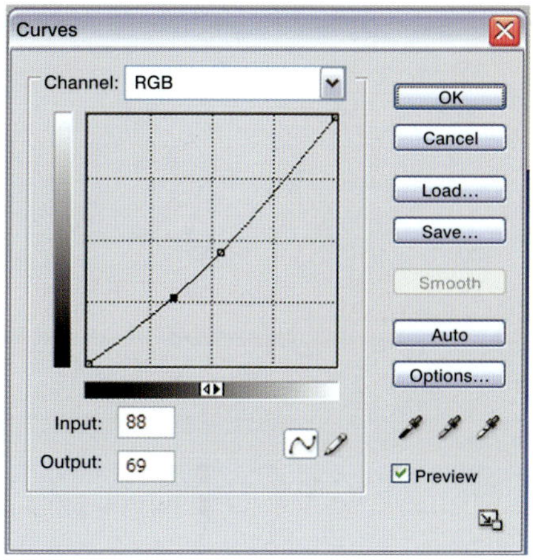

itep 2
low I opened the Selective Color vindow (Image › Adjustments › elective Color) and chose the Reds rom the Colors dropdown menu at the op of the window. This allowed me to djust the color of the red hues, first f all using the Cyan slider. Ensuring hat the Preview option was enabled, value of –33% Cyan was found to ive the best result. Then the Magenta nd Yellow sliders were adjusted to ncrease the warmth of the reds, using 20 and +23 respectively.

Step 3
Once the reds had been adjusted, I turned my attention to the yellow by choosing this Color dropdown menu. To increase the saturation of this, a value of +23 was set on the Yellow slider. A similar amount was added to the Magenta slider to increase the warmth of the yellows, while the Cyan slider was set to –26 to remove some of the cooler tones. Once I was happy with the image, I clicked OK to confirm the adjustments.

Step 4
To darken the shadow areas around the spice barrels I used the Curve control (Image › Adjustments › Curves), dragging the line slightly downward. This made the colors more apparent against the dark background. Once I got the final result I wanted, I clicked OK. Happy with the image, I then went to Layer › Flatten Image to reduce it back to a single layer in order to save it.

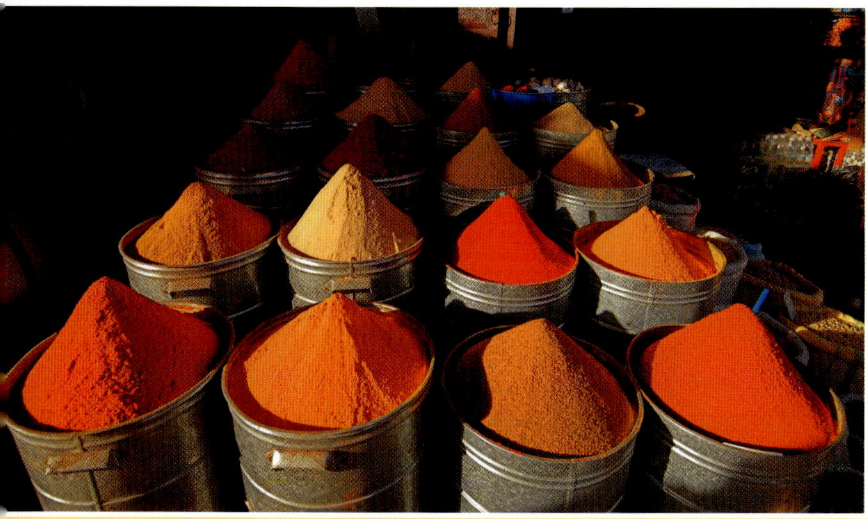

By using the Selective Color controls, the reds and yellows of the spices could be adjusted without affecting the overall color of the image.

Replicating Fuji Velvia

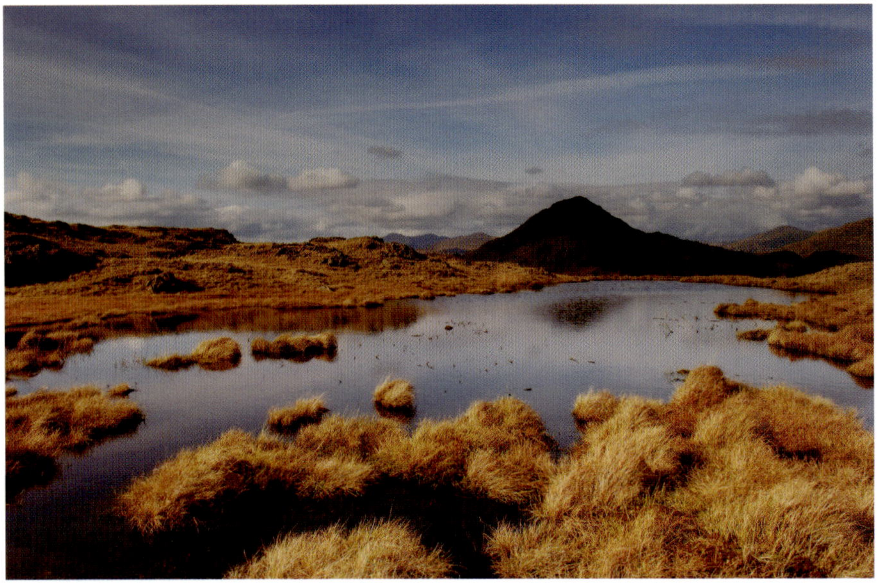

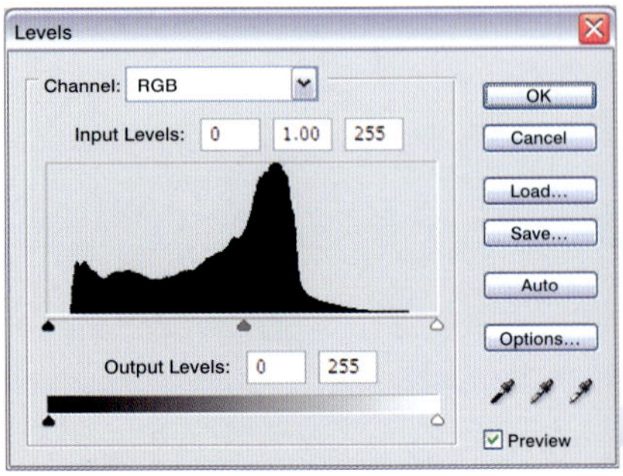

Step 1

The first thing to check on your image is the tone distribution; do this by opening the Levels window (Image › Adjustments › Levels). With a low-contrast image, you will see that there are gaps between the ends of the histogram and the edges of the box. To increase the contrast of the image, drag the small triangle sliders at the extreme left and right to meet the body of the histogram. Ensure that you don't go too far with the sliders, as any areas of the image outside of these will result in loss of shadow or highlight detail.

The contrast and color of digitally captured images can often be less punchy and saturated than the results achieved from films such as Fuji Velvia.

With its highly saturated colors and punchy contrast, Fuji Velvia color slide film is the film of choice for many landscape and nature photographers. For those used to the impact of this classic emulsion, digital capture can prove a frustrating experience. It is all too easy for the images to be far less saturated and lower in contrast, leading to a disappointing rendition of the original colors that you remember.

This does not have to be the case, though, as with a few simple adjustments in your imaging software you can add extra contrast, saturation, and fine-tune the images to suit your personal taste. The precise adjustments depend on your image, but follow these steps and you can get that Velvia look.

A few simple adjustments in your software will bring out the best in your images.

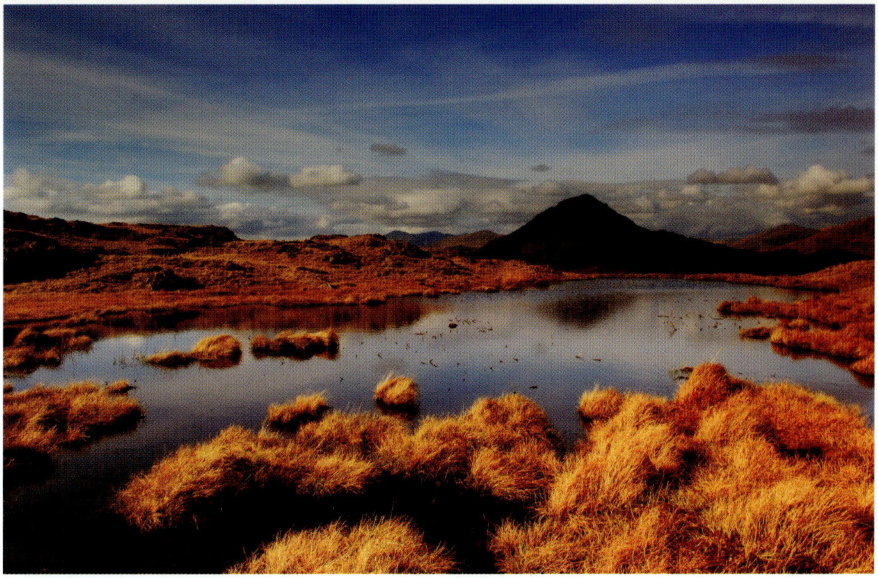

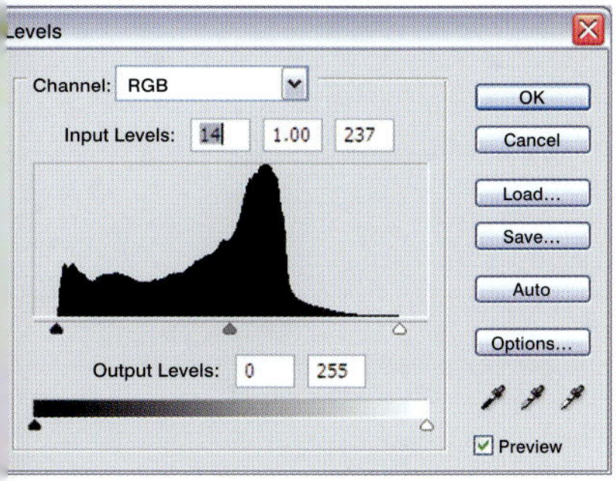

tep 2
lthough the levels adjustment will ncrease contrast, the image will still ack the punch that is characteristic of elvia; you need to adjust the Curves mage › Adjustments › Curves) to ive the image more impact. With the ialog box open, click on the diagonal ne in the center and drag the curve ownward slightly to darken the idtones of the image. Then click alfway between the center and the op of the line and drag this up to pproximately the original position n the diagonal line. At this stage you ay want to fine-tune the adjustments; ragging the left-hand side of the urve will affect the shadows, dragging e right-hand will affect the highlights. e careful not to overdo this; aim to raw a gentle S-shaped curve.

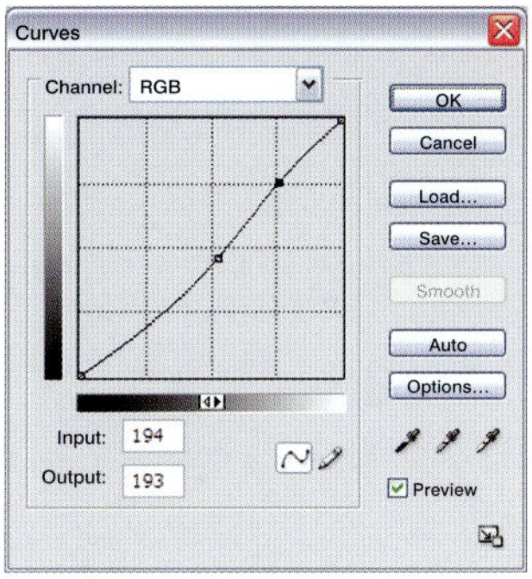

Step 3
Once you are happy with the contrast, you will need to add some extra saturation (Image › Adjustments › Hue/Saturation) to match the film's results. Drag the Saturation slider to the right in the Hue/Saturation dialog box to create the result you want. A value of between +10 and +30 should give enough of a boost to the colors without going out of gamut, although if you are in any doubt turn on the Gamut Warning (View › Gamut Warning).

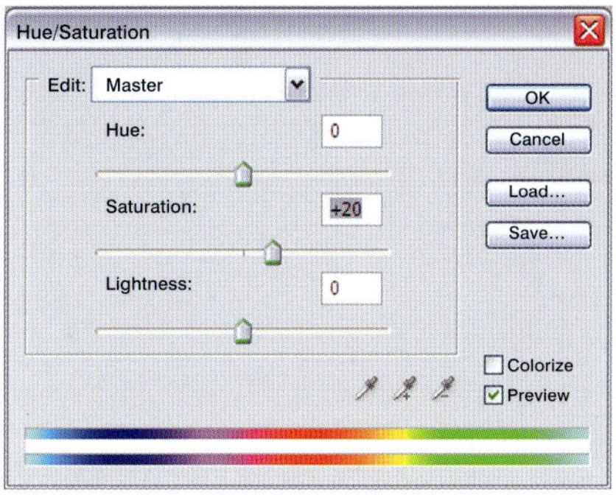

Step 4
Assuming your original image has a neutral color balance, you may need to adjust the colors to match the color rendition of Velvia. Open the Color Balance window (Image › Adjustments › Color Balance) and drag the color sliders to give a Velvia-like appearance. Start off with the values of +8 red, +2 green, and –4 yellow. You will need to experiment with different values for various images, as the adjustment depends on the color of the original.

Other Film Looks

Although most films currently available are designed to give fine grain and saturated colors, this has not always been the case. Many films that have passed into photographic history were loved for their "golf-ball"-like grain and soft, muted colors. These emulsions, such as some of the faster color slide and print film made by Scotch and Fuji, had a cult following among more arty photographers because of their unique characteristics. Despite their technical shortcomings compared to modern emulsions, the look of these films can impart a completely different feel to your images, which it is possible to recreate digitally.

The obvious solution would be to use a high ISO when shooting your digital images. At low ISO settings, modern digital cameras are excellent at producing smooth colors and low noise (the equivalent of grain). Unfortunately, when you increase the ISO setting, the effect lacks the subtlety and smoothness that you need to create an effective grainy image. The best solution, therefore, is to shoot your images at the lowest ISO setting possible for the conditions and then achieve the effect in your software.

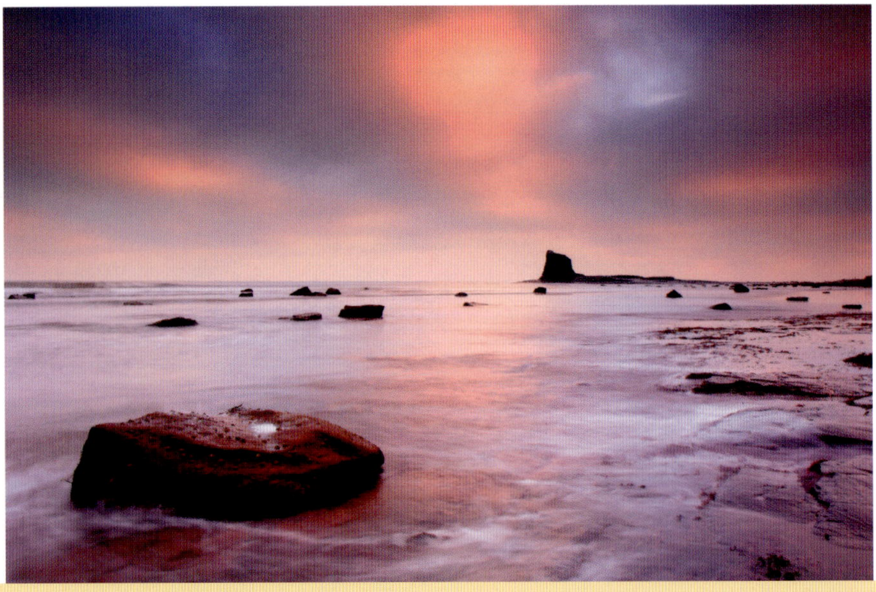

Recreating Film Grain and Low Color Saturation

Step 1

I wanted to fine-tune the final effect of this technique. I created a copy of the image as a new layer by going to Laye › New Layer Via Copy. First ensuring that I was working on this new layer, I went to Filter › Artistic › Film Grain. This opens a new editing window, giving you individual controls for the Grain, Highlight Area, and Intensity for the filter. The precise adjustments you need will depend on both your origina image and the intensity of the effect that you want; I found that values of 5 Grain, 0 Highlight Area, and 1 Intensity created the subtlety that I wanted. You can check how your image will appear in the preview window to the left of the screen. Once I was happy with the result, I clicked OK to confirm the filte

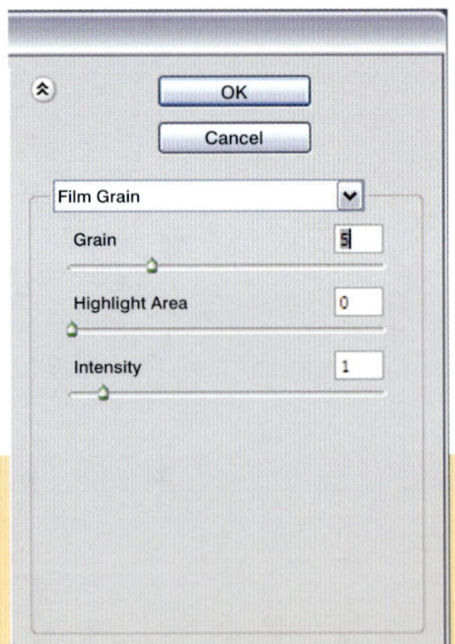

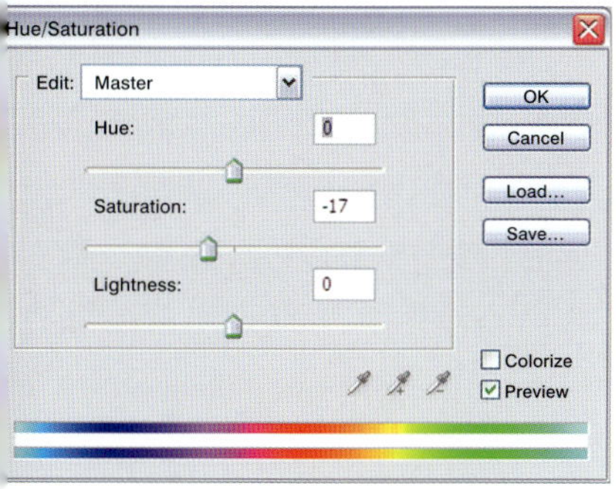

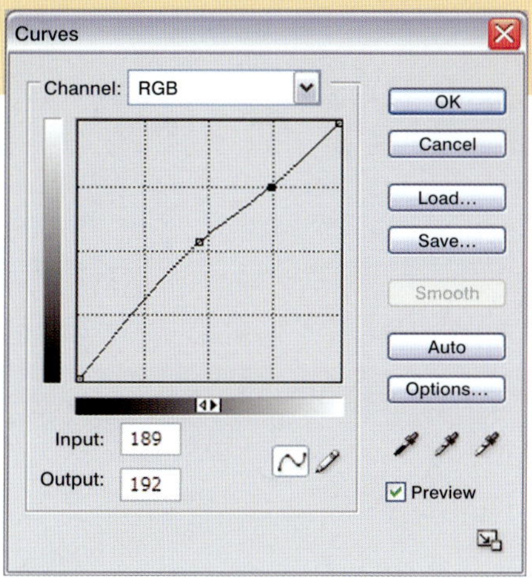

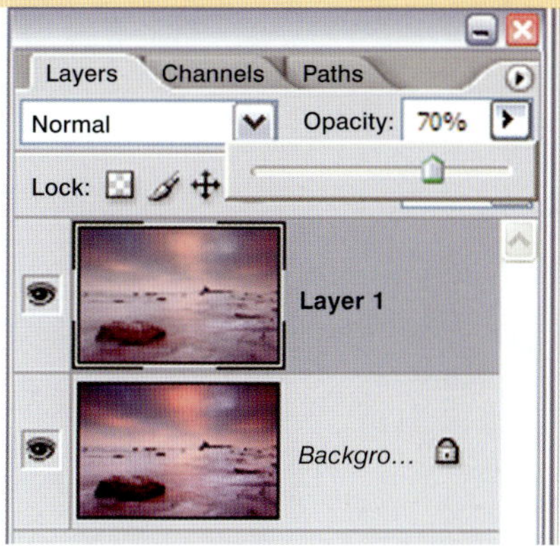

itep 2

itill working on the top layer, then went to the Hue/Saturation ontrols (Image › Adjustments › lue/Saturation) to adjust the colors. 'or the effect of a high-speed film, he Saturation should be reduced y between –5 and –20, depending n the intensity of the colors in our original image. For this early-norning shot, I needed only to educe the saturation to –7 to give nuted colors. To confirm the effect, clicked OK.

Step 3

To lower the contrast, I used the Curves control (Image › Adjustments › Curves) on the top layer of the image. I clicked on the top portion of the line to lock the highlights and then dragged the middle of the line upward slightly to lift the density of the shadows, and clicked OK. Once again, this is an area in which you can experiment. Bear in mind that most high-speed films had a low-contrast appearance, so aim for a curve with a shallow angle rather than a steep one.

Step 4

The final stage was to adjust the density of the layer that I had been working on to give a more believable appearance to the final image. In the top right corner of the Layers palette, I clicked on the arrow to the right of the Opacity value. This opened a slider that I used to lower the Opacity to 70% so I could just about see some of the original image showing through. This gave the subtlety that I was looking to create, so I reduced the image back to a single layer by going to Layers › Flatten Image before saving it.

By using the Film Grain filter and Hue/Saturation controls in Photoshop, you can add extra mood and recreate the ffects of using an old-fashioned igh-speed color film.

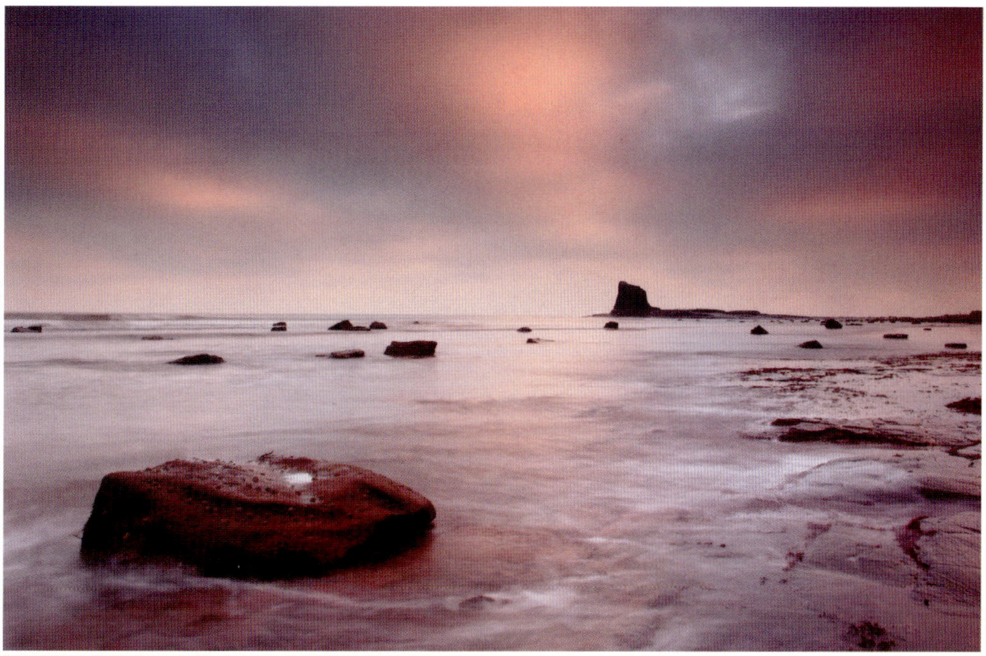

Black and White

Your color digital images can easily be converted to black and white. Using the Channel Mixer gives you the option of adjusting the tones of the final result to suit your requirements.

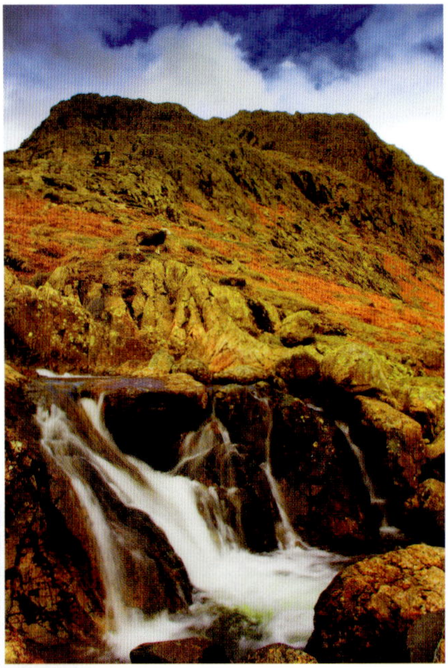

It may seem strange to include black and white images in a book on color, but digital photography has blurred the boundaries created by film capture. Rather than choose a specific film when you shoot your images, you can simply shoot everything in color and worry about the final image later on. Being able to use these adjustments successfully requires a basic understanding of color, however. So although it does not immediately appear to be related, black and white is simply an alternative to the color that we see around us, and opens up a whole range of opportunities for toning and other techniques that rely on color for their effect.

There are many ways of converting your color images to black and white in Photoshop, but the Channel Mixer offers some of the most versatile options simply by ticking the Monochrome option. By offering control over how the red, green, and blue channels are combined, this technique allows you to adjust how

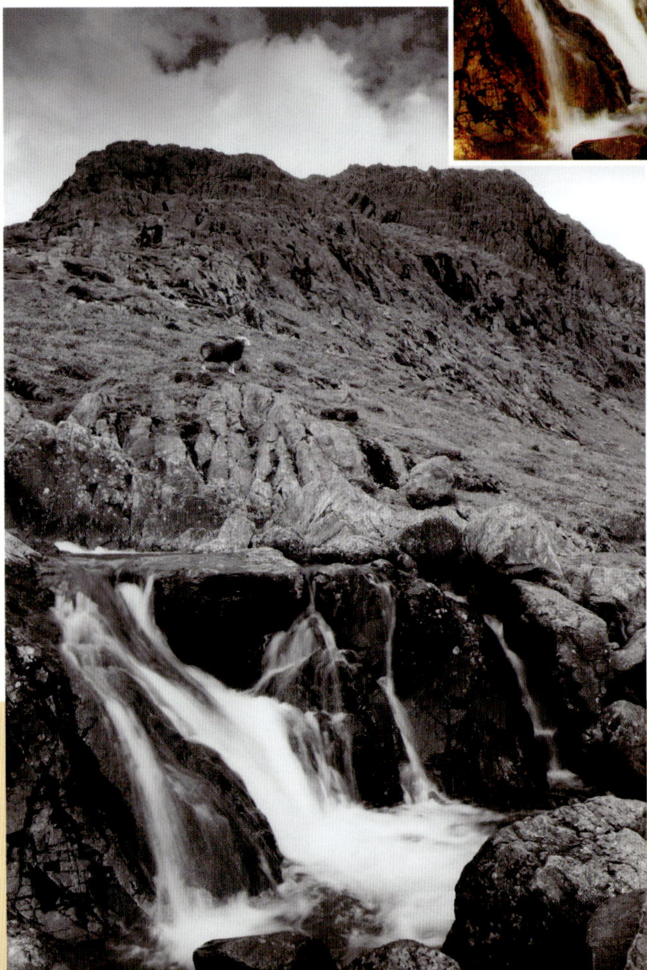

Standard conversion: using the settings below gives results similar to using a standard black and white film. The image has a wide tonal range, although lacks contrast for my taste.

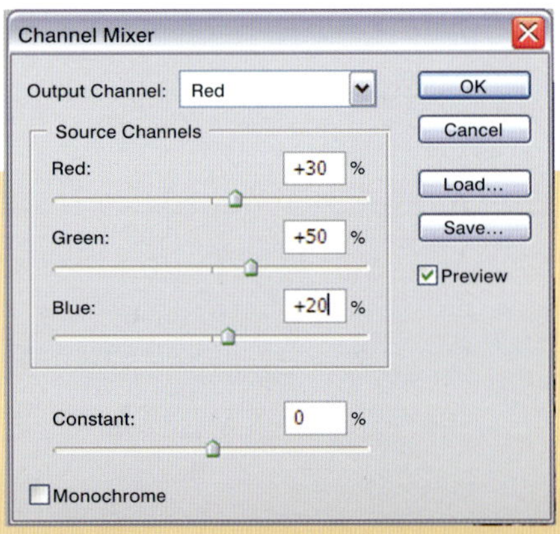

he original colors in the image are
;onverted. This gives you the ability
o recreate the effects of using colored
ilters on traditional film from your
:olor images. This is achieved by
ıdjusting the three color sliders to
hange the tones. You darken the tone
rom a color in your image by adding
nore of the opposite color, and lighten
t by adding the same color. For
xample, to replicate the effect of
ısing a red filter, you need to use
low value for the blue channel and a
igh one for the red channel. To control
he overall exposure, there is also a
lider marked Constant—this should
ot usually be needed as long as you
nsure that the values you enter in the
olor sliders add up to 100.

Here is how you use the Channel
Aixer to convert to black and white.

Once you have opened the Channel
Aixer window (Image › Adjustments ›
:hannel Mixer), ensure that the
Aonochrome box at the bottom of
he window is ticked. As a starting
oint for recreating the sort of result
ou would get from standard black
nd white film, enter values of +30
ed, +50 green, and +20 blue. You can
ne-tune these values for your own
nages, but I find that these are good
ɔr most images.

Replicating Using a Red Filter

Open the Channel Mixer as with the standard conversion, but this time enter values of 100 red, +20 green, and −20 red. As before, you can adjust these values to suit your image, but make sure that they add up to 100.

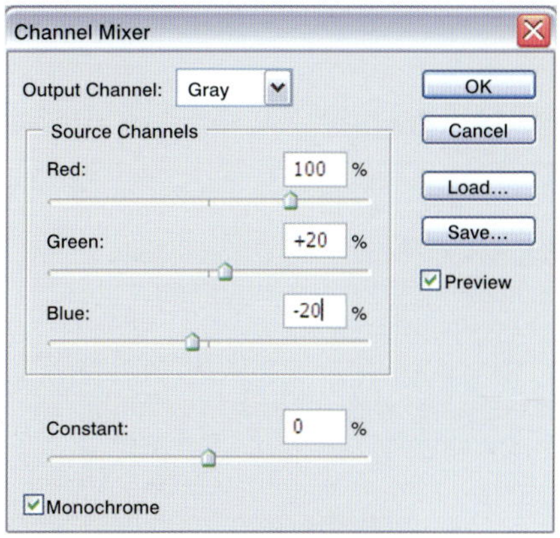

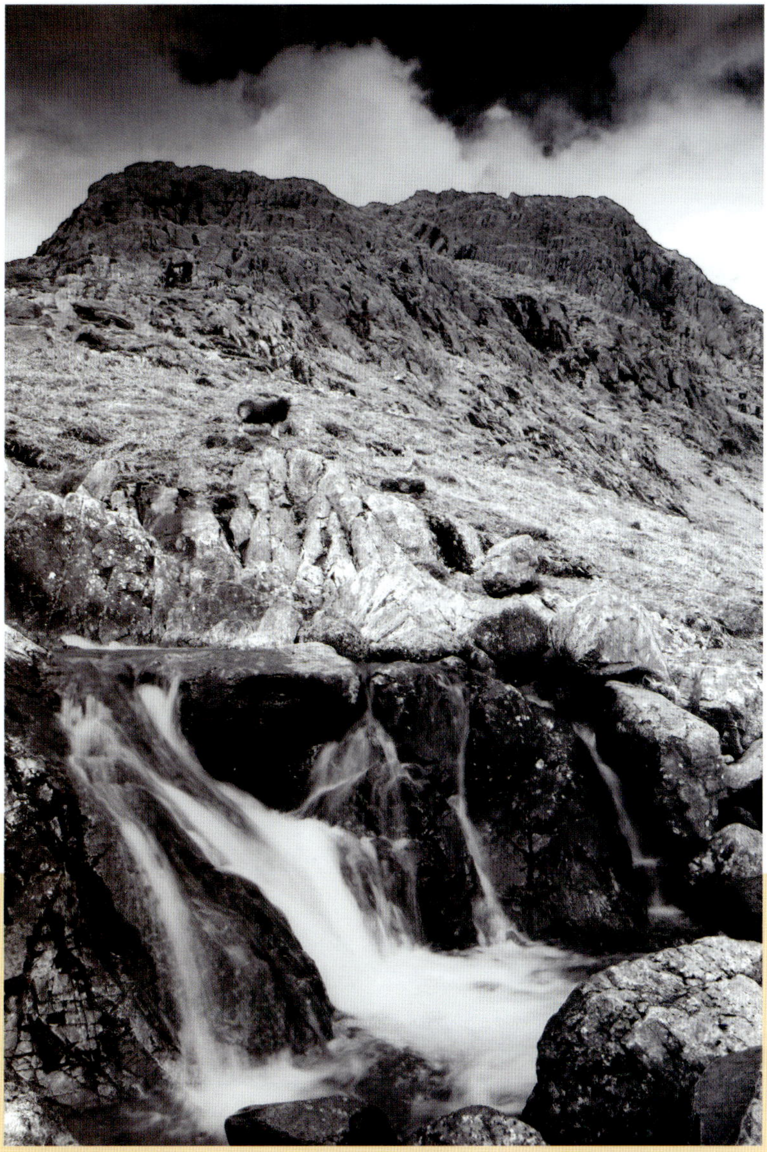

› The settings used for this conversion have added much more contrast to the image, just like using a red filter on black and white film. Notice how the white ouds and blue sky stand out compared to e standard conversion, and the browns of e landscape are much lighter.

Duotones and Tritones

We have already discussed how to achieve limited color ranges in your images and how these can create different looks and moods. But here is a simple way of achieving a limited color range no matter what the original colors of the subject. Toning is traditionally the arena of black-and-white photography, but digital photography means that you no longer have to conform to the usual black-and-white or color rules when shooting images. Adding tone and color to monochrome images is a great way of using colors to create specific moods.

One of the most versatile ways of toning your images is to use the Duotone option in Photoshop. This technique has its roots in traditional black-and-white printing, but the digital option does not involve messy chemicals or the potential health risks of working in the darkroom. This tool gives the option of using up to four separate colors to tone your images; these can be targeted at specific density ranges in the original image. For the main tutorial, we will be dealing with two tones (duotones), although using three (tritones) or four (quadtones) tones can produce dramatically colored results.

Step 1

If your image is color, the first thing to do is to convert it to grayscale (Image › Mode › Grayscale) to use the Duotone mode. You then need to convert the image to Duotone by going to Image › Mode › Duotone. This brings up an option window for you to customize the exact tones of the image. We chose Duotone from the Type dropdown menu, as we wanted only two tones. For our image, we used black as the first color. We then clicked on the white color box and chose a Pantone blue as the second color.

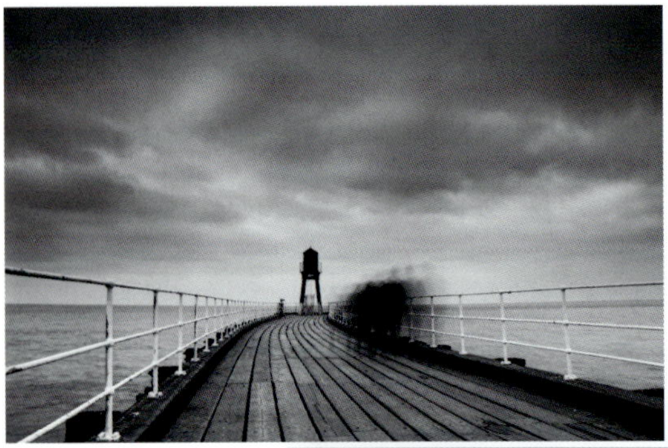

You need to start with a grayscale image to work with duotones in Photoshop. In black and white, this image lacked the atmosphere that I was looking to create.

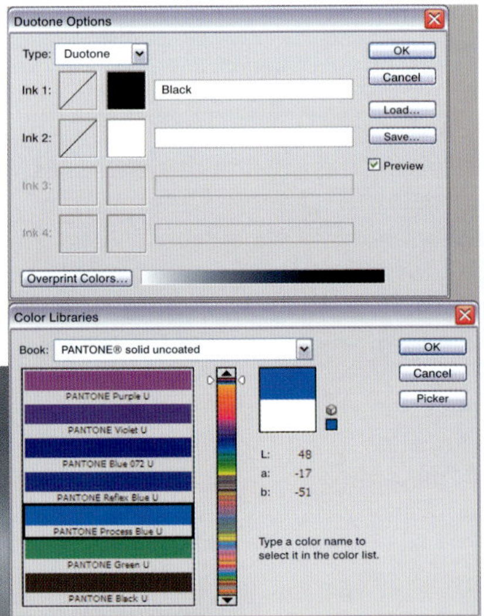

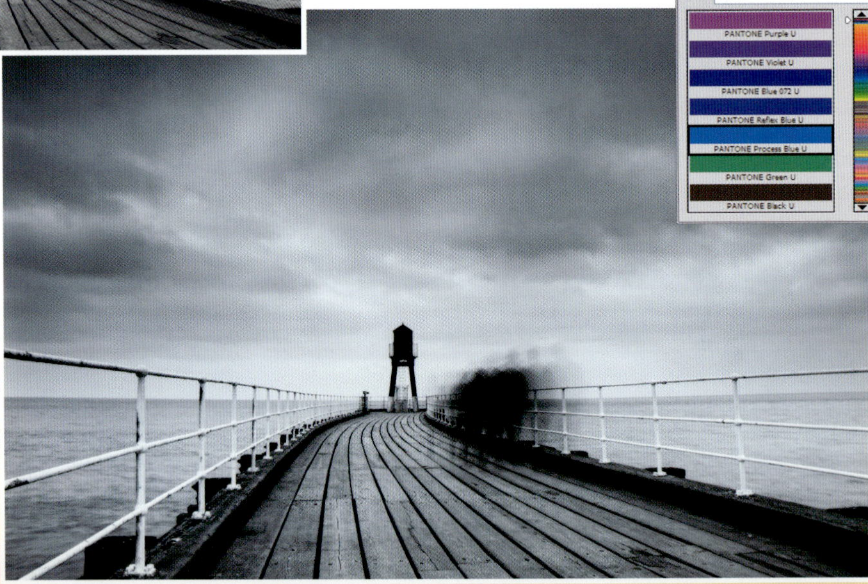

By adding a blue and black duotone, the image has been given a cool, mysterious mood that was lacking in the original.

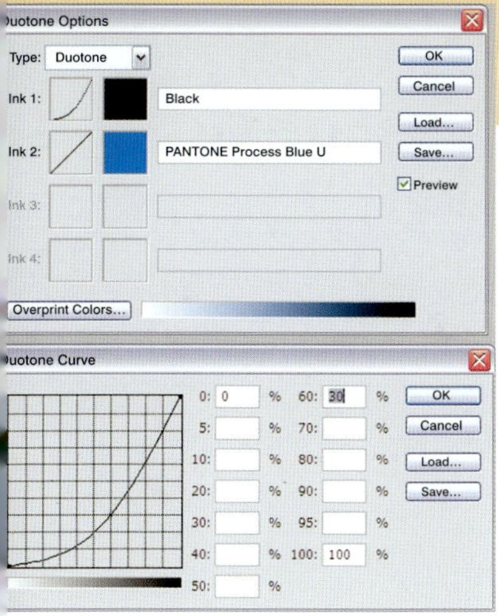

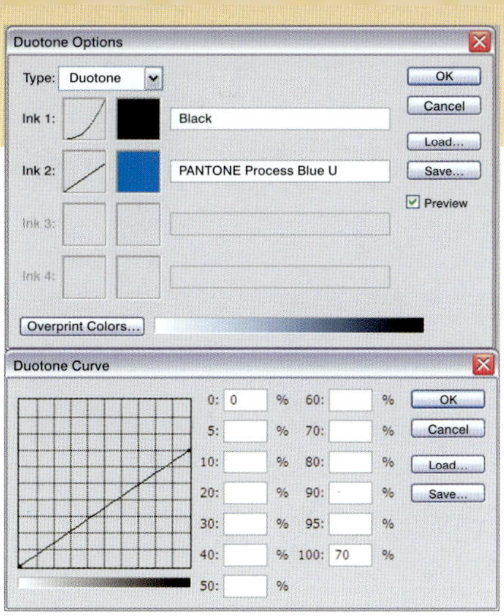

Tip

Black-and-white conversions
Simply converting from color to grayscale sometimes does not give a suitable tonal range to your image. For more control over the final image, you can use the Channel Mixer to fine-tune how the colors translate to black and white before converting to grayscale to use the Duotone option.

'tep 2
o adjust the density areas that the 'uotones will affect, click on the graph ext to the color box. With the graph djustment window for the black we ntered a value of 30 in the 60% box o give the curve a steeper angle to dd a little contrast to the black tones. o confirm your changes, click OK in he Duotone Curve window, but keep he Duotone Options window open.

Step 3
Now click on the graph next to the blue and enter 70 in the 100% box. This will drop the line to give the blue tones lower contrast, and leave the lighter areas of the image clear. Once happy with the result, click OK. These values are correct for our image, but you can experiment with different ones, or even click and drag on the curve itself to alter its shape. Try not to introduce heavily shaped curves or the image may start to solarize (have reversed tones like a negative).

ritones

he techniques for producing tritones re very similar to duotones, but you eed to select this option from the ype dropdown menu. This will give he option of three different tones. Ve left the black and blue tones as he duotone example, but added an range tone to replicate a classic epia/blue split-tone effect.

In the orange tone graph adjustment 'indow, we entered values of 0 in the 00% box and 30 in the 50% box to roduce an upturned U-shaped curve. his shape means that the orange tones would mainly affect the midtones of the image, leaving the blue and black tones visible in other areas.

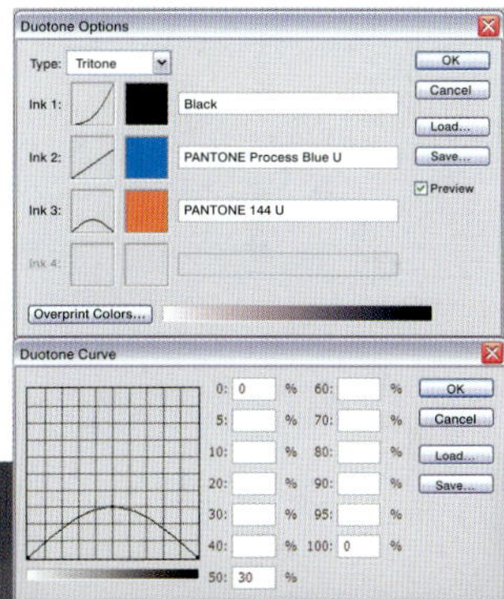

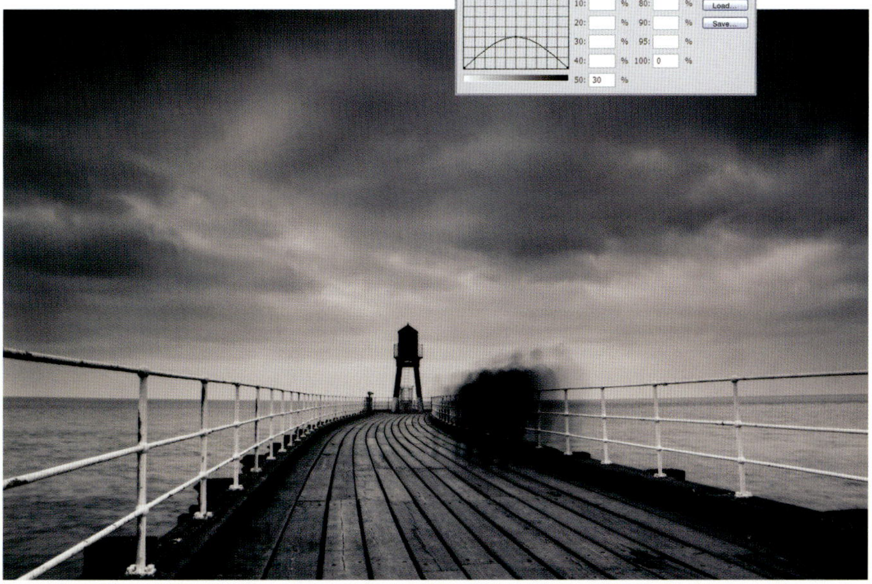

Tritones can be used to echo the split-toning techniques such as sepia/blue, as with this image.

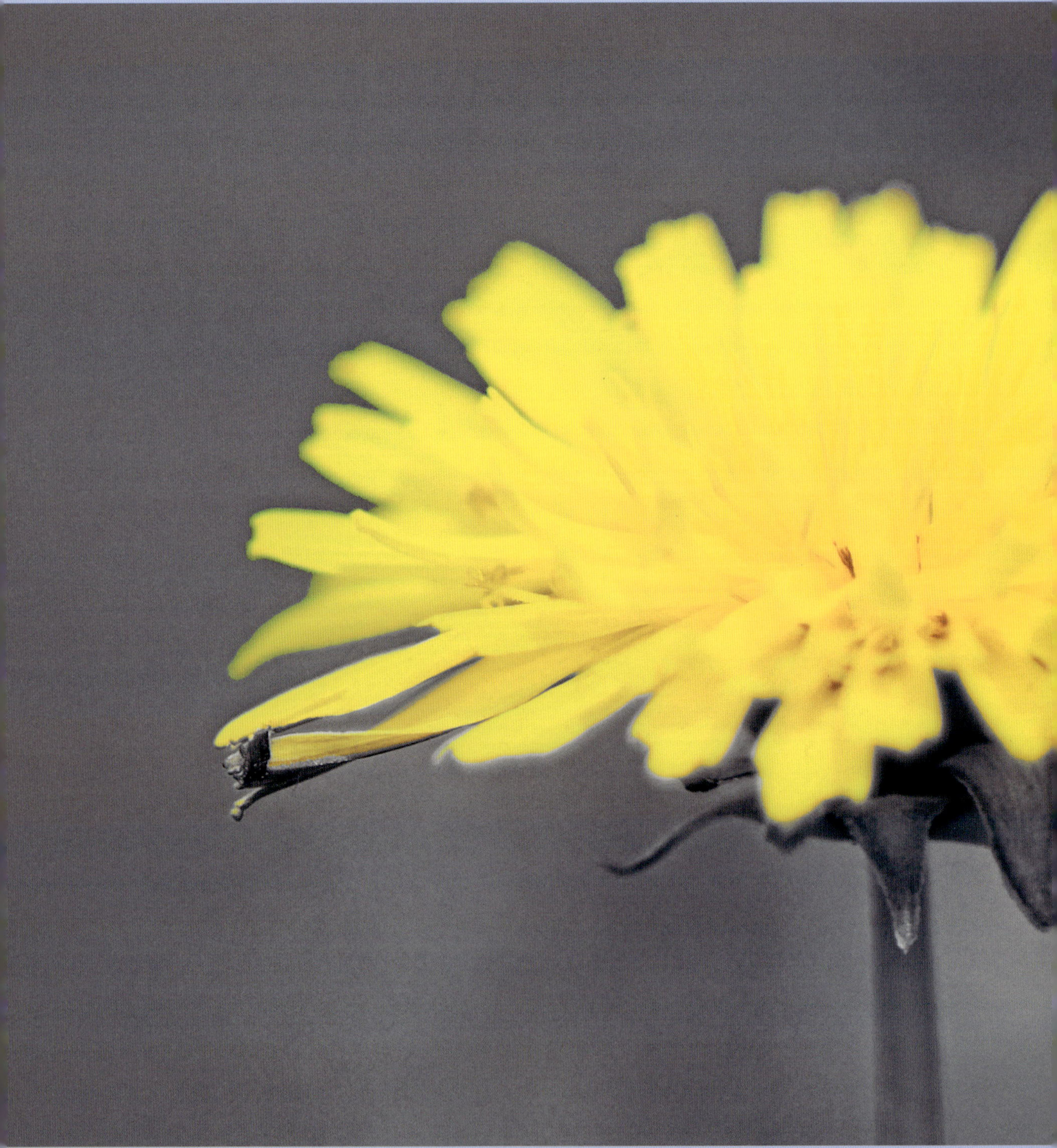

Beyond Visible Color

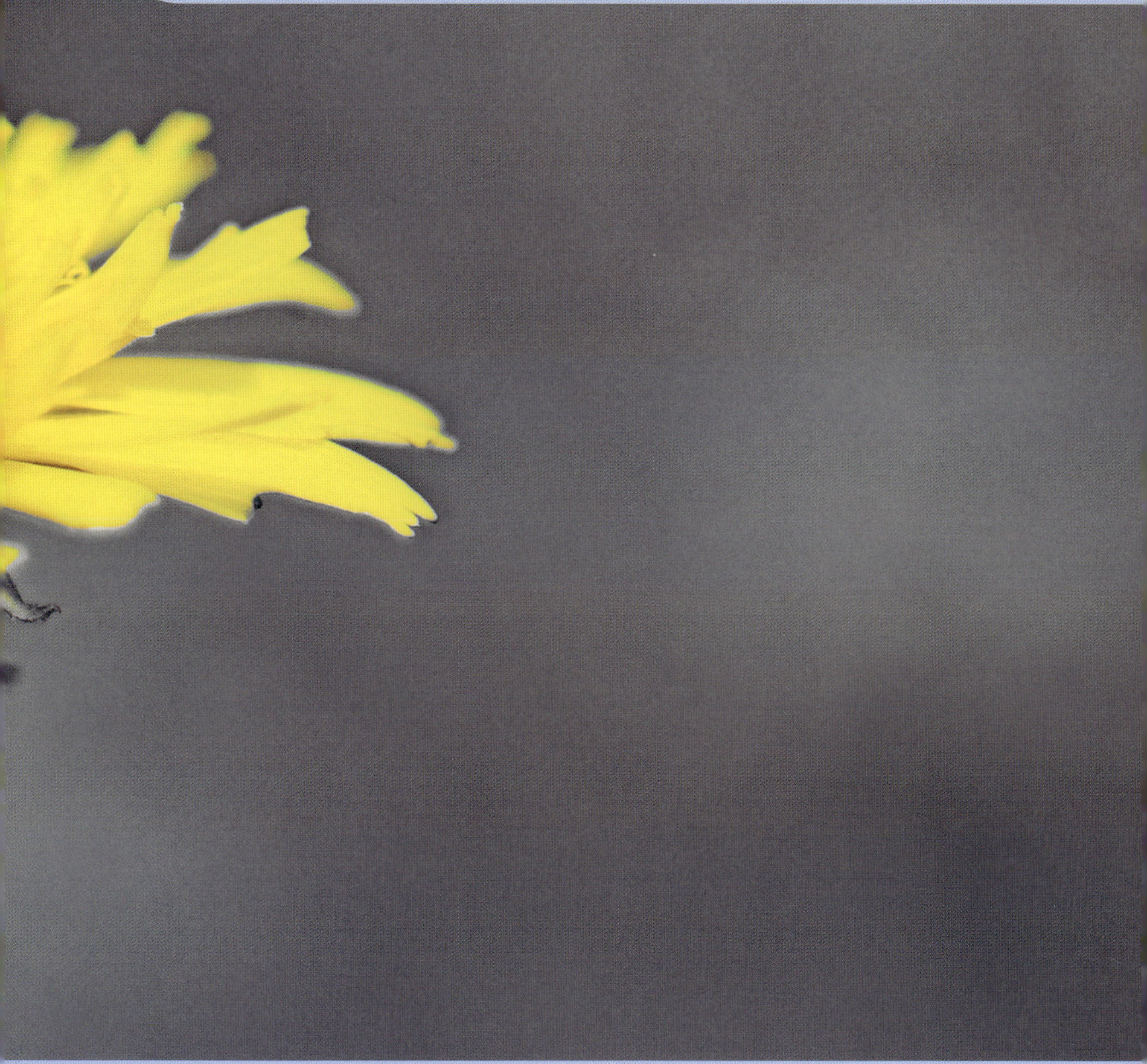

Color Popping

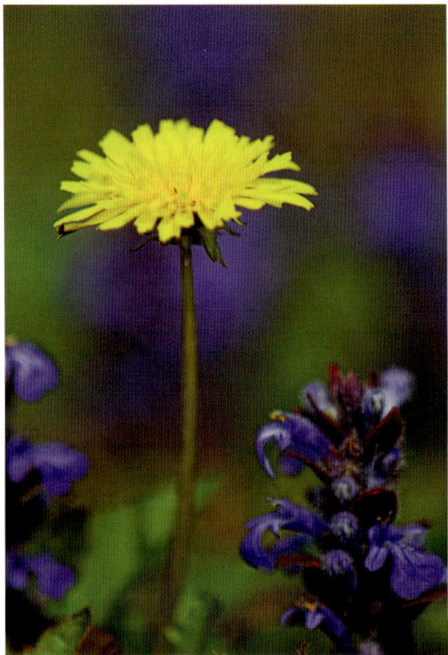

Although this yellow flower gives a strong focal point to the image, the brightly colored background and the blue flowers in the foreground detract from its impact.

You do not have to choose between just color or black and white images. The power and versatility of digital gives you the option of combining the two in one image. This technique, where you selectively turn parts of your image monochrome while leaving others in color, is commonly known as "color popping," and can create striking images.

This technique is most successful when your original image contains an easily recognizable primary-colored object to use as the colored subject. Leaving strong primary colors isolated against a black-and-white background makes them really stand out in the image, creating maximum impact.

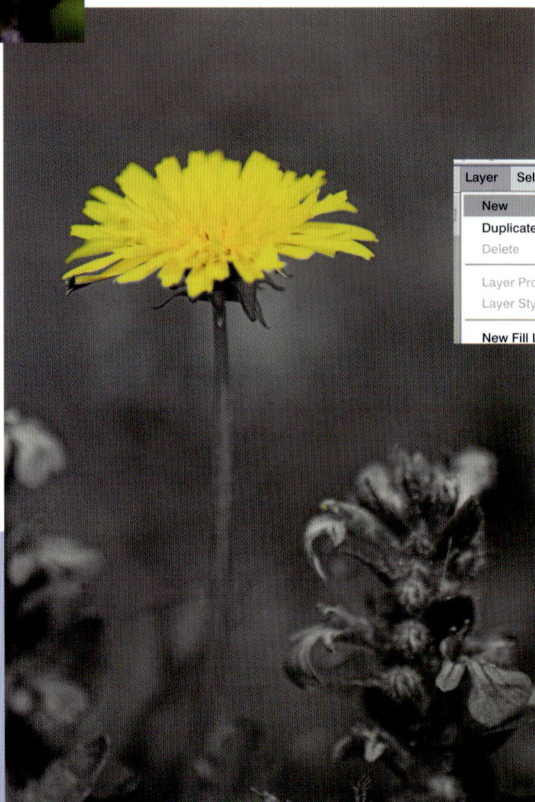

Leaving the yellow flower colored while removing the color from the rest of the image produces a much more eye catching result, as the flower becomes far more dominant in the frame.

Color selection

Step 1
Before you start this technique, it is best to create a new layer by going to Layer › Layer Via Copy to leave your original image untouched. This will also give you more options for combining your adjusted image with the original for other effects (see panel).

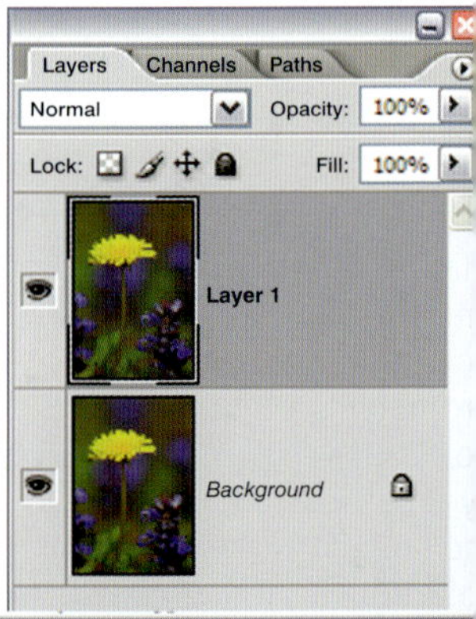

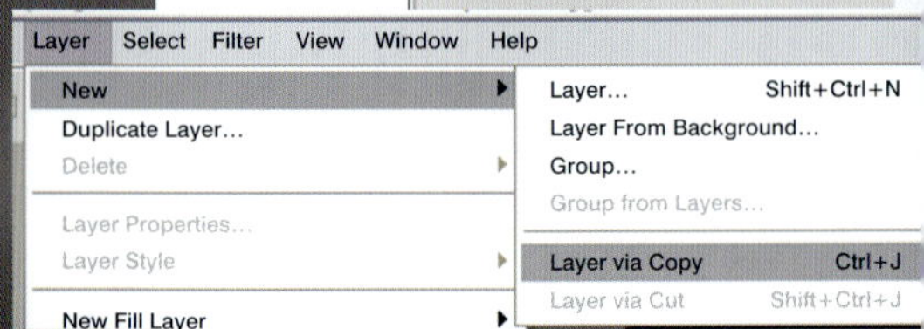

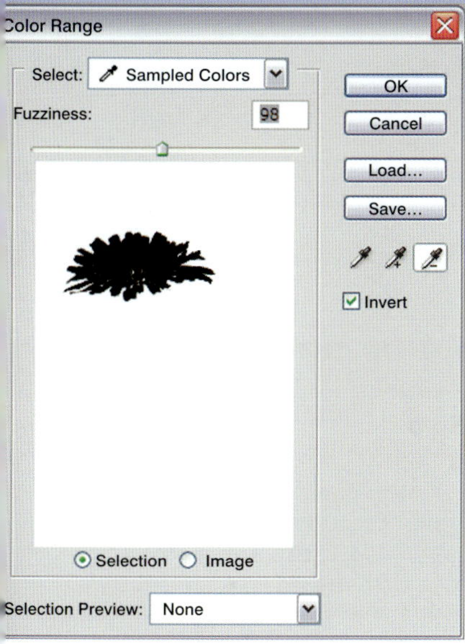

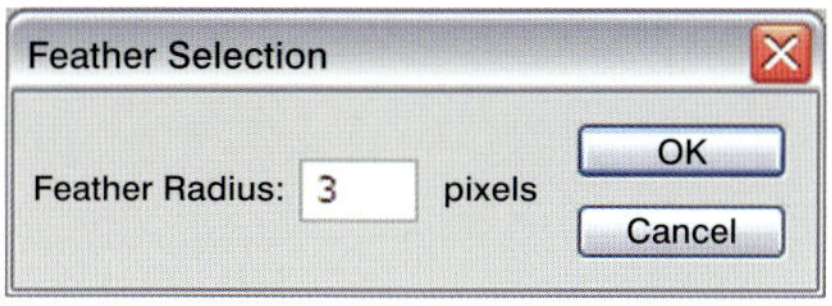

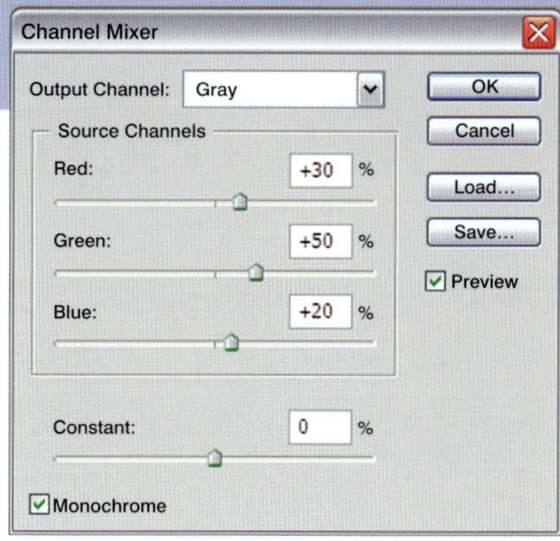

tep 2
nsuring that the new layer is ighlighted in the Layers palette, you ow need to select the area that you ant to remove the color from. The asiest way is to use the Color Range election tool (Select › Color Range). n the Color Range window, ensure hat the Selection option is ticked nder the image preview, the Sampled olors is selected in the Select ropdown menu, and the Invert tick ox is checked. Using the main yedropper tool, click on the area of he image that you want to remain in olor. Adjust the Fuzziness slider until nly this area is visible in the preview. ou may need to add or remove areas om the selection using the + and – yedroppers to fine-tune your election. Once you are happy with he selection, click OK.

Step 3
You now need to feather the selection by going to Selection › Feather. This will smooth the transition between the areas to compensate for any slight inaccuracies in the selection. A value between 2 and 5 pixels should be fine; I used a value of 3 pixels for this image, as there was a lot of fine detail. Then click OK to confirm this value.

Step 4
To remove the color from the selection, you can use any of the usual Photoshop options. I used the Channel Mixer for maximum control over the tones in the image to allow me to ensure the background was just as I wanted. For a simpler conversion, you could use the Image › Adjustments › Desaturate option. Once you are happy with your image, you need to reduce it to a single layer (Layer › Flatten Image) before saving.

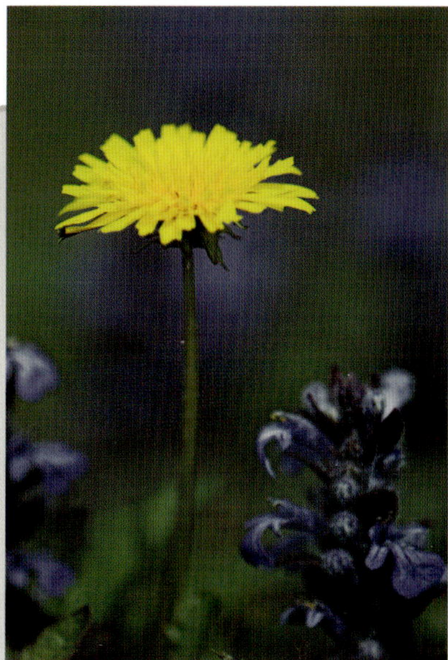

By using Layers, you can leave just a hint of color rather than remove it all together for a more subtle effect.

Reducing the Color

Reduce the Opacity of the black and white layer by using the slider in the top right of the Layers palette. The exact value is down to personal preference, but to leave just a little color in the image, a value of between 60% and 80% will give the best results.

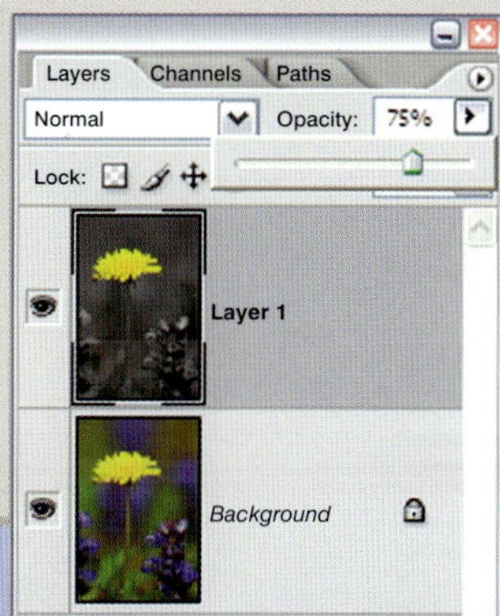

Solarization

When a film or piece of photographic paper is exposed to light part-way during its development, and the development is then continued as normal, some tones in the image become reversed. This technique, known as solarization, was used most notably in black and white by the photographers Man Ray (1890–1976) and Lee Miller (1907–1977), whose images portrayed a distorted reality much like the surrealist artists of the period.

This effect works only on part-developed images, as the light exposure will not affect the areas that have already developed as much as the clear areas. The edges between these two areas are also often affected, and visible lines appear at areas between dark and light tones of the original image.

The effect, although tricky, can be done fairly easily by anyone with their own darkroom using black and white materials. Solarizing color images is almost impossible to control in any predictable way, so this technique has historically been the reserve of monochrome workers.

All this has changed with digital imaging, as you can create effects easily without damaging the originals, or wasting precious materials on trying to achieve the result you want. You can recreate solarization techniques on black-and-white and color images.

Color Solarization

Before you start, you need to create a new layer with a copy of your background image by going to Layer › New › Layer Via Copy. Once you have done this, the technique for solarizing your images uses the Curves adjustments (Image › Adjustments › Curves) to reverse colors and tones in your images selectively. You access the different Color Channels by using the Channel dropdown menu at the top of the Curves Adjustment window. Use the examples here as a starting point for your own images and experiment to achieve the results that you want.

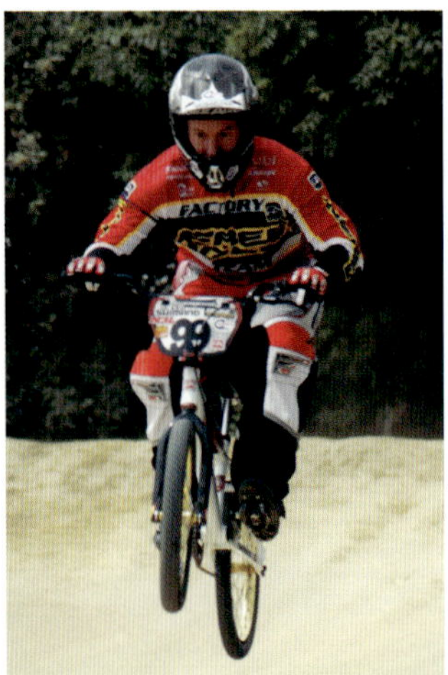

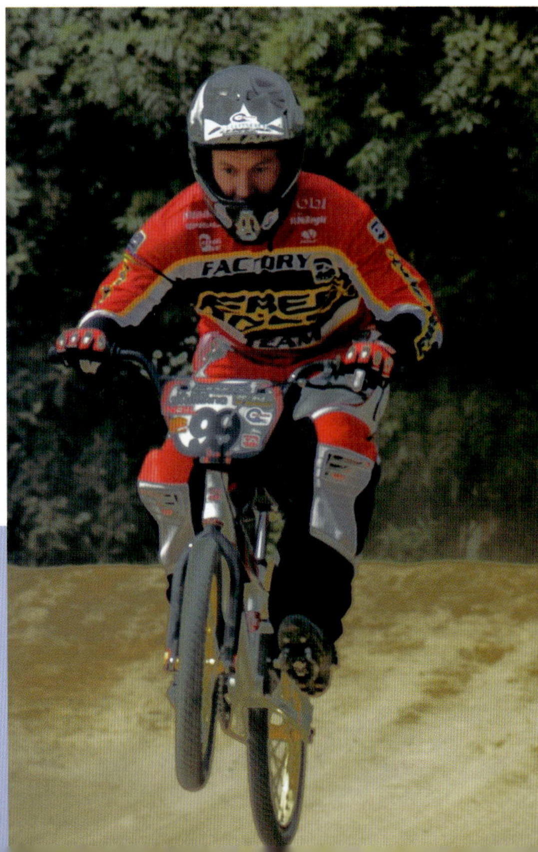

This technique does not work for every image, but by reversing some of the colors in the image you can produce graphic, striking images.

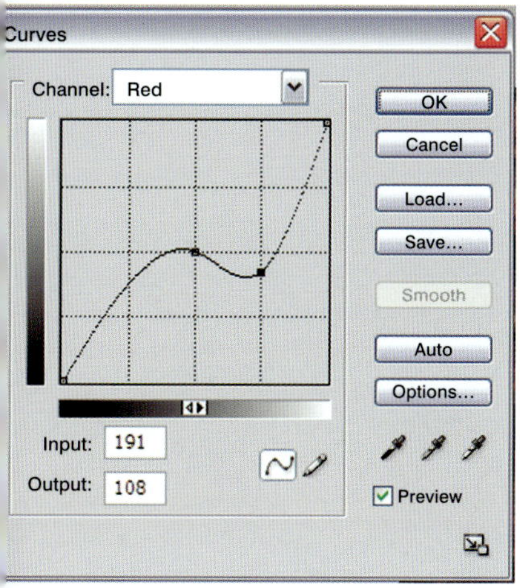

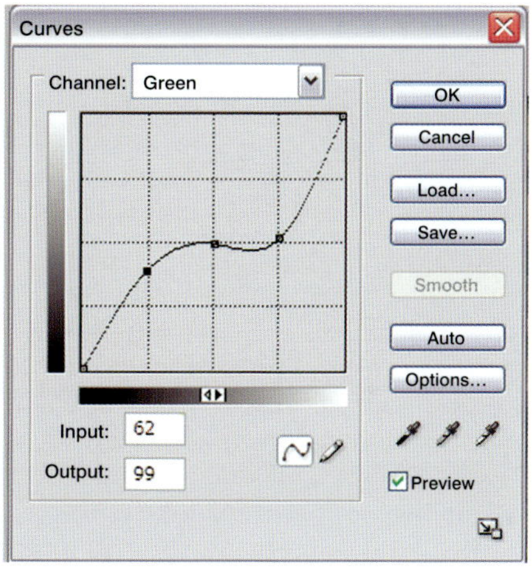

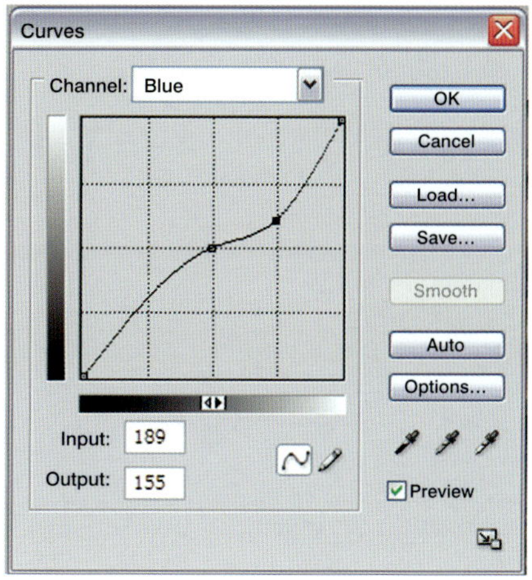

ed Channel
/ith all the channels, begin by locking
ıe mid-point of the line by clicking on
once. You will see a black dot appear
here the line is locked. For our image,
e needed to apply a very strong curve
› the line in the Red Channel. You do
ıis by dragging the top half of the line
own, and then the bottom half up.
›u get the reversed tones anywhere
hen this line becomes horizontal
· beyond.

Green Channel
We wanted only a slight reversal in the green tones, so we applied a less extreme curve than for the Red Channel. There is still some solarization in this color, however.

Blue Channel
Our image contained very little blue, so we applied only a very slight curve, mainly in the highlights (the top half of the line).

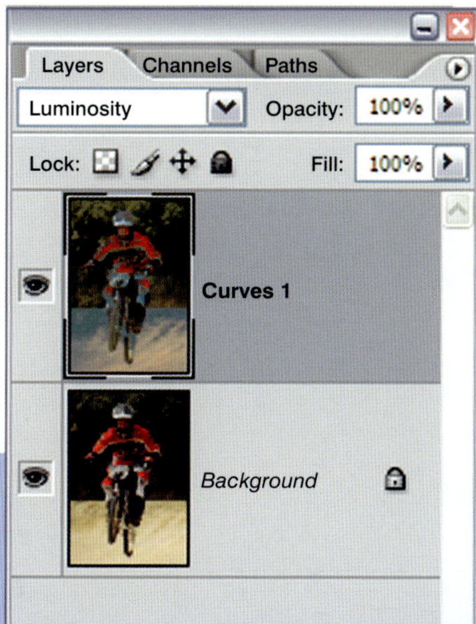

Blend Mode
To mix the adjusted layer and the original image to give a more realistic result, we changed the Blend Mode at the top of the Layers palette to Luminosity. To save the image, you need to reduce it to a single layer by going to Layer › Flatten Image.

Cross-processing

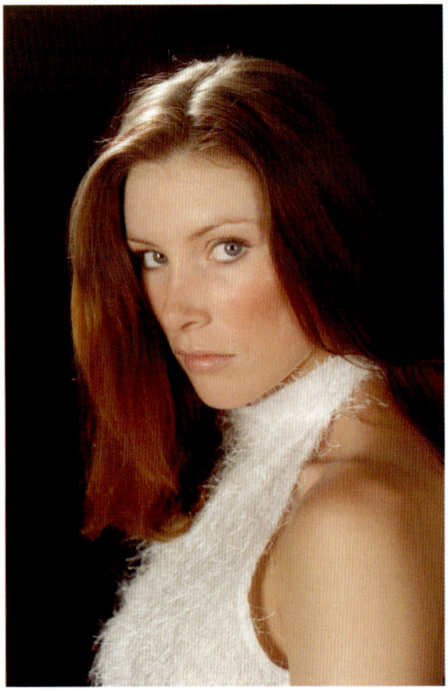

The effect of processing films in the wrong chemicals was probably discovered by accident, but it has become popular, especially among portrait and fashion photographers, because of the distinctive colors and tones it produces. This technique is known as cross-processing and there are two main ways to do it: using color slide film and processing it as if it were a color print film, and vice versa.

Both methods can produce striking results, but the most popular for many years was to use a color print film designed for weddings or portraits such as Kodak VPS and process it in E-6 chemicals to produce color slides. The colors and contrast of the resultin slides bear little resemblance to the original tones. The contrast of the highlights is compressed, making ther appear much lighter, and the shadows typically have a cyan color cast.

While this effect is easy to produce with film, many processing labs are unwilling to put the wrong film throug their machines for fear of damage, and predicting the final result takes practice—and wasted film—before yo achieve the desired effect.

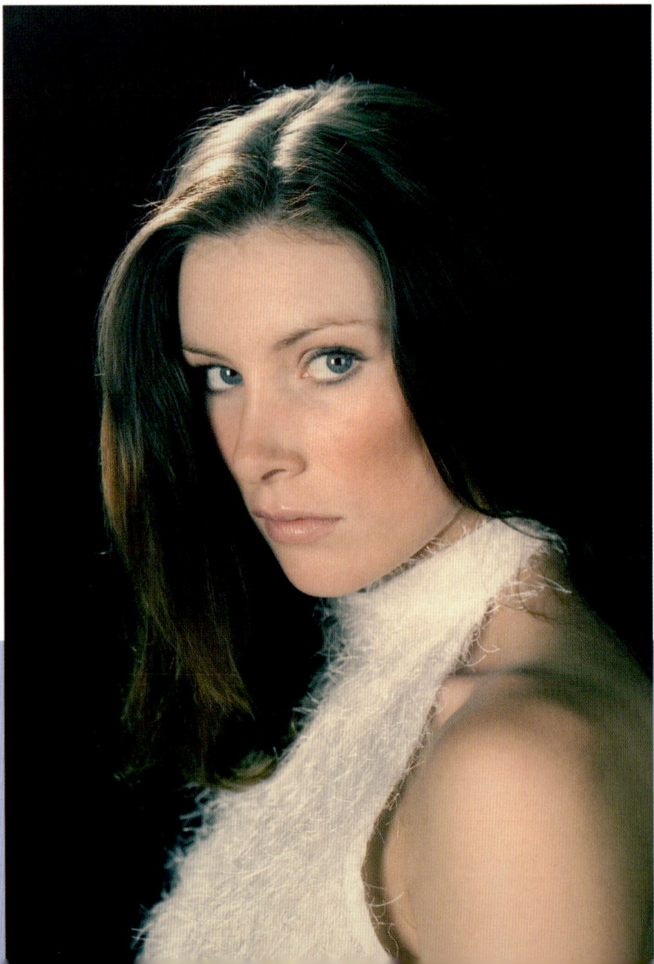

Using the Curves adjustment allows you to give your images the look of a cross-processed film image. The cyan-colored shadows and pale skin tones are characteristic of processing color print film in chemicals designed for color slides.

Vith digital images, you can
:xperiment to your heart's content
vithout fear of ruining a precious
›hotograph as long as you save a
:opy of the original. So, here is how
o recreate a cross-processed look.

Master Channel
Apply a single mouse click on the bottom quarter of the line to lock the shadow density, then drag the top quarter of the line upward to lighten the midtones and highlights.

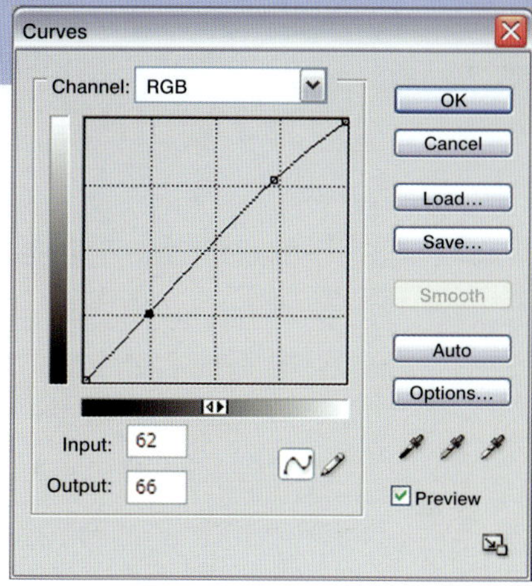

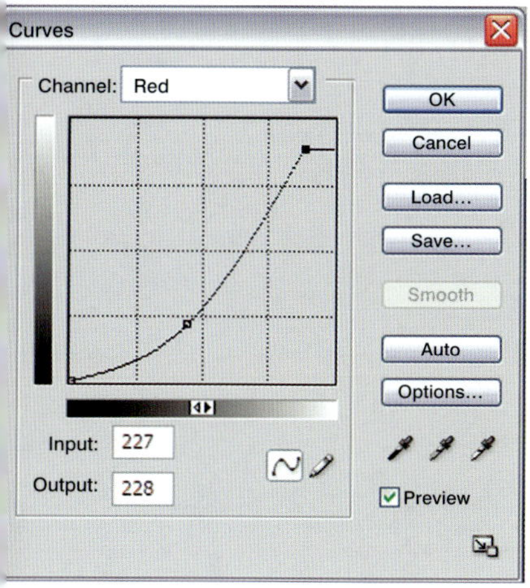

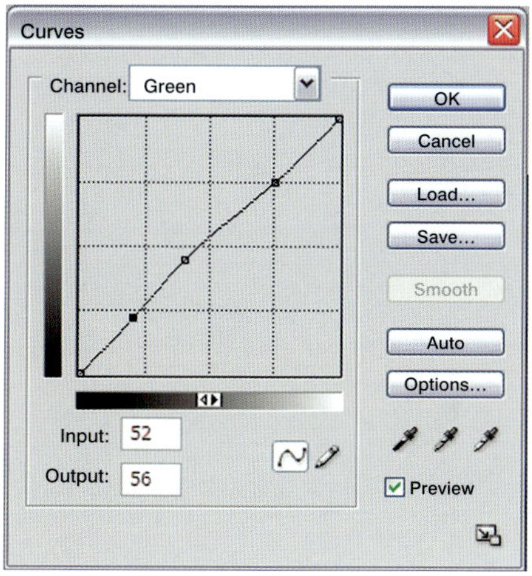

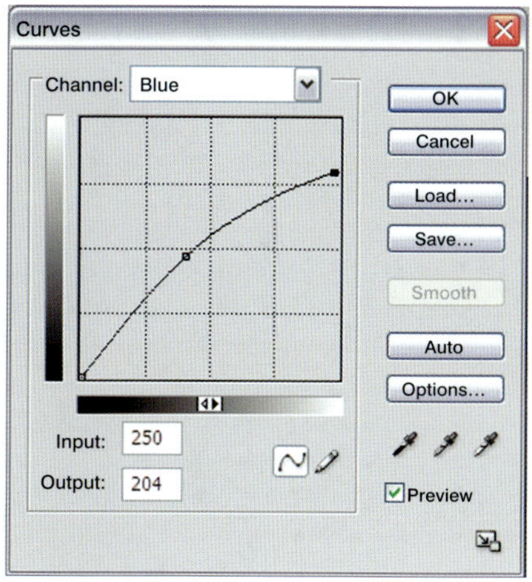

:ed Channel
ı this channel, single-click on the
ne around halfway inside the top
ght box, then drag the very top
orner of the graph down the vertical
xis slightly to remove reds from the
ighlights. Now drag the lower portion
own slightly to change the color of
ıe shadows.

Green Channel
Only a slight adjustment is needed for this channel. Single-click to lock both the bottom and top quarters of the line, then drag the middle upward very slightly to lighten the midtones.

Blue Channel
In the Blue Channel, drag the very top right corner of the graph down the vertical axis. To remove blue from the highlights, drag the center of the line upward.

Infrared

There is a whole range of radiation that we never see because it is outside the wavelengths of our visual spectrum. That does not mean that it can be entirely ignored when it comes to photography, however, as both film and digital sensors can be sensitive to these "invisible" wavelengths.

These wavelengths can occur at both infrared and ultraviolet wavelengths; it is the infrared end that is most useful to photographers. There are special films in both black and white and color that are designed to be sensitive to this radiation and can produce startling and unique results.

Most digital sensors are also sensitive to this infrared radiation, but many manufacturers use a glass filter in front of the sensor to stop them being recorded. This is to allow the camera to record images that more closely match the way we see the world, rather than how the sensor would see it. Many of these filters still let some wavelengths of infrared radiation through, however, so with some experimentation can still be used to produce infrared images.

Because we cannot see these rays, the normal convention of recreating the visual world is thrown away, and the only limit is either the technology or your own imagination. So, how do you go about recording this invisible world?

Color Infrared Film

There are few photographic products to match color infrared film when it comes to producing striking, almost unbelievable, results. Using these emulsions requires some careful handling, as they need to be loaded and unloaded from the camera in complete darkness, and predicting the results takes plenty of practice. The images are characterized by bright and punchy colors, especially in bright conditions. Foliage often records as a bright red or magenta, and blue skies as anything from cyan to green. The effect can be altered by using traditional colored filters, especially the deep red that is normally used to darken skies in black and white. This film can also be used with an opaque infrared filter for the most extreme results. Forget any thoughts of color accuracy, and you will not be disappointed if you want your images to have plenty of impact.

Black-and-White Infrared Film

The grainy images with an almost supernatural glow produced by black-and-white infrared film have long been a favorite among the more arty monochrome workers.

Like the color infrared films, these have to be loaded and unloaded in complete darkness, and the results depend on both the amount of infrared radiation present and the filter used. All infrared shooting is best done in bright, sunny conditions, when there is more of this radiation present.

With a deep red filter in place to cut out most of the visible light, the results are striking. Foliage, especially fresh new growth, has an unearthly glow as the chlorophyll reflects infrared very well. Skin tones are generally much paler than they normally appear, again due to reflected infrared radiation.

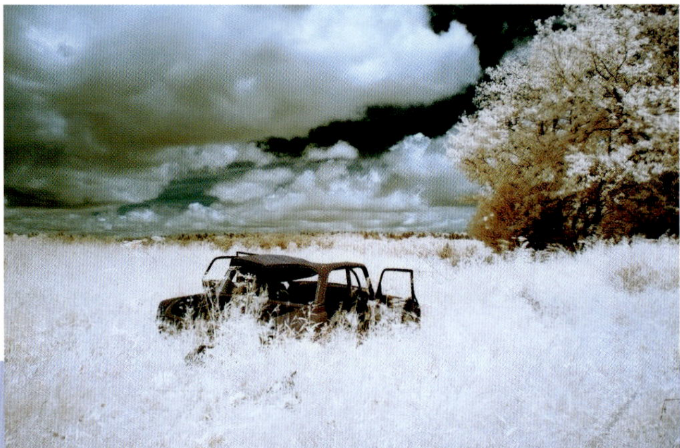

« The colors from infrared film can produce stunning results for those looking for a break from the reality of the normal scene.

Tip

Infrared radiation is focused in a slightly different plane to visible light, so it is recommended that you slightly defocus the lens to account for this. Many lenses have a small dot to indicate this position next to the normal focusing mark. This is only a problem when using an infrared filter, though, and using a small aperture setting for maximum depth of field will usually deal with the issue anyway.

Digital Infrared

Many digital cameras can be used to capture black-and-white infrared images. All you need is a special filter that cuts out all of the visual light, and lets only infrared radiation through. Before buying one, it is worth checking to see whether your camera is sensitive to this radiation.

Placing this filter over the lens means the viewfinder will often go very dark or even completely black. You need to frame up your shot beforehand, making a tripod pretty much essential. The metering can also give completely wrong exposures, as it will not "see" the infrared radiation, so experiment with the settings on your camera.

Post-capture Adjustments

Once you have captured the scene you will be faced with a strange, eerie red or deep magenta image. This is perfectly normal and can soon be corrected by going to Image › Adjustments › Desaturate. The result is likely to look very flat, so go to Image › Adjustments › Levels and drag the triangles at either end of the graph to meet the body of the histogram to correct the contrast. You may also need to adjust the contrast further using Curves (Image › Adjustments › Curves) for your own images.

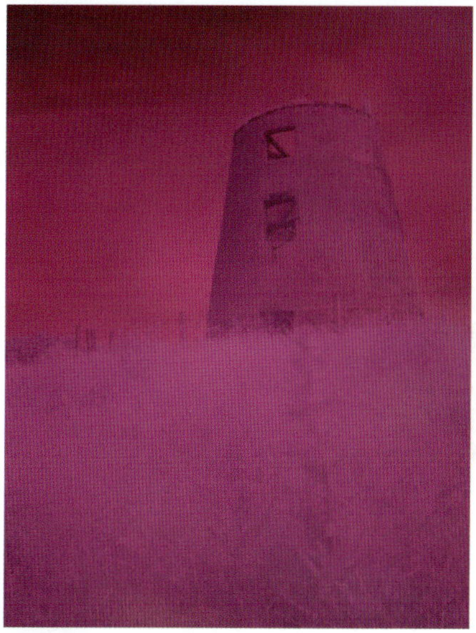

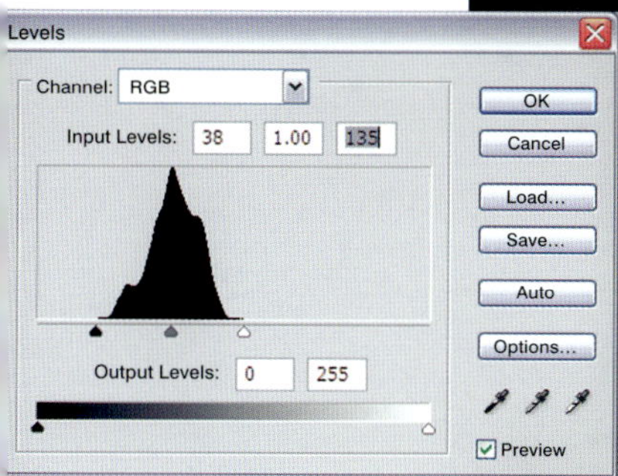

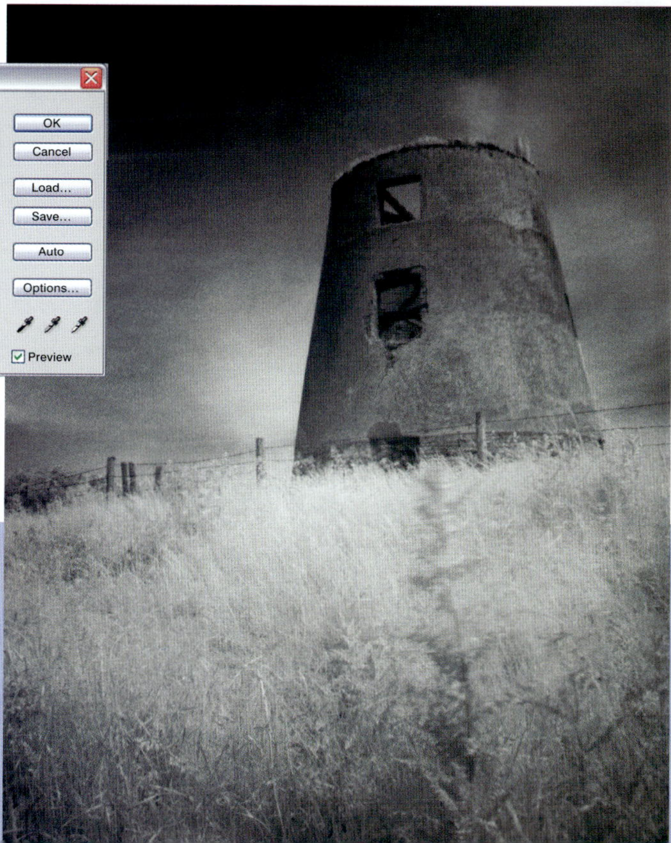

The results using an infrared filter on your digital camera do not look great straight from the camera (above). However, the strong color cast and contrast are easily adjusted to give a striking black and white result.

Recreating a Black and White Infrared Image in Photoshop

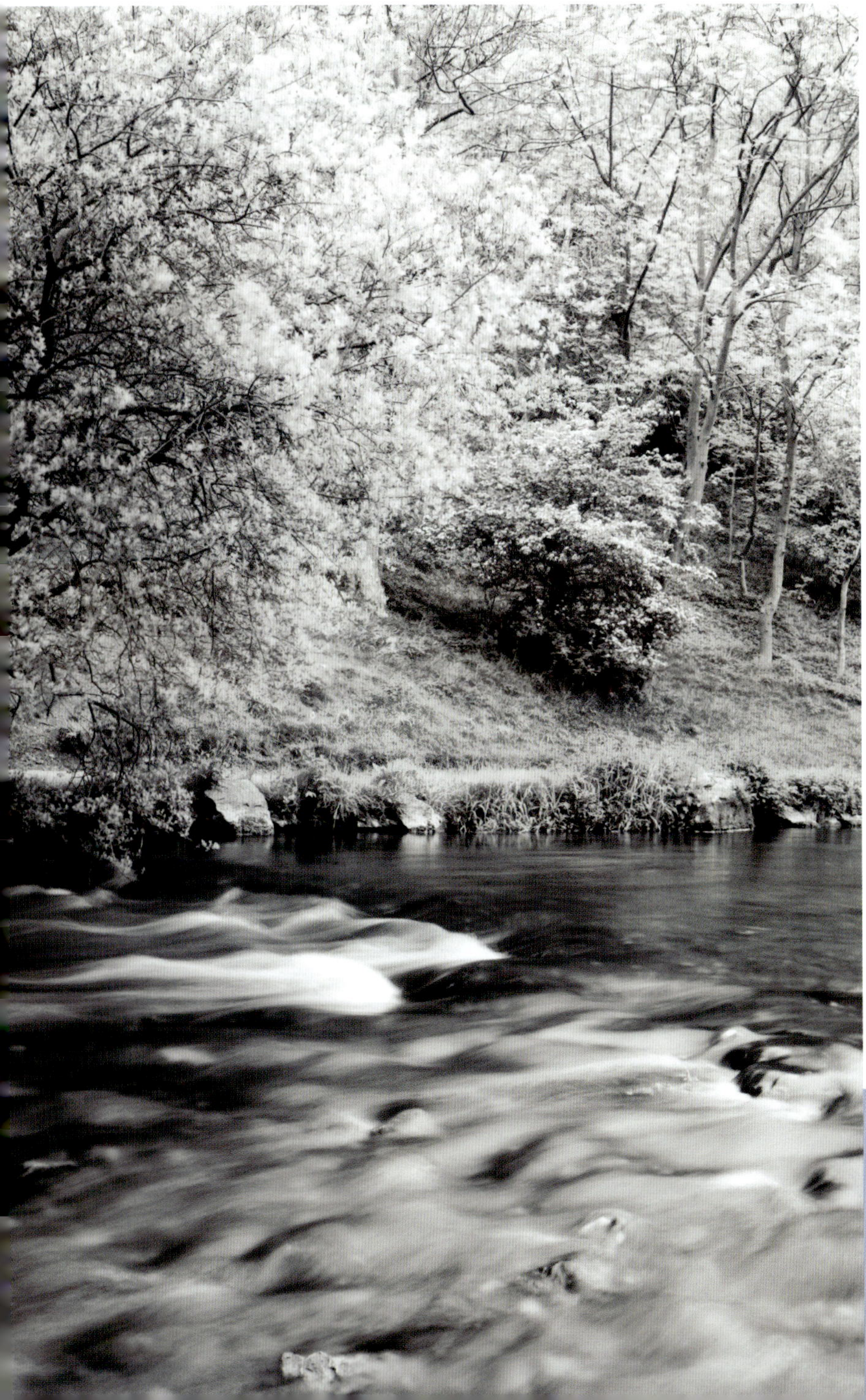

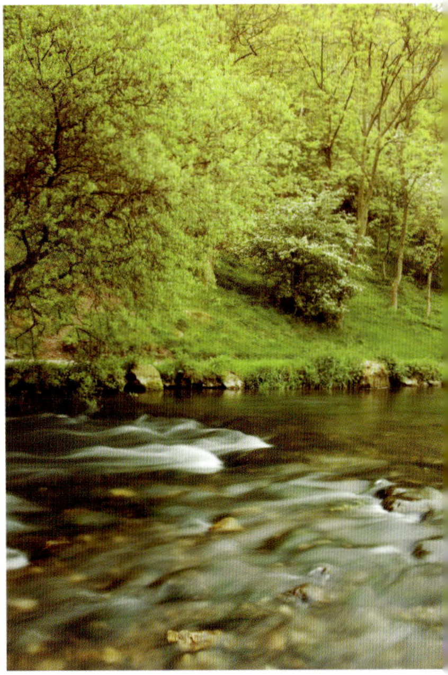

If you do not have an infrared filter or your camera is not sensitive to infrared, you can still achieve a similar result from a color original. Similar to infrared capture, this effect works best on shots with bright, fresh green foliage, as in our spring image, here.

Tip

For those who want to take digital infrared photography further, there are a number of specialist repairers who will remove the filter from the sensor to allow the camera to record this radiation.

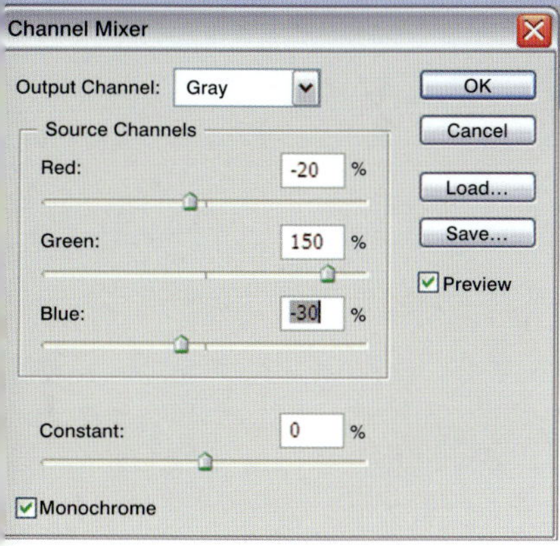

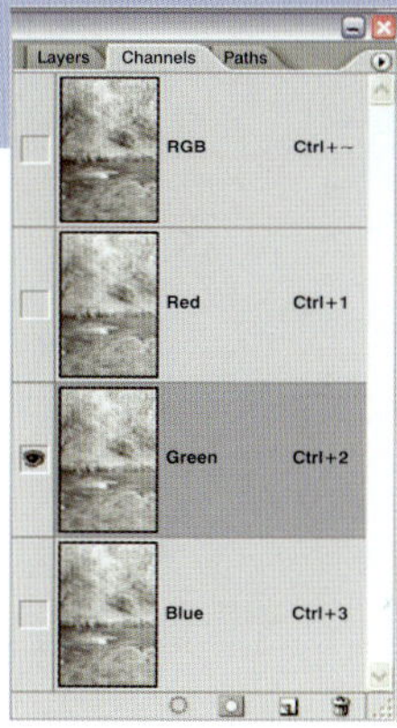

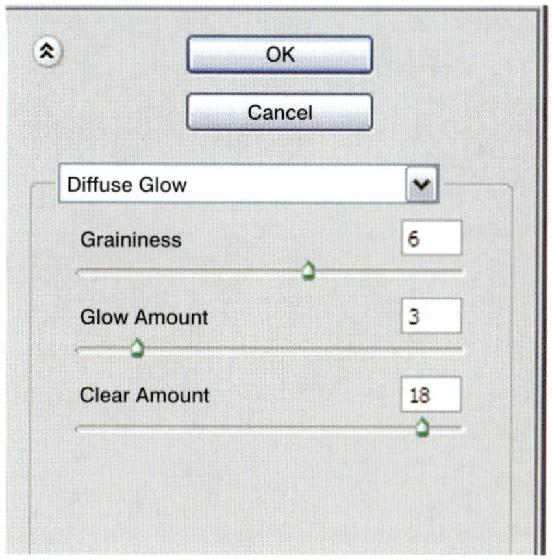

Step 1
You need to create a new layer by going to Layer › New › Layer Via Copy before you start creating this effect. With this new layer active, you then go to Image › Adjustments › Channel Mixer and select the Monochrome option in the Window. Then adjust the color sliders as we did in the black and white conversion. Use settings of -20 Red, +150 Green, and –30 Blue as a starting point. When adjusting these settings, you are looking to make the foliage lighter.

Step 2
Once you have the right black and white look for the top layer, click back onto the background in the Layers palette, then open the Channels palette by clicking on the tab. You now want to add the characteristic glow to the highlights of infrared, so click on the Green Channel, then go to Filter › Distort › Diffuse Glow.

In the new window, start with settings of 6 Graininess, 3 Glow Amount, and 18 Clear Amount. What you are looking for is a subtle glow without too many blown highlights.

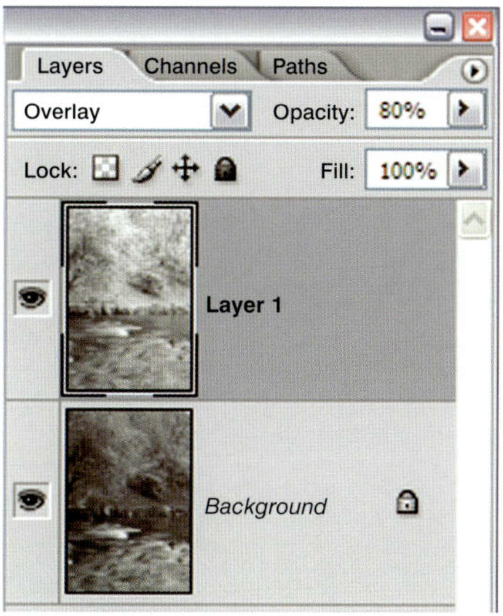

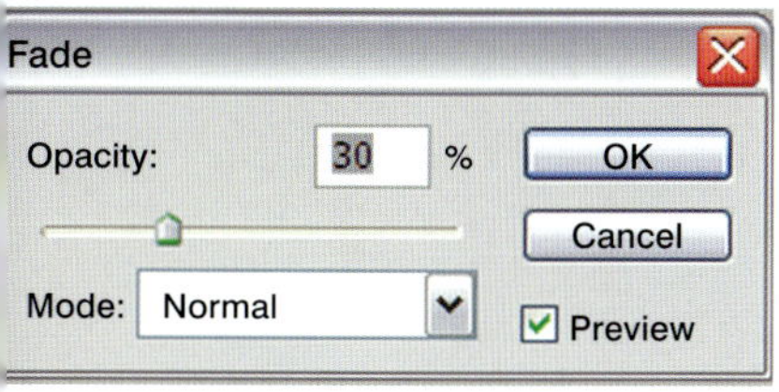

Step 3
Once you are happy with the settings, click OK and then go to Edit › Fade Diffuse Glow. Enter a value of 30% on the Opacity slider and click OK.

With the main effect achieved, click back to the RGB option in the Channels palette and remove the color by going to Image › Adjustments › Desaturate. Then click back onto the top layer in the Layers palette and change the blend mode to Overlay to allow the two images to work together more effectively. To fine-tune the effect, we set the Opacity of the top layer to 80% to allow a little more of the background to show through.

Tip

A handy (although not foolproof) way of checking whether your digital camera is infrared sensitive is to use a standard television remote control. Point it at the lens of the camera and take some shots to find out if it can "see" the infrared beam emitted by the remote.

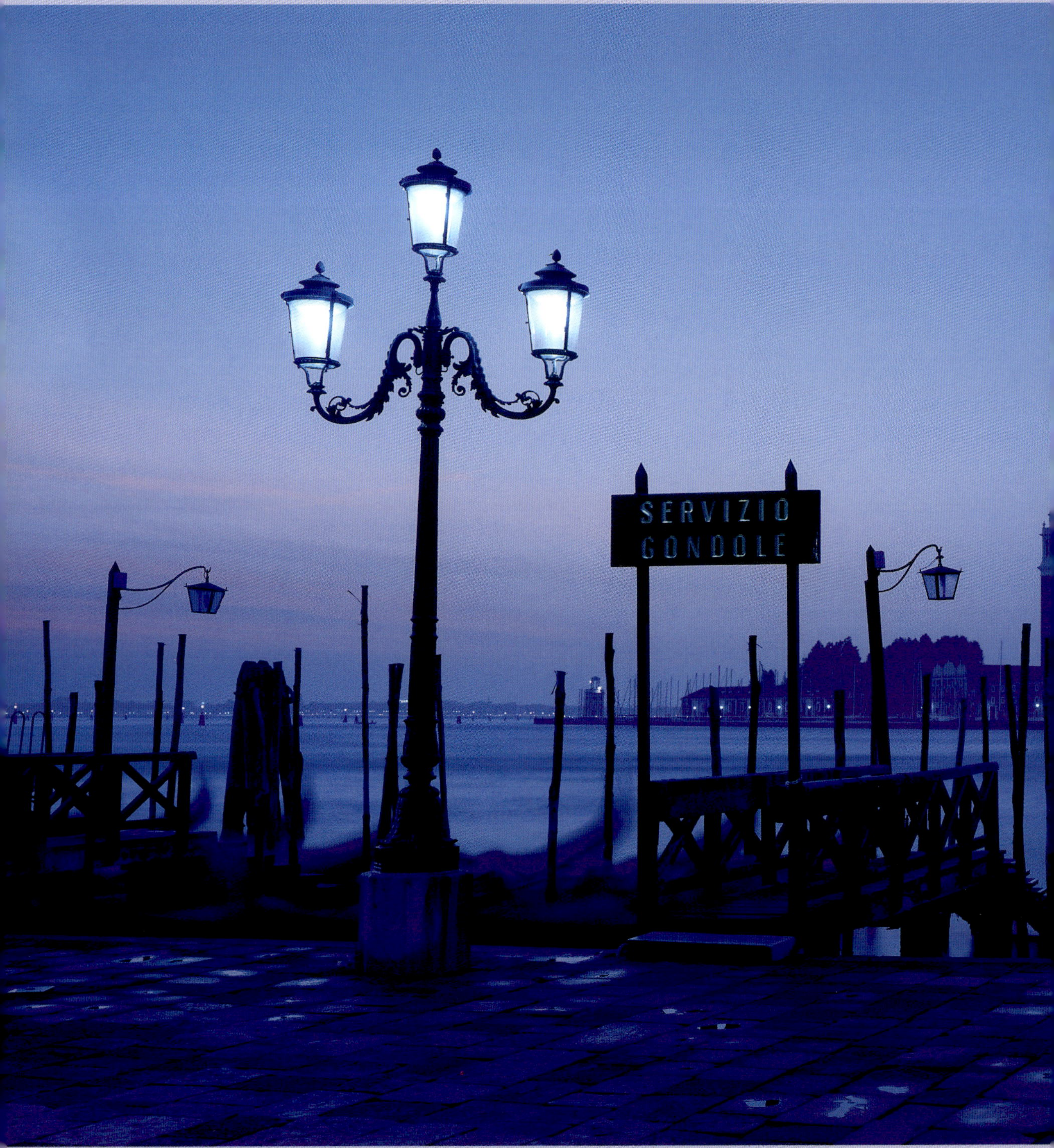
SERVIZIO
GONDOLE

Photographers' Profiles

10

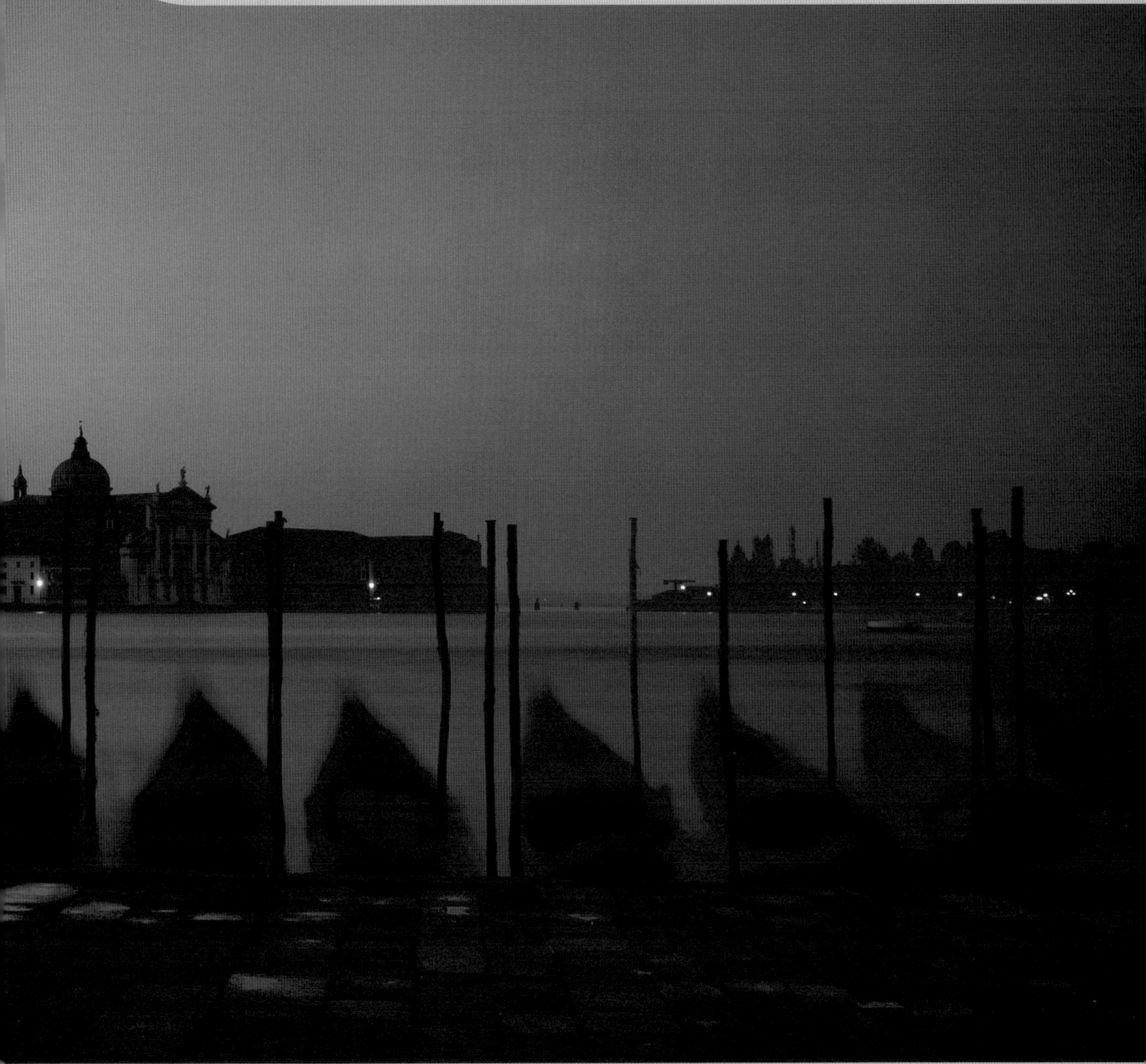

Photographer's Profile

Color can be used in every area of photography, from portraits to landscapes. In the following pages are the profiles of four leading exponents of the art of color photography from very different fields.

Martin Barraud

Constructing complicated sets involving several exposures on a single sheet of 5x4in film at art college was the starting point for Martin Barraud's preference for photography as a conceptual artform rather than the more descriptive approach of many of his contemporaries. During these first experiments, Barraud explored the effect of color in his images. A distinct style began to emerge involving bold use of color, especially blue tones, which has become an essential element of Martin's work ever since.

In 1985, Barraud got his big break in the difficult world of commercial photography when he had the opportunity to work with top special effects photographer Pete Seaward. After a year learning about the realities of working long hours for sometimes demanding clients, his employer announced that he was going to give up the studio to concentrate on location photography.

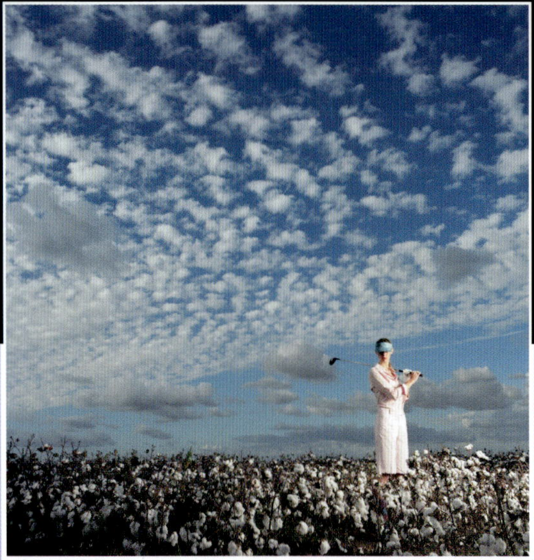

Cotton Golf.

After taking up the offer to buy some of Seaward's studio equipment, Barraud took the plunge to go solo and started a small London studio supplying images for magazine and editorial clients. His use of strong, bold colors helped to bring in the work, especially for covers that needed to stand out on the newsstand.

This desire for images with simple, striking colors has become more important over the years, especially when shooting for picture libraries such as Getty Images. With many thousands of images vying for attention from buyers, Barraud has found that only by using color in tandem with composition and subject matter, can his images stand out in the crowded commercial marketplace.

Although much of Barraud's work relies on complicated sets and choreographing his models into position, nature and luck still play a part in the success of his images. The light and weather conditions can make or break a photoshoot, and has a huge effect on the mood of both the crew and the results. The image of the girl playing golf in a cotton field took meticulous planning to find the right location, but nature played its part by providing the perfect backdrop of "cotton wool" clouds against the deep blue sky just when Barraud was ready to take the shot.

He freely admits that blue is one of the dominant colors in his work, as it suits his style and works well for the images required by his clients. In the shot of 24 people carrying beanbags across the wide-open space of South Africa, the red of the beanbags was deliberately chosen to contrast with the blue sky, although the combination of so many models and the location made organizing the shoot very tough. The result shows how important choice of color is, both for the image itself and its marketability.

With many shoots taking a month of pre-production, including set-building, Barraud cannot afford to leave his choice of colors down to luck. But when the whole thing comes together as the image that he first imagined, it still creates the same sense of excitement and satisfaction as those original experiments at college. You can see some of his stunning images at *www.barraud.com* and expect to see many more of his images on billboards near you soon.

Beanbags 2.

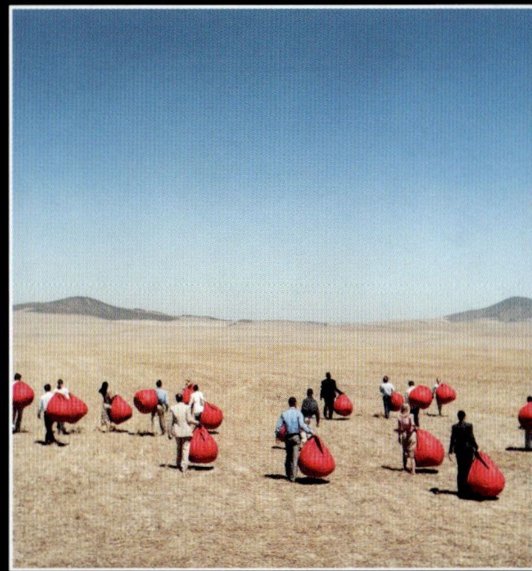

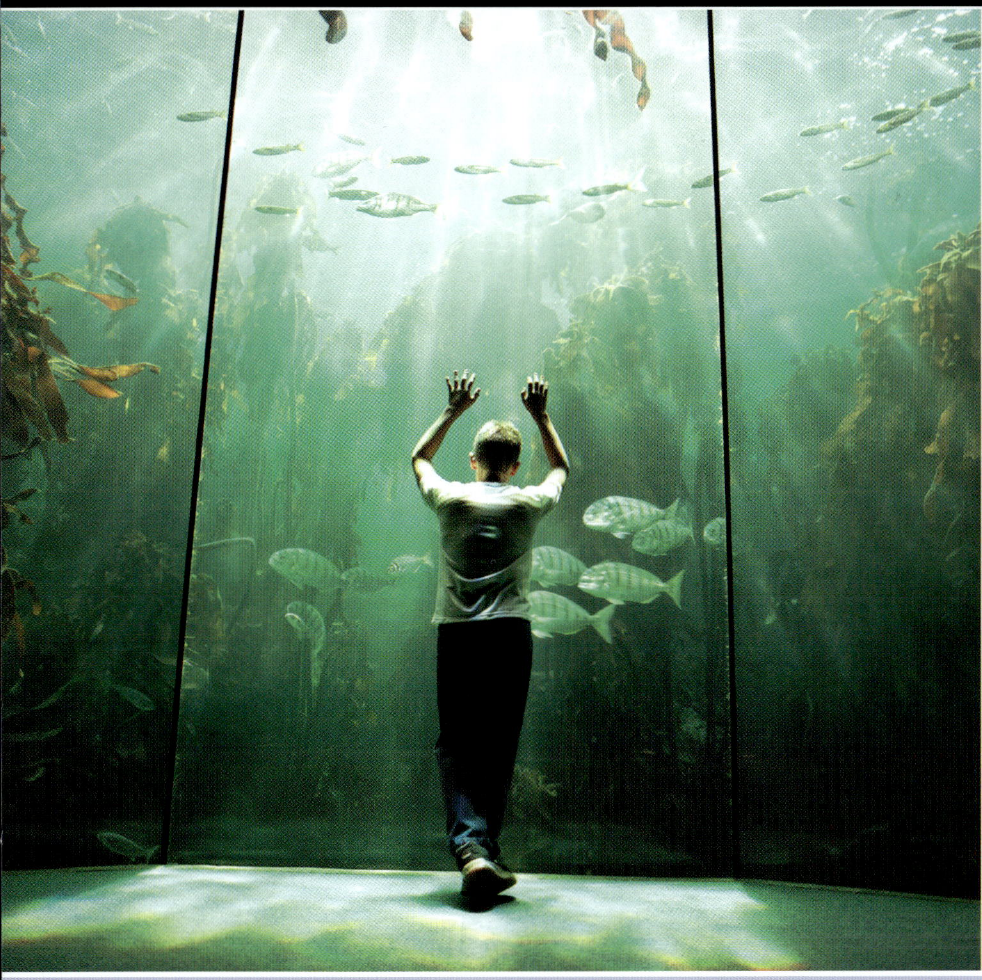

Aquarium.

Photographer's Profile

David Churchill

After assisting the highly respected architectural photographer Richard Bryant for eight years, David Churchill turned freelance in 1992. Best known for his work for architects, designers, and advertising agencies in the UK and worldwide, in 1999 Churchill became principal photographer for "Glasgow 1999 City of Architecture and Design." He has also published two books of his architecture images: *The Lighthouse* and *Homes for the Future*.

From creating a mood, to helping to indicate where you are in a building, color is an integral part of the design and architecture of the majority of Churchill's subjects. Deciding how best to shoot this is an integral part of the decision-making process. He is naturally drawn to color, as is evident in the strong, saturated colors that are a trademark of many of his images. This apparent simplicity often takes considerable time and effort to achieve. Isolating large blocks of color has become one of Churchill's favorite ways of conveying the sense of design and impact of modern buildings. Careful composition and framing ensures that these colors are the most powerful elements of the image, while giving a sense of the building's character.

Having learnt his trade with film, Churchill now uses a high-end Phase One medium-format digital back. The move to digital capture has simplified his need for additional lighting on location, thanks to the greater tonal range and ability to deal with mixed lighting conditions. The post-production work now plays an even more important part in the process. The ability to combine two shots taken with different exposures and the opportunity to fine-tune the lighting and contrast replaces some of the time and cost it would have taken to achieve the effect on location.

Churchill often uses the color casts caused by mixed lighting to his advantage. Setting the white balance for the artificial tungsten lighting used for many interiors at dusk can turn the sky a strong blue. This effect relies on perfect timing to work successfully—if you do it too early, the blue is too weak; if you wait too long, the sky turns black. So despite the advantages of digital, it is still the skill and eye of the photographer that really matters.

Although architectural work still plays a huge part in Churchill's work, over recent years his photographic style has resulted in commissions from many other clients seeking to give their products a strong identity. From *Formula 1* magazine to top yacht designers Bannenberg, His ability to convey design and space is in demand around the world. You can see more of his work at *www.davidchurchill.co.uk*.

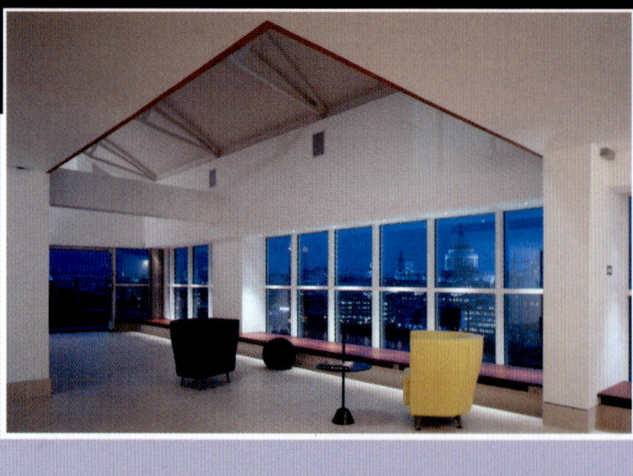

Benbow House, UK.

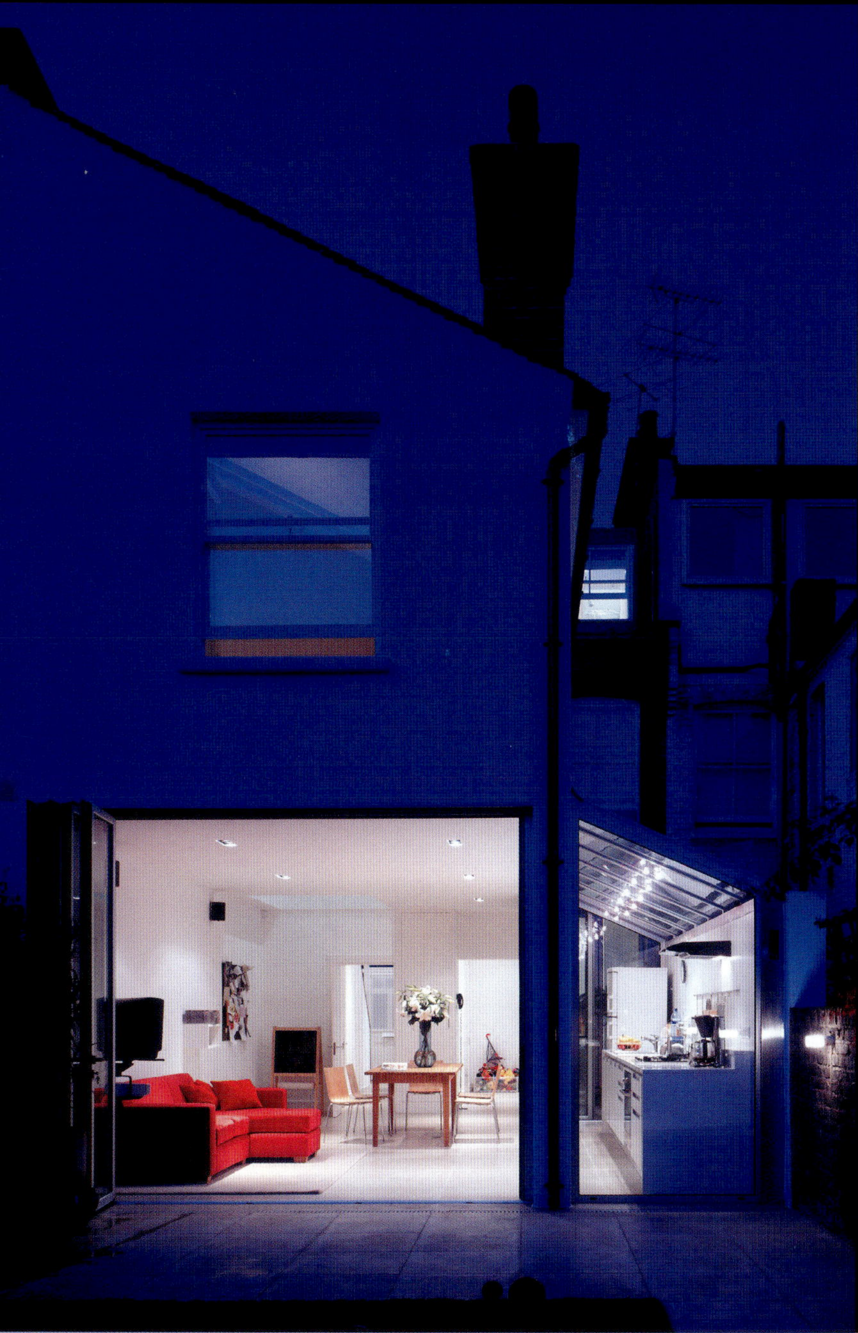

Offenbach House, UK.

Art TM, UK.

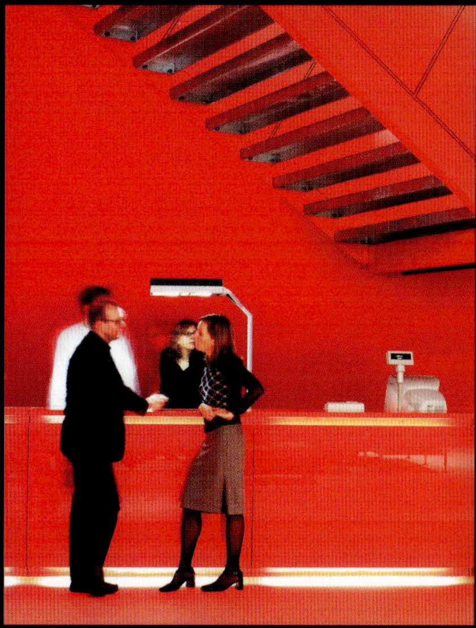

Habitat, Germany.

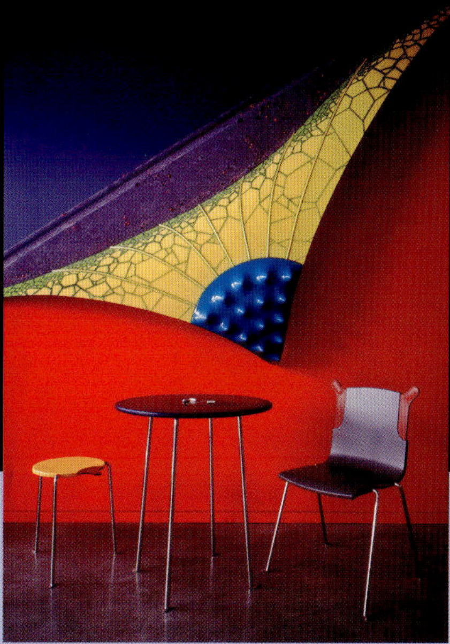

Photographer's Profile

Andrea Jones

Andrea Jones is a fine art and editorial photographer. She prefers to simply frame the subject rather than tamper with the natural beauty and colors of the plants that provide her with most of her subjects. These plants and gardens provide Jones with a fabulous source of color, so this wish to capture the colors accurately rather than employ filters or sophisticated image manipulation is understandable.

Jones shoots on both medium-format film cameras and on digital, and she finds that each method has its strengths and weaknesses when it comes to capturing colors accurately. Using Fuji Velvia 100 color transparency film gives very intense and saturated greens and reds, which is ideal for more general shots, although it can struggle to capture the subtle yellow tones of many plants. For plant portraits, she prefers to shoot digitally, as the extra control over the subtleties of the colors makes digital a more versatile medium. In her search for accuracy, Jones would use watercolor paint to match the colors of the plants, but time and commercial pressures mean that she usually has to rely on memory to get the color balance and tones she requires.

Of all her subjects, it is the blue flowering plants that offer the greatest challenge. To attract insects, these flowers reflect a great deal of ultraviolet light that is invisible to our eyes but can be recorded on many photographic materials. On film especially this can give the flowers a completely different color to how we see them, and so demands particular shooting conditions to minimize the effect. Jones shoots early or late in the day when the light is low to record these flowers as accurately as possible.

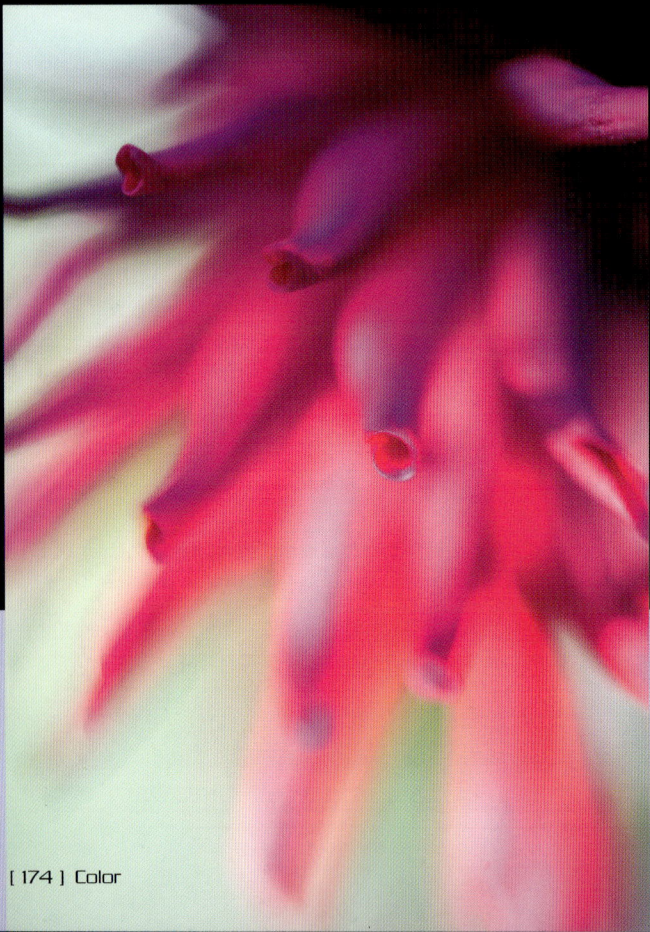

Red Dahlia.

«

Passiflora "Anastasia."

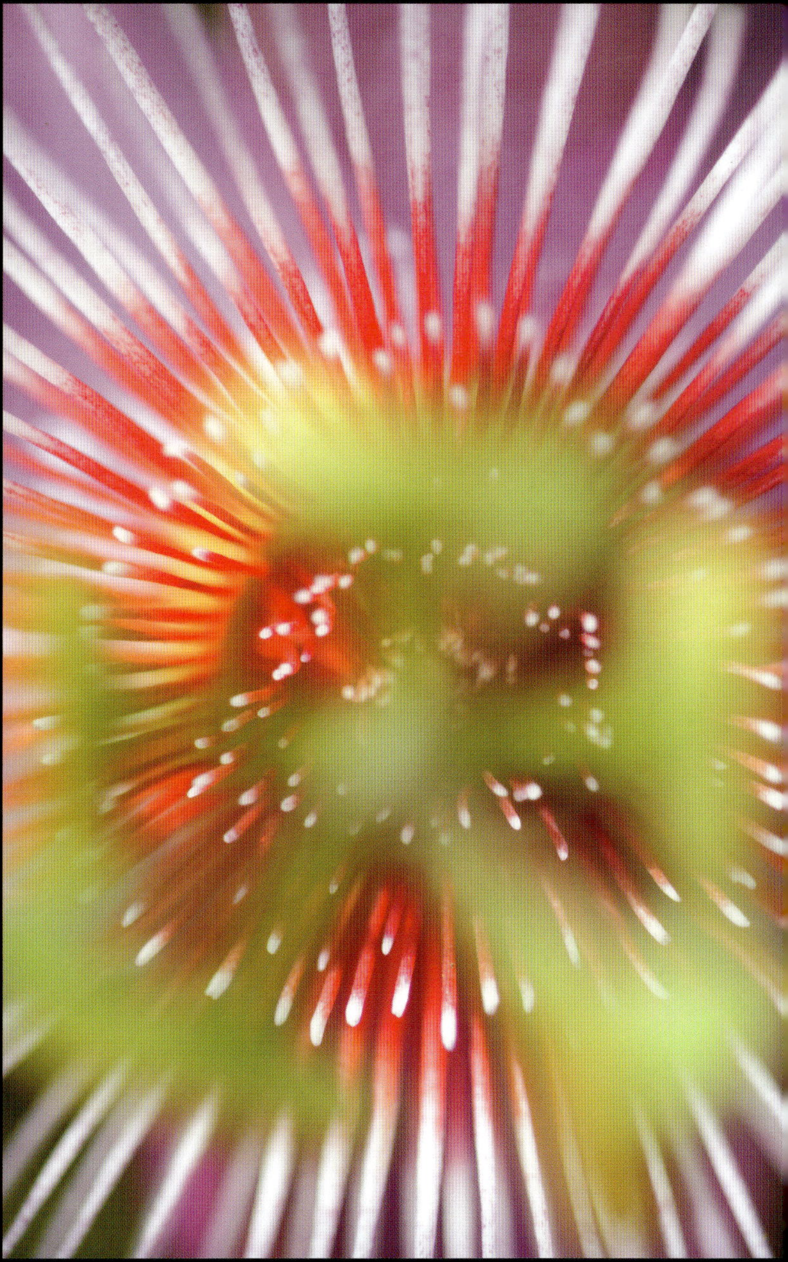

'or most images, she prefers to shoot during ıe early morning, as the soft golden light gives ıe colors a magical quality that is not present t other times of the day. She finds the light ater in the day more contrasty, and lacking the tmosphere of the morning, although the warm ght of early evening can also produce good esults. Her perfect day would involve a soft mist arly in the morning, then a light haze during ıe middle of the day, finishing with a clear ky during the evening—she admits that it is a truggle to put her camera down when the light s perfect.

Accompanying plant-hunters Sue and Bleddyn Vynn-Jones on trips to Vietnam, Korea, and uatemala has provided Jones with even more ıspiration for her plant portraits, as well as roviding images for her fine art prints. She as set up her own image library—*www. ardenexposures.com*—and her work has been sed in many gardening magazines and books, long with calendars and prints.

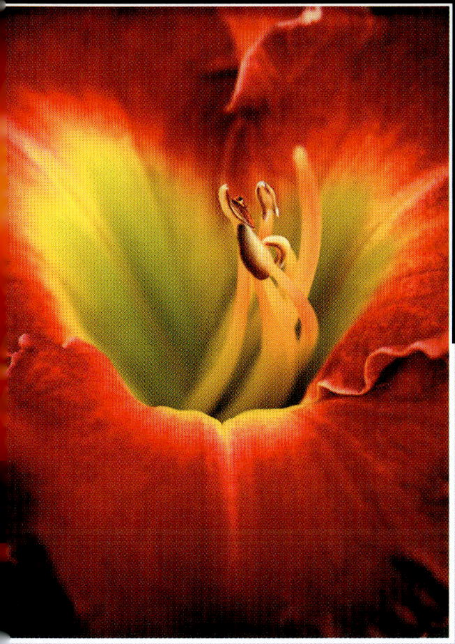

Hermerocallis "Dragon King."

Photographer's Profile

Jeremy Walker

The apparent simplicity of Jeremy Walker's stunning landscape images does not come about by chance. It is the understanding of how color, and crucially light, can affect the feel and mood of his images that sets his work apart from many other landscape photographers.

After studying at art college for four years, Walker started his photographic career assisting in a London studio, then ran a commercial studio for five years. But the lure of landscape and location photography proved too much, and he took the plunge to go freelance, shooting mainly landscape and travel images. Since then he has provided images for many stock libraries and clients worldwide.

The success of Walker's work is due in no small part to the attention to detail that he learned while working in the more controlled environment of the commercial studio. Simple, strong graphic shapes and patterns appear in many of his images, often with a single color dominating the frame. These compositions create a strong sense of the mood and feel of the location, and it is often what he leaves out rather than what he includes in the frame that is most important.

This strong color does not come from image manipulation or enhancement; he simply works with the elements that nature presents. Searching out the right location and shooting at the right time of day is the key to his photography. Using the subtle (or not-so-subtle) changes in light through the day, he often spends days at a location determining the right conditions for a single shot.

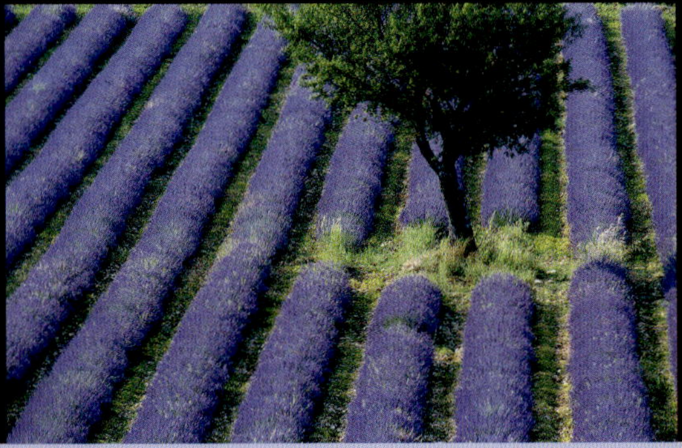

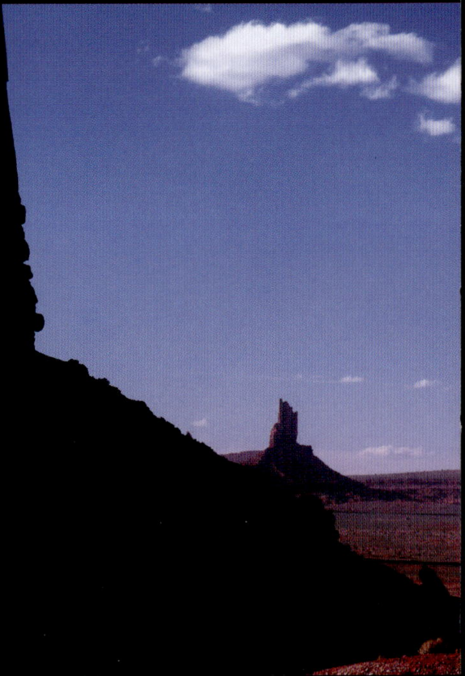

Lavender, France.

Monument Valley, US.

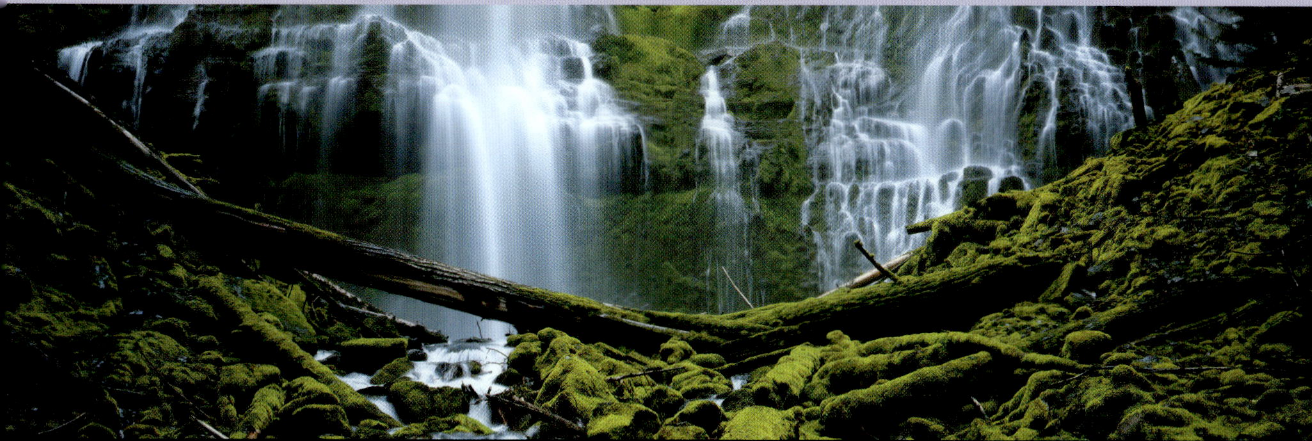

Proxy Falls, US.

·lis shot of Monument Valley is a great example f this dedication, with the contrast between he warm rock and deep blue sky dominating he frame. The inclusion of a single white cloud ıst visible at the top of the frame rounds off he image. Without this simple but essential ·lement, the image would not have such impact.

Although he now shoots many of his images ligitally, this philosophy has not changed—color, ght, and location are everything in landscape hotography. Only adjusting the Levels or Curves or fine-tuning, Walker prefers to leave nature to ıake the image. He believes that capturing this eauty is more about patience and dedication han the quick-fixes offered by modern technology.

After 12 years of freelance photography, Walker's enthusiasm for and dedication to his art has not diminished. Working with natural light means that every shoot and location creates a whole new set of challenges and opportunities. See more of his images at *www.jeremywalker.co.uk*.

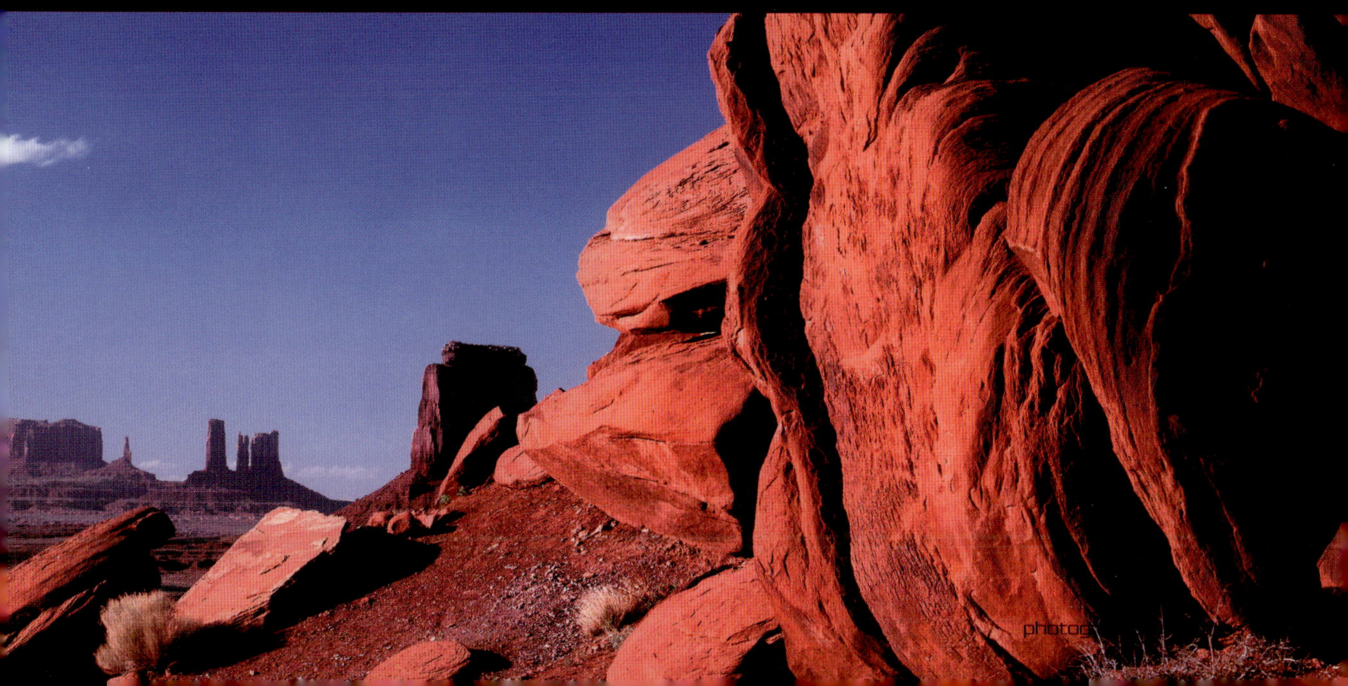

Appendix

Adjustment Layers

Although not essential for successful image editing, Photoshop offers a more versatile method of applying adjustments to the simple Layers option. Instead of creating a layer containing all of the image information, an adjustment layer contains only the information regarding the settings that you have applied. The great advantage over standard layers is the ability to alter these adjustments at any time, rather than applying them to the image.

Most of the commands available under the Image › Adjustments menu can be used as adjustment layers. These appear in the normal way in the Layers palette, and the settings will affect the layers beneath the adjustment layer, but not those above it in the stack.

You create these by going to Layer › New Adjustment Layer, and choosing the image adjustment type that you want to apply. After making any changes, you can alter the settings by double-clicking on the Layer thumbnail in the Layers palette; this will bring up the adjustment window with your current settings.

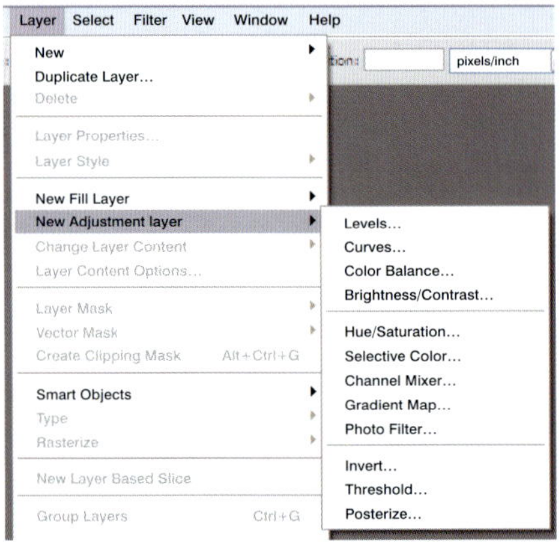

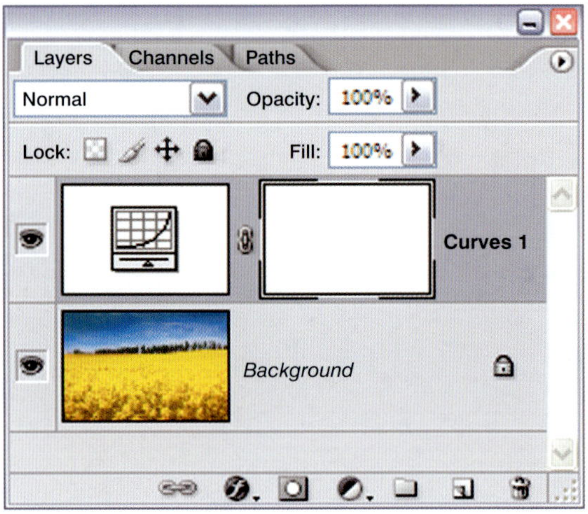

Online Resources

Here are some useful Web sites for further information on photographic products and color science and technology.

Product and software manufacturers

Adobe
www.adobe.com
Imaging software

Apple
www.apple.com
Computer hardware and software

Canon
www.canon.com
Cameras, lenses, and printers

Epson
www.epson.com
Ink-jet printers

Fuji
www.fuji.com
Cameras, film, and dye-sublimation printers

Hasselblad
www.hasselblad.se
Cameras and lenses

Kodak
www.kodak.com
Cameras, film, and dye-sublimation printers

LaCie
www.lacie.com
Monitors

Nikon
www.nikon.com
Cameras and lenses

Olympus
www.olympus.com
Cameras and lenses

Pentax
www.pentax.com
Cameras and lenses

Sigma
www.sigma-imaging-uk.com
Lenses

Sony
www.sonystyle.com
Digital cameras and accessories

Color management and color information

Colour Confidence
www.colourconfidence.com
Color-management solutions

Pantone
www.pantone.com
Color management and color products

International Color Consortium
www.color.org
Web site for the International Color Consortium (ICC)

London College of Communication
www.digitalcolour.org
Web site for the color-imaging group at the London College of Communication

Print Longevity

However much effort and care you put into getting the best results from your color images, there's one harsh fact that you have to face: all photographic materials deteriorate over time. The colors will fade until eventually all your hard work will disappear into oblivion. With traditional photographic materials the problem still occurs, but the effects are more predictable and measurable than for the more recent technologies available for making prints from digital files.

The popularity of home ink-jet printers has been accompanied by many fears about how long the resulting prints will last. These fears were fueled by the poor longevity of the images produced by many of the early models, which in many cases struggled to resist fading and deterioration for more than a few months rather than the years that we were used to with traditional materials.

These problems have caused a great deal of people to dismiss ink-jet prints for photography. The manufacturers have been quick to address these fears, and have taken steps to increase the lifespan of the prints produced using their ink and paper.

How Long Will Prints Last?

There's no simple answer to this question, as there are so many factors that will affect your prints. Many of the manufacturers claim some impressive figures for their own materials, but there's also an independent source of information for those looking for greater reassurance. The Wilhelm Institute in Iowa, US, has pioneered the research into print longevity. By using accelerated exposure to light techniques they can predict the likely lifespan for many of the materials in use today. Their results have shown that the best ink-jet materials actually outlast many traditional photographic materials.

In controlled conditions traditional photographic prints using standard papers have a lifespan of around 40 years, with the latest pigment based inks and dedicated papers achieving a predicted life of over 100 years. Both dye-based ink-jet materials and dye-sublimation prints lag behind the results for the best pigment-based media, but even these achieve figures similar to traditional materials. So with care you should be able to ensure that your precious prints will last as long as your previous images.

These results are all based on using the printer manufacturers own materials, though, so if you start using other manufacturers materials it's much more difficult to predict. While there are savings to be made using cheap inks and papers, there are plenty of pitfalls, with print longevity being key. Having said this there are some high quality materials, particularly papers, that are used by many with great results. When looking at these materials ensure that the paper is acid-free and find out if there is any independent information available for the paper when used in your model of printer. This way you can at least minimize the risk of faded prints.

What Can You Do To Ensure Your Prints Will Resist Fading?

Although there are few certainties in the area of print longevity, there are several steps you can take to ensure that you get the maximum lifespan from your ink-jet prints:

- Use the best quality inks, preferably pigment-based.
- Use high quality, acid-free papers from a reputable brand.
- Never display your prints in direct sunlight.
- Use a high quality, sealed frame for displaying your prints, and ensure that the print isn't in direct contact with the surface of the glass.
- Avoid using adhesives to fix the print to the frame or display board.
- When storing prints use archival quality protective sleeves, and inside an acid-free storage container.

Glossary

Aperture
A variable opening inside a lens that governs how much light passes to the film or sensor. Numerically known as f-numbers, these are commonly arranged as f/2.8, f/4, f/5.6, f/8, f/11, f/16, and f/22. F/2.8 lets in the most light and f/22 the least.

Artifacts
Incorrectly valued pixels that are by-products of digital image processing. Often visible as small marks or dots similar to digital noise.

Assign Profile
A method used for color management, the color profile of the incoming image file is replaced by the working profile of the software application.

Autoexposure
An in-camera system for setting the shutter speed and aperture automatically.

Auto White Balance
Using a sensor inside the camera, the white balance is set automatically according to the color temperature of the light and color of the subject.

Bit
A binary digit, represented by 0 and 1, this is the building block of all digital files. These values represent black and white, or off and on, and are the smallest unit of data in a digital system.

Bit Depth
Describes the size of the number of tones used to make an image. Also known as color depth when applied across the three color channels.

Bitmap (BMP)
A term used for any pixel-based image using a checkerboard-like arrangement.

Brightness
A measurable scale used in digital images with values from 0 (black) to 255 (white).

Calibration
Adjusting a digital-imaging device to give accurate colors. Commonly used for scanners, monitors, and printers in a color-managed system.

CCD
Charge Coupled Device. The most common type of light-sensitive sensor found in digital cameras and scanners.

Channels
The individual color information used to form a digital image. In an RGB file, this consists of three separate grayscale images for the red, green, and blue components of the image.

Channel Mixer
A tool in Photoshop that allows the color values for the channels to be altered. Especially useful for black-and-white conversion.

Clipping
When tones in the image close to the highlight or shadow values are translated as pure white or black. The result is lost detail in the final image.

CMOS
Complementary Metal Oxide Semiconductor. An alternative type of light-sensitive sensor to the CCD.

CMYK
Cyan, Magenta, Yellow, and Black (or "key"). An image mode used to prepare images for lithographic printing used in all magazines and books. CMYK has the smallest color space of the three-color modes commonly used.

Color-balancing Filter
Pale colored filters used to make small adjustments to the color of the image.

Color Cast
Usually an unwanted overall color tint that appears when the color temperature of the light does not match the white balance of the camera or film. Can be corrected using correction filters on the camera, a white balance setting that corresponds to the lighting, or by adjusting the colors in imaging software.

Color-correction Filter
Strongly colored filters used to correct differences between the color temperature of the light source and the color temperature sensitivity of the film or sensor.

Color Management
Using a system to define the color spaces and profiles used by the different devices used in a digital darkroom. Used to ensure consistent colors when the image is transferred between devices.

Color Space
Image modes that give different color characteristics and range of available colors. The basic modes are RGB, CMYK, and LAB, used by different devices for color reproduction.

Color Target
A product consisting of colors of known and measurable values used to calibrate a device or system. IT-8 and GretagMacbeth ColorChecker are two common types used for scanners and cameras.

Color Temperature
A measurement of the color of the light produced by a light source, commonly expressed in degrees Kelvin.

Color Wheel
A visual representation of how colors interact together by arranging them in order around the edge of a circle.

Complementary Colors
Two colors that are opposite each other on the color wheel. Combining light of these two colors will produce white light.

Compression
A means of making digital files smaller by using complex formula to group pixels together, rather than save every pixel. There are two basic types: "lossy," where some information from the original file is lost during the process, and "lossless," where all the original data is retained.

Curves
A Photoshop tool that allows you to adjust the contrast, color, and brightness of images by setting points along a line representing the image.

Cyan
A blue-green color whose complementary color is red.

Digital Darkroom
A generic term used to describe any computer and input or output devices used for digital imaging.

Duotone
A black and white toning technique using two colors in different parts of the image to produce the final result. In digital imaging it can also be replicated using a Photoshop tool of the same name.

Dye-sublimation
A printing process that uses tiny heating elements to transfer printing dyes onto paper.

Dynamic Range
A measurement of the range of brightness in photographic materials or digital sensors. The higher the number, the greater the range of tones that can be recorded.

Electromagnetic Spectrum
The complete range of wavelengths or frequencies of electromagnetic radiation. Visible light is contained within this spectrum, along with other radiation such as infrared and ultraviolet that can have an effect on photographic materials.

Fluorescent Light Source
An artificial light source that uses a fluorescent gas to emit light. Usually takes the form of tube or strip lights, and emits light containing strong "spikes" of particular wavelengths. These are very good for simulating daylight for viewing, but can prove difficult to achieve the correct color photographically as they do not conform to standard color temperature measurements.

Gamut
An expression of the range of colors used to create, display, or output a digital image.

Gray Card
A neutral-colored card that reflects 18% of the light falling on it. Can be used for accurate exposure metering or for taking a reading to set the white balance.

Grayscale
The simplest form of a digital image, containing no color information. Can be used to create and save black-and-white images. The lowest quality used for photography is an 8-bit grayscale containing 256 tones from black to white.

Harmonious Colors
Colors next to each other on the color wheel. Used together, these colors usually create gentle, harmonious images.

Highlight
The brightest part of the image, represented by the value 255 on the 0–255 scale used in digital images.

Histogram
A graphic representation of a digital image showing the range of tones present as a series of vertical columns.

Hue
An alternative expression for color that can be given a numerical value.

ICC
The International Color Consortium. An organization founded to develop and set standards for the representation and measurement of colors, to allow these to be used across a range of devices.

Incandescent Light Source
An artificial light source usually used to define the white balance setting for indoor lighting such as tungsten bulbs.

Ink-jet Printer
An output device that sprays tiny droplets of ink onto a medium to produce an image.

Interpolation
Adding extra pixels to a digital image by assessing the existing information to create new data. Usually used to increase the size of the image for printing.

ISO (Speed)
International Standards Organization. A rating used to determine the sensitivity of a film or sensor to light. A low number such as ISO 50 or 100 needs more light to form an image than a higher number such as ISO 400 or 800.

JPEG
Joint Photographic Experts Group. A universal image file type that uses compression to shrink the size of the file. Known as a "lossy" type of compression as some information is lost during the process.

LAB Mode
A color space with a very wide color gamut used when processing images. It is not used by any device to produce images, so cannot be used for printing, creating, or outputting images.

Layer
A means of stacking images on top of one another in Photoshop, used for creating composite images or creating copies of the original image to allow adjustments to be made without affecting the original.

Levels
A tool in Photoshop allowing you to control the brightness of the image. Takes the form of a histogram with moveable points to allow adjustments.

Magenta
A blue-red color whose complementary color is green.

Noise
Unwanted, random pixels containing incorrect tone or color information that degrades the image quality. Most visible in shadow or even-toned areas of the image. Similar to grain in traditional film emulsions, this can be a consequence of shooting at high ISO settings. Can also be caused by using very long exposures.

Overexposure
When too much light reaches the film or sensor due to incorrect exposure. Causes the image to look too light, with lost highlight detail.

Pantone
An internationally recognized color library that uses a code for specifying specific colors. Used primarily in the printing industry to identify and mix ink colors.

Photoshop
The industry-standard image-editing software produced by Adobe.

Pixel
Short for "picture element," the pixel is the individual building block of a digital image. Arranged in a gridlike pattern called a bitmap to form the overall image.

Polarizing Filter
A filter that only allows light through that is vibrating in a particular direction. Used to cut out reflections, increase color saturation, and darken blue skies.

Profile
A way of defining the colors produced by a device, allowing its characteristics to be translated accurately when an image is transferred from one device to another in an imaging system.

Quadtone
A black-and-white toning technique using four colors affecting different areas of the image. Can be replicated in Photoshop using the appropriate settings in Duotone mode.

RAW
A file format that takes data directly from the image sensor and stores it in a format that needs to be decoded by dedicated software to form the image. Most camera manufacturers use their own proprietary RAW format.

RGB
Red, Green, and Blue. The three primary colors used by most digital imaging devices to form images.

Saturation
An expression for the purity of a color, the more white, gray, or black is present in a color the lower the saturation.

Shadow
The darkest part of the image, in digital imaging it is represented by a zero value on the 0–255 scale.

TIFF
Tagged Image File Format. A high-quality file format used to store digital images, recognized by most imaging software. Can be uncompressed or compressed using a "lossless" system.

Tritone
A black-and-white toning technique using three colors affecting different areas of the image. Can be replicated in Photoshop using the appropriate settings in Duotone mode.

Underexposure
When too little light passes to the film or sensor, giving very dark images with little or no shadow detail.

White Balance
A camera setting used to correct for changes in the color temperature of the lighting that would otherwise cause color casts on an image.

Index

D

Acknowledgments

I would like to thank everyone for their help and assistance in producing this book, in particular all at *Practical Photography* and EMAP for allowing me the time and opportunity to complete this project alongside my normal work, and my commissioning editor, Chris Middleton at RotoVision, for getting the book underway in the first place, and giving continued help along the way.

Special thanks go to my friend and colleague Bob Martin for supplying some of the portrait images, and to all my friends and family, without whose support and kind words the book would never have happened—in particular Pete and Amanda, who persuaded me to take on the project.

There are also many companies and individuals who assisted with the technical areas, illustrations, and products:

Paul Reynolds at Sigma Imaging
Javan Bramall at Colour Confidence
Chris Wallace at GretagMacbeth
All at Nikon UK
All at Epson UK

Finally, I would like to dedicate this book to the memory of my parents, Jeff and Sheila Rutter.